Bartolomé Mitre, William Spilling

The Emancipation of South America

Bartolomé Mitre, William Spilling

The Emancipation of South America

ISBN/EAN: 9783743332393

Manufactured in Europe, USA, Canada, Australia, Japa

Cover: Foto ©ninafisch / pixelio.de

Manufactured and distributed by brebook publishing software (www.brebook.com)

Bartolomé Mitre, William Spilling

The Emancipation of South America

THE EMANCIPATION OF SOUTH AMERICA

BEING A CONDENSED TRANSLATION

BY

WILLIAM PILLING

OF

THE HISTORY OF SAN MARTIN

BY

GENERAL DON BARTOLOMÉ MITRE
FIRST CONSTITUTIONAL PRESIDENT OF THE ARGENTINE REPUBLIC

With Maps

LONDON: CHAPMAN & HALL, Ltd.
1893

TRANSLATOR'S PREFACE.

THE title of this translation is the second title of the original "History of San Martin." This transposition of title is an index to the relation which the translation bears to the original. This latter is truly a biography of San Martin, whose life could not be understood unless very full account were given of the events in which he took so prominent a part, therefore the biography is also a history.

No man who plays a prominent part in the history of a revolution can escape becoming involved in disputes with his contemporaries, and in many intricate questions which are of interest only to a very small number of their successors. These disputes and these questions greatly affect the career of a man, but have small influence upon the history of a Nation. Of such troubles San Martin had his full share, his biographer has entered fully into them, and with much detail has given proofs of the correctness of the view he takes of them. These details are, for the most part, suppressed in the translation, and all matters concerning San Martin himself are greatly curtailed, while prominence is given to the events of the times in which the scene passes. The translation is thus a history in which enter the biographies of the two principal personages, San Martin and Bolívar.

This translation is intended only for the general mass of English-speaking readers, to whom minute details are wearisome, and is thus in every part a condensation of the copious accounts which are given in the original of the stirring events described. The student of history will not find in it that ample information which he requires, in order fully to understand the subject in all its bearings; for him the original provides a mine of historic wealth, enriched as it is with notes and with a voluminous appendix.

WILLIAM PILLING.

LONDON, *March*, 1893.

CONTENTS.

	PAGE
TRANSLATOR'S PREFACE	vii
PROLOGUE	xxvii

CHAPTER I.

HISTORICAL INTRODUCTION.

The Argument of the Book—Synopsis of the South American Revolution—The Action of America upon Europe—The Colonization of Spanish America—The Colonization of North America—Colonial Policy in both Americas—The Emancipation of North America—The Affiliation of the Revolution of South America—The Moral Revolution of South America—The Precursor of the Emancipation of South America—The Races of South America; the Creole—The First Throes of Revolution—The Growth of the Revolution—Attempts at Monarchy in South America—Retrospection 1

CHAPTER II.

SAN MARTIN IN EUROPE AND IN AMERICA.

1778—1812.

His Birth and Parentage—Leaves for Spain—His Career in the Spanish Army—Africa—France—St. Vincent—Portugal—Cadiz—Society of Lautaro—Argonilla—Baylen—Tudela—Albuera—Lord Macduff—London—Buenos Ayres—Outbreak of the Revolution—Experiments in Government—The Influence of San Martin—Personal Appearance and Character of San Martin . 31

CHAPTER III.

THE LAUTARO LODGE.

1812—1813.

The First Triumvirate—Political Parties—The Mounted Grenadiers —Military School—The Lautaro Lodge—Battle of Tucuman— Revolution of 8th October—The Second Triumvirate—Military Plans 43

CHAPTER IV.

SAN LORENZO.

1813—1814.

Battle of the Cerrito—Meeting of the Constituent Assembly—Reforms —Spanish Depredations on the Fluvial Coasts—The Action of San Lorenzo—Battle of Salta—Influence of the Lodge—Disasters of Vilcapugio and Ayohuma—Argentine Generals—San Martin takes Command of the Army of the North—Appointment of the Supreme Director 53

CHAPTER V.

UPPER PERU.

1814.

The Problem of the Argentine Revolution—The Geography and Ethnology of Upper Peru—Outbreak and Progress of the Revolution in Upper Peru—Cruelties of the Spaniards—Composition of the Royalist Army—Arenales—His Campaign from Cochabamba to Santa Cruz—Battle of La Florida—Results of these Operations 64

CHAPTER VI.

THE WAR IN THE NORTH.

1814.

The Army of Tucuman—Preparations of Pezuela—Plans of San Martin—The New Military School—Popular Movement in Salta—Martin Güemes—The Gauchos of Salta—Operations of the Royalists—The Fall of Monte Video—Retreat of Pezuela— San Martin's Secret Plan—His Illness—Is appointed Governor of Cuyo 72

CHAPTER VII.

THE CHILENO-ARGENTINE REVOLUTION.

1810—1811.

Chilian and Argentine Society compared—Martinez Rozas—Popular Excitement—Loss of Power by Governor Carrasco—The South of Chile—O'Higgins—Deposition of Carrasco—Establishment of a Junta—Resemblances of the Two Revolutions—Argentine-Chilian Alliance—Freedom of Commerce—Mutiny in Santiago—Installation of the First General Congress—Defeat of the Radicals—Rozas at Concepcion 80

CHAPTER VIII.

PROGRESS AND FALL OF THE CHILIAN REVOLUTION.

1811—1814.

The Three Carreras—A New Junta—Dissolution of Congress—Armed Protest by Rozas—Valdivia—The First Newspaper—Death of Rozas—The Chilian Flag—Carrera again Dictator—Abascal—Pareja lands at Valdivia—Battle of San Carlos—Siege of Chillán — O'Higgins made General-in-Chief — Argentine Auxiliaries — Arrival of Gainza—Lastra named Supreme Director — Capture of Talca — Mackenna at Membrillar — Defence of Quecheraguas—Mediation of the British Commodore—Treaty of Lircay—The Carreras again in Power—Invasion of Osorio—Siege of Rancagua—Flight of O'Higgins and Carrera . 91

CHAPTER IX.

CUYO.

1814—1815.

The District of Cuyo—Policy of San Martin—Reception of Chilian Refugees—Trouble with Carrera—Fall of Alvear—Cuyo becomes an Independant State—Self-sacrifice of the People of Cuyo—Revenues of Cuyo—Characteristics of San Martin—Anecdotes of San Martin—Royalist Successes—The Banquet at Mendoza 108

CHAPTER X.

THE SPY SYSTEM OF THE PATRIOTS.

1815—1816.

The Restoration of Spanish Domination in Chile—Cruelties of the Royalists—Nationalist Reaction—The Plans of Abascal—San

Martin establishes Secret Agencies in Chile—His Spy System—Preparations of the Chilian Patriots—Marcó del Pont—Manuel Rodriguez—Brown and the Argentine Privateers—Loss of the *Uribe*—Capture of the *Consequencia*—Blockade of Callao—Attack on Guayaquil—Loss of the *Trinidad*—Return of the Squadron 117

CHAPTER XI.

THE IDEA OF THE PASSAGE OF THE ANDES.

1815—1816.

Opposition to the Plans of San Martin—He receives Permission to assume the Offensive—Also Supplies of Guns and War Material—Collects the Grenadiers—Balcarce Provisional Director—The Lodge in Mendoza—Tomas Guido 124

CHAPTER XII.

THE ARMY OF THE ANDES.

1816—1817.

Composition of the Army—Freeing the Slaves—Fray Beltran—The Arsenal—Powder Factory—Cloth Factory—Pueyrredón elected President—Declaration of Independence—Interview at Córdoba—Condarco—Maps of the Passes of the Andes—Concentration of the Army—The Function of the 17th January, 1817—The Flag of the Army of the Andes 126

CHAPTER XIII.

THE PASSAGE OF THE ANDES.

1817.

The Southern Andes—Passes of the Andes—Stratagems of San Martin—The Pehuenche Indians—Preparations of Marcó—Preparations at Mendoza—Pueyrredón—Detachments flanking the Main Army—Instructions from Government—The Sierra of Chacabuco—Occupation of Coquimbo by Cabot—Capture of Copiapó—Capture of Talca—March of the Main Army—The Affair at Pichueta—Capture of Achupallas—Juan Lavalle—Capture of the Guardia Vieja—Putaendo—Defeat of Atero—Concentration of the Army at the Foot of Chacabuco—The Judgment of Posterity 132

CONTENTS. xiii

CHAPTER XIV.

CHACABUCO.

1817.

PAGE

The Sierra of Chacabuco—Atero occupies Chacabuco—Maroto appointed to command the Royalist Army—Moonlight March of the Patriots—The Royalist Vanguard driven in—Advance of the Main Body—Repulse of O'Higgins—Soler takes the Position in Flank—Total Rout of the Royalists—Barañao—Occupation of Santiago—O'Higgins elected Supreme Director—Marcó taken Prisoner—San Bruno shot—Reception of the News in Buenos Ayres—San Martin returns to Buenos Ayres . . 144

CHAPTER XV.

THE FIRST CAMPAIGN IN THE SOUTH OF CHILE.

1817.

The Mistakes committed by San Martin—Ordoñez—Las Heras marches to the South—Occupation of Concepcion—The Action of Gavilán—O'Higgins takes Command—Freyre captures the Forts of Arauco—Treaty with the Indians of Arauco—Operations against Talcahuano—French Officers—The Assault of the Morro—Las Heras is withdrawn from the captured Outwork . 151

CHAPTER XVI.

ARGENTINE-CHILENO ALLIANCE.

1817.

Origin and Results of this Alliance—San Martin in Buenos Ayres—Carrera's Trip to North America—His Return and Arrest by Pueyrredón—The Mission of Condarco to London—Quintana Deputy Director—Coinage of Chilian Money—" The Legion of Merit "—Guido as Argentine Representative—Irizarri appointed Chilian Agent in Europe—Monarchical Ideas—Chilian Jealousy of Argentine Influence—The Conspiracy of the Carreras—Two of the Brothers imprisoned at Mendoza—Life of San Martin at Santiago—The " Tertulias "—Commodore Bowles takes a Secret Agent to Lima 157

CHAPTER XVII.

CANCHA-RAYADA.

1817—1818.

The Political State of Chile—Pezuela appointed Viceroy of Peru—His Policy—Osorio lands at Talcahuano with Reinforcements—The Patriot Forces—Retreat of O'Higgins—March of Osorio on Santiago—Proclamation of Independence—Concentration of the Patriot Army—Affair on the Lontué—Retreat of Osorio—The Halt at Talca—The Night Attack at Cancha-rayada—Dispersion of the Patriot Army—O'Higgins wounded—Masterly Retreat of Las Heras—Panic in the Capital—Return of O'Higgins and San Martin—Reorganization of the Army—The Camp on the Plain of Maipó 165

CHAPTER XVIII.

MAIPÓ.

1818.

Confusion of the Royalists after Cancha-rayada—They march on Santiago—The Plain of Maipó—Position of the Patriots—Desertion of General Brayer—Battle of Maipó—Results of the Battle—Osorio collects a Small Force at Talcahuano—Zapiola takes Command in the South—Osorio evacuates Talcahuano . 174

CHAPTER XIX.

AFTER MAIPÓ.

1818.

Execution at Mendoza of Don Luis and Don Juan José Carrera—Constitutional Reform in Chile—Tragic Fate of Dr. Rodriguez—The Secret Correspondence of Osorio—San Martin leaves for Buenos Ayres—His Arrangements with Pueyrredón—Monarchical Illusions—Bolívar—Spain 181

CHAPTER XX.

THE FIRST NAVAL CAMPAIGN ON THE PACIFIC.

1818.

The Naval Resources of Chile—Ships purchased by Government—Affair of the *Esmeralda*—Blanco Encalada—Another Convoy from Spain—The Mutiny of the *Trinidad*—The Chilian

CONTENTS.

Squadron leaves Valparaiso—The Capture of the *Maria Isabel*—Capture of Five Transports—The Return of the Squadron—Cochrane—The Two Wives. 186

CHAPTER XXI.

THE REPASSAGE OF THE ANDES.

1818—1819.

The Last Campaign in Chile—Another Conspiracy of Carrera's—Proclamation to the Peruvian People—Correspondence with Bolívar—San Martin withdraws a Division to Mendoza—The Tragedy at San Luis—Definite Arrangements for the Expedition to Peru—Retirement of Pueyrredón 194

CHAPTER XXII.

COCHRANE—CALLAO—VALDIVIA.

1819—1820.

The Character of Cochrane—He sails for Callao—The Spanish Squadron—The First Attack on Callao—Loss of a Fireship—Capture of the *Montezuma*—Return to Valparaiso—Manufacture of War Rockets—Second Attack on Callao—Inefficiency of the Rockets—Guise captures Pisco—Death of Colonel Charles—Capture of Transports at Guayaquil—Escape of the *Prueba*—Cochrane's New Scheme—Valdivia—Capture of the *Potrillo*—Reinforcements at Talcahuano—Return to Valdivia—Capture of the Southern Forts—Evacuation of the Northern Forts—Wreck of the *Intrepido*—Surrender of the City—Repulse at Chiloe—Return 200

CHAPTER XXIII.

THE DISOBEDIENCE OF SAN MARTIN.

1819—1820.

The Perplexities of San Martin—Popular Sentiment in Spain—The Expedition assembling at Cadiz—Discontent among the Troops—O'Donnell crushes the Conspiracy—San Martin summoned to Buenos Ayres—His Proposal to O'Higgins and Cochrane—The Gaucho Chieftains—San Martin again ordered to Buenos Ayres—The Plans of Government—The Duc de Luca—Uprising of the Argentine People—San Martin still hesitates—Mutiny of the Army of the North—San Martin sends in his Resignation—Critique on his Behaviour 210

CHAPTER XXIV.

THE CONVENTION OF RANCAGUA.

1820.

The Spanish Revolution of 1820—Return of San Martin to Chile—Mutiny of the Detachment at San Juan—The Remnant of the Division crosses the Andes to Chile—Rout of Cepeda—The Reign of Anarchy in the United Provinces—The Convention of Officers at Rancagua—The Disobedience of San Martin endorsed by the Army—Cochrane aspires to the Command-in-Chief—San Martin appointed Generalissimo—The Presence of the Army of the Andes a Danger to Chile 216

CHAPTER XXV.

PERU.

1820.

The Colonial Era in Peru—Lima—The Peruvian People—Viceroy Abascal—The Native Army—Pezuela—La Serna—Revolutionary Outbreaks — The Insurrection of Cuzco—Secret Societies—Correspondence with San Martin—Dissolution of the Native Army—Olañeta—Camba—Valdés—The Royalist Forces . . 223

CHAPTER XXVI.

THE EXPEDITION TO PERU.

1820.

San Martin's Address to the Argentine People—Composition of the Expedition—Sailing of the Expedition—Disembarkation at Pisco—Occupation of Pisco by Las Heras—Proclamation by San Martin—Pezuela proposes Peace—The Commissioners meet at Miraflores—Arrange an Armistice—The Terms proposed—Negotiations broken off—Expedition of Arenales to the Highlands—Re-embarkation of the Army 230

CHAPTER XXVII.

THE OPENING OF THE CAMPAIGN.

1820—1821.

The Coming Campaigns—The Pageant at Callao—Expedition from Ancon—Guayaquil—Revolution of Guayaquil—The *Esmeralda*

CONTENTS. xvii

Frigate cut out by Cochrane—The Expedition lands at Huacho — Huara — Cavalry Skirmish at Chancay — The Numancia Battalion joins the Patriots—Discontent in Peru—The Independence of Trujillo—Torre-Tagle—Junction with Arenales—The Guerillas—The Provisional Regulation 235

CHAPTER XXVIII.

THE FIRST CAMPAIGN IN THE HIGHLANDS.

1820—1821.

The Natural Division of Peru—The Highlands of Peru—The Flying Column under Arenales—Defeat of Quimper—The Invasion of the Highlands—The Battle of Pasco—Retreat of Aldao from Ica—Massacres of Indians by Ricafort—The Sack of Cangallo and Huancayo—Aldao establishes himself at Huancayo—Arenales rejoins San Martin 245

CHAPTER XXIX.

THE ARMISTICE OF PUNCHAUCA.

1821.

Prospects of the Royalists—Spanish Councils of War—Deposition of Pezuela—Proposals of Peace—The Conference at Retes—State of the Two Armies—The Royal Commissioner—The Patriot Army moves to Ancon—Proclamation from King Ferdinand—Effect in Columbia—Effect in Mexico—Course of the Revolution in Mexico—Iturbide—The " Plan de Iguala "—Success of the Plan—Fate of Iturbide—The Conference of Punchauca—Armistice of Punchauca—Interview between San Martin and La Serna—Mistaken Policy of San Martin—The Conference renewed at Miraflores—Prolongation of the Armistice—Captain Basil Hall—Canterac moves to the Highlands—Return of the Patriot Army to Huacho—La Serna evacuates Lima—Occupation of Lima by the Patriots—Proclamation and Inactivity of San Martin 249

CHAPTER XXX.

THE SECOND CAMPAIGN IN THE HIGHLANDS.

1821.

Aldao and his Indian Levies—Gamarra takes Command—Is driven out by Ricafort—Ricafort returns to Lima—Arenales marches from Huara—The Successes of Arenales cut short by the

Armistice—Character of Arenales—His Expostulations against the Mistaken Policy of San Martin being unheeded he rejoins him at Lima—Repulse of La Serna by the Mountaineers of Jauja 261

CHAPTER XXXI.

THE EXPEDITION TO THE SOUTH.

1821.

Conspiracy to capture Callao—Miller sent South with a small Force—Lands at Pisco—Insurrection at Cuzco—Cochrane applies to Chile for Aid—Ravages of Fever at Chincha—Cochrane sails for Arica—Capture of Arica—Evacuation of Tacna—Miller marches Inland—Capture of Mirave—Occupation of Moquegua—Miller retreats to Tacna and to Arica—Miller establishes himself at Ica—Loss of the *San Martin* 265

CHAPTER XXXII.

PERU INDEPENDENT.

1821.

The Continental Campaign—Lack of National Spirit in Peru—Convention of Notables at Lima—Declaration of Independence—Capture of Ships by Cochrane at Callao—Attempted Surprise by Las Heras—Overtures of Cochrane to La Mar—San Martin appoints himself "Protector of Peru"—Decree against the Spaniards—Banishment of the Archbishop—Tragic Fate of José Miguel Carrera 270

CHAPTER XXXIII.

THE PROTECTORATE OF PERU.

1821—1822.

The Captain of the Army of the Andes—Royalist Expedition for the Relief of Callao—The Defile of Espiritu Santo—Outburst of Enthusiasm in Lima—Manœuvres in Front of Lima—Retreat of Canterac—Feeble Pursuit of the Royalists—Capitulation of Callao—Reforms of San Martin—The Order of the Sun—Deterioration in the Spirit of the Army—Subsidy from the City of Lima—Conspiracy in the Army—Monarchical Ideas of San Martin—Monteagudo and the "Patriotic Society of Lima"—Mission of Garcia del Rio to Europe 277

CHAPTER XXXIV.

SAN MARTIN AND COCHRANE.

1821—1822.

Mutual Invectives of Two Heroes—San Martin fails to fulfil his Promises to the Fleet—A Stormy Interview—Cochrane seizes Treasure—Cochrane pays his Men with Government Funds—And sails for Guayaquil—Surrender of Two Spanish Frigates to Peruvian Agents—Cochrane attempts to seize the *Venganza*—Returns to Callao and Captures the *Montezuma*—Returns to Chile and abandons the Pacific—The New Peruvian Navy . 287

CHAPTER XXXV.

THE DISASTER AT ICA.

1821—1822.

Royalist Headquarters established at Cuzco—Expedition under Loriga against Pasco—Defeat of Otero—Burning of Cangallo—San Martin sends a Contingent to the Assistance of Bolívar—And Summons the First Peruvian Congress—Torre-Tagle Deputy-Protector—Expedition to Ica—Rout of the Patriots by Canterac—Barbarous Treatment of Spaniards by Monteagudo . 292

CHAPTER XXXVI.

THE REVOLUTIONS IN QUITO AND VENEZUELA.

1809—1812.

The Northern Zone of South America—The First Outbreak at Quito —The Revolution at Caracas—Commencement of the Reaction —SIMON BOLIVAR—His Appearance and Character—His Education—His First Visit to Europe—His Second Visit to Europe —His Life at Caracas—Reception of the Envoys by the British Government—Bolívar meets Miranda in London—Brings him back with him to Venezuela—Action of the Regency of Cadiz—The Patriot Junta sends an Army against Coro—Reception of Miranda—His Plan for a Constitution — First Congress of Venezuela—Declaration of Independence — Revolt of the Canarians—Revolt at Valencia—Capture of Valencia by Miranda —Adoption of a Federal Constitution—General Discontent—Carora sacked by Monteverde—The Royalists of Guayana—Destruction of the Patriot Flotilla—The Great Earthquake—San Carlos burned by Monteverde—Miranda is appointed Dictator—Successes of the Royalists—Monteverde is repulsed in an Attack on the Entrenched Camp at Victoria—Insurrection of the Slaves—Loss of Puerto-Cabello—Miranda treats for Peace —The Capitulation—Miranda is imprisoned by his Officers—Cruelties of Monteverde—Death of Miranda 296

CHAPTER XXXVII.

THE REVOLUTIONS IN NEW GRANADA AND QUITO.

1809—1813.

Excitement in New Granada—Expedition against Quito—Réinstallation of the late Captain-General of Quito—Massacres by the Royalist Soldiery—Revolution at Cartagena—Outbreak on the Plains of Casanare—A Junta established at Pamplona—And at Socorro—Pacific Revolution at Bogotá—Establishment of a Junta—Social Anarchy—Proposals to summon a Congress—The State of Cundinamarca—Nariño appointed Dictator—Congress adopts the Federal System of Government and retires to Ibague—The Province of Cartagena declares itself an Independent State—Preparations of the Royalists—Torices named Dictator of Cartagena—Operations against Santa Marta—Arrival of a New Viceroy—The First Victory of the Patriots—Another Insurrection in Quito — Successes of Montufar and Macaulay— Treachery of the Pastusos—La Vendée of the Revolution— Installation of a Junta at Quito—Operations in the South—Quito declares itself an Independent State—Murder of Ruiz de Castillo—Victory of the Royalists at Mocha—Capture of Quito— Massacres at Popayán—The Policy of Nariño—The Congress at Leiva—Dr. Camilo Torres named President—Civil War—Arrival of another Viceroy—Cundinamarca and Antioquia declare themselves Independent States—Congress places Nariño in Command of the Army—Successes of Nariño—His Passage of the River Juanambú—Dispersion of his Army—He is sent in Irons to Spain—Operations of Bolívar against Santa Marta— Defeat of an Expedition from Cartagena—Bolívar conceives the Idea of Reconquering Venezuela—He crosses the Cordillera— His Memorial to the People of New Granada—President Torres adopts his Idea 312

CHAPTER XXXVIII.

THE RECONQUEST OF VENEZUELA.

1813.

" Pacification " by Monteverde—The Signal for Revolt—Triste— The Expedition to the Mainland—Cruelties of Zuazola—Defeat of the Royalists at Maturin—The Island of Margarita—Arismendi—Siege of Cumaná—Cajigal retreats to Guayana—Mariño named Dictator of the Eastern Provinces—The Expedition of Briceño—Defeat of Correa by Castillo—Bolívar's Commission from the Congress of Granada—Capture of Mérida and Trujillo —Bolívar fulminates a Decree of Extermination against all Royalists—Marti Defeated by Rivas—Rout of Izquierdo—Valencia and Caracas evacuated by Royalists—The Genius of Bolívar —His Triumphant Entry into Caracas—He proclaims Himself

Dictator—Lays Siege to Puerto Cabello—The Reaction—Second Decree of Bolívar—Arrival of Reinforcements at Puerto Cabello—Death of Girardot—Victory of Las Trincheras—Honours to Bolívar at Caracas—The Order of the "Liberators"—Boves, Morales, and Yañez—They rouse the Llaneros—Campo-Elias—Defeat of Boves at Mosquitero—Massacre of Royalists at Calabozo—Repulse of Patriots at Barquisimeto—Battle of Araure—Effects of the Dual Dictatorship—Reappearance of Boves on the Scene—The Patriots are driven from the Plains—General Revulsion of Feeling 324

CHAPTER XXXIX.

THE SECOND FALL OF VENEZUELA.

1814.

Bolívar discloses a New Phase of his Character—The Assembly of Caracas—His Treaty with Mariño—Defeat and Death of Yañez—Action at La Puerta—Repulse of Morales at Victoria—Successes of Rivas—The Massacres of Caracas and La Guayra—Preparations of Bolívar—His Defence of the Entrenchments of San Mateo—Heroism of Recaurte—Defence of Caracas by Rivas—Of Valencia by Urdaneta—Action at Boca Chica—Mariño defeated at San Carlos—First Battle at Carabobo—Rout of the Patriots at La Puerta — Capitulation of Valencia— D'Eluyar raises the Siege of Puerto-Cabello—Bolívar evacuates Caracas—Entrenches Himself at Aragua—Retreats to Barcelona—Capture of Aragua by Morales—Bolívar is accused of Treachery—Retires to Curaçoa—Repulse of Morales at Maturin—Massacre at Cumaná—Rout of the Patriots at Urica—Death of Boves—Capture of Maturin by Morales—Death of Rivas—The Last Patriot Army under Urdaneta seeks Refuge in New Granada . 343

CHAPTER XL.

THE DISSOLUTION OF NEW GRANADA.

1815—1817.

The Fall of Constitutional Government in Spain—Jealousy of Native Troops—Bolívar takes Command of the Army of New Granada—Capture of Bogotá—Fresh Honours to Bolívar—Bolívar makes War on Cartagena—And retires to Jamaica—His Memorials—Morillo arrives from Spain with a Powerful Squadron, and takes Command of the Royalists—Miyares secures the Isthmus of Panamá—Morillo's Instructions—Reduction of the Island of Margarita—Loss of the *San Pedro*—Morillo occupies Caracas—And sails thence for Cartagena—Cartagena—The Siege of Cartagena—The Fortress and City are evacuated by the Patriots

—Repulse of Calzada from the Plains of Casanare—Defeat of the Patriots at Balaga—Further Successes of Calzada—Madrid is defeated by Sámano in the South—Fresh Disturbances in Venezuela—Offers of Amnesty—Establishment of Military Rule at Bogotá—Executions—Morillo returns to Venezuela—Cruelties of Sámano—Death of La Pola—Sámano is appointed Viceroy by Morillo 353

CHAPTER XLI.

THE THIRD WAR IN VENEZUELA.

1815—1817.

Position of Affairs in Venezuela—The Fresh Outbreak on the Island of Margarita—Paez—His First Action—Revulsion of Opinion among the Llaneros—The Army of the Apure—Successes of Cedeño—Attempt to assassinate Bolívar—Bolívar goes to Haití—The Expedition from Cayos—The Landing at Margarita—Bolívar is named Supreme Chief—The Expedition proceeds to Carúpano—Bolívar proceeds to Ocumare—Defeat of Bolívar by Morales—Bolívar's Flight from Ocumare—Successes of Mac-Gregor—The Army of the Centre—Bolívar returns to Haití—Defeat of Lopez by MacGregor—Piar defeats Morales at Juncal—Paez lays Siege to San Fernando—The Spaniards evacuate the Island of Margarita—Bolívar leaves Haití with a Second Expedition—Piar marches on Guayana—Forces the Passage of the Cauca—Occupies the Missions of Coroní—Bolívar again defeated—And leaves for Guayana—Capture of Barcelona by the Royalists—The True Base of Operations—Advance of La Torre from New Granada—Is totally defeated by Paez—And descends the River to Angostura—Is again defeated by Piar at San Felix—Mariño summons a Congress—Morillo puts an End to the Farce—Brion forces his Way up the Orinoco—Flight of La Torre—Conspiracy of Piar and Mariño—Execution of Piar—Banishment of Mariño 365

CHAPTER XLII.

THE REORGANIZATION OF VENEZUELA.

1817—1819.

The Expedition of Morillo and Canterac against the Island of Margarita—The Action at Matasiete—The Massacre at Juan Griego—Morillo returns to Caracas—Position of Patriots and of Royalists—The Civil Administration of Bolívar—Rout of Saraza at Hogaza—The Horse Marines—Bolívar surprises Morillo at Calabozo—Retreat of the Royalists to Sombrero—Defeat of Bolívar at La Puerta—Capture of San Fernando by Paez—

CONTENTS. xxiii

PAGE

Defeat of Paez at Cojedes—Defeat of Cedeño by Morales—And of Morales by Paez—Mariño takes Cumaná, and refuses Allegiance to the Liberator—Bolívar raises a New Army, and is reconciled to Mariño—Santander sent to Casanare—Bolívar's Idea of a Constitution—The Congress of Angostura—Bolívar is named President of Venezuela—The Foreign Auxiliaries—Luis Mendez—Colonel Hippisley—Colonel Wilson—Campbell—Gilmour—General English—Colonel Elsom—General MacGregor—General Devereux—Colonel Montilla—Morillo opens the Campaign—Tactics of Paez—Morillo reoccupies San Fernando—The Affair of " Las Queseras del Medio "—Bolívar's New Idea . 380

CHAPTER XLIII.

BOYACA—COLUMBIA—CARABOBO.

1819—1822.

Bolívar joins Santander—The Passage of the Cordillera—The Expedition halts in the Valley of Sagamoso—Skilful Manœuvres of Bolívar—He captures the City of Tunja—Battle of Boyacá—Bolívar occupies Bogotá—His Activity and the Honours paid Him—Founds the Republic of Columbia—Cruelty of Santander—Bolívar returns to Angostura—Changes during his Absence .—Decrees of Congress—Bolívar named Provisional President of Columbia—Military Operations on the North Coast—Arrival of the Irish Legion at Margarita—Paez retakes San Fernando—The Armistice of Trujillo—Morillo returns to Spain—Revolution in Maracaibo—Operations of Montilla—Bolívar again takes the Field—Battle of Carabobo—Bolívar for the Second Time enters Caracas in Triumph—The Constituent Congress—Bolívar is named President—Capitulation of Cartagena—The Provinces of the Isthmus declare their Independence—Fall of Chagres and Portobello—Bolívar leaves for the South—Activity of Morales —He capitulates—Puerto Cabello is taken by Paez . . . 394

CHAPTER XLIV.

THE WAR IN QUITO.

1821—1822.

Operations in the South of Columbia—Sucre—He leads an Expedition to Guayaquil—His Victory at Yahuachí—His Defeat at Ambato—Arrival of Murgeón from Spain—Bolívar marches on Quito with a Fresh Army—Battle of Bombená—He retreats to Patia—San Martin sends a Contingent to aid Sucre—Manœuvres of the Opposing Armies—The Cavalry Affair at Rio Bamba—Battle of Pichincha—Surrender of Quito—Capitulation of Garcia and of the Pastusos—Prætorianism—Bolívar enters Quito in Triumph 406

CHAPTER XLV.

GUAYAQUIL.

1822.

The Meeting and Merging of Two Revolutions—The Protectorate of Guayaquil—Defeat of the Provincial Army at Ambato—Arrival of Sucre—The Revolt of Puerto-Viejo—Arrival of Salazar—La Mar takes Command of the Provincial Forces—The Question of Guayaquil 414

CHAPTER XLVI.

THE INTERVIEW AT GUAYAQUIL.

1822.

The Influence of Individuals—The Illusions of San Martin—Bolívar becomes jealous of Argentine Influence—The Entry of Bolívar into Guayaquil—He annexes the Province to Columbia—The Arrival of San Martin—The Conference—The Banquet—The Ball—Departure of San Martin—Result of the Conference—Remarkable Letter from San Martin to Bolívar 418

CHAPTER XLVII.

THE ABDICATION OF SAN MARTIN.

1822.

Disturbances in Lima—Banishment of Monteagudo—Return of San Martin—The First Congress of Peru—The Resignation of San Martin—Honours decreed to him by Congress—He leaves Peru—His Illness in Chile—He retires to Mendoza . . . 426

CHAPTER XLVIII.

THE FIRST NATIONAL GOVERNMENT OF PERU.

1822—1823.

The State of Peru—Appointment of a Junta—Bolívar offers Assistance, which is declined—The Plan of Campaign—The Army of the South—Dilatory Movements of Alvarado—The Advance of the Royalists—Battle of Torata—The Rout of Moquegua—Activity of Miller—Withdrawal of the Columbian Contingent—Arenales leaves Peru—Riva-Agüero named President—Preparations for a Fresh Campaign—English Loan—Despatch of a

Peruvian Army to the South under Santa Cruz—Capture of Lima by Canterac—Sucre brings another Columbian Contingent to Peru—Bolívar is named Generalissimo—Canterac returns to the Highlands—Plans of Sucre—Manœuvres of Santa Cruz—He captures La Paz—Gamarra occupies Oruro—Retreat of Santa Cruz—Indecisive Action at Zepita—Dispersion of the Patriot Army—Orderly Retreat of Sucre—Appeals to San Martin for Help—Reconstruction of Congress—Arrival of Bolívar—His Reception—His Appearance—He is Master of Peru . . . 431

CHAPTER XLIX.

JUNIN—AYACUCHO.

1823—1824.

The Day-Dreams of Bolívar—Rivadavia—Treaty between Columbia and Buenos Ayres—Overtures from Spain to Buenos Ayres—The Mission of Alzaga to the West and North—Treatment of the Argentine Contingent by Peru—Mutiny of the Garrison of Callao—Hoisting the Flag of Spain—Falucho—Dissolution of the Army of the Andes—Monet occupies Lima and Callao—Treachery of Torre-Tagle—Ships burned by Guise in Harbour—Bolívar named Dictator—Execution of Argentine Officers by Monet—Illness of Bolívar—His Preparations—Olañeta rebels against the Viceroy—Bolívar marches on Jauja—Advance of Canterac—Cavalry Action at Junin—Rapid Retreat of Canterac—Bolívar returns to Lima—Movement against him in the Congress of Columbia—The Spanish Naval Squadron—Manœuvres of Sucre—Advance of Royalists from Cuzco—Sucre concentrates his Forces—The Royalists gain his Rear—Victory or Death—Victory of Ayacucho 443

CHAPTER L.

APOGEE, DECLINE, AND FALL OF BOLIVAR.

1824—1830.

Results of the Victory of Ayacucho—The Twofold Nature of the Revolution—Assassination of Monteagudo—Bolívar summons a Congress at Panama—His Theatrical Proceedings—Upper Peru becomes an Independent State—Tendency of the Policy of Bolívar—He leaves Lima for Potosí—The Banquet at Arequipa—Bolívar meets Argentine Envoys at Potosí—His Proposals to them—Opinions of the Press of Buenos Ayres—He draws up a Constitution for Bolivia—Attempt to assassinate Bolívar at Lima—Adoption of a New Constitution by Peru—The Grand Confederation of the Andes—The Nature of the Proposed Monocracy—Revolution in Venezuela—Bolívar Returns to Columbia—

Revolutions in Peru and Bolívia—The Convention of Ocaña—Bolívar is again named Dictator of New Granada—Conspiracy against him at Bogotá—He declares War against Peru—His Monarchical Proposals—Rebellion at Antioquia—Venezuela becomes an Independent State—The Constituent Congress at Bogotá—Bolívar resigns—Mosquera is elected President of New Granada—Pension assigned to Bolívar 458

EPILOGUE.

The Verdict of Posterity—The Tragedy of Emancipation—San Martin goes to Europe—His Return to Buenos Ayres—Bolívar in Retirement—Anarchy in New Granada—Establishment of the Republic of Ecuador—Death of Bolívar—His Last Words—Life of San Martin in Exile—His Death—His Remains are brought back to Buenos Ayres—The Work of the Two Liberators compared—The Nature of True Greatness 470

TRANSLATOR'S APPENDIX.

I.—The Spanish Colonial System 477
II.—Personal Appearance of San Martin 478
III.—The Rocket-Tubes at Callao 478
IV.—Description of a Suspension Bridge 478
V.—The Ideas of San Martin 479
VI.—A Venezuelan Picture presented to the City of New York . 480
VII.—The Battle of Carabobo 481

BIOGRAPHICAL NOTES.

Alvarado—Arenales—Brown—Cochrane—Güemes—Las Heras—Lavalle—Miller—Necochea—O'Higgins—Paez. . . . 484

PROLOGUE.

THE object of this book is to give a biography of GENERAL JOSÉ DE SAN MARTIN, combining therewith the history of the emancipation of South America. It is a necessary complement to the HISTORY OF BELGRANO, written thirty years ago. These two histories display the Argentine Revolution in its two principal aspects; one relates the development of a nation, the other the effect of this development upon the emancipation of a continent.

This history is based, for the most part, upon documents hitherto unpublished, some of which are truly posthumous revelations which throw new light upon mysterious or little known events, or correct errors resulting from defective information.

I believe I have consulted all the books, pamphlets, newspapers and fly-sheets which have ever been printed concerning San Martin, and of manuscripts I have a collection of at least 10,000 documents, bound in 73 thick volumes, which it is my purpose to deposit in the National Library.

The most important of these sources of information has been the archive of General San Martin himself, which was placed at my disposal by his son-in-law, the late Don Mariano Balcarce. I have also consulted the archives of this city from the year 1812 to the year 1824, without which it would have been impossible to compile a complete history. The archives of the Director Pueyrredón, which were given to me by his son, have also been of great service to me, as also those of General O'Higgins, Don Tomás Godoy Cruz, General Las Heras, and others. I have also acquired much verbal information from conversations held with many of the contemporaries of San Martin, and with some of his companions in arms.

In addition to consulting all available maps and plans relating to the campaigns of San Martin, I have inspected in person the routes followed by the army of the Andes and have made sketches myself of the scene of memorable events when plans were not forthcoming.

* * * * * * *

This book will not be the historical monument which posterity will some day consecrate to the immortal memory of San Martin, but those who do at some future date erect it, will herein find abundant materials, stones finished or but roughly cut, with which solidly to lay out the foundations.

BARTOLOMÉ MITRE.

BUENOS AYRES, 1887.

HERE follows, on 25 pages, a list of unpublished manuscripts consulted in the compilation of this work, which manuscripts will be deposited in the National Library of Buenos Ayres.

WILLIAM PILLING.

THE EMANCIPATION OF SOUTH AMERICA.

CHAPTER I.
HISTORICAL INTRODUCTION.

THE ARGUMENT OF THE BOOK.

THREE great names stand forth conspicuous in the annals of America, those of WASHINGTON, BOLIVAR, SAN MARTIN. Of Washington, the great leader of the Democracy of the North; of Bolívar and of San Martin, who were the emancipators of the southern half of the continent. The story of the life-work of the latter of these two is the Argument of this book.

The scene of action passes on a vast theatre, a territory extending for more than fifty degrees of latitude, from Cape Horn to the Tropic of Cancer, and occupies twenty years of strife. The starting-point of this history is the Argentine revolution; it follows the course of this revolution as it spreads over the continent, and its object is to explain the laws which governed the establishment of a family of new Republics, and the fundamental principles from which they sprang.

This argument is dual and complex, for it treats both of political revolution and of social evolution. It shows how the Argentine revolution became a propaganda to the world outside, of the principles upon which it was based, and how under these auspices independent and sovereign nations sprang into existence, with forms and tendencies in the same likeness and similitude. It shows the proclamation of a new international law, which only permits of alliance against an enemy in the name of a common destiny, and forbids conquests and annexations. It shows also the failure of the attempt in Columbia to unite the emancipated colonies artificially into a monocracy in opposition to natural law and to the new idea of the rights of man inaugurated by the Argentine revolution.

The two hegemonies, the Argentine and the Columbian, unite to set the seal upon the emancipation of South America. San Martin and Bolívar cross the continent from the Atlantic to the Pacific by different routes, giving liberty to enslaved peoples, founding new nations, and meeting as together they enclose the colonial system in its last entrenchments, they bring the two opposing systems face to face, the shock resulting in the triumph of the superior principle.

Thus considered, the history of the emancipation of South America presents a homogeneous character, with unity of action and with one dominant idea, which in the midst of accidental deviations reveals the existence of a law giving one accordant significance to facts accomplished.

The study of the theatre of the war of independence shows that the scene passes in two distinct revolutionary areas—one at the south, comprehending the United Provinces of the River Plate, Chile, and Upper Peru; the other, at the north, comprehending Venezuela, New Granada, and Quito. The strife and the triumph proceed simultaneously in each area until the two revolutions, like to two masses obeying a reciprocal attraction, converge towards the centre. This plan, drawn up and carried out by the two great Liberators, emancipates South America by the combined military action of the revolted colonies, which action has at once the ideal unity of a poem and the precision of a machine.

The unity of this action is clearly displayed in the general lines of the life of San Martin, and gives to his historic figure an importance far transcending both his deeds and his designs. He was born in an obscure American town, which disappeared as he commenced to figure upon the scene; thus America in its entirety became his country. He grew up as a soldier in the Old World, fighting by sea and on land in company with the first soldiers of the age, and so prepared himself for his warlike mission, unwitting of his destiny. In the New World he commenced his career by establishing tactics and discipline as his base of operations, and from their combination produced his machine of war. He consolidated the independence of the United Provinces of the River Plate as the point from which he might start for the conquest of South America. In command of the army of the North, his name is associated with the revolution of Upper Peru; as he passed the Andes in prosecution of his own plan, he became identified with the revolution of Chile, and after consolidating the independence of this country he initiated the first international alliance in America. He secured the command of the Pacific, without which the independence of America was at that time impossible, and gave liberty to Lower Peru. He then carried the revolutionary standard of the allies to the foot of Pichincha, where he met the liberator of Columbia. Under the equator, which divides the two theatres of the war, he clasped hands with Bolívar. Thus ended his grand campaign; at the apogee of his power he disappeared from the scene, knowing that his mission was fulfilled, that his strength was exhausted, and condemned himself to exile, faithful to the ruling maxim of his life, *Serás lo que debes ser ; y sinó, no serás nada.**

From exile he looked upon the results of his life-work: the definitive political organization of South America in

* "Thou shalt be that which thou oughtest to be; if not, thou shalt be nothing."

accordance with geographical divisions, the foundation of a new constellation of independent States in obedience to natural laws as by him instinctively foreseen. He saw without envy that Bolívar, with whom he shared the glory of the redemption of a new world, wore the crown of the final triumph, though he knew that both as a politician and as a soldier he was his superior. Then the wild dream of Bolívar that he could found an empire of dependent republics under the auspices of Columbia faded away, and gave place to the Argentine plan of independent republics heralded by San Martin.

Synopsis of the South American Revolution.

It has been said that posterity will look upon the emancipation of South America as the most important political phenomenon of the nineteenth century, both in itself and from the probable extent of its future consequences. The immediate result was to bring into existence a new group of independent nations, founded on democratic principles, in open opposition to the right of conquest and to the dogmas of monarchy and absolutism which yet prevailed in the Old World. These new nations were organized on the principle of equality, and were emancipated from privilege, and thus offered an entirely fresh field for experiment in the development of the physical and moral faculties of man. This movement thus constitutes one of the most drastic changes ever effected in the condition of the human race.

The first throes of this revolution were felt at the two extremities and in the centre of South America in the year 1809. In 1810 all the Spanish American colonies rose up in rebellion as by one innate impulse, and proclaimed the principle of self-government. Six years later all, save one, of these insurrections were quelled.

The United Provinces of the River Plate alone maintained their position, and after declaring their own independence they gave to the conquered colonies the signal for the great and final struggle by making common cause with them.

In 1817 the Argentine revolution drew up a plan for the emancipation of the continent, took the offensive, crossed the Andes, and liberated Chile; in union with Chile obtained command of the Pacific, liberated Peru and carried her arms to the equator in aid of the revolution of Columbia. This vigorous impulse was felt in the extreme north of this southern continent, which in its turn defeated and expelled the champions of the old system, went through a similar evolution, and crossed the Andes to the point where the two forces united. The Highlands of Peru became the scene of the final struggle. Then the Spanish American colonies were free by their own strength, and from the chaos sprang up a new world.

During the progress of these events, the United States of the North, the pioneers of the Republican era, recognised the independence of the new republics (1822), as " an expression of the simple truth," and declared—

" The peoples of South America have a right to break the chains which bind them to their mother country, to assume the rank of nations among the sovereign nations of the world, and to establish institutions in accordance with natural laws dictated by God himself."

As a consequence of this recognition the United States, in the year 1823, promulgated the famous Monroe Doctrine which, in opposition to the Bull of Alexander VI., established a new principle of international law under the formula—" America for the Americans."

Free England, who at first looked favourably upon the revolution, began, in 1818, to lean towards Spain and the Holy Alliance, advocating an arrangement on the basis of the "commercial freedom" of the colonies. The diplomatists of Washington interfered in favour of their complete emancipation, and Lafayette, in support of this idea, declared to the Government of France:—

"Any opposition which may be made to the independence of the New World may cause suffering but will not imperil the idea."

Thus, much before the final triumph, the emancipation of the new continent was accepted as an accomplished fact, and the attitude of the United States supported by England turned the scales of diplomacy in its favour in 1823. When at the Congress of Verona the party of reaction proposed a contrary policy, Canning, Prime Minister of Great Britain, wrote to Grenville those memorable words which re-echoed through two hemispheres:—

"The battle has been fierce, but it is won. The nail is clenched; Spanish America is free. *Novus sæclorum nascitur ordo!*"

The battle of Ayacucho was the response to these words, and Canning could then exclaim:—

"I have called a new world into existence to redress the balance of the old."

The Action of America upon Europe.

The land discovered by Christopher Columbus, which completed the physical world, was destined to re-establish its general equilibrium at the moment the base thereof was shaken.

Before the end of the fifteenth century Europe had lost its moral and political equilibrium. After the invasion of the barbarians, which imbued it with a new principle of life without destroying the germ of decay left by the fall of the Roman Empire, its civilization was again on the point of collapse. Not one homogeneous nation there existed, her productive energy was exhausted, liberty was but a latent hope, privilege was the dominant law, politics were founded on the principles of Macchiavelli, all healthy evolution in the path of progress was impossible.

A fresh invasion from the East advanced under the standard of the Crescent, and the despotism of Mussulman fanaticism was the last hope of the people. Europe, shut in between the Danube and the Pillars of Hercules, seemed lost; the discovery of a new world alone could save her. This discovery restored harmony to the discordant elements, gave new life to Christianity, and saved the liberties of mankind. The Reformation, which came immediately afterwards, engrafted upon the consciences of men the germ of the democratic principles of the Bible, which, transplanted to a new world, later on regenerated the effete civilization brought from Europe, and spread it as a vital principle of politics all the world over.

The popular belief that the fountain of eternal youth was to be found on the new continent discovered by Columbus, was no vain imagination. The decrepit civilization of the Old World drew fresh youth and strength from the virgin soil of America, the genius of progress therein latent developed rapidly in the genial air. The opening of this new and vast field to human activity, was truly a renovation of social order in accordance with natural law, and resulted in the organization of a democracy based upon labour. To this end it was only necessary that the European, leaving his old traditions behind him, should, on a vacant continent, work out his own destiny under the guidance of healthy instinct.

The Colonization of Spanish America.

In the repartition of the new continent the worst lot fell to the southern half. Spain and Portugal carried their feudal absolutism to their colonies, but they could not plant there their systems of privilege, of aristocracy, or of social inequality. The good and the bad seed alike were modified by cultivation in a new soil, the natural product being democracy. The mode of colonization contributed to this result. The most trustworthy annals of the Indies recognise the fact that the conquest was achieved at the expense of the conquerors, without any drafts on the royal treasury. Hence arose that spirit of self-reliance which they bequeathed to their descendants. A rebel world grew up under the auspices of absolutism. The colonial constitution, which inculcated a personal despotism and excluded the idea of a common country, contributed fatally to this result. Spanish America was looked upon as the personal property of the Spanish monarch, in virtue of the Bull of Alexander VI. Thus the colony did not form a part of the nation, and was united to her only by allegiance to a common sovereign. When the monarch disappeared, his power lapsed to his vassals; the logical and legal result being the separation of the colonies from the mother country.

The government of the colonies was entrusted to the Council of the Indies, represented politically by a Viceroy, and in law by the Audiencia, the bounds of whose authority were ill-defined. In municipal affairs, the Cabildos, derived from the free communities of the mother country, were nominally the representatives of the people. In them lay the germs of democracy, as they possessed the right to call public meetings for the settlement of their own affairs by vote, which right, for long in abeyance, became an active power when supported by popular force.

The great extent of the country, the want of moral cohesion, the admixture of races, the general corruption of manners, the absence of an ideal, the lack of political and industrial activity, and the profound ignorance of the masses, all contributed to produce a state of semi-barbarism by the side of a weakly civilization, and vitiated the entire social organism. From this embryo was to spring a new republican world, the product of the germs latent within it.

The Colonization of North America.

North America, more fortunate, was colonized by a nation which had practical notions of liberty, and by a race better prepared for self-government. The process commenced a century later. The colonists easily adapted themselves to a climate similar to that of the mother country, and founded there a new home to which they were bound by free institutions. Originally the English colonies were looked upon as Crown provinces, and were ruled by privileged companies, and by a Council similar to that of the Indies, the monarch reserving to himself, as in Spain, the supreme legislative authority and the right of appointment, without giving any legislative rights. The colonists of Virginia, by their own energy, soon acquired some political rights, which were secured to them by royal charters. This example was followed by the colonists of Maryland. Colonial assemblies absorbed the privileges of the companies, and the royal charters formed later on the basis of republican institutions.

After the planters of Virginia and Maryland came the PILGRIM FATHERS of New England, who, flying from persecution in Europe, sought liberty of conscience in the New World. Authors of the great revolution, they were deeply imbued with the republican spirit, and with the democratic spirit of Switzerland and of the Netherlands, in which latter country they had seen their ideal of the ruler of a free people in the austere person of William of Orange, the antetype of Washington. In accordance with these ideas, they established at once a form of popular government hitherto unknown, based upon just laws. Finally came the Quakers, who proclaimed freedom of the intellect as an innate and inalienable right, and drew up their constitution on the basis of democratic equality, absolute and universal; in this anticipating the most advanced of the modern era. Under William Penn they established the representative colony of Pennsylvania, the nucleus and the type of the great republic of the United States.

Such was the genesis of democratic liberty, destined to become universal.

Colonial Policy in both Americas.

The commercial monopoly which Spain adopted as a system on the discovery of America, had an influence quite as evil upon herself as upon her colonies. The intention was that Spain should draw to herself the wealth of the New World, by keeping in her own hands the exchange of European manufactures for the products of America. Every industry which might compete with those of the Peninsula was prohibited in America. At first Seville, and afterwards Cadiz, was declared to be the only port from which ships laden with merchandise could sail, or at which they could land cargoes of colonial produce. All direct trade between the colonies themselves was forbidden. The restrictive system was completed by collecting all the merchant vessels into annual or biennial convoys sailing in charge of ships of war to or from Portobello and Panama. Merchandise so introduced, was carried across the isthmus and distributed by way of the Pacific and by land to Potosi, where the Southern and Atlantic Provinces could supply themselves at prices five or six hundred per cent. over the original cost. Such a system could only spring from a mind enfeebled by the possession of absolute power, and could only be tolerated by a race of slaves.

Before one century had elapsed, the population of Spain was reduced by one-half, her manufacturing industries were ruined, her mercantile marine no longer existed, her trade was in the hands of foreign smugglers, and the gold and silver of the New World went everywhere except to Spain.* When Spain, taught by experience, sought to

* See Appendix I.

remedy the evil, it was already too late, her colonies on the southern continent were lost to her. Neither force nor love, nor a common interest, bound the disinherited children to their parent; the separation was complete, and the independence of the colonies a question of time and of opportunity.

The colonial system of Spain was not an invention, it was an ancient tradition, it was the economic theory of the epoch reduced to practice. England followed the same system, committing even greater errors in the establishment of privileged companies, such as the East India Company, giving territories to them on a feudal basis, the monarch reserving absolute authority over commercial relations.

In practice these errors furnished their own remedies. Tyrannical laws fell into disuse from the resistance of colonies armed with municipal rights. Thus the results sought by England were achieved without great violence and with advantage both to the mother country and to her colonies. The navigation laws of 1650—1666 gave supremacy to the mercantile marine of England, and by shutting out foreign competition from her markets, monopolised the trade with the colonies. This monopoly in skilful hands, colonized North America and corrected to some extent the errors of the system. In 1652, under Cromwell, freedom of commerce was established between England and her colonies, the right being given to the colonists to tax themselves by the votes of their representatives and to regulate their own Customs duties. This was almost independence. Even when their charters were mutilated or abrogated by the Stuarts, this doctrine was respected by common consent. When England disregarded it came the revolution.

THE EMANCIPATION OF NORTH AMERICA.

A special question of constitutional law concerning

Customs duties, was the immediate cause of the revolution in North America. The revolution of South America arose from a question of fundamental principles.

The Stamp Tax imposed by England on her colonies was repealed on the ground that it was an *internal* tax, but Parliament sanctioned the imposition of Customs duties on the ground that they were an *external* tax, the produce of the colonies being subject to the will of the king. The colonists protested and took a further step by declaring that the *Mutiny Act* had nothing to do with them, as it was sanctioned by a Parliament in which they were not represented. They called out their municipal militia, and so in 1774 commenced the great struggle for the emancipation of America. During ten years their resistance had been kept within the limits of the laws, but from this moment they took their stand on the wide basis of natural and ideal right, independent of law and of tradition.

The Declaration of Independence on the 4th July, 1776, was the proclamation of an innate universal human right, of a new theory of government independent of precedent, inspired by natural law, by philosophy, and by political science. This declaration became, as has been said,

"The profession of faith of all the liberals of the world."

The echo of these theories was heard in France, and by her was transmitted to the Latin nations of both hemispheres. The people embraced them with enthusiasm. Up to that time two schools of politics had divided the empire of free thought. The historical school, led by Montesquieu, looked upon the constitution of England as the finished work of experience and of human logic. The philosophical school, led by Rousseau, denied the value of experience and thought to establish liberty and the sovereignty of the people by seeking "the best form of association for the defence and protection of each associate against the force of all, so that each one should obey only himself and remain free as before." This second doctrine formulated in the constitution of the United States, became a new principle in political science, and as such met with general acceptance throughout the colonies of South America.

The most important feature of the revolution of North America is not the achievement of her national independence, but her emancipation, political, intellectual, and moral, in the name of human rights and in constitutional form. From this moment, English constitutionalism ceased to be a model, and the English constitution to be an ideal, even among the English themselves, who have had to recognise their descendants and political pupils as their masters.

The spirit of free England, anticipating the verdict of posterity, justified insurrection in America. Statesmen and thinkers such as Chatham and Burke, sympathised in the movement, declaring, "There is no monopoly of principle," but its effect upon France was still more marked, being the outcome of the reasonings of her philosophers.

Thus it was that America reacted for the second time upon Europe with most beneficial effect. On the third occasion the part of teacher is played by South America.

The Affiliation of the Revolution of South America.

Hardly was Peru conquered by the Spanish race, than it became the theatre of civil war. The conquerors, headed by Gonzalo Pizarro, rebelled against their king in the name of their rights as conquerors, cut off the head of the king's representative and burned the Royal Standard. Hardly had one generation time to grow up in America, ere a son of Hernan Cortez, in whose veins flowed the blood of the celebrated Indian Doña Marina, conspired to give independence to Mexico in the name of the same territorial rights invoked by Pizarro. The far off colony of Paraguay was from the first a turbulent municipal republic. The colonists deposed their royally appointed governors with shouts of "Death to Tyrants," elected rulers of their own, and did as they liked for more than twenty-five years (1535-60). These and many other similar facts, prove that the colonization of South America was imbued from the commencement with the principle of individuality and with the instinct of independence, which naturally resulted in emancipation and democracy.

These insurrections were outbursts of Castillian spirit, but early in the eighteenth century, Creoles begin to call themselves with pride Americans, and for the first time is heard in Potosi the cry of *Liberty*. In 1711 the half-breeds proclaimed a mulatto King of Venezuela. In 1733 the Creoles rose in arms and compelled the abrogation of the commercial monopoly of the "Compania Guipuzcoana de Caracas." In 1730 two thousand half-breeds at Cochabamba (Upper Peru), made armed protest against the poll-tax, and acquired the right to elect Creoles as officers of justice to the exclusion of Spaniards. In 1765 the Creoles of Quito rose in armed insurrection against the imposition of direct taxes. None of these outbreaks had as yet any definite political character. The embryonic republic of Paraguay gave the first example of a revolutionary movement based upon the sovereignty of the people.

José Antequera, by birth an American but educated in Spain, appeared on the scene during a dispute between the governor of Paraguay and the Cabildo of Asuncion. The people named him governor by acclamation. He placed himself at their head, in opposition to the theocratic rule of the Jesuits, who were ruining the country. He fought pitched battles against the royal troops and was blessed as a saviour, but died on the scaffold as a traitor to his king.

After his death, his pupil Fernando Mompox organized the popular party under the name of the *Comuneros*, deposed another governor and established a governing Junta, but was also overcome.

In 1781 the *Comuneros* broke out in insurrection in New Granada, but the movement was suppressed.

These were not events of great historical importance, but they show that throughout the period of Spanish domination, the rule of the mother country was irksome to the Spaniards themselves, and was hateful to all Americans.

The Moral Revolution of South America.

There can be no revolution until the ideas of men become the conscience of the mass, and until the passions of men become a public force, because "it is man and not events which constitute the world." The revolution was accomplished in the man of South America before the end of the eighteenth century; after that all his actions have one object and one meaning. Emancipation was no longer an instinct, it became an active passion.

Spain through jealousy of England joined France in aiding the rebels of the North, and her recognition of the independence of the new republic was virtually the abdication of her own authority over the South. Aranda, one of the first statesmen of his time, advised his sovereign in 1783 to forestall the inevitable future by making one *infante* King of Mexico, one King of Peru, and one King of the Mainland, taking to himself the rank of Emperor. The King of Spain shut his ears to these counsels.

The revolution of 1789 proved that the ideas embodied in the Declaration of Independence were of universal application. The monarchs of Europe took the alarm and formed reactionary leagues. To South America these ideas were conveyed by educated Creoles, who travelling in Europe learned them from French writers. "The Rights of Man" was translated, printed in secret, and circulated through New Granada by Antonio Nariño.

Charged with this as a crime, no proof could be brought against him as no copy of the book could be found, tortures failing to extract information from suspects. He was banished to Africa, his property confiscated, and his original copy of the work was burnt by the public executioner. From the men of culture the new ideas filtered to the masses, transforming their minds by the creation of an ideal, which each one interpreted in accordance with his own talents, interests, or prejudices.

The Precursor of the Emancipation of South America.

During some years previously an ardent apostle of human liberty had wandered about the world. He was a dreamer with confused ideas and undisciplined attainments, a generous minded warrior, above all, a man of strong will. A soldier of Washington, a comrade of Lafayette, a general under Dumouriez,* a companion of Madame Roland in her prison, a confidant of Pitt in his schemes of insurrection in the colonies of Spanish America, distinguished by Catharine II. of Russia, whose favours he put aside in deference to his austere mission, looked upon by Napoleon as a lunatic with a spark of the sacred fire, Francisco Miranda, a native of Caracas, was the first to foresee the great destinies of republican America, and the first to raise the banner of freedom on the southern continent.

He it was who organised the revolutionary efforts of South Americans in Europe; establishing an understanding with the Creoles of the colonies. It was he who towards the close of the eighteenth century founded in

* Miranda served with great distinction in the campaigns of Valmy and Jemappes, and commanded the right wing of the Republican army at the disastrous affair of Neerwinden. He was afterwards imprisoned by the Directory on suspicion of being implicated in the defection of Dumouriez, whose treachery he had denounced, but escaped and fled to England.—Tr.

London the political society, the "Gran Reunion Americana," to which they were all affiliated. In this society were initiated in the mysteries of future liberty, O'Higgins of Chile, Nariño of New Granada, Montufar and Rocafuerte of Quito, Caro of Cuba, who represented the patriots of Peru, Alvear, an Argentine, and others who later on became illustrious. Here the two great liberators, BOLIVAR and SAN MARTIN, took an oath to work out the triumph of the cause of the emancipation of South America.

This society was the type of the secret societies which, transplanted to the theatre of action, impressed its seal upon the characters of those who directed the revolution of South America. They inoculated it with the true American idea, which, heedless of frontiers and disregarding all obstacles, looked upon the enslaved colonies as one, with one aspiration, with one love, and with one hatred of their common master. This gave cohesion to the revolution in America, and ensured triumph by the union of all forces to one common end. Here was the point of contact of all Creoles, wherever they might work for independence and for liberty. Here is the explanation of the identity of the original movements in spite of the isolation of each colony.

Miranda sought to interest the whole world in the cause of independence; chiefly he sought the help of England. Three times (1790—1801) he obtained a promise of moral and material support from Pitt, with the co-operation of the United States. European complications and the hesitation of the cabinet at Washington, prevented the fulfilment of these promises. In 1791 he published a letter to the Americans, in which he attacked the colonial system of Spain, declaring that nature had separated America from Spain by the interposition of the ocean, thus emancipating her sons from the mother country, and that they—

"Were free by natural right received from the Creator; that the moment had arrived for opening up a new era of prosperity; and with the aid of Providence, to raise up in America a grand family of brothers united by a common interest."

Failing in his attempt to secure the help of England and the United States, Miranda ventured upon the enterprise by himself. In the year 1806 he made two attempts to kindle the fire of revolution in his native country. He landed on the mainland at Ocumare with two hundred men, and at Vela de Coro with five hundred. None responded to his call, but the cry was heard, and its echo resounded through two worlds.

England, on the death of Pitt, abandoning his projects for the emancipation of the colonies of Spanish America, attempted to conquer them for herself, and was twice defeated at Buenos Ayres in 1806 and 1807. Miranda was pleased at this defeat, and in 1808 wrote to congratulate the Cabildo of Buenos Ayres. At the same time he wrote to the Cabildo of Caracas, giving notice of the invasion of Spain by Napoleon, advising them to take charge of the government and to send deputies to London to arrange the future course of the New World. At the same time he published in London a pamphlet written in English by an Englishman, in which from the defeat of the English was drawn a lesson, based upon the opinion of General Auchmuty, that the Creoles would only make alliance with England on condition of their own independence. Miranda translated this pamphlet into Spanish, and added a sketch of a constitution for the new States proposed, the dominant idea of which was a federal republic on a basis of independent Cabildos.

As the victory of Buenos Ayres made a great noise in the world, and more especially in the hearts of Americans, this propaganda fell in with the new sentiment of nationality, disclosed in the words of Don Cornelio Saavedra in his address to the Patricios* of Buenos Ayres in 1807 :

* A native regiment which had taken a prominent part in the repulse of the English.—TR.

"Those born in the Indies, whose spirits are undaunted, are in no way inferior to the Spaniards of Europe, and in valour give place to none."

THE RACES OF SOUTH AMERICA.—THE CREOLE.

Five races, which for historic purposes may be looked upon as three only, peopled the Southern Continent at the outbreak of the War of Independence: the European Spaniards, the Spanish-American Creoles, and the half-breeds; also the indigenous Indians, and the negroes from Africa. The Spaniards formed a privileged class, and by reason of their origin enjoyed both political and social pre-eminence. The Indians and the negroes formed the servile class. The half-breeds, derived from a mixture of three races, formed an intermediate class, and in some places were in a large majority. The Creoles, direct descendants of Spaniards, of pure blood, but modified in character by contact with the half-breeds, were the true sons of the soil, and constituted the basis of society. Generally the most numerous, they were always the civilising force of the colony. They were the most energetic, the most intelligent and imaginative; and with all their inherited vices and their want of preparation for freedom, were the only ones animated by an innate sentiment of patriotism.

Those born in South America thus formed a race apart, an oppressed race, who saw in their ancestors and in their contemporaries not fathers and brothers, but masters. The colonial system placed, to a certain extent, all natives of the soil upon the same level, and drew a broad line of distinction between the Spanish-American colonists and their mother country. Spain, by reason of distance, yielded to her colonists greater freedom and more municipal rights than she gave to her own sons in their own land, but her absolute government could not bind her colonies to her by the tie of nationality. Men of Spanish birth looked upon the colonies as feudal territory, over which they, as beings of a superior race, were the natural lords, and thought that if only a shoemaker remained in Castile, this shoemaker had the right to govern all America.

The natural aspiration of slaves is for freedom, and that of oppressed races who know their own strength is to assume their place in the human family. In this double aspiration lay the germ of revolution in America. In 1780 the indigenous race under Tupac-Amarú, a descendant of the Incas, rose *en masse* in Peru against their oppressors, but were naturally defeated. They possessed no great social force, and did not represent the cause of civilized America. The day of the Creoles had not yet come, but they saw nothing to admire, to love, or to respect in Spain. An absolute King, generally an imbecile, was the sole point of contact between them. Their mother country was to them neither a country nor a mother. The instinct of independence became a passion, even more vehement in those who resided in Spain than in those who had never left their own hearths. Thus it was that the leaders who did most for the revolution came from Spain.

In the struggle each race took its own special part. The Creoles formed the vanguard and directed the movements. The indigenous races formed the first line in Mexico, but elsewhere they were only useful as auxiliaries. In South America the half-breeds formed the rank and file of the armies of the revolution. The Argentine *gaucho*, with the fatalism of the Arab and the strength of the Cossack, gave the type to the cavalry, renowned for the impetuosity of their charge from La Plata to Chimborazo. The *llaneros** of Venezuela, half-breeds for the most part, formed the famous squadrons of Columbia, whose feats were celebrated from the Orinoco to Potosi. The *rotos*† of Chile, mostly of Indian blood, formed with Argentines in solid battalions, who measured their strength with Spanish

---

* Men of the plains, from *llano* = a plain. † Countrymen.

regiments, victors over the soldiers of Napoleon in the Peninsula. The manumitted negroes gave their contingent to the American infantry, showing the warlike qualities of their race. In Upper Peru the indigenous races kept alive for ten years the flames of insurrection when the patriot armies were defeated. The *cholos* of the Highlands of Peru espoused the cause of the king, and were highly esteemed as infantry by the Spanish generals, more especially on account of the extraordinary rapidity of their marches.

The Creole of South America is a sturdy off-shoot of that civilizing Indo-European race to which is reserved the government of the world. It is his mission to complete the democratization of the American continent and to found a new order of things destined to live and progress. He has impressed the peculiarities of his character upon the new nationalities.

When the revolution broke out in 1810, it was said that South America would become English or French; when it triumphed, that the continent would sink back into barbarism. By the will and the work of the Creole, it became American, republican, and civilized.

The First Throes of Revolution.

The initial outbreaks of the year 1809, were in some parts of a more radical character than were those of the following year, when the first political formula of the rebellion was merely a demand for relative and provisional independence, for a compromise between democracy and monarchy upon the basis of autonomy.

The doctrine that on the disappearance of the monarch his sovereignty reverted to his people, was for the first time boldly proclaimed in Mexico. From this it was deduced that they had the right to appoint governing Juntas for their own security, and owed no allegiance to those established in Spain at the time of the French invasion. Hence arose disputes between the Creoles and the Spaniards, and between the Audiencia and the Viceroy, which at the end of 1809 changed the movement into a conspiracy for independence.

In Quito the commotion assumed more definite forms. The colonial authorities were overturned and a governing Junta was set up, which took to itself the attributes of sovereignty and raised troops for its own defence. They exhorted the peoples of America by a proclamation to follow the example, announcing that "law has resumed its authority under the equator," and that "the rights of man were, by the disappearance of despotism, no longer at the mercy of arbitrary power." The authors of this premature revolution were overcome and put to death in prison.

In Upper Peru, the city of Chuquisaca was the first to move. In May, 1809, the Creoles, at the instigation of the Audiencia, tumultuously deposed the constituted authorities, and set up an independent government. In July the city of La Paz followed the example. Under the name of the *Junta Tuitiva*, an independent government composed exclusively of Americans was established, which raised an army, and hung on a gallows those who denied its authority. Both these revolts were suppressed by the combined arms of the neighbouring Viceroyalties of Peru and La Plata. The leaders of the insurrection of La Paz died either on the field of battle or on the gallows. One of the latter before being thrown off cried out :—"The fire which I have lighted shall never be quenched." Their heads and limbs were nailed to the posts which mark out the public roads in that country, but before they had rotted away the fire was again burning in Upper Peru.

By the quelling of these conspiracies it was thought that the danger was averted, but as was said by the Viceroy of Peru fifty years before, on the first revolt of the Comuneros of Paraguay, "it was but a covering up of the fire with ashes."

The Growth of the Revolution.

In the year 1810 the drama of revolution unfolded itself upon a vast continental scene, with a unity of action which from the first attracted the attention of the world. All the Spanish American colonies with the exception of Lower Peru, arose in rebellion simultaneously, and proclaimed one political doctrine. Some historians have thought that this movement was the result of an external impulse, and that the subsequent separation was as the falling of unripe fruit. Others, better informed, look upon this separation as a necessity: "The union of Spain with America, possible under an absolute *régime*, was incompatible with representative government and with the political equality of the citizens." The truth is that the South American revolution was inspired by an innate sentiment of patriotism, in obedience to conservative instinct, and by its nature tended to independence.

The divorce of the colonies from the mother country took place at a critical moment, when their union was hurtful to them both. If America was not prepared for self-government, and if her attempts at self-government almost exhausted the forces already weakened by the struggle, what would then have been her condition had she remained under the rule of unnatural laws which condemned her to a lingering death, a prey to vices inoculated by an evil system?

It cannot be denied that without the invasion of Spain by Napoleon in 1808, and the consequent disappearance of the dynasty of Spain, the revolution would have been delayed; but this does not imply that America was not ripe for emancipation, the opportunity was nothing more than the spark setting fire to the combustibles already prepared for burning.

The Provisional Government established in Spain anticipated the complaints of the colonists, and recognised by its acts the justice of their cause, fomenting their resistance as much by its concessions as by its refusals. The Regency of Cadiz called upon Americans to join the national Cortes, thus raising them to the rank of freemen, but at the same time gave them only one deputy, chosen by itself, for each million of inhabitants, while to the natives of the Peninsula, for the most part under the yoke of the foreigner, it gave one deputy for each hundred thousand. The essential difference lay in the divergence of their political opinions. The Regency maintained "The American dominions are an integral part of Spain," from which it deduced the right of Spain to rule America in the absence of the sovereign. Americans, as we have already seen, maintained that the crown was the only link between them. Take away this fundamental divergence of opinion, and the reason for the revolution disappears, the insurrection loses its legality, and the question becomes one of national representation, having no relation either to independence or to autonomy.

The colonial authorities were deposed without resistance by the force of public opinion, and new ones were instituted without any rupture of relations with the mother country, though all foresaw the logical end of the process. In answer to this moderate policy, the Regency refused to the colonies that freedom of trade which it had proposed to give them, avoided the mediation of England, and, without attempting to arrive peacefully at an understanding, stigmatised the Americans as rebels and declared war against them, punishing as high treason in them that which the Spaniards themselves had done in Spain. It was then (1811) that Venezuela declared herself independent, and gave herself a republican constitution.

South America was ill-prepared for the struggle; she had neither soldiers nor politicians, she had to improvise all she needed. Spain in alliance with England and supported by the first nations of the world, was mistress of the seas, her armies triumphant in Europe, were stronger than before the French invasion, nevertheless South America unaided accepted the challenge, and triumphed all alone.

The meeting of the Cortes and the promulgation of the Constitution of 1812, instead of reconciling the mother country with her colonies, fanned the flames of insurrection, and by concessions encouraged the spirit of independence. When in 1814 the King was restored, America was still governed in his name, and the movement having been crushed in Venezuela the revolution was placed in a false position. The refusal of America to surrender without conditions to absolute power, was replied·to by the proclamation of a war of reconquest, and amicable arrangement was no longer possible.

In 1820 despotism triumphed in Europe under the banners of absolute kings allied against the liberties of the people, but in South America the cause of independence, fostered by the example of the United States, was successful. From this epoch the reaction of American thought is felt in the Parliament of England, and influences even Spain herself, where the armies collected to stamp out revolution in America, turn against the absolute king and re-establish a constitutional *régime*. This is a critical moment: upon the triumph or the defeat of revolution in South America depend the destinies of two worlds.

Five years later on, victory crowned her efforts, America is republican, independent, and free. From this moment the current of history, which has for three centuries carried despotism from the East to the West, now turns back; the action of the principles of American regeneration flows from West to East and spreads over Europe until stopped by the barrier of Islamism. Greece cries out for emancipation, and Europe instead of joining to crush her aspirations, runs to help her. Portugal becomes free by the example and influence of her American colonies, who send back to her her absolute kings, transformed into constitutional rulers. In France the revolution of 1789 revives in a compromise between monarchy and a republic, its champions being a comrade of Washington and an emigrant prince who had studied American democracy at close quarters. Take away the South American revolution of the year '10, suppose it to be suppressed in 1820, or eliminate the final triumph of 1825, and the republic of the United States remains the sole representative of liberty; and the world, even with the help of free England, lies grovelling under the sway of absolutism.

Attempts at Monarchy in South America.

Had the idea of Aranda been adopted in 1783, it is probable that a bastard monarchy would have been established in America, upon which time would have impressed the seal of democracy. Had the King of Spain removed his throne to America in 1808, as did he of Portugal, it is possible that the course of the revolution might have been changed under dynastic auspices, delaying the advent of the republic and perchance accelerating constitutional stability. These two opportunities being lost, the revolution could only develop in accordance with its own nature and become essentially a republican movement.

The Pilgrim Fathers of New England and the Quakers of Pennsylvania carried with them the seed of republicanism. The Cavaliers who colonized Virginia became republicans by founding a new country of a distinct type, which produced Washington. The Spanish colonists of South America brought with them no such ideas but only germs of individualism, from which time developed desires for independence and for equality. The indigenous races knew nothing of any form of government except monarchy. The Creoles were born republicans. The idea of establishing a monarchy never sprang from a Creole brain, and when proposed was looked upon by them only as a compromise or as an artificial expedient when it was not folly. In 1808 the English constitution was the ideal of thinkers trained in the school of Montesquieu. In 1810 the *social contract* of Rousseau was their gospel, and the revolution of that year assumed spontaneously a popular form, producing municipal republics, whereby the course of opinion became exclusively democratic.

When early reverses damped the republican hopes of Argentine leaders, they looked to the establishment of a monarchy under the protection of the Great Powers as a means of securing independence and constitutional freedom. In 1814 it was proposed to crown an Infante of Spain King of La Plata. In 1816 that same Congress which declared the independence of the Argentine Provinces, embraced the idea of crowning a descendant of the Incas at Cuzco, and uniting Peru and the River Plate under his rule, a proposition quenched in ridicule. The same Congress, in 1819, after swearing to and promulgating a republican constitution, sought in Europe for a king, lowering their character in the eyes of the world, and bringing accusations of treachery upon themselves from their own countrymen.

This reaction took place precisely at the time when the perseverance of the republicans had gained for them universal sympathy, when the United States threw her shield over the infant peoples to protect them from the attacks of the Holy Alliance, and when England, after declaring that she would not recognise " the revolutionary governments of America," became convinced of her mistake. The agents of this policy were men such as Rivadavia, who stands in America second alone to Washington as the representative statesman of a free people; such as Belgrano, the type of republican virtue; and such as San Martin, who, a republican at heart, had no faith in democracy, yet founded republics which by natural law became democracies. When San Martin ignored this law, his career as a liberator came to an end. So also, later on, fell Bolívar in the attempt to convert democracy into monocracy. The only American liberator who in his folly crowned himself emperor—Iturbide in Mexico—died on the scaffold, a presage of the sad end of another emperor, whose corpse was sent back to Europe as a protest against the imposition of monarchy.

The Empire of Brazil is apparently a proof of the possibility of establishing monarchy in America, but the contrary is the fact. Brazil is a democratic empire, founded upon the principle of the sovereignty of the people, without any privileged class or hereditary nobility, and has nothing monarchical about it except the name.

Retrospection.

When the war was over and the continent at peace, Bolívar exclaimed, "I blush to say it, independence is the only good we have achieved at the cost of all else." Even at this price independence was solid gain, for it was life. The continuance of the colonial system was death by decomposition. Independence was, moreover, the establishment of the democratic republic, a system under which all losses may be retrieved. South America has no reason to complain of the task allotted to her in working out the destiny of humanity.

In the first decade of this century the republic of the United States was a sun without satellites. The apparition of a group of new nations from the colonial nebula of the South, formed, for the first time in the political world, a planetary system of republics governed by natural laws. An entire continent, almost one half the globe, extending from pole to pole and washed by the two greatest of the oceans, became republican.

At that time there were but two republics in the world—in Europe, Switzerland; in America, the United States. The influence of the latter was not yet felt, but the new system of republics soon became a power of the first rank.

The republics of South America were strong enough to conquer their independence, but they lacked the elements of self-government. They had passed at one bound from slavery to freedom, and it took them more than one generation to eradicate evils produced by three centuries of misgovernment. In the war they had expended not only their blood, their treasure, and their vital energy, but also their intellectual strength. Wealth came to them with independence, but the want of the elements of self-government made them an easy prey to anarchy and despotism, from which the conservative instinct at length saved them. Still they suffer the evils of inexperience, but nothing is lost while republican institutions, the great work of the revolution, are preserved.

No people so ill-prepared for the change could have done better. Even the United States passed through a critical period of transition, which imperilled their existence as an organised nation. The republics of South America have suffered greatly from misgovernment, but the instincts of the people have ever been superior to the incapacity of their rulers. Had they continued subject to Spain, they would have died of inanition; had the English invasion been successful, they might now be colonies of England, such as Australia and Canada, and might possibly be richer in material wealth than they are, but they would not be independent nations, charged with the mission of creating new elements of progress; they would but feebly reflect a far-off light. South America would but exist as an appendage of Europe, and Europe would be subject to the Holy Alliance of absolute kings.

If South America has not realised all the hopes awakened by the revolution, still it cannot be said that she has faltered in her course. She has resolved for herself the problem of life, educated herself in the hard school of experience, and by sorrow has purged away her vices. Giving the lie to sinister presage, which condemned her to absorption by inferior races, the energetic Creole has assimilated them, giving them freedom and dignity, or, when necessary, has suppressed them. With help from the most superior races of the world, acclimatized upon her hospitable shores, the reins of government have been secured to him. Her regenerated population doubles itself in twenty or thirty years; before the end of the next century South America will number four hundred millions of freemen, North America five hundred millions, and all America will be Republican and Democratic.

To these great results, following the example of Washington and equal to Bolívar, will have contributed, with such talents as he possessed, the founder of three republics, the emancipator of one-half of South America, whose history will now be told.

CHAPTER II.

SAN MARTIN IN EUROPE AND IN AMERICA.

1778—1812.

JOSE DE SAN MARTIN was born on the 25th February, 1778, at the town of Yapeyu in Misiones, and was the fourth son of Captain Don Juan de San Martin who was at that time Lieutenant-Governor of the Department of Yapeyu. When he was eight years old the family went to Spain, and he became a pupil in the Seminary of Nobles at Madrid, where he remained only two years, and learned little beyond the rudiments of mathematics and something of drawing. Before he was twelve years old, he joined the "Murcia" regiment as a cadet. The uniform of this regiment was white and blue, the same colours the mature soldier afterwards carried in triumph over half a continent.

His first campaign was in Africa, where he received his baptism of fire in battle against the Moors. When in garrison at Oran in 1791, the city, at that time besieged by the Moors, was destroyed by an earthquake. In 1793 he joined the army of Aragon, and served under Ricardos against the republicans of France on their own territory. This experience was of great value to him, as Ricardos was the best tactician among the Spanish generals of that day. After two successful actions at Masden and Truilles, Ricardos was forced to retire to the foot of the mountains, where he maintained his position for twenty days against the constant attacks of the enemy, and San Martin so distinguished himself that he was promoted to the rank of sub-lieutenant.

In the following May, after the death of Ricardos, the "Murcia" formed part of the garrison of Port Vendres, which, after beating off two attacks of the French, was forced to retreat to Collioure and there surrendered. San Martin gained another step by his conduct in these affairs.

In 1795 the peace of Basilea freed the young lieutenant from his *parole*. In the following year his father died, and the treaty of San Ildefonso brought Spain as an ally of the French republic into collision with Great Britain. On the 14th February, 1797, the "Murcia," on board the Spanish Mediterranean squadron, took part in the disastrous affair off Cape Saint Vincent. On the 15th August, 1798, San Martin was marine officer on the *Santa Dorotea*, when that ship was captured after a desperate defence, by the English 64-gun ship *Lion*, and being thus for the second time debarred from active service, he devoted his leisure to the study of mathematics and drawing.

In the year 1800 at the head of a company of his old regiment, he took part in the serio-comic war with Portugal known as the "War of the Oranges," and was present at the siege of Olivenza. After the Peace of Amiens in 1802, his regiment was employed in the blockade of Gibraltar and Ceuta, and in 1804 we find him in garrison at Cadiz, as second captain of a light infantry regiment, where his conduct during a pestilence was as honourable to him as had been his conduct in the field.

By the Treaty of Fontainebleau, in 1807, France and Spain divided Portugal and her colonies between them, and a column of 6,000 Spanish troops under Solano invaded Portugal. The regiment to which San Martin was attached, captured the town of Yelves, but took no further part in the campaign.

The *émeute* of the 2nd May at Madrid, gave the signal for an outbreak of popular indignation, against the usurpations of Napoleon. The news reached the army of Solano when on the march for Cadiz. Solano was at first undecided what course to adopt, but his appointment as Captain-General of Andalucia and Governor of Cadiz being confirmed by the French, he on the 28th May issued a proclamation condemning the insurrection. The people flocked in crowds to the palace, shouting for an immediate attack upon the French squadron lying in the harbour; in the confusion some shots were fired. San Martin, who was officer of the guard, withdrew his troops into the house and closed the door. It was blown in by a cannon-shot, but time had been gained for the escape of Solano across the roof to a neighbouring house, where, however, he was soon afterwards found and cruelly butchered.

This tragedy was never effaced from the memory of San Martin, and without doubt greatly affected his policy on many subsequent occasions. In spite of his love of liberty he ever after looked with horror upon mobs, and upon governments who relied upon them. He considered that intelligence supported by orderly strength should hold the government of the world. Nevertheless his reason and his heart must have told him that the cause of Spain was just, and that the executions on the Prado of Madrid on the 2nd May were more barbarous and less justifiable than was the murder of Solano.

About this time it is said that Miranda visited Cadiz in disguise, but for this report we can find no foundation. He was the founder and organiser of the secret societies to which South Americans throughout Europe were already affiliated, but Spain was the last country in Europe in which such societies were established. Cadiz being the one port open to American trade, became naturally at this time the centre of the revolutionary propaganda.

In the early years of the nineteenth century an association styled " Sociedad de Lautaro," or " Caballeros Racionales," had ramifications all over Spain, and was affiliated with the "Gran Reunion Americana" established in London by Miranda. This society had in Cadiz alone in the year 1808 more than forty members, some of them grandees of Spain. Those of the first grade were pledged to work for the independence of America; those of the second swore " to recognise no government in America as legitimate unless it was elected by the free and spontaneous will of the people, and to work for the foundation of the republican system." Of this society San Martin became a member. An American by birth, a revolutionist by instinct, and a republican by conviction, he was, perchance, without knowing it, an adept of Miranda, and was destined to make the dream of the master a reality, when the bones of that master lay rotting on the mud banks upon which his eye might at this time often rest.

At the same time with San Martin three other members joined the lodge; Alvear, who was his confidant till he became jealous of his fame; José Miguel Carrera, who was to die cursing him; and, most modest of all, the naval lieutenant Matias Zapiola, who was afterwards his right arm on many a hard-fought field. San Martin was the least brilliant and the poorest of them all; his comrades recognised the superiority of his talents as a soldier, and said that he did the thinking for them all, but in the great revolutionary drama that all foresaw they assigned to him only the place of a stern warrior; Alvear and Carrera, the most arrogant and the most ambitious, were to be the heroes.

The general rising in Spain found San Martin in his place as an officer of light infantry under the command of Colonel Menacho. He was soon promoted, and his regiment joined the second division of the army of Andalucia, commanded by the Marquis of Coupigni. When the French under Dupont crossed the Sierra Morena, he was placed in charge of the line of the Guadalquivir. On the 28th June, 1808, he led a mixed column against the advanced guard of the enemy, and charged a detachment of cavalry with such impetuosity at the head of twenty-one hussars, that he killed seventeen of the enemy, took four prisoners and all their horses, and retired in triumph, in the face of very superior numbers. This action was greatly applauded by the whole army, a badge of honour was given to all who charged with him, and he was appointed captain in the Bourbon regiment "on account of distinguished conduct in the action at Argonilla."

This small triumph was the precursor of one of the greatest victories of the epoch. Before one month had elapsed, the imperial eagles of Napoleon were beaten by an army of recruits inspired by patriotism, and Captain San Martin was mentioned with distinction in the order of the day of the battle of Baylen.

The road to Madrid being opened by this victory the army of Andalucia entered the capital in triumph, and San Martin received, with his commission as lieutenant-colonel, a gold medal for his conduct in the battle.

He was afterwards present at the disaster of Tudela, and in the retreat to Cadiz, and in 1810 was appointed aide-de-camp to the Marquis of Coupigni. In 1811 he took part in the bloody battle of Albuera, where the French were defeated by an allied army under General Beresford, the same who five years previously had capitulated to Liniers at Buenos Ayres. The same year he joined the Sagunto regiment, the escutcheon of which was a sun with this motto "Hœ nubila tolunt obstantia solvens"—dissipates clouds and removes obstacles. This was the last Spanish standard under which San Martin fought, and its symbol was identical with that of the flag of the as yet unthought of army of the Andes.

The prophecy of the dying Pitt was realised. Napoleon had stirred up against himself a national war and was irremediably lost. Spain allied with Great Britain, in saving herself, saved Europe from his brutal domination, and the American Creole having paid with usury his debt to the mother country could now honourably leave her. San Martin had fought under her flag for twenty years, he had seen the strategy of great generals, had learned the tactics of every arm in the service; the pupil was now a master able to give lessons. He turned his eyes to his own country, and seeing her in difficulty resolved to return and consecrate his life to her service.

The confidant of his projects and sentiments on this occasion was a singular personage. Lord Macduff, afterwards Earl of Fife, was a Scotch noble descended from that Shakespearean hero who slew Macbeth. He was in Vienna when the Spanish insurrection broke out in 1808, he came over at once and enlisted as a simple volunteer. As such he took part in most of the great battles of the time, in one of which he was seriously wounded, and was given the rank of a General of Spain for his services. Then it was that San Martin and Macduff became acquainted; their generous natures had a profound sympathy each for the other, their friendship was enhanced by the dangers they shared, and continued so long as both lived. By his help and by the interposition of Sir Charles Stuart, a diplomatic agent in Spain, San Martin obtained a passport for London, and received from his friend letters of introduction, and letters of credit of which he made no use.

In London he met his comrades Alvear and Zapiola, and other South Americans who were there at the time. All belonged to the secret society founded in London by Miranda, in which Bolívar had just taken the oath, before leaving for Venezuela in company with the illustrious master. San Martin and his two comrades were initiated in the fifth and last grade, and in January, 1812, embarked on the *George Canning* for the River Plate. On the 9th March they reached Buenos Ayres, accompanied by various officers who came to offer their swords in the cause of independence.

The moment was a critical one in the history of the

American revolution; the serious work was just commencing; the real struggle between Patriots and Royalists was yet to come, and the discordance of the various elements of society only now became apparent.

The Argentine revolution had provoked insurrection in Chile, both by diplomacy and by example. Her first army of volunteers had marched to Upper Peru with the object of striking the enemy in the centre of his power; and in November, 1810, had won the first victory of the war at Suipacha, but was eight months later defeated at Huaqui, and compelled to retreat to Tucuman. Buenos Ayres had attempted to gain command of the rivers by arming a small squadron, which was destroyed by the enemy in the Paraná. A Portuguese army of four thousand men held the line of the Uruguay. Paraguay had commenced a system of isolation, almost of hostility.

The movement in Chile, at first successful, was in 1812 threatened by an expedition from Peru, and the young Republic unfortunately put her trust in José Miguel Carrera, who, with some attractive qualities, possessed no solid talents, either military or political.

In this same month of March an earthquake destroyed the city of Caracas. Reaction triumphed over Miranda in Venezuela; only in New Granada did the revolutionary cause maintain a footing for some time longer. In 1815 all the insurrections in South America had been suppressed, save only the Argentine revolution, which was never overpowered.

Meantime the viceroyalty of Peru, holding a central position, with a strong army and the command of the sea, was the centre of reaction; and the masses of the people not yet implicated in the revolution, began to look unfavourably upon it, as their eyes were opened to the perils it invoked and to the sacrifices it involved.

The Argentine revolution had as yet no fixed plan. In so rudimentary a state of society the actual leaders had but little power to direct the latent strength of the people, and even among themselves opinions were divided, some believing that the centralisation of power in the city of Buenos Ayres was the only means of ensuring the success of the revolutionary movement, while to others decentralization seemed the one necessary condition of national life. The revolution arose in the cities; its legality was based upon municipal rights, and could not long maintain its original form. It could only live by a wider popularity based upon the sovereignty of the people at large. Fortunately the men at this time at the helm were the most intelligent, energetic, and foreseeing who ever acted together on this stage.

The first Executive Government, installed on the 25th May, 1810, was a Junta, in imitation of those established in Spain to resist the domination of the French. Modified a year later by the admission of deputies from the provinces, it became a many-headed monster, useless alike for debate and for administration. It was succeeded by a Triumvirate under the name of "The Executive Government," which, by the aid of those men, saved the State from shipwreck.

Such was the situation of THE UNITED PROVINCES OF THE RIVER PLATE when SAN MARTIN landed on Argentine soil.

Twenty-six years before, while yet a child, he had left his native land; now he returned in the ripeness of manhood, tempered in the struggles of life, tutored in the art of war, initiated in the mysteries of secret societies formed for the propagation of the new ideas of liberty. The new champion brought to the American cause tactics and discipline applied both to politics and to war; and, in embryo, a vast plan for a continental campaign which should embrace half a world and should result in its independence.

It has been said that San Martin was not a man but a mission, and, in truth, seldom has the influence of one man upon the destinies of humanity been greater than was his. He was at once the arm and the head of the Argentine hegemony; he combined the evolutions of armies with those of nations, marking each evolution with some achievement either political or military; obtained great results with the least possible means, and without waste of strength; and showed how a people may be redeemed without being oppressed. His character is even yet an historical enigma.

The grandeur of those whose names attain immortality is measured not so much by their deeds or by their talents as by the effect their memory has upon the consciences of men, causing them to vibrate from one generation to another in sympathy with an idea or with a passion. The moral grandeur of San Martin consists in this: that nothing is known of the secret ambitions of his life; that he was in everything disinterested; that he confined himself strictly to his mission; and that he died in silence, showing neither weakness, pride, nor bitterness at seeing his work triumphant and his part in it forgotten.

San Martin was a man of stalwart frame; his face was the reflex of his mind, a fiery spirit hidden under a studious reserve of manner, which at times exploded. His head, which was of medium size, he carried very erect. His thick black hair he always wore cut short; the straight high forehead indicated the presence of a strong and healthy brain. The darkness of his complexion was deepened by exposure; his large black eyes were fringed by long lashes and overhung by heavy eyebrows, which met when he frowned; these eyes were the characteristic feature of his face, disclosing the intensity of his nature, but hiding his purpose. His nose was long, aquiline, and prominent; mouth small, with firm red lips; teeth strong and white. His chin and jaw showed strength of will and the absence of animal passions. His voice was rough, his gestures simple, and his whole person inspired at once respect and sympathy.*

* See Appendix II.

San Martin gave verbal orders with great precision, and in ordinary conversation was fond of a joke. He wrote laconically in a style of his own, and was much given to reading French authors. Very reserved and of warm affections, he was a great observer of men, studying how he might best avail himself of such talents as they possessed. Haughty by nature, unobtrusive both by temperament and by system, he forced upon himself a stoical disregard of injuries. He was studiously moderate, and patient in the elaboration of his plans. A slave to duty himself, he was tolerant of human frailty in others, but could be severe when severity was requisite. He was, as with truth and with posthumous justice he has been styled by Vicuña Mackenna, "the greatest of the Creoles of the New World."

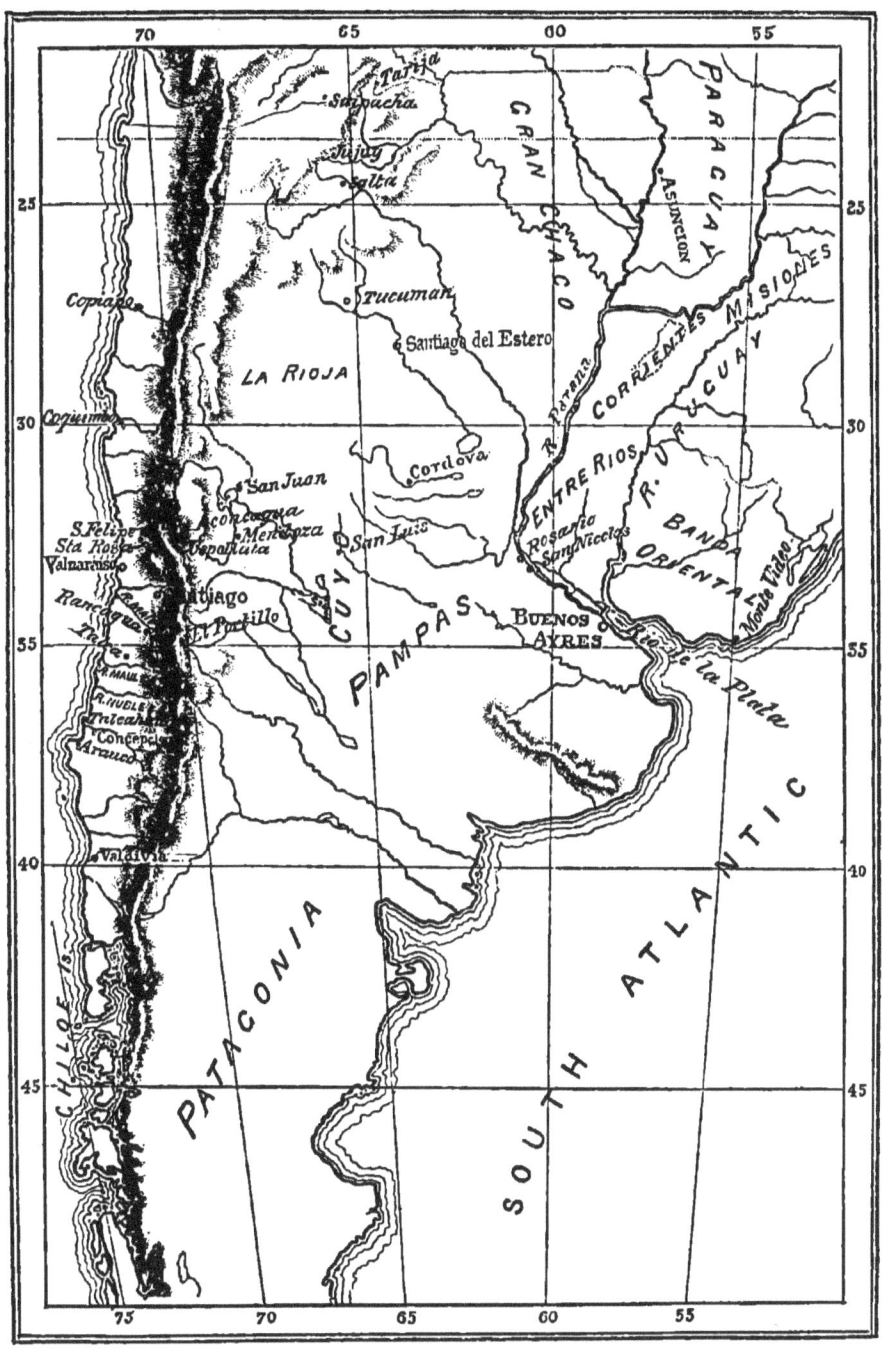

I.—MAP OF THE VICEROYALTY OF LA PLATA AND OF THE KINGDOM OF CHILE, EXCLUDING UPPER PERU AND SOUTHERN PATAGONIA.

CHAPTER III.

THE LAUTARO LODGE.

1812—1813.

THE Provisional Junta, which was established at Buenos Ayres on the 25th May, 1810, was a simple evolution of historic and municipal rights, and was legalised by the election of deputies to it from the Cabildos. This body was subsequently reconstructed, but this measure and the creation of Provincial Juntas were retrograde movements, arising from a latent tendency to decentralisation, in which lay the germ of the federal system of a later day. The next step was the creation of a Triumvirate, which, being a more centralised form of government, responded to the immediate needs of the revolution, and was a necessity of the time.

In the Junta the conservative and revolutionary elements of society were both represented, but the Triumvirate represented no party, and was merely an anonymous Dictator. The revolution had as yet no defined policy, and thus afforded no basis for the development of the democratic idea.

A Legislative Assembly was convened, formed of deputies from the various provinces, which drew up a constitution which virtually gave back the executive power to the Cabildos. This Assembly was dissolved by the Triumvirate, a measure greatly applauded by the public, but which attacked the fundamental principle of government.

The Triumvirate then drew up and decreed a constitution of its own, providing for the periodical election of the Executive by a mixed assembly of notables and of representatives of different towns, who should also act as a legislative council until the convention of a National Congress.

These measures were far from satisfying the requirements of the democratic party, who called for the immediate convocation of a National Congress, which would give form and life to the Republic, though government was still carried on in the name of the King. The Triumvirate opposed the convocation of a Constituent Assembly, considering the time for this had not yet come. Hence came about a fourth political evolution, more dangerous and more important than any of the others.

San Martin returned to his native country a man unknown, but with a certain repute as a brave soldier and a skilful tactician. His comrade, Alvear, on the contrary, came of a family already well known in the River Plate. Ambitious of glory and of power, and of a brilliant imagination, he was a great contrast to San Martin, and assumed an attitude of protection to him, recommending him to the Government of the United Provinces as a good soldier.

Eight days after his arrival San Martin was confirmed in his rank as a lieutenant-colonel, and was entrusted with the organization of a squadron of cavalry, in which Alvear held the rank of major and Zapiola that of captain. This was the origin of the famous regiment of mounted grenadiers, which fought in all the battles of the War of Independence, which gave to America nineteen generals and more than two hundred officers, and of which, after shedding its blood and spreading its bones across the continent from La Plata to Pichincha, a remnant returned under the command of a trooper who in thirteen years had fought his way up to the rank of colonel, and brought back their old standard with them.

The experience of San Martin in Spain had taught him that success is not possible in a long war without a solid military organization. He had seen the Spanish armies, ever routed in spite of their heroism, when remoulded under English discipline triumph over the first soldiers of Europe. He knew that Spain, once free from war in the Peninsula, would send her best troops and her best generals to America. Coolly he studied the situation, and came to the conclusion that the war was but commencing, that the armies of the revolution had no consistence, that there was no plan of operations and no preparation for future emergencies. He said nothing of this publicly, but quietly set to work to found a new military school. Under his command the first squadron of the mounted grenadiers became the school of a generation of heroes. He did as Cromwell did in his day; he made one regiment the model for an army. Under strict discipline, which did not repress individual energy, he formed soldier and officer alike, one by one, instilling into them a passion for duty and that cool courage which is the secret of success.

His first work was to instruct the officers, who under his guidance became the monitors of the future school. To the companions of his voyage he added men who had already seen service in the war, preferring those who had risen from the ranks, but took none of higher rank than lieutenant. To them he added cadets, chosen from respectable families of the city of Buenos Ayres. He was their master both in tactics and in the use of arms, and taught them both to study and to manœuvre with heads erect. Their nerves he tried by nocturnal surprises, those who failed being dismissed, as he wished "to have only lions in the regiment."

He also established a sort of vigilance committee among them, and in extreme cases gave permission to fight duels. On the first Sunday in each month he presided at a meeting of this committee. In an adjoining room each officer wrote on a blank ticket an account of any misconduct he had observed. These tickets were folded and dropped into the hat of the Major, and were then inspected by himself. If among them was any accusation, the accused was sent from the room while the matter was discussed. A committee of inquiry was named and directed to report at a special meeting, where each officer gave his opinion in writing, and a secret ballot decided whether the accused should remain in the corps or not. In the first case the president, in the name of the committee and in their presence, gave a full apology to the accused; in the second, a special committee was appointed to wait upon him and procure his resignation, he being at the same time notified that if he continued to wear the uniform he would be forcibly stripped of it by the first officer he met.

This tribunal had a concise and severe code which classified transgressions worthy of punishment, from the act of ducking the head in danger to that of refusing to fight a duel, be it just or unjust; also striking a woman, even if insulted by her; and included all sorts of personal misconduct.

The troopers were all carefully selected, short men not being admitted. He subjected them to strict discipline, and armed them with the long sabre of Napoleon's cuirassiers, telling them that with this weapon they could split like a melon the head of any *Goth** they met. In their first skirmish they gave practical proof of the truth of this lesson. Finally, he gave to each trooper a war-name, forbidding him to answer to any other.

Other squadrons were formed on the model of this one till a regiment was embodied, and Government sent San Martin his commission as colonel with these words :—

"Government sends you a commission as colonel of the mounted grenadiers, and hopes that by the continuance of your steadiness and zeal you may present the country with a corps capable alone of securing the liberties of your fellow-citizens."

* A term of opprobrium given at that time to Spaniards.—TR.

Meantime San Martin had married Doña Maria de los Remedios Escalada, a beautiful girl of one of the first families of the city.

San Martin made no pretence of being a politician, but among friends he spoke plainly his opinions :—

"Until now the United Provinces have fought for no one knows what, without a flag, and without any avowed principles to explain the origin and tendency of the insurrection. We must declare ourselves independent if we wish to be known and respected."

With these ideas he did not hesitate to join those who desired the convocation of a Constituent Congress, but he saw the necessity of establishing some powerful nucleus of political force which should bring superior intelligence to influence popular movements, preparing among a few that which should be the apparent will of all. This idea he, aided by Alvear, carried into effect by the installation of the celebrated secret society known as THE LAUTARO LODGE, which exercised so great and so mysterious an influence upon the destinies of the revolution.

This Lodge was established in Buenos Ayres about the middle of the year 1812. Its members were of all political parties, but the majority were of the party at that time dominant in the State. The society was organised in various grades ; in the first, neophytes were initiated according to the ritual of the Masonic lodges which were introduced into Buenos Ayres prior to the outbreak of the revolution ; in the higher grades they were initiated into the higher purposes of the society, and behind these was hidden the central lodge (Logia Matriz), in which lay the supreme power of the society.

The declared object of the Lodge was :—

"To work systematically for the independence and happiness of America, proceeding with honour and justice."

Thus membership was exclusively confined to men of American birth. By its constitution, if any of the brotherhood was elected supreme ruler of the State, he could take no important step without consulting the Lodge; he could not appoint a diplomatic agent, general-in-chief, governor of a province, judge of an upper court, high church dignitary, nor general officers, and could not punish any member of the brotherhood, by his own authority. It was a law of the Society that all members should mutually assist each other in all the exigencies of civil life; that at the risk of life they should uphold the decrees of the Lodge; and should inform it of anything which could influence public opinion, or affect the public security. To reveal the secret of the existence of the Lodge "by word or by sign" was punishable by death by such means "as might be found convenient." This penalty, was, however, only intended to have a moral effect. By an addition to the constitution, it was arranged that when any brother of the *Logia Matriz* was named general of an army or governor of a province, he should have power to establish an affiliated society, with a smaller number of members.

The Society failed to secure the adhesion of the members of the then Government, but most of the popular leaders joined the Lodge, and its ramifications soon extended to all classes, the most notable adherent being Dr. Don Bernardo Monteagudo, who had great influence among the younger citizens.

Very exaggerated ideas have been held as to the influence of the Lautaro Lodge. Events have been attributed to its action and it has been held responsible for executions and crimes with which the Society had nothing whatever to do. It has been made the scapegoat of all the mistakes and errors of the epoch. The Lodge of Lautaro was not a machine of government or of speculative propaganda, it was an engine of revolution, of war against a common enemy, and of defence against internal dangers. In this sense it greatly contributed to give tone and direction to the revolution, concentrating the forces of government, giving unity and regularity to political evolutions, and a vigorous impulse to military operations. Under its auspices was created the first popular Assembly which gave form to the sovereignty of the people; to it was due that spirit of propaganda which characterized the Argentine revolution, and the maintenance of the alliance with Chile, which gave independence to half the continent; but there was danger in the secrecy of its debates, and in the irresponsibility of its collective power, which was manifest when it became a tool in the hands of personal ambition. The limited sphere in which its influence was felt proves that the Argentine revolution was impelled by forces of much greater power, and obeyed general laws over which it had no control.

The Portuguese army, then holding the left bank of the Uruguay, had agreed to retire within the frontier in pursuance of an armistice arranged, on the 26th May, 1812, by the interposition of the English minister, between the United Provinces and the Court of Rio Janeiro. The Spanish flag yet floated on the walls of Monte Video, but the road was now open and a strong patriot army was concentrated on the right bank of the Uruguay.

In Buenos Ayres public spirit revived on the discovery of a vast conspiracy of European Spaniards under Alzaga, which was to have broken out on the 5th July, in concert with the forces in Monte Video and the Spanish squadron in the roadstead, aided by the Portuguese army, which had not yet retired. The Triumvirate punished the conspirators with great severity, and the base of operations was solidly secured.

In the North the situation was less promising. The Royalist army, after completing the subjugation of Upper Peru, advanced in triumph to the heart of the United Provinces, and invaded the Province of Tucuman. The relics of the Patriot army were in retreat, under command of Belgrano, and it was only hoped that they might reach Cordoba in safety. At this critical juncture Belgrano, disregarding the positive orders of Government, turned on the enemy, who were double in number to his own forces, and completely routed them on the 24th September, near to the city of Tucuman, capturing flags and cannon, and thus saved the Argentine revolution.

By the constitution drawn up by the Triumvirate, it was established that one of their number should retire every six months. On the expiration of the first six months, they convened another Assembly to elect one in place of the outgoing Triumvir. This Assembly, repeating the errors of the previous one, took upon itself the attributes of a representative body. Government dissolved it as it had the former one, and called upon Don Juan Martin Pueyrredon to fill the vacant chair; but the national spirit was no longer confined within the limits of the municipality of Buenos Ayres, and demanded the immediate convocation of a National Congress, elected by the people. The Triumvirate proposed that a third Assembly should devote itself to drawing up a plan for the election of the Congress. This Assembly accordingly met on the 6th October, in the midst of the excitement caused by the news of the victory of Tucuman, and elected as Triumvir a nominee of the Executive. Public opinion saw in this only a continuance of the provisional system and was greatly incensed, both against the Triumvirate and against the Assembly.

Behind the popular movement was the Lautaro Lodge under the direction of Monteagudo, who secured the concurrence of San Martin and his grenadiers, as also that of Alvear. This movement was much more carefully prepared than that of the 25th May, 1810, or than that of the 5th and 6th April, 1811. The leaders drew up a plan of operations, defining the parts to be played by the people, by the corporations, and by the troops. They chose beforehand the members of the future Government, and even made a programme of the policy they should pursue.

At half-past eleven on the night of the 7th October the

troops of the garrison commenced to defile into the Plaza Victoria, and took up positions in front of the Cabildo. The grenadiers, with sabres sheathed, were headed by San Martin and Alvear; after them came Colonel Ortiz Ocampo with the 2nd regiment, and Lieutenant-Colonel Pinto with the cavalry. At daybreak on the 8th, the bell of the municipality was rung and the people commenced to assemble. Soon three hundred persons, among whom were the principal members of the religious orders, occupied the galleries of the Chamber and presented to the Cabildo a petition with more than three hundred signatures, asking—

"Under protection of the military for the suspension of the Assembly and the deposition of the Triumvirate, so that the Cabildo, reassuming the authority delegated to it by the people on the 22nd May, 1810, might immediately create a new Executive encharged to convene a truly national Assembly."

The Cabildo acceded to everything, declaring by proclamation that the Assembly when convened should have supreme power within limits defined by the towns, in order to draw up a Constitution. They also appointed an executive, consisting of Don Juan José Passo, Don Nicolas Rodriguez Peña, and Don Antonio Alvarez Jonte, under the rules of the Provisional Statute. All which was submitted to the people and approved of by acclamation.

This revolution, which was municipal in its form, was essentially national aud democratic in its tendency. The principle of the sovereignty of the people was recognised by calling a general Congress; the old traditions, which gave supremacy to the capital, were set aside; and the first bold step was taken in the path of independence.

The new Triumvirate lost no time in setting about their appointed task; the Constituent Assembly was speedily convened, the victorious army of Tucuman was strongly reinforced, and another army was despatched to besiege Monte Video.

Thus in the space of seven months from the arrival of San Martin in Buenos Ayres the aspect of affairs was completely changed. Government was consolidated, its policy defined, public spirit was aroused, and the revolution, with two armies, boldly displayed the flag of independence. But the military situation was precarious, everything depended upon the result of a battle.

Monte Video was a fortress of the second class, was defended by 335 guns, of which 175 were in battery, was garrisoned by more than 3,000 troops and by 2,000 militia, and was further protected by a squadron of 14 ships of war, mounting 210 guns, and by a flotilla, while the United Provinces had not even a gunboat. Here was the centre of reaction and the natural base for any expedition from the Peninsula, while the state of relations with Brazil increased the danger from this quarter.

The Royalist army, beaten at Tucuman, had been strongly reinforced, and lay entrenched at Salta, waiting the arrival of another army from Upper Peru.

Government summoned a council of military chiefs—of whom San Martin was one—and of influential citizens, to aid the Cabildo in devising measures to meet these threatening dangers. It was decided that Monte Video must be taken at any cost, and that Belgrano should be instructed to drive the enemy from Salta, in order to open the road to the centre of the Spanish power at Lima.

CHAPTER IV.

SAN LORENZO.

1813—1814.

ON the 31st December, 1812, the vanguard of the army sent against Monte Video, under the command of Colonel Rondeau, completely defeated a strong sortie of the garrison and laid siege to the city.

On the 31st January, 1813, the general Constituent Assembly met in Buenos Ayres. The majority were members of the Lautaro Lodge, so there was no longer that anarchy of opinion which had neutralized the former Assemblies. For the moment it fulfilled popular aspirations; the nominal sovereignty of the King of Spain was eclipsed, his name disappeared for ever from public documents, the escutcheons of Spain were torn down, titles of nobility, the Inquisition, and judicial torture were abolished. The effigy of former monarchs was substituted on coins by the seal of the United Provinces—a sun with rays and a Phrygian cap, within a wreath of laurel. The colours of the Spanish flag were replaced by the blue and white of the Patriot cockade, and the last link with the mother country was broken by declaring the supremacy of the National Courts of Law. Everything was reformed, even to the prayers of the priests and the songs of the people, who now in inspired verse saluted,

"A new and glorious Nation,
With a conquered lion at her feet." *

---

* A quotation from "Oid Mortales !" the Argentine national hymn.

So was inaugurated the sovereignty of the Argentine people; a formal Declaration of Independence was now all that was wanting for the establishment of a republic.

The armies in the field swore obedience to the Assembly and marched with enthusiasm under the new flag upon the fortifications of Monte Video and upon the entrenchments of Salta; only upon the water did the spirit of revolution as yet make no progress. The maritime power of Spain seemed invincible in America; her ships of war dominated the coasts from California on the Pacific to the Gulf of Mexico on the Atlantic. The sailors of Monte Video dominated the River Plate and its affluents. One day they bombarded Buenos Ayres, another they spread terror along the banks of the Uruguay, and sacked defenceless towns on the Parana. Batteries were thrown up on the banks in front of Rosario and at Punta Gorda, which only diverted attack from these points to others more defenceless.

In October, 1812, the towns of San Nicolas and San Pedro, on the western bank of the Parana, were cannonaded and sacked. Then, with the object of diverting the attention of the Patriots from the siege of Monte Video, cutting off all communication by the rivers with the interior, and of procuring supplies for the garrison of Monte Video, a flotilla was organised under the command of a noted smuggler, Ruiz by name, on which was shipped a detachment of infantry, led by a red-haired Biscayan, named Zabala, a man of colossal stature and of approved valour.

The Government of Buenos Ayres, hearing of this expedition, ordered the battery at Rosario to be dismantled and the guns to be sent higher up the Parana, to Punta Gorda, where the garrison was strengthened. The colonel of the mounted grenadiers also received orders to march with two squadrons for the protection of the coast from Zarate to Santa Fé.

The Royalist expedition, under convoy of three small

ships of war, concentrated at the mouth of the Guazu, below the delta of the Parana, about the middle of January, and were there delayed by a north wind, so that when San Martin reached the coast they were only commencing the ascent of the main river. Keeping his troops out of sight, San Martin, disguised in the hat and poncho of a countryman, kept watch upon their movements from the bank, by day and by night. On the 28th January they passed San Nicolas, and on the 29th anchored above Rosario, without having as yet made any attempt to land.

Escalada, commandant of Rosario, collected twenty-two men, carrying muskets, and thirty horsemen, and with a small gun prepared to make what resistance he could. At daybreak on the 30th the flotilla cast anchor inside the island of San Lorenzo, which lies in the middle of the river about seventeen miles to the north of Rosario. The western bank here consists of high bluffs, affording no landing-places except where narrow paths were cut through them to the water's edge; in front of one of these cuttings the flotilla anchored. Beyond the low trees which bordered the edge of the bluff stood the lonely monastery of San Carlos, a two-storey building with a belfry on the roof.

About a hundred men landed, but all the provisions they could obtain from the peaceful friars were a few fowls and melons; all cattle had been withdrawn from the coast. As the monastery bell struck half-past seven, a cloud of dust was seen on the Rosario road. It was Escalada, with his fifty men and his one small gun. The Spaniards retreated with drums beating to their boats, and Escalada opened fire upon them from the edge of the bluff, but was obliged to draw off as the guns of the flotilla had much longer range than his one piece.

On the night of the 31st, a Paraguayan prisoner escaped from the flotilla, swimming ashore on a bundle of sticks. From him the Patriots learned that the whole force of the enemy did not exceed three hundred and fifty men, that they were mounting two small guns, intending to land next day in greater force for the purpose of searching the monastery for treasure which they supposed to be there hidden, and that after securing the treasure they intended to proceed up the river, passing the batteries of Punta Gorda by night, if they could not destroy them, and so cut off the trade with Paraguay.

Escalada sent out messengers with this news, one of whom met San Martin and his grenadiers, who, following the windings of the river had been left behind by the flotilla, which was favoured by a southerly breeze. Fortunately the wind now chopped round to the north and delayed the intended landing, so that when San Martin, by forced marches, reached the post-house of San Lorenzo, three miles from the monastery, on the night of the 2nd February, nothing had yet been done. At the post-house he found fresh horses waiting for him, sent there by Escalada.

In front of the post-house stood an old carriage without horses. Two troopers rode up to it, and asked :—

"Who is here?"

"A traveller," answered a sleepy voice.

Another horseman rode up saying—

"Be careful; this is not an enemy, but an Englishman on his way to Paraguay."

The traveller put his head out of one of the windows of the coach, and thinking he recognized the figure and voice, said :—

"Surely you are Colonel San Martin?"

"If so, you have a friend here, Mr. Robertson," answered the other.

And so it was; this was the well-known traveller, William Parish Robertson, who was destined to witness the memorable events of the next day, and to record what he saw.

The two friends laughed together at their unexpected

meeting in the dark, and San Martin spoke of his project.

"The enemy has double the number of men that we have, but I doubt if they get the better of us."

"So say I," replied the Englishman, offering his visitors wine to drink to their success, and asking permission to go with them.

"Agreed," answered San Martin, "but take care; it is no part of your duty to fight. I will give you a horse, but if the day goes against us you must run for it."

Then, giving the order to mount, he put himself with his friend at the head of the silent troopers, and soon after midnight reached the monastery, which they entered by a gateway in the rear of the edifice.

All the cells were vacant: not a sound was to be heard in the cloisters. The gate being shut the troopers dismounted in the large courtyard. The Colonel enjoined silence upon them, and forbade them to light fires.

"It brought to mind," says the English traveller, "the Greek host hidden in the bowels of the wooden horse, so fatal to Troy."

San Martin, with a night-glass, ascended the tower of the church, and saw by their lanterns that the enemy was yet there. He then carefully reconnoitered the country round him, and from information furnished by Escalada formed his plans.

On the river face of the monastery a level plain, apt for cavalry manœuvres, extended for three hundred and fifty yards to the edge of the bluff. Two winding paths, one only of which was practicable for infantry in formation, led to the beach below. He then withdrew his men from the courtyard and formed them, holding their horses by the bridle, behind the cloisters and outhouses, leaving Escalada and his volunteers within the edifice. At dawn he again mounted the tower. At five o'clock, as the shades of night melted away, boats laden with armed men, were seen to leave the flotilla for the shore. At half-past five, two small columns of infantry marched up the main path.

Then San Martin came down from his post of observation, and, meeting Robertson at the foot of the stairs, said:—

"In two minutes more we shall be upon them, sword in hand."

A few paces off his orderly held his charger ready, a fine cream-coloured horse, fully caparisoned. In a moment he was in the saddle. Drawing his curved sabre he galloped off to his grenadiers, who were now to enter into action for the first time, and in a few words exhorted them to remember his lessons, and, above all, not to fire a shot, but to trust to their lances and sabres. He put himself at the head of the second squadron and gave command of the first to Captain José Bermudez, directing him to attack the flank and cut off the retreat of the invaders, and added :—

"We will meet in the centre of the enemy's columns; there I will give you further orders."

The enemy, about two hundred and fifty strong, had in the meantime advanced some two hundred and odd yards. They came on quickly to the sound of drums and fifes, and with a flag, in two parallel columns of half companies, with two four-pound guns between the columns and a little in advance. Then was heard for the first time the war clarion of the mounted grenadiers.

From the right and from the left of the monastery the two squadrons dashed forward at full gallop, sabre in hand. San Martin led the attack on the left, Bermudez that on the right. San Martin being nearest was the first to fall on the enemy. The fire of the two guns failed to check the onset; the heads of the Spanish columns were thrown into disorder, but, falling back, opened a heavy fire of musketry. San Martin with his squadron encountered the column led by Zabala in person; his horse was killed by the first volley, and a fierce hand-to-hand fight raged round him as he lay upon the ground caught by the leg by his fallen steed, in which he received a slight sabre cut in the face. A Spanish soldier ran forward to bayonet him, but was run through the body with a lance by a grenadier named Baigorria. Another trooper, named Juan Bautista Cabral, sprang from the saddle and released his leader from the fallen horse, and fell himself pierced by two mortal wounds, shouting:—

"I die content! We have beaten the enemy."

Almost at the same moment, Cornet Bouchard killed the bearer of the Spanish ensign and captured the flag.

The other column was also driven back by the charge of the squadron led by Bermudez, and the Spaniards abandoning their guns, retreated to the bluff, where they attempted to form square under protection of the guns of the flotilla. Bermudez leading a second charge upon them was mortally wounded by a cannon-shot, and Lieutenant Manuel Diaz Velez, carried away by his enthusiasm, fell with his horse over the bluff, with a ball in his forehead, and two bayonet wounds in his chest, but the Spaniards were driven headlong to the beach, leaving behind them, besides their flag, their guns and fifty muskets, forty dead and fourteen prisoners. Many of those who escaped were wounded, one of these being Zabala, their leader.

The grenadiers had fifteen killed and twenty-seven wounded, among whom each of the United Provinces had at least one representative. Lieutenant Diaz Velez, being taken prisoner, was carried on board the flotilla.

San Martin assisted by Robertson, generously furnished the flotilla with fresh supplies for their wounded, and arranged for an exchange of prisoners, giving up those he had captured for three previously taken by the boats and for his wounded officer; but Velez died in the arms of his comrades a few hours after. One of these released prisoners was a Paraguayan named José Felix Bogado; he at once enlisted in the regiment, and during thirteen years' service with it, from San Lorenzo to Ayacucho, won his way up to the rank of Colonel, and then returned to

Buenos Ayres, accompanied by seven of the original troopers of the corps.

Still covered with the blood and dust of the fight, San Martin signed the despatch announcing his victory, under the shade of an old pine-tree which still stands in the garden of San Lorenzo.

The affair of San Lorenzo, though of little military importance, had a most beneficial effect upon the Patriot cause. The safety of the towns on the banks of the Parana and Uruguay was secured; communication with Entre Rios, which was the base of the army besieging Monte Video, was maintained; the expected supplies to this city were cut off; the trade with Paraguay was preserved; and above all, a new general given to the army and new vigour to the spirits of the men.

Three days afterwards, the discomfited flotilla descended the Parana, laden with wounded instead of plunder, and carried the news to Monte Video. At the same time San Martin returned to Buenos Ayres, and the enthusiasm of his reception somewhat deadened the calumnies which already began to embitter his life.

On the 20th February the Spanish army entrenched at Salta was completely routed by General Belgrano; the third victory in less than three months. The revolution of the 8th October and the influence of the Lautaro Lodge were justified by these results.

When San Martin returned to Buenos Ayres, he found that political parties, confined within the limits of the capital, weakened by local animosities, and ultimately enclosed by the four walls of the Lodge, had degenerated into circles ruled by personal influences, and like most of the influential men of that day he became imbued with the belief that a constitutional monarchy backed by Europe was the true solution of the political problem. Neither he nor they saw that the sentiment of the people was essentially republican.

Secret societies have been at times the only means of

organization left to an enslaved people, but they have never accompanied the development of revolutionary ideas; as a general rule they have produced nothing beyond abortive conspiracies; among a free people they are impotent. Thus the continuance of the secret and irresponsible influence of the Lautaro Lodge, could have no other effect than to weaken the power of the General Assembly, its own creation.

Within the Lodge itself there soon arose two distinct parties, one strove only for democratic independence, the other was a personal party with Alvear at its head, which presently absorbed the whole society.

The dream of Alvear was military glory and a dictatorship. His friend Carrera was at this time (May, 1813), both a dictator and a general in his own country; he took him as his model, but was clear-sighted enough to see that their circumstances were not identical.

In June, 1813, the army of the North a second time invaded Upper Peru under the orders of Belgrano, but was badly beaten at Vilcapugio on the 1st October, and almost destroyed at Ayohuma on the 14th November. The remnant retreated to its former position, and Belgrano requested to be relieved of the command.

The United Provinces had not at this time any general conspicuous for military genius. The laurels gained by Don Antonio Gonsalez Balcarce at Suipacha were blighted at the Desaguadero. His brother, Don Martin Balcarce, was in Chili in command of Argentine auxiliaries. The victory of Don José Rondeau, in front of Monte Video, was the first and last of his career; he lacked the qualities of a commander-in-chief. Belgrano was wanting both in technical knowledge and in warlike instinct, but was the best of them all. Of the generals of division, none had as yet shown any capacity for separate command. The revolution which had been so far opposed by mediocre generals and badly-organized troops, had now to contend against skilful generals and well-disciplined troops.

Alvear applied for the command of the army of the North. San Martin, who considered the expedition against Monte Video of more importance, willingly gave place to him, but Alvear, ever vacillating and loth to leave the field of politics, changed his mind and recommended San Martin for the post. San Martin was anxious to free himself from the trammels of party in order to gain freedom of action in the course he had marked out for himself; he accordingly accepted the command of a reinforcement for the army of the North, and received instructions to assume the command-in-chief if he should deem it advisable.

This reinforcement consisted of the 7th battalion of infantry, 700 strong, two squadrons of the mounted grenadiers, and 100 artillerymen, and reached Tucuman before the close of the year 1813. Soon after San Martin and Belgrano met at Yatasto on the road to Salta, and swore friendship to each other, an oath most faithfully kept by both.

These two celebrated men had never met before, but had for some time corresponded. San Martin presented himself as a subordinate, but Belgrano looked to him as a master in the art of war, and regarded him as his successor. After some delay, due to the reluctance of San Martin to supersede his friend, he at length assumed the command on receipt of positive orders to that effect from Government, Belgrano remaining with him in command of a regiment. Belgrano died in the belief that San Martin was the tutelar genius of South America, and San Martin to the end of his days honoured the memory of his illustrious friend as that of one of the purest patriots of the New World.

On the 22nd January, 1814, the executive power was concentrated in one person, who took the title of Supreme Director. Don Gervasio Antonio Posadas was selected by the Lodge to fill this post, and was duly elected by the General Assembly. No one was more surprised than himself at this appointment, for which his only special recommendation was that he was the uncle of Alvear, who for the present contented himself with the command of the army of the capital, until such time as he could take command of the army of Monte Video, and there achieve such military glory as should entitle him to supreme power.

The first care of San Martin, on assuming command of the army of the North, was to insist upon the regular payment of his men. There existed in the army chest a sum of thirty-six thousand dollars, drawn from Upper Peru, which Government had directed should be paid over to the General Treasury. San Martin disobeyed the order and applied the money as he wished, giving Government at the same time his reasons for so doing. Government approved of his conduct as justified by necessity, for the army was at the time in the last stage of destitution.

CHAPTER V

UPPER PERU.

1814.

THE military policy of the United Provinces had three distinct ends: first, to construct a new nation within the geographical limits of the old Viceroyalty of the River Plate; second, to aid in the establishment of other South American nations, who would be their natural allies; and third, to carry their arms beyond their frontiers for the removal of obstacles to their expansion. Hence the expeditions to Paraguay and Monte Video, the aid given to the insurgents in Chile, and the war waged with the Viceroyalty of Peru. The army of the North, as the embodiment of this threefold policy, was styled "The Auxiliary Army of Peru," and its mission was to incorporate the Provinces of Upper Peru as a portion of the old Viceroyalty, to capture Lima, the centre of Spanish power in South America, and to bring Lower Peru into an alliance similar to that already contracted with Chile.

For four years Upper Peru had been the battlefield of the Patriots and Royalists; it was now completely in the power of the latter. The four provinces known as Upper Peru are shut in by mountain ranges, and have no fluvial communication with either ocean. Situate within the tropics, their high tablelands and intervening valleys furnish at once examples of perpetual winter and perpetual spring, and yield all the natural products of the globe.

Upper Peru is divided by two spurs from the Andes into three districts. The western range runs parallel to the Pacific Ocean from the desert of Atacama—which is a high tableland—to the first valleys of Lower Peru on the coast, cutting off an arid and thinly-peopled district. The central plain, well peopled but inclement, is the natural road from the Argentine Republic to Lower Peru, and was the theatre of operations during the preceding campaigns. The eastern range, with lofty peaks covered with perpetual snow, looks down upon a truly intertropical paradise. At its foot extends to the west the smiling valley of Clisa, where stands the city of Cochabamba, with easy access over the hills to the central plateau, and to Chuquisaca by valleys on the south-east. Behind Cochabamba and to the east of the range lies the Valle Grande, which collects the mountain streams and delivers them to the Amazon. More to the north-east lies Santa Cruz da la Sierra in the midst of a vast grassy plain, which slopes gradually away to the confines of Brazil, Paraguay, and the Argentine Chaco.

The social organization of Upper Peru was a continuation of the system of the Incas, complicated by the antagonism of races. Europeans had established themselves in six cities, whose former inhabitants, driven out to the ice-covered hills or to the torrid valleys, worked as serfs for their lords and masters as cultivators of the soil or as miners. The lower class in these cities consisted of half-breeds, and formed the greater part of the population. All the rest of the country was peopled exclusively by two indigenous races, who paid a capitation tax, and had no civil rights. The language of the conquerors was unintelligible to the mass of the people.

In this country the first rebellion against the domination of Spain was quenched in blood in 1809, but news of the revolution of Buenos Ayres in 1810 rekindled the smouldering embers. The movement was supported by Argentine troops under Balcarce, who won the first victory of the war at Suipacha, but was afterwards totally defeated on the Desaguadero. The Patriots of Cochabamba being thus left alone, fought another battle by themselves at Sipe-Sipe on the 13th August, 1811, but were defeated. The repulse of the second invasion under Belgrano in 1813 was another great disappointment to them, but still the spirit of the people was not crushed. There was, however, no cohesion among them; they had the courage to resist and to die on the field of battle or on the scaffold, but they were unable to concert any plan of action; thus these successive disasters greatly weakened the ties which bound them to the Patriots of Buenos Ayres, but vain were the efforts of the Spaniards to overcome the passive resistance of the people. Heads of rebels were exposed along the public roads, the properties of such as had fled were confiscated and sold, towns were sacked, military commissions terrorized the country, prisoners taken in the last campaign were sold as slaves to the owners of the vineyards and plantations of Peru, but still insurrectionary movements constantly broke out; even the Indians, armed with nothing more than clubs, slings, and arrows, braved death with the utmost stoicism, certain that they would be avenged. The Spanish general, unable either to retreat or to advance, established his headquarters at Tupiza; and while a portion of his army kept open communications in the rear, his vanguard advanced to Salta, constantly harassed by the country people, who rose in arms on the retreat of the Patriot army to Tucuman.

The army which had twice defeated the armies of the United Provinces was almost entirely composed of natives of the Highlands of Lower Peru. They were men inured to hardships and privations, untiring on the march, faithful to their flag, obedient to their officers, and undaunted under fire. They were half-breeds, who spoke the same language as the people of the country in which they fought. The climate of this country was the same as that of their own, and they were accustomed to the peculiar requirements of mountain warfare. All this gave them great advantages over the Argentine troops on that field of action, and the remembrance of defeats disheartened the Patriot army.

Belgrano after the rout of Ayohuma had left Colonel Don JUAN ANTONIO ALVAREZ DE ARENALES as governor of Cochabamba and commandant of the Patriot forces in the rear of the enemy, and Colonel Don Ignacio Warnes as governor of Santa Cruz de la Sierra, under the orders of Arenales. Only men of their stamp could have undertaken the desperate enterprise of keeping alive the flames of insurrection in the mountains of Upper Peru after such disasters.

Arenales is one of the most extraordinary characters of the Argentine revolution. Born in Spain and educated in Buenos Ayres, he embraced with ardour the American cause, and took a prominent part in the insurrection at Chuquisaca in 1809. Taken prisoner, he was sent to Peru, and remained in the casemates of Callao till set at liberty by the Cortes of Cadiz in 1812. At the time of the battle of Tucuman he was in Salta, and there headed a patriotic movement which was immediately quelled. Previous to the battle of Salta he had joined the army of Belgrano, and accompanied it to Upper Peru. To austere manners, tenacity of purpose, and untiring activity he added the virtues of a good citizen, great talents as an administrator, inflexible will, and a brain fertile in warlike stratagems. His face never displayed any signs of either pleasure or pain, and his stern look and voice joined to his lion-like head, marked him as one born to command; but under all lay a warm heart, more anxious to do right than to win glory.

Warnes was of English descent, but was born in Buenos Ayres, and in 1807 had distinguished himself in defence of his native city.

San Martin, on learning from Belgrano the character of Arenales, at once opened communications with him, and on two occasions sent him arms and ammunition, with officers, to aid him in his operations.

While Belgrano was in Upper Peru, Colonel Landivar, a Spaniard, was made prisoner at Santa Cruz de la Sierra. This man had been one of the most merciless agents of

Goyeneche, and he was kept for trial by the General, "not for having fought against our system, but for the murders, robberies, burnings, violences, extortions, and other excesses perpetrated by him in contravention of the laws of war." It was proved that he had executed fifty-four prisoners of war, whose heads and arms had been cut off and nailed to posts on the public roads. The accused alleged that he had only ordered the execution of thirty-three individuals, and that in obedience to express orders from Goyeneche, which he produced in evidence. The defence was ably conducted by an officer of the Grenadiers, who pleaded that the prisoner having acted only in obedience to the orders of his superior could not be looked upon as other than a prisoner of war. The Court pronounced sentence of death, which sentence was laid before San Martin on the 13th January, 1814, who at once signed it without consulting Government.

This trial gives an idea of the mode in which war was waged in Upper Peru. The cruelties of the Spaniards produced reprisals on the part of the insurgents, which so filled the land with bloodshed that "the inhabitants looked calmly upon these scenes; no one hesitated to risk his own life, and all sought to shed the blood of those of the other party." Such was the war into which Arenales now entered as leader of the fifth insurrection of Cochabamba.

The Royalist army being in possession of the central plateau the position of Arenales at Cochabamba was untenable, but the road by the Valle Grande was open to him; he could join Warnes at Santa Cruz de la Sierra, and communicate with the Argentine Provinces by the Chaco, and from Santa Cruz he could march over well-wooded plains to Chuquisaca.

On the 29th November he commenced his retreat with sixty musketeers, four small guns, a few cavalry, and a crowd of countrymen armed with clubs and slings, who covered his flanks and rear. In the valley of Misque he attempted to make a stand, but was forced across the

Cordillera to the head waters of the eastern streams. Overtaken at Chillán, he beat off his pursuers, and reached the Valle Grande, where he recruited his forces, forming an infantry battalion of one hundred and sixty-five men, and two squadrons of cavalry, and was joined by some guerilla chiefs.

The insurrection spread, and Pezuela despatched Colonel Blanco with six hundred men and three light guns, to subdue it. On his march Blanco met with six heads nailed to posts, a gage of defiance from the guerillas who swarmed in the adjacent valleys.

On the 4th February the two armies met. The Patriots had at first the advantage, till a part of their raw troops were seized with panic; the Royalists captured their guns and remained masters of the field. Blanco shot his prisoners, and cut off the heads of three leaders, after which he retreated to Chillán for reinforcements.

Arenales retreated to the frontier of Santa Cruz, taking his arms and spare ammunition with him on mule-back. Reinforced by Warnes he halted at Abapo on the Rio Grande, and in March had two hundred and four infantry and four small guns. Warnes refused to recognise his authority, and took up a position for himself at Horcas with a thousand men, advancing his outposts to Herradura and Petacas, passes of the Cordillera considered impregnable, as they were nothing more than flights of stairs cut in the sides of the mountain.

At the same time the Indians of the Chaco along the banks of the river Pilcomayo rose up in favour of the Patriots; guerilla chiefs aroused a part of the Province of La Plata; and the towns in Blanco's rear were again in insurrection. Pezuela despatched Colonel Benavente with five hundred men, against this new insurrection; but in spite of sundry advantages gained by both columns, Benavente was so weakened that he was soon reduced to inaction, and Blanco, whose troops suffered greatly from fever, was forced to evacuate the Valle Grande early in April and to retreat to Misque.

Arenales, while encamped at Tumina, received information that Blanco, resuming the offensive, had forced the passes of Herradura and Petacas, and had dispersed the division under Warnes. He at once marched towards the scene of action, and met Warnes at the head of only three hundred men. The latter, learning wisdom by his reverses, placed himself under his orders. Blanco had in the meantime taken the city of Santa Cruz, and was now coming in search of them with six hundred men, of whom one-half were regular infantry.

On the 24th May the Royalists came in sight, and the Patriots retreated by a narrow defile, leaving a small party to draw on the enemy. At dawn on the 25th they reached the town of LA FLORIDA, on the river Piray. Arenales took up a position on the right of this small river, in an open space where the bank was about two yards high. Below, the river spread out, while in front lay a wide plain. His flanks were protected by dense brushwood; the town was behind him. He planted his guns on the open, placed his cavalry in ambuscade on each flank, with Warnes in command on the right and De la Riva on the left. At the foot of the bank he opened a trench, concealed by sand and brushwood, where he stationed his infantry, kneeling, and awaited the attack. His entire force numbered about eight hundred men.

Just before noon the same day a dropping fire was heard in the woods in front. It came from the outpost, who were retreating before the enemy. Soon after that the Royalist column debouched from the wood, preceded by skirmishers. Blanco drew up his men on the plain, with strong cavalry reserves on the flanks, and opened fire with his four-pounders. Then, as the infantry advanced firing, the Patriot guns opened upon them. When the skirmishers entered the river, the entrenched infantry poured in a volley, and, springing from their shelter, charged through the smoke with such impetuosity that, aided by the cavalry on the left, they completely routed the enemy, Colonel Blanco remaining dead upon the field.

Arenales headed the pursuit in person with so little caution that he was attacked by a group of fugitives, who left him for dead with fourteen wounds, three of them in the face. His men rushed in and saved him, carrying him on their shoulders back to the camp.

Two flags, two guns, two hundred muskets, one hundred killed, and ninety-nine prisoners, were the trophies of this victory, while the Patriots lost only one man killed and twenty-one wounded, including their leader.

Such was the action of La Florida, which saved Santa Cruz de la Sierra and compelled the retreat of the Royalist army from Salta. It gives the name to one of the principal streets of Buenos Ayres. For it Arenales was raised to the rank of general, and a badge of honour was decreed to the troops engaged.

Arenales was no sooner well of his wounds than he marched with his division and reoccupied the Valle Grande, routing a Royalist force of two hundred men at Postrer Valle on the 4th July, but was on the 5th August himself defeated at Sumapaita. Afterwards reinforced by Padilla with a body of Indian slingers, he forced Benavente to retreat from Tomina, and again reoccupied the Valle Grande.

Eighteen months he maintained this extraordinary war at a cost to the enemy of 1,300 men in killed, wounded, and missing, entering Cochabamba at last in triumph, and joining the Argentine army with 1,200 men.

Over the vast plains of La Plata the revolutionary spirit had spread almost unopposed, but where mountain ranges marked out the limits of Upper Peru the movement could only advance by force of arms. The map of the old Viceroyalty did not coincide with that of the social revolution of the United Provinces. Upper Peru had been the high road from Buenos Ayres to Lima in time of peace; it now remained for San Martin to decide whether the same road was strategically the proper road to Lima or not, in time of war.

CHAPTER VI.

THE WAR IN THE NORTH.

1814.

The Army of the North when reinforced, barely numbered 2,000 men, mostly recruits, among whom desertion was frequent. Disorganized, short of officers, and badly clothed, it was quite incapable of making head against the enemy. Jujui and Salta were held by the victorious Spaniards, who threatened the whole of the northern frontier. San Martin was more especially troubled by the lack of officers and the general want of discipline in the troops.

Pezuela, the Spanish general who had defeated Belgrano at Vilcapugio and Ayohuma, had established his headquarters at Tupiza on the frontier of Upper Peru, and ordered a levy of two to three thousand men in the Highlands of Lower Peru. He also formed two battalions out of contingents from the nearer valleys of Chichas and Ciuti, raising his army to about four thousand regulars. His vanguard under Ramirez, one thousand five hundred to two thousand strong, with eight guns, occupied Jujui, and his cavalry scoured the country as far as Salta. San Martin's outposts also reached almost to this city, and at this time the men of the city and of the country round about, rose *en masse* and formed a sort of vanguard to the Army of the North.

San Martin had at that time no regular plan, he neither knew his own resources nor the designs of the enemy, and

confined his efforts to the reorganization of the army.
After consultation with Colonel Dorrego, who commanded
the advanced posts, he determined to confide these positions to the district militia and to concentrate his regular
forces in Tucuman. In carrying out this plan he received
most valuable assistance from the devotion of the country
people, who masked all his movements and prevented the
enemy from discovering anything either of his intentions
or of his strength.

His first step was the construction of an entrenched
camp to the north of the city, which put a stop to desertion, and he increased the number of his troops by recruiting. Here he stood on the defensive and limited his
efforts to aiding the popular movements in Salta, Cochabamba, and Santa Cruz de la Sierra.

In this entrenched camp, which is known to history as
the citadel of Tucuman, he established a school of instruction, holding up the mounted grenadiers as a model for
the rest of his force. Belgrano was a most docile pupil,
but Dorrego, though his talents were highly esteemed by
San Martin, was sent off to Santiago del Estero for insubordinate conduct. Belgrano soon afterwards left the
army, giving as his last advice to his friends the maxim,
"that war must be waged not with arms alone but with
the force of public opinion," which maxim was at that
time exemplified by facts, for the Royalist armies held only
the ground on which they stood, and their movements were
paralyzed by the popular insurrections all around them.

In the Province of Salta the revolutionary movement
was most pronounced. The first popular manifestation in
the city produced the organization of the civic militia. In
1810 the urban guard was raised by the voluntary enlistment of youths of respectable families. Then arose spontaneously among the peasants of the campaña, a corps
of cavalry, with the instincts of the Cossacks, and the
qualities of the Mamelukes, headed by a chieftain who
made his name famous for deeds of prowess.

MARTIN GUEMES had first borne arms against the English in the reconquest of Buenos Ayres in 1806 and in the memorable defence of 1807. He with his men, formed the vanguard of the first Patriot army which invaded Upper Peru. His horsemen penetrated as far as Potosi, and covered every movement of the Patriots. At Suipacha he did good service. In 1811 he escorted the prisoners of the campaign to Buenos Ayres, where he was appointed to the general staff with the rank of captain. In 1813 he took part in the second siege of Monte Video, and was absent from his native province at the time of Belgrano's expedition, but when San Martin took command of the army he was at Santiago del Estero on his way back.

The insurrection of Salta in the face of the victorious enemy, was carried out with equal deliberation and courage. The population emigrated *en masse*, the peasants abandoned their huts and the towns were left desolate. In the capital even the tongues were taken from the church bells, lest the enemy should use them to celebrate their victories. Two old friars alone remained in each convent to administer the sacraments to the sick and aged who could not go away.

When the Royalist vanguard occupied the city of Salta a lieutenant, named Ezenarro, was detached with thirty men to occupy a district thirty-two miles to the south in the valley of Lerma. The first Sunday after his arrival, one of the men of the place after morning mass, said:—

" We must rise against this canalla."

" With what arms ? " asked another.

" With those we take from them," said yet another.

A proprietor, named Luis Burela, put himself at their head, surprised the guard, disarmed Ezenarro and his men, and sent them prisoners to Tucuman. Then, with the arms they had captured, they marched to within ten miles of Salta, where they were met by a company of Spanish troops, whom they charged at once, and completely routed, taking most of the men with their leader prisoners, and sending them also to Tucuman. Another proprietor, named Pedro Zabala, followed the example of Burela, armed his peons and some volunteers and took the field.

So began the resistance to the enemy, in which the whole people speedily joined, so that Salta became a bulwark to the United Provinces impregnable to Royalist arms, solely by the force of public opinion roused to action.

The Province of Salta, which at that time formed a part of the jurisdiction of Jujui, enters within the first spurs of the Andes which branch from the second of the two ranges which enclose Upper Peru, and has the same physical characteristics, plains, mountains, and an intermediate tropical zone. Its possession was thus of great importance to the invaders, as it was the gate to Argentine territory. The occupation of Jujui opened the road to the plains and valleys of Salta, but even the occupation of Salta itself did not secure their position. The agricultural lands, from which alone supplies could be drawn, lay in valleys to the south of the capital, and it was this part of the Province the guerillas undertook to defend. The nature of the country eminently adapted it to guerilla warfare. The inhabitants were a hard-working race of men, strong, active, and inured to hardships, individually brave, and with a natural instinct for the class of warfare they waged. They were horsemen, accustomed to go either up or down hill at full speed, whose ordinary equipment enabled them to gallop unharmed through thorny brushwood. They were good marksmen, either from the tree-tops or from horseback, or on foot from behind their horses if need were. San Martin made no mistake when he entrusted to them the task of keeping the Royalists at bay while he was engaged in the reorganization of the regular army at Tucuman. He had seen in Spain what might be accomplished by this class of irregular troops.

Pezuela, deceived by false despatches which San Martin caused to fall into his hands, believed that these raw levies were the vanguard of the Patriot army advancing on Salta, and in consequence lost much valuable time waiting for reinforcements.

In March the Royalist vanguard advanced from Salta into the valley of Lerma, in search of supplies, under the command of Colonel Saturnino Castro, a native of Salta, who had the repute of being the first cavalry officer of the Royalist army of Peru, and whose valour had decided the day at Vilcapugio. The guerillas, who became known to history as the GAUCHOS of Salta, greatly harassed the progress of the expedition, swarming in the woods along the line of march, cutting off stragglers, driving in small detachments, and firing upon the main body from any convenient shelter.

On the 24th, videttes on the Guachipas River at the end of the valley, descried fifty-six of the enemy, under Captain Fajardo, approaching them. Captain Saravia collected thirty men armed with short muskets, and a group of peasantry with clubs and pikes, charged upon them and completely routed them, killing eleven including the captain, and making twenty-seven prisoners, while he had only three men killed and one wounded.

Meantime Güemes had entered the Sierra to the east of Salta, and on the 9th and 18th, two parties of his Gauchos surprised two detachments of the enemy. On the 29th he came so close to the city that Castro sallied out against him for about a league with eighty men, but was completely routed, with the loss of half his force.

For this feat Güemes was named Commandant-General of the Vanguard, and on the recommendation of San Martin, was raised to the rank of Lieutenant-Colonel.

Güemes then occupied the approaches to the city and harassed the garrison by daily attacks upon the suburbs. Being reinforced from Jujui, the Royalists then organised two expeditions of 500 men each. One, composed of a battalion of infantry and a squadron of light horse under Colonel Alvarez, marched early in June into the valley of Lerma. At the town of Sumalao, Alvarez found the vanguard of the Guachipas awaiting him. The Patriot outposts were driven in, but the main body sheltered by trees and broken ground, poured so heavy a fire upon him that he was forced to return to the city, with many killed and wounded, and with the loss of all the supplies he had seized.

The other column, also composed of infantry and cavalry, was under the command of Colonel Marquiegui, who like Castro was a native of Salta, and of great repute for skill and knowledge of the country. This column marched to the east and was met by Güemes in person, who made so stubborn a resistance that it was also forced back to the city, and the siege was re-established.

Pezuela had drawn in his reserves and advanced to Jujui. Thence he sent orders to Colonel Marquiegui to march with one hundred infantry and one hundred and fifty horse, by the north-eastern frontiers of Tucuman and Santiago del Estero, to the rear of the advanced guard of the Patriots on the river Pasaje. Marquiegui carried out his instructions with great skill, captured several forts, and learned from prisoners that the army of San Martin consisted only of three thousand recruits, and that the vanguard which gave them so much trouble, was nothing but a swarm of undisciplined Gauchos; but he also learned that the object of the campaign, which was the relief of Monte Video, was now impossible, that city having already fallen.

When news of this expedition reached Tucuman, Güemes was immediately reinforced by one hundred infantry and one hundred mounted grenadiers, and Marquiegui retreated, marching one hundred leagues in a semicircle, but was prevented from carrying off either horses or cattle.

This was the last attempt at invasion; five thousand men were not enough to capture Tucuman, much less to conquer the country. Pezuela withdrew his troops beyond the frontier, and sent off a strong detachment to Cuzco to crush an insurrection which had broken out in that city.

The object of the Royalist invasion was, by a powerful diversion, to compel the Argentine Government to withdraw their army from the Banda Oriental for the protection of the northern provinces, but meantime that government had armed and equipped a small naval force, which, under the command of an Irishman named BROWN, had, on the 16th May, defeated and almost destroyed the Spanish squadron stationed at Monte Video, which city soon after surrendered to the Argentine army then besieging it under the command of Alvear.

Before the conclusion of these events, the General of the Army of the North had disappeared from the theatre of war. San Martin, after careful study of the question, had clearly discerned that the road by Upper Peru was not the true strategical line of the South American revolution. His idea was to carry the war to the West, to pass the Andes, to occupy Chile, to secure the dominion of the Pacific, and to attack Lower Peru on the flank, continuing military operations to the North merely as a subordinate detail of the main design.

This plan, the merits of which were not appreciated by his contemporaries until it was crowned with victory, is looked upon by posterity as not merely the most simple, but as the only possible plan which could give the desired result. It was then held to be folly, whilst in reality the folly lay in persevering in the attempt to reach Lima with insufficient means and by an impracticable route. Knowing that it would be looked upon as folly, San Martin kept his idea to himself, as *his secret*, as he himself styled it in confidential intercourse, waiting to disclose it for the day when he should hold in his hand the thunderbolt which was to shatter the power of Spain in America. Three months after taking command of the Army of the North, he wrote to his friend, Don Nicolas Rodriguez Peña :—

"Don't flatter yourself with thinking of what I can do here. I shall do nothing, and nothing here pleases me. Our country can do nothing more here than act on the defensive, for which war the brave Gauchos of Salta suffice, if aided by two squadrons of regular troops. To think otherwise is to throw men and money into an abyss. I have already told you *my secret*. A small, well-disciplined army in Mendoza, to cross to Chile and finish off the Goths there, aiding a government of trusty friends to put an end to the anarchy which reigns. Allying our forces, we shall then go by sea to Lima. This is our course, and no other."

This idea, which was a secret in 1814, and which would, if divulged, have caused its author to be looked upon as a lunatic, is the idea which has given San Martin his place in the history of the world, and which finally changed the destinies of South America.

With such plans in his head, San Martin could not rest content with the command of the Army of the North. Further, his rival, Alvear, after crowning himself with the laurels of victory at Monte Video, aspired also to those of Peru. Doubtless, with his enterprising character and sparks of genius, he would have broken the routine of the previous campaigns, and San Martin was willing to yield his post to him, asking for himself, as for a resting-place, the government of the obscure province of Mendoza, by which he threw dust in the eyes, not only of the enemies of America but also in those of his own friends, imitating the tactics of William the Silent, to whose character his own bears some analogy.

In addition he was, towards the end of April, attacked by an affection of the lungs, which obliged him to leave Don Francisco Fernandez de la Cruz in command of the army, and to retire, by the advice of his physician, to the Sierra of Cordoba, in search of a drier climate.

On the 10th August, 1814, the ex-General of the Army of the North was appointed Governor of Cuyo. From that moment he lived only for his idea. Mendoza was the starting-point in the realization of his plans; it was the soil whence sprang the legions which were to liberate America.

CHAPTER VII.

THE CHILENO-ARGENTINE REVOLUTION.

1810—1811.

IN September, 1814, San Martin took charge of the Government of Cuyo. The revolution in Chile had then lasted four years and was about to succumb, a prey to intestine discords and to the arms of Peru. In order to understand what followed we must first know what preceded the appearance of San Martin upon the scene.

Never were two peoples more analogous and less alike than the peoples of Chile and of the United Provinces. Both countries were situate at the southern extremity of the new continent, under the same degrees of latitude, but while one was shut up between the mountains and the sea, the other spread over vast plains. The first was agricultural, the second pastoral and commercial. Chile possessed a territorial aristocracy, and a population of half-breeds, whose relations were somewhat feudal in character. The Argentine people were by nature democratic. Both people sprang from the same origin, and were in temperament alike.

The colonization of Mexico and Peru was an imitation of the feudal system of Europe; the labour of an enslaved race was utilized for the production of the precious metals. The colonization of the River Plate and of Chile was effected by the colonists themselves. Assimilating in some degree the indigenous races, they conquered their territories from a warlike people, and, in so doing, developed their own aptitude for war, while they supplied themselves with the first necessaries of life by their own labour.

While the colonists of the River Plate crossed immense deserts and reached the Pacific by way of Upper Peru, the colonists of Chile crossed the Andes from Arauco and established themselves to the east of the Cordillera at Mendoza, opening for themselves a road to the Atlantic. Thus the city of Mendoza, capital of the Argentine Province of Cuyo, was a bond of union between the two countries.

During the colonial epoch Chile had vegetated in obscurity amid peace and plenty, but the Provinces of the River Plate had lived in a state of almost constant warfare with their neighbours the Portuguese, with the English, and with the Indians, which gave them some knowledge of their own strength, and inoculated them with new ideas. These ideas filtered across the Cordillera to Chile, and there smouldered till, in the year 1810, the flames of revolution burst out in both countries almost simultaneously.

The kingdom of Chile, as it was called, was colonized under the auspices of Peru, but was, in 1778, separated from this Viceroyalty and placed under the orders of a governor, who was at the same time President of the Real Audiencia. These two authorities, with the Cabildos granted to some cities, constituted the whole political, judicial, and municipal system of the colony. The separation from Peru inspired the colonists with instinctive ideas of independent autonomy, till the death of the then governor, Muñoz Guzman, on the 10th February, 1808, plunged the hitherto pacific colony into a fever of expectancy.

The Home Government followed no fixed system in the appointment of the superior authorities in the colonies. Their nomination came from the Crown direct; sometimes vacancies were provided for beforehand, sometimes the

G

colonists were empowered to make a provisional appointment; but, latterly, that power was, as a rule, vested in the Audiencia. In 1806 all this was changed by Royal decree, which enacted that, in case of a vacancy, the military official of the highest rank then in the colony should assume the vacant post. On the death of Muñoz Guzman, the Audiencia of Chile raised its own President to the vacant office. The officers stationed on the frontier of Araucania protested against this appointment, and proclaimed Colonel Don Francisco Garcia Carrasco Provisional Governor and Captain-General, and the Audiencia was forced to yield.

The new Captain-General took with him to the capital, as his secretary and councillor, a man who had for many years resided at Concepcion, who had great influence in the south and was highly thought of throughout the country. This was Dr. Don Juan Martinez de Rozas, an Argentine, born in Mendoza, who was at that time forty-nine years of age. He was a graduate of the University of Cordoba, and a fellow-student with Dr. Castelli, through whom he afterwards entered into political relations with Belgrano. In various official positions in Chile he had gained experience of public affairs, and his wife was a daughter of one of the principal families of the South. Of a passionate character, he was at the same time prudent, was well read in the current literature of the day, and was the leading spirit in a group of men who discussed among themselves the future destinies of America.

The new Captain-General was a man of limited intelligence, violent in his proceedings, and with no firmness of character. Thus he soon made himself hated, and was despised by all. His one passion was cock-fighting, his greatest pleasure was in listening to jokes, and his affections were concentrated upon a domestic of African race, through whose hands all favours were bestowed. The whole aim of Rozas was to make him an instrument for social and political reform. To this end he strove to raise the Cabildo of Santiago into a position analogous to that of Buenos Ayres, and to use it as a counterpoise to that of the Audiencia. The Governor, by his advice, added twelve new members to this body, influential citizens, most of whom were men of advanced opinions. The immediate result of this innovation was to inoculate this assembly with revolutionary ideas.

Ferdinand VII. being now a prisoner of Napoleon, the Creoles thought that the time had come to replace the colonial system by a government of their own, but the Spaniards, who thought only of preserving their own privileges, protested against the idea. The two parties soon came into collision. The Governor cancelled the decree which added twelve members to the Cabildo, and quarrelled first with the Audiencia and then with Dr. Rozas.

The Spaniards strove to reconcile him with the Audiencia, and advised him to fortify the hill of Santa Lucia which commands the city, and to arm their partisans; but finding their counsels set at nought, they denounced him to the Viceroy of Buenos Ayres as unfit for the post he held. He, on his part, appealed for help both to the Viceroy of Buenos Ayres and to him of Peru.

At the same time several leading Chilians, aided by young Argentines resident at Santiago, opened communications with the popular leaders of Buenos Ayres. Carrasco then tried what intimidation would do. On the 25th May, 1810, the same day on which the Viceroy of Buenos Ayres was deposed by the people, he ordered the arrest of three of the principal citizens of Santiago, as advocates of revolutionary ideas. The municipal authorities protested, and convened an open Cabildo, which cited the Governor before them. He thought at first of resistance, but 3,000 men filled the Plaza. He could not depend upon the troops, and at the request of the Audiencia he presented himself, amid the shouts of the populace who clamoured for his deposition.

. A new Procurator, elected by the Cabildo, the previous one being among the prisoners, opened the case by declaring that it was the will of the people that the prisoners should be set free, and that the Cabildo would remain sitting till it was done. This was the first time that such a thing as "the will of the people" had been heard of in Chile, and the speech of the new tribune was loudly applauded.

Carrasco yielded, and decreed not only the liberation of the prisoners, but also the dismissal from their posts of those who had aided in the arbitrary measure. He also accepted the control of an Assessor, without whose authorization his judicial acts should, in future, be invalid. These decrees were endorsed by the Audiencia, which was a virtual dismissal from office of the last Governor and Captain-General of Chile.

From that day the latent spirit of revolution gained ground, but the efforts of the Patriots were as yet limited to theoretical discussions. Their head-quarters were in Santiago, the warlike Province of Concepcion was their base, and their teaching came from Buenos Ayres, "the Athens of the New World," as it is styled by a Chilian historian. The growth of public opinion in Santiago, and the news constantly arriving from Spain, more especially that of the battle of Ocaña, kept the interest alive.

The south of Chile, whose capital was Concepcion, virtually formed a distinct country. The people called themselves "Penquistos," to distinguish themselves from their northern neighbours, who styled themselves "Chilians." Their troublesome neighbours, the Indians of Araucania, had accustomed them to war; their pastoral and agricultural pursuits made them strong and hardy. Their society included a class of free peasantry, among whom the army of the frontier found recruits, and from whom sprang the most distinguished leaders on both sides in the war which followed. The man of most influence in this district in 1809 was Dr. Rozas, who, after his quarrel with Carrasco, returned to Concepcion and began openly to work for independence.

He advised that Chile, without renouncing her allegiance to her captive sovereign, should provisionally appoint a National government, after the example set by the Provinces of Spain, which idea he advocated in a manuscript circular, for at that day there was no printing-press in Chile.

Among the co-workers with Rozas was a wealthy proprietor of the South named DON BERNARDO O'HIGGINS, son of the celebrated Viceroy of the same name. Educated in Europe he spoke English, and was, by reason of his Irish descent, partial to the institutions of England. A disciple and confidant of Miranda he had been affiliated in his lodge, swearing as did San Martin and Bolivar to work for the liberty of the New World.

Carrasco kept the prisoners in gaol in spite of his promise to the Cabildo, and issued a decree establishing a special Junta to keep watch over the advocates of the new ideas. The excitement in Santiago increased, and eight hundred armed citizens demanded the institution of a governing Junta, in imitation of that established in Buenos Ayres on the 25th May. The Audiencia prevailed upon Carrasco to resign his power into the hands of the Count de la Conquista, a Chilian noble, who was eighty-five years of age. The Patriots were not satisfied, but as they succeeded in surrounding the new Governor by councillors in whom they could trust, they for a time acquiesced.

About the end of July an emissary from Belgrano and Castelli crossed the Andes. The Patriots, stimulated by the news he brought, determined to persist in their previous design, and induced the Count to convene an open Cabildo on the 18th September. To ensure their triumph the Cabildo called out the city militia, and the proprietors of Santiago filled the suburbs with their armed tenantry. They were also joined by some officers of the garrison. In spite of the protest of the Audiencia, the Count laid down his baton of command, and the Cabildo appointed a governing Junta of seven members, of whom Dr. Rozas was one, the Count being named President.

The new Government was accepted by the whole country, but nothing was changed until the arrival of Dr. Rozas, who on the 2nd November entered the capital in triumph, between lines of troops, amid salvoes of artillery, the clang of bells, music, and loud acclamations. All that night the city was illuminated and fireworks blazed in his honour. Never had Santiago witnessed such an ovation.

The Chilian revolution resembled that of Buenos Ayres, in that it was Parliamentary and legal, initiated and carried out within the precincts of the municipal forum; and that it triumphed by the force of opinion, without violence, in the name of the public weal. Both followed the same formula, the resumption of their own rights, without a rupture with the mother country and protesting fidelity to the legitimate sovereign. The first was an aristocratic revolution, the second was democratic and radical; but, both were essentially American and obeyed the same historic law. Thus from the beginning, the two nations were bound together by fraternal ties and by a common cause.

The news of the installation of the Junta of Chile was received in Buenos Ayres with transports of joy, and the thunder of their guns on the 11th October, reverberated in the hearts of the Chilian people. Buenos Ayres proposed at once an alliance offensive and defensive, assuring the Chilians that England would recognise any constitution they might give themselves, now that Spain had fallen. Rozas, in return, presented a plan for a vast continental confederation, which idea found an eager advocate in Alvarez Jonte, the Argentine envoy, who as a practical exposition of it, asked Chile for an auxiliary force in aid of the Argentine Government against the reactionary movement which had its headquarters in Monte Video.

The Cabildo opposed the project, but Rozas had the majority of the Junta with him, and in 1811 a decree was published for the despatch of an auxiliary force of 500 men, and authorizing the Argentine envoy to enlist 2,000 recruits. This sealed the alliance of the two countries and united their destinies for good or evil. Of the promised contingent, 100 dragoons and 200 infantry reached Buenos Ayres on the 14th June, 1811, and met with an enthusiastic reception.

The Patriot party soon became divided into two factions. The Radicals, who aimed at independence, were headed by Rozas, and had in their front line the Argentine residents. The death of the Count de la Conquista in February, 1811, left Rozas at the head of affairs, but his power was more apparent than real. Against him, at the head of the Moderate party, was ranged the Cabildo, sustained by the Creole aristocracy, whose timid temporising policy almost placed them in line with the party of reaction. The Royalist, called the Goth or Saracen party, recognized the leadership of the Audiencia, accused Rozas of personal ambition and even of aspiring to the crown. Rozas had no such ambition and lacked even the spontaneous courage of the man of action. Through all this opposition he carried on his plan of reform, of which freedom of commerce was the most important feature. This was proclaimed in February, 1811, with the result that in a few months the revenue was doubled and was soon after quadrupled. He also raised troops and summoned a general Congress of Deputies from the Provinces, whose election was based upon the limitations established by municipal precedent.

The 1st April was the day appointed for the elections. That same day a part of the garrison of Santiago mutinied under Colonel Figueroa, who was a friend of Rozas. At first the daring Royalist was successful, and occupied the Plaza, placing himself under the orders of the Audiencia, who however, declined all responsibility. Rozas, who alone of his colleagues preserved his presence of mind, ordered the rest of the troops to march against the mutineers. The two forces met in the Plaza and opened fire on each other simultaneously, at close quarters. The affair soon ended in favour of the Patriots, young Manuel Dorrego, of Buenos Ayres, at that time a student of the University, particularly distinguishing himself in the fight.

Figueroa took refuge in a convent, where he was captured by Rozas at the head of a party of citizens, was tried that same night, sentenced to death "as a traitor to his country and the government," and was shot the next morning at four o'clock. The bodies of five of the mutineers who had been killed, were hung on a gallows in the Plaza on the afternoon of the 1st, and next day proclamation was made that all who conspired against the State would be similarly punished.

Immediately afterwards the Audiencia was dissolved, and with it disappeared the last semblance of monarchical authority in Chile.

Meantime the elections passed off quietly in the rest of the country. In the Centre the Creole oligarchy triumphed, the great proprietors being elected by their tenants without opposition; but in the South and in some of the northern districts, the Radicals were successful.

Following the example of Buenos Ayres, the Deputies were incorporated with the executive, in spite of the just protest of the Cabildo, which revenged itself by procuring the election of twelve deputies for the capital in place of the six it ought to have had according to the electoral census.

On the 6th May the interrupted election took place in Santiago. The candidates of Rozas being defeated from this day his power waned.

Congress met on the 4th July. Out of forty members Rozas could only count upon thirteen votes. On the same day the Junta resigned, and the "High Congress" assumed the executive power. Rozas in an eloquent speech gave a sketch of his policy, which he recommended for their adoption, and was listened to with deep attention by the whole Assembly; for the moment all the discordant opinions vibrated in harmony.

It is an interesting question whether this early establishment of the Parliamentary system was of benefit or was an evil to Chile. The Chilian historian, Vicuña Mackenna, considers it premature. He says, "the dictatorship of a Cæsar rather than that of a Cicero" would have been preferable for a people without constitutional education. Gervinus thinks that it assured to Chile, later on, that tranquillity so wanting in the other republics of South America. Lastarria, more philosophical than either, observes that the establishment of the doctrine of the sovereignty of the people, even under such restrictions as placed them in the hands of a few only, was the true way to weaken colonial prejudices and to arouse the idea of the dignity of man. The fact is that it was the natural outcome of the feudal character of Chilian society. In the Parliamentary drama the people played the part of the Greek chorus, which repeated the words of the principal actor. Chile soon remedied the error, copied from Buenos Ayres, of incorporating Congress with the Executive, which shows the existence of a hidden force neutralising the effect of an evil example.

The revolutions of Holland and the United States had shown the world that a regulating Congress was compatible with a dictatorship; and even in South America it was seen later on that no dictatorship, however powerful, could disregard the will of the people from whom its authority was derived. In Chile less than in any other colony was this possible; nevertheless it is certain that Rozas convened this Congress in obedience to a solemn promise exacted from him by O'Higgins as a condition of his support.

The Moderate party, which had a large majority in Congress, knew not what use to make of their power; they were without experience, without plans, and had no fixed ideas; most of them desired only peace and security for their properties. The minority had clearer views; they aimed at raising their leader to the head of the State, and at independence.

On the 27th July an English ship of war reached Valparaiso, whose captain was commissioned by the Viceroy of Peru, with credentials from the Regency of Spain, to receive the subsidy which Chile was expected to contribute for the maintenance of the war in the Peninsula. One million six hundred thousand dollars had been deposited in the treasury for this purpose. The Moderates and the Royalists were for paying the amount at once, but O'Higgins, speaking for the Liberals, said:—

"Although we are in a minority we shall know how to supply that defect by our energy and our courage; we are sufficient to oppose effectually the delivery of this money, of which our country threatened with invasion has need." This bold protest decided the question in the negative.

The Liberals afterwards proposed the appointment of an Executive of three; one for each of the three territorial divisions of the country, the North, the South, and the Centre. The Moderates accepted the idea but put off the election. The Liberals then attempted to intimidate Congress by popular tumults, sadly compromising their leader by these sinister manœuvres. Congress showed more firmness than could have been expected from its composition, and the defeated minority seceded from the Assembly. The majority then named three of their own party as the Junta, and Rozas, looking upon his cause as lost, retired to Concepcion, where he was received in triumph, and set up an opposition Junta, the South recalling its members from Congress.

Congress then drew up a constitution, so unworkable that it only served to show their utter lack of all political knowledge. It never came into operation.

CHAPTER VIII.

PROGRESS AND FALL OF THE CHILIAN REVOLUTION.

1811—1814.

THE disappearance of the Radical party in Congress, the reactionary policy of the Conservatives, and the proceedings of Rozas at Concepcion, had most evil effect upon the course of the revolution in Chile. Liberalism became anarchy, and the Moderates became mixed up with the Spanish party. At this juncture Don José Miguel Carrera returned to his native land.

Carrera was a scion of one of the most distinguished families of Chile, and was at that time twenty-seven years of age. He had fought in Spain against the French, and brought with him a major's commission, granted by the Junta of Galicia, and the brilliant uniform of an hussar. He had two brothers, officers in the army of Chile. The elder, Juan José, was a man of herculean strength, but of feeble intellect, wanting in moral courage, and full of envy of his more talented brother. The youngest and most amiable of the three, was named Luis, and was at that time twenty years of age. In danger he was always found in the front rank, and was devoted to José Miguel. These three had a sister, Javiera, of great beauty and of masculine strength of mind; she was skilful in intrigue and ambitious, but was distinguished both by social and domestic virtues; her intrepid spirit made her the Egeria of her brothers.

José Miguel was a man of action, and a thinker so far as his unruly nature would permit; of vehement passions, and licentious life, a ready writer and a brilliant speaker, of good presence and of attractive manners, but with an overweening sense of his own importance. He was a sort of an Alcibiades shorn of his great qualities.

Carrera presented himself publicly to Congress, dressed in his brilliant uniform, offered his services and his sword, and then entered into secret negotiations with the Liberal party, through the powerful family of Larrain. With them he organized a popular demonstration by which the Government was upset on the 4th September, a new Junta of five members was appointed, six of the members of Congress for the capital were dismissed as illegally elected, and three seats were declared vacant.

Congress had hesitated to grant the request of the Government of Buenos Ayres for forty quintals of gunpowder from the factory in Chile; the new Government sent off two hundred quintals. It reduced the taxes, reformed some abuses in administration, encouraged industry, armed the militia, and had the glory of making Chile the first nation in America to abolish slavery.

The principal posts were monopolised by the Larrain family, greatly to the disgust of Carrera. One of this family boasting that the legislative, executive, and judicial presidencies were all held by them, Carrera asked :—

"And who has the presidency of the bayonets?"

Dazzled by his popularity, he now only thought of how to overturn the new Government, and even sought and obtained help from the Spanish party to this end.

On the 15th November Juan José Carrera mutinied with his battalion and seized the barracks of the artillery. Luis headed the artillerymen and dragged the guns into the street, the roll of their wheels on the pavement giving the signal for a fresh revolution. José Miguel put himself at the head of the mutiny, and summoned the Executive and Congress to meet and hear the petitions of the people.

He was joined only by the Spanish party, who shouted for the dissolution of the Junta and of Congress. The next day an open Cabildo was convened, which named a new Junta, composed of José Miguel Carrera, as representative of the capital, Gaspar Marin for the North, and Rozas, or in his absence Don Bernardo O'Higgins, for the South. This resolution was presented to Congress by the military chiefs, and Congress, after some delay, authorised the appointment of the new Junta.

On the 27th November, on pretext that he was in danger of assassination, Carrera made several arrests. He himself took one of the prisoners to the barracks, made him kneel before a crucifix, and by threatening him with immediate execution, forced from him a declaration against the others. The trial which followed proved the innocence of the accused. Called to account by his colleagues and by Congress, he, on the 2nd December, demanded the dissolution of the latter, occupied the Legislative Palace with troops, and forced from the Assembly a decree to that effect. Marin and O'Higgins protested and withdrew from the Junta. Carrera replaced them by one of his own partisans and by a noted leader of the Spanish party.

The two political parties, which represented the aristocracy and democracy of Chile, disappeared, and the country fell under the domination of a military oligarchy, which setting aside laws, juntas, and congresses, depended only on the army for support. Juan José Carrera was raised to the rank of brigadier-general, and his brothers were made lieutenant-colonels, with special decorations for their services.

Public opinion was entirely against the Carreras, all eyes turned to the South and to Rozas as the only man who could vindicate the law. Rozas protested against the mutiny and offered his assistance to Congress, but he was in an anomalous position. By leaving the capital and setting up an opposition Junta at Concepcion, he had entered upon dangerous ground and had sapped the base of his moral power; he had destroyed the territorial unity of the revolution and had aroused provincial jealousies. Thus Carrera, though destitute of political principle, and seeking only his own aggrandisement, was the true representative of the cause of national unity.

The Centre of Chile is divided from the South by the river Maule. Carrera stationed an army on the north bank, while, through the intervention of O'Higgins, he conferred with Rozas. On the 12th January, 1812, a convention was drawn up by three plenipotentiaries, which recognised the South, Centre, and North as three distinct provinces, each of which should name one member of an Executive, until a Constituent Congress could be convened. Carrera was in no haste to ratify this convention, till an army from the South advanced to the line of the Maule. A collision was prevented by an interview on the 25th April between the two leaders, who verbally agreed to the ratification of the convention and the re-installation of Congress. This agreement was hailed with joy throughout the country, and Carrera was received in triumph on his return to Santiago.

It was not patriotism nor fear of the Penquistos, which induced Carrera to restore the Congress he had dissolved; the Argentine Government, appealed to by the Government of Concepcion, had offered their mediation, but the most serious matter was that the province of Valdivia had on the 12th March declared itself Royalist, and proclaimed Carrera Captain-General of the kingdom, an appointment which he indignantly rejected.

Valdivia occupied the extreme south of the country, had a seaport with fortifications which were considered impregnable, and was supported by the Archipelago of Chiloe, where the people were all Royalists and had a Royalist garrison.

Early in 1812 the first printing-press was established in Chile, and on the 13th February appeared the first newspaper, entitled *La Aurora de Chile*, edited by Camilo Enriquez, a priest, assisted by an Argentine named Vera y Pintado, and by Irrizarra of Guatemala. From the United States, together with the printing-press, came Mr. Poinsett as consular agent, who introduced a new element into the political opinions of the country, democratic ideas, which new ideas found at first little acceptance save in the army, where they were fostered by Carrera as a counterpoise to the federal ideas which had gained strength during the recent events.

On the night of the 9th July a revolutionary movement broke out in Concepcion, headed by the partisans of Rozas, but secretly fomented by the Spanish party, which dissolved the Provincial Junta. Rozas went to Santiago, whence he was banished by Carrera to Mendoza, and died there on the 3rd March, 1813.

Carrera was now without a rival, and the revolution gained in unity and in strength. The various parties commenced to fuse together, with his authority as a common centre, and the desire for independence became more marked. When Consul Poinsett celebrated his national anniversary of the 4th July, the flag of the stars and stripes was seen entwined with an unknown tri-coloured flag, bearing a lone star in one of its corners. This unknown flag was the new flag of Chile. On the 16th July the tricoloured cockade was worn by all the citizens of Santiago, and on the 30th September the new flag was formally recognised as the national ensign. Nevertheless independence was not then declared, still government was carried on in the name of Ferdinand VII., while the Carreras went about the city at night in disguise, with groups of young men, pulling down the escutcheons of the Creole aristocracy.

In order to test his popularity, Carrera then sent in his resignation, which the Cabildo refused to accept. In consequence of a misunderstanding with his brother, Juan José, who was still envious of him, he repeated his resignation, but in conjunction with his brother Luis, reserved the command of the army. His father, Don Ignacio, was appointed to succeed him, and supported by Don Juan José adopted a reactionary policy, which was opposed by José Miguel and Luis, at the head of the troops.

The two brothers, assisted by two friends, then drew up a plan for a constitution, which was presented to the Junta by one of their adherents. This plan created a Senate of seven members, and contained two clauses which provided that :—

"Ferdinand VII. was king on condition of accepting and swearing the Constitution made by the people," and " no decree emanating from authority outside the territory shall have any effect, those who obey it being punished as traitors to the State."

These clauses were accepted by the Junta, but Don Ignacio Carrera, being afraid to sign them, retired from the Government, and Don José Miguel returned to office.

Carrera was again dictator, and opposition was silent in the face of a new danger. A Royalist army had invaded Chilian territory and occupied the South. He was now the champion of a noble cause; all the military chiefs, even those who opposed his policy, obeyed him willingly; the people saw in danger the justification of a strong government; the military repute he had brought with him from Europe caused him to be regarded as the first soldier of his country.

Abascal, Viceroy of Peru, was then more than seventy years old. By firmness and prudence he had maintained peace in his Viceroyalty in the midst of the commotions which stirred all Spanish America. More than that, he had made Peru the centre of the Royalist reaction, had crushed rebellion in Upper Peru, had made war on the Argentine provinces, had sent an expedition to Quito, and had kept Chiloe under his orders. He had watched the Chilian revolution from its commencement, waiting for a favourable opportunity to attack it. Antonio Pareja, an experienced soldier, was named Commandant-General ot Valdivia and Chiloe, and early in 1813 reached the island with five vessels, a number of officers, fifty soldiers, and fifty thousand dollars.

He quickly organised the militia of the Archipelago, with the garrison as a nucleus, and crossed to Valdivia with 1,400 men, where he incorporated the garrison of that fortress, raising his force to over 2,000 men. These he arranged in three divisions, each with six guns, and re-embarking, sailed northwards, keeping his destination secret. Three days afterwards, on the 26th March, he landed in the bay of San Vicente, taking the town of Talcahuano in the rear, and threatening Concepcion in front. Talcahuano was taken by assault; the garrison of Concepcion mutinied and gave up the city. Thus speedily he was master of the South, and further strengthened his force by the garrisons of Arauco.

With 2,000 regulars, from 2,000 to 3,000 militia, and with twenty-five guns, he opened the campaign early in April. At Chillán the country rose in his favour, increasing his force to 6,000 men, with whom he occupied the line of the river Nuble, which lies to the south of the Maule.

Carrera was equally active; he proclaimed himself General-in-chief with full powers, declared war against the Viceroy of Peru, set up a gibbet in the Plaza of Santiago, on which to hang all who should hold communication with the enemy, and caused the imposition of a forced loan of two hundred and sixty thousand dollars upon those hostile to the revolution, which measures inspired general enthusiasm and confidence.

On the 1st April he established his headquarters to the north of the Maule, with merely an escort, and gave orders for the concentration of the army at Talca. His friend, Consul Poinsett, accompanied him as a volunteer, and the same day he was joined by O'Higgins, who forgot his resentment, an example followed by Mackenna, who was a talented engineer. Calling in the militia of the South, who remained faithful, in twenty days he was at the head of 10,000 men, from whom he organised an army of 2,500 regulars, badly armed, and as many lancers of the militia, with sixteen field-pieces.

The campaign opened with a piece of good fortune which greatly encouraged the Patriots. It chanced that an officer sent with 500 men to surprise the vanguard of the enemy at a pass on the Maule, misunderstood his orders, and on the night of the 27th April fell in with the main body of the Royalists, some five or six thousand strong. Not knowing who they were, he attacked them and captured the whole of the artillery. At dawn the enemy recovered from their panic, pursued him and recaptured the guns and prisoners. The loss of the Patriots in killed and wounded was four times that of the Royalists, but the moral effect was that of a victory. The greater part of the irregular cavalry deserted from Pareja, who nevertheless advanced to the Maule. The army was drawn up to force the passage, when the men from Chiloe and Valdivia threw down their arms and refused to go further; they cared nothing for the Royalist cause beyond the Maule. Pareja, lying on a stretcher, stricken with a mortal disease, ordered a retreat, on which the rest of the irregulars dispersed, and he was left with little more than a thousand men.

Carrera knew nothing of what had occurred, and let fifteen days pass before he made up his mind to cross the river. The Patriot vanguard under Luis Carrera came up with Pareja on the 15th May, as he was about to pass the Nuble. The Royalists halted, the dying general mounted on horseback for the last time, and placed Captain Sanchez in command. Sanchez at once occupied some rising ground, where he threw up an entrenchment with his baggage, and formed his infantry in square, and opened fire with twenty-seven guns upon the Patriots, checking their advance. Carrera then took the command, and on the arrival of Don Juan José with the second division, drew up his infantry in line with cavalry on the flanks to surround the enemy. Don Juan José, without waiting for orders, attacked the position and was driven back; the same fate befell another battalion which followed his example. The guns were dismounted at the first shot. The cavalry which had passed to the rear of the enemy, were dispersed by artillery fire, and the infantry fell back in disorder. The third division, under O'Higgins and Mackenna, then came up and prevented the advance of the enemy, which would have turned the repulse into a rout. Night put a stop to this strange affair, and Carrera retreated in disorder to San Carlos.

Sanchez crossed the Nuble with all his artillery, without further molestation, and retreated to Chillán, with a loss of six killed and fifteen wounded.

This battle of San Carlos showed that Carrera was destitute of military talent; but he had the strength of mind to reject the councils of his disheartened officers, who advised him to withdraw the army beyond the Maule, and for the first time drew up a definite plan of operations. With one part of his army he occupied Concepcion and Talcahuano, cutting off the retreat of the enemy by sea, and despatched O'Higgins with his division to Arauco, securing the South, but in these manœuvres he lost much time, and one detachment of 650 men left in reserve on the Nuble, was captured by a Royalist force from Chillán.

Sanchez was an obscure soldier, born in Galicia, of no real genius, but quick-sighted, of great tenacity, and devoted to the cause he served. At Chillán he entrenched himself, aided by the people, who were all Royalists, and by the preaching friars, who had there a convent, which soon became a well-provisioned citadel.

When Carrera, against the advice of O'Higgins and Mackenna, determined at the end of July to besiege Chillán, it was already winter, the season of heavy rains

On the 3rd August, Mackenna established a battery of six guns, at four hundred and fifty yards from the trenches. The following morning Sanchez made a vigorous sally but was driven back. The same afternoon he made another attack upon a reserve battery, under the fire of his own redoubts, a ball from which blew up the ammunition of the battery, causing great confusion. Carrera ordered the battery to be abandoned, but his officers disobeyed him, and O'Higgins coming up to the rescue, the enemy was again repulsed.

The losses were considerable on both sides, but the sufferings of the besiegers were augmented by the inclemency of the weather. A convoy of ammunition for Carrera was intercepted by Royalist guerillas, thirty miles from the encampment, and delivered to Sanchez, whose supplies were running short. On the 5th Sanchez made another attack upon the advanced battery, which was bravely repelled by Luis Carrera. The Patriot general then ordered an assault upon the town, which was beaten off by the townspeople themselves. The spirit of the Patriot army was broken, deaths and desertions greatly reduced their numbers. Carrera summoned the garrison to surrender. Sanchez replied by proposing an armistice, during which the Patriots should recross the Maule. A council of war was called, and against the advice of Mackenna the siege was raised. On the 14th August the Patriot army encamped on the banks of the Itata, and from this moment their cause declined.

Carrera again fell into the error of dividing his army. He posted one division near the mouth of the Itata, under command of his brother Juan José, to protect the line of the Maule, and O'Higgins was despatched with a weak division to secure the frontier on the Bio-Bio. With the rest of his forces he went to Concepcion, while his guerillas scoured the country in every direction. This was just what suited Sanchez, who could do nothing with a strong force in front of him. He had plenty of irregulars who knew the country well, and split up his force into flying columns to the north and south. The depredations of the Patriots stirred up the resistance of the people, and various detachments were cut up in detail. O'Higgins could not prevent the reconquest of the line of the Bio-Bio and the occupation of Arauco, by which supplies were drawn by the Royalists from Valdivia and Chiloe.

At the end of September Carrera was shut up in Concepcion, and the Patriot army was blockaded in three separate divisions. He ordered their concentration at Concepcion. Juan José Carrera reached the Membrillar near to the junction of the Diguillin with the Itata early in October, where he was forced to entrench himself. Carrera then marched to meet O'Higgins, and joined him at the pass of " El Roble," some ten miles to the east of Membrillar. The united forces, about 1,000 strong, encamped on ground badly chosen. Sanchez, joining the irregulars with a division from Chillán, attacked them there on the night of the 19th October. In the confusion Carrera jumped his horse into the river and went off to join his brother, receiving a lance wound in his flight. His absence was not noticed, but O'Higgins, after three hours' firing, led a bayonet charge upon the enemy, and drove them across the river. When Carrera returned to the camp he saluted O'Higgins as " the saviour of the division and of the country," and in his official despatch spoke of him as " the first of soldiers, capable of uniting in himself the glories of Chile." These words were his own abdication, his military star was eclipsed.

After this affair Carrera again changed his plan. He left his brother and O'Higgins at the confluence of the Diguillin and Itata, protected by fieldworks, and returned to Concepcion. This destroyed his prestige in the army and in public opinion; the Press gave the signal of general discontent; even from the pulpit the disastrous influence of the three Carreras was condemned.

When Carrera took command of the army his place as

Dictator was for a time filled by his brother Juan José; when he also took the field his two colleagues resigned. The Corporations and the Senate then named a new Junta of three, chosen from the Moderate party, two of whom were enemies of Carrera. The new Junta were active in furnishing supplies until the raising of the siege of Chillán and the revolt of the province of Concepcion produced strained relations between them and Carrera.

The capital became excited by the adverse course of the war, and the Liberals of 1811 clamoured for a change in the constitution. The Press advocated the adoption of a more Republican system. On the 8th October a meeting of the corporations, convened by the Junta, confirmed them in power, but directed that the seat of Government should be removed to Talca. Don José Ignacio Cienfuegos, a man of great influence in the South and an enemy of Carrera, joined the Junta, and Larrain, ex-President of the late Congress, and also an enemy of Carrera, was left in charge of the affairs at Santiago. Government had organized in the capital a new battalion officered by their own adherents, and had asked for a supply of arms from Buenos Ayres. The 300 Chilian auxiliaries came back from that city, and the Argentine Government, in return for their services, had decreed that an Argentine auxiliary force of equal number should march to the assistance of Chile. This column, raised in the provinces of Cordoba and Mendoza, crossed the Andes under the command of DON JUAN GREGORIO LAS HERAS, and were warmly welcomed. Their first duty was to escort the Junta to Talca, where Colonel Don Marcos Balcarce took command of the contingent.

The Junta, on receiving news of the affair at El Roble, resolved to remove Carrera from the command, and first thought of replacing him by Balcarce, but, yielding to national sentiment, decided to appoint Colonel O'Higgins, whose tried valour and civic virtues gave him great popularity, both in the army and throughout the country. This appointment in February, 1814, had an evil effect upon the army, where Carrera had still many partizans, splitting it into two parties. Carrera left for the capital accompanied by his brother Luis, but on the road they were taken prisoners by a party of Royalist irregulars under Barañao, and carried off to Chillán.

The army of which O'Higgins took command consisted of about 2,500 men dispersed in fractions, disheartened, and badly armed and equipped. On the 31st January a reinforcement of Royalist troops landed at Arauco, consisting of 800 men and six guns under Brigadier-General Gainza, appointed by the Viceroy as successor to Pareja. Eight days later he crossed the Bio-Bio and joined Sanchez at Chillán, without meeting an insurgent on his march.

O'Higgins stationed one division of his army at Membrillar, while with the rest he marched to the line of the Bio-Bio to intercept the supplies of the enemy. This plan was as bad as those of Carrera. Mackenna, left in command at Membrillar, had under his orders on the 14th February, 800 infantry, 100 dragoons, and sixteen guns. Soon after the country around was occupied by the light troops of the enemy, so that he was obliged to make sallies in force to procure supplies and forage. On one of these occasions, when he had taken a considerable number of cattle his rear-guard was attacked by a much stronger force, which was driven off with heavy loss by Las Heras with 100 of the Argentine auxiliaries.

Meantime a Royalist detachment of 300 men had crossed the Maule, and on the 4th March attacked the city of Talca, from which the Junta had already withdrawn. The feeble garrison made a stout resistance under Colonel Spano, a Spaniard who had joined the Patriots in 1809, but was overpowered, Spano dying wrapped in the tricoloured flag he had so bravely defended.

This blow spread consternation in Santiago. The people crowded to the Plaza, and Irizarri proposed the appointment of a Dictator, following the example of the Roman

Republic in times of danger, and Colonel Lastra, Governor of Valparaiso, was named Supreme Director. The new Government in a few days organized a force of 1,500 men with six guns, and placed in command a young man named DON MANUEL BLANCO ENCALADA, but these raw troops were repulsed in an attack upon Talca, and were afterwards completely routed at Cancha-Rayada on the 27th March.

The position of Mackenna at Membrillar became very difficult. The loss of Talca cut his communications with the capital; he threw up more entrenchments and remained steadily on the defensive. O'Higgins started to his assistance on the 16th March, leaving weak garrisons in Concepcion and Talcahuana. It was time; Gainza was already between them. On the 19th O'Higgins drove in the Royalist vanguard at Quilo, and Gainza, withdrawing the garrison from Chillán, fell next day upon Mackenna, but was beaten off with the loss of eighty killed.

On the 23rd O'Higgins joined Mackenna, and next day moved off northwards with 2,600 infantry, 600 cavalry, and twenty guns. Gainza, harassing his rear, marched in the same direction; victory would lie with him who could first cross the Maule. O'Higgins, by a skilful manœuvre, captured a pass, and throwing up defences of brushwood in his rear, beat off an attack, and crossed on the 4th April. Gainza crossed by a different pass on the same day, and tried to stop the march of the Patriot army at a pass on the Claro River. On the 7th O'Higgins forced the pass, and the two armies faced each other between that river and the Lontué. At Quecheraguas O'Higgins threw up entrenchments, and on the 8th and 9th beat off attacks of the enemy, giving time for the arrival of reinforcements from Santiago. Gainza then retreated to Talca, and the garrisons of Concepcion and Talcahuano capitulated.

By this time the Anglo-Spanish armies had driven the French from Spain, and the Government of Spain called upon the insurgent colonies to send deputies to Cortes. In

Mexico the Royalist arms were triumphant; the rising star of Bolívar at Caracas was about to suffer eclipse; the revolutions of Quito, Venezuela, and New Granada were crushed; Lima, still the great centre of reaction, prepared yet another expedition for the conquest of Chile; only in the united provinces of the River Plate did the revolution still hold its ground. In these circumstances Hillyar, commodore of the British squadron of the Pacific, offered his mediation to the Viceroy of Peru for the pacification of Chile. His offer was accepted, and he reached Santiago just after the successful defence of Quecheraguas. Government appointed O'Higgins and Mackenna to conduct the negotiation. It was accordingly arranged on the 3rd May that Chile should return to the state of the year 1811, under the rule of a provisional Junta subject to the Regency of Spain; that the Royalist troops should withdraw from Chile within one month; that Chile should send deputies to the Peninsula to settle all disputes, and should do what she could to help the cause of Spain. This arrangement, which is known as the Treaty of Lircay, was badly received in the Royalist camp, and also by public opinion in Chile, and resulted in nothing more than a truce.

It is a question whether these terms were agreed upon in good faith by either party. So far as Gainza was concerned, they saved him from certain defeat.

Don Francisco Antonio Pinto, diplomatic agent of Chile in London, was instructed to repair to Madrid in representation of her interests, but the Royalist troops were not withdrawn, and the Government remained in the hands of Lastra as Supreme Director. Chile was resolved upon liberty at any cost, and public opinion, which had forced on the treaty, was now equally pronounced against it.

The alliance between Chile and the United Provinces was *de facto* at an end, and the Argentine auxiliaries were withdrawn from the army to Santiago. On the 22nd July a mutiny in the barracks restored the Carreras to power. They proclaimed themselves the saviours of the country.

By the Treaty of Lircay Don José Miguel and Don Luis were excluded from the arrangement for a mutual exchange of prisoners; they were to be sent by sea to Valparaiso, and thence banished into honourable exile; but, escaping from their prison at Chillán, they had reached the capital and raised this mutiny, in which style of work Don José Miguel displayed more skill than he had done in the field against the national enemy. A provisional Junta was named by the noisy shouts of an open Cabildo, of which Carrera made himself president.

Had Carrera torn up the Treaty of Lircay, he would have had both reason and patriotism on his side, but his first step was to confirm the clause relating to freedom of commerce with Peru and to exhort the people to preserve peace. As before, he had neither ideas nor courage, and in his hands Congress, army, and revolution were all lost together. In spite of the protests of Las Heras, the Argentine auxiliaries were ignominiously expelled from the capital, on the pretext that it was their duty to assist the Government when called upon. O'Higgins counselled them to observe absolute neutrality in all civil disputes, following the example of the Chilian auxiliaries in Buenos Ayres in the revolution of 1812, and at the invitation of the Cabildo marched his army upon Santiago. Carrera met him on the plains of Maipó, where, for the first time, Chilian blood was shed by Chilians, and O'Higgins was defeated.

Meantime, the Viceroy of Peru had refused to ratify the treaty of peace, had despatched a fresh expedition to Talcahuano, and General Osorio at the head of 5,000 men was now marching on the capital. In this emergency O'Higgins put himself and the remnants of his force under the orders of Carrera, who speedily collected five or six thousand men, who might have done something had they been well led, but neither he nor O'Higgins showed any capacity for command. The latter, with 1,700 men, was cut off from the main body and shut up in Rancagua, where he defended himself with desperate valour for thirty-two hours against the whole army of the Royalists, till, his ammunition being exhausted, he cut his way through the enemy at the head of 300 men, and rejoined Carrera, who had retreated to Santiago.

Here all was confusion; and the people having lost confidence in their own leaders were ready to shout for the King. Las Heras, marching south with the Argentine auxiliaries, met O'Higgins in full retreat towards the Cordillera, and protected the rear until the fugitives from Santiago were safe on Argentine soil.

Carrera busied himself only in trying to secure the public treasure, which he packed on mules and carried off with him beyond Santa Rosa, but he was overtaken and the treasure fell into the hands of his pursuers on the slopes of Los Papeles on the 11th October. On the night of the 13th he crossed the snow-line on the summit, bidding farewell to his country, which he was never to see again.

So ended the first period of the revolution of Chile, which is styled "the time of the old country." The new country was yet to come. Argentines and Chilians in alliance were yet to raise from the dust the banners of Rancagua, and to bear them triumphant to the Equator.

CHAPTER IX.

CUYO.

1814—1815.

THE district of Cuyo lies to the east of the Cordillera, between 31° and 35° south latitude, and extends eastward to the 66° of west longitude, where the Andean formation dies away in the vast plain of the Argentine Pampa. Here the snow waters flowing from the mountain ranges lose themselves in lakes, or cut for themselves channels through the sandy soil, forming a network of inland rivers, which flow on undeterminately till they disappear. Peopled by colonists from East and West, this region was the point of union between two separate peoples, in whose alliance lay the destinies of all the Spanish colonies washed by the Pacific.

Mendoza, San Juan, and San Luis, were grouped together to form the Province of Cuyo, when San Martin was named Governor in 1814. Here he found the materials he required for the great enterprise he had in view. In 1810 the inhabitants of this province were barely 40,000 in number, but they were a hard-working, thrifty race, easily amenable to discipline. Traders from Mendoza and San Juan crossed the Andes to Chile, and the Pampa to Buenos Ayres, with troops of carts drawn by bullocks, or with troops of pack-mules, laden with wine, dried fruits, and flour. The men of San Luis were graziers of cattle and of sheep, famed for their skill as horsemen and as Indian fighters. Without knowledge of the character of this people it is impossible to comprehend how San Martin could in this one Province raise an invincible army which, sustained by it alone for three years, liberated two republics and spread the principles of the Argentine revolution over an entire continent.

Determined to keep free from all personal obligations to the instruments of his policy, San Martin refused to occupy the house allotted to him by the Cabildo of Mendoza, gave up half his salary as Governor, and, in 1815, sent his wife back to Buenos Ayres in pursuance of the system of rigid economy which he imposed upon himself and carried out ruthlessly in every department of his administration. In January, 1815, he was promoted by Government to the rank of General of Brigade, which appointment he accepted only on the understanding that he should resign it as soon as the State was secured from Spanish domination, and steadily refused any further promotion. Some historians have seen in this systematic self-abnegation, an imitation of the Cardinal who hobbled on crutches to seize the keys of Saint Peter. Doubtless he had his ambitions, but no such design appears in the course of his life, which was consecrated to his own people to the complete sacrifice of all personal interest.

According to him Chile was the citadel of America, and must be reconquered at any cost. In Mendoza he met many of the fugitives who crossed the Andes after the disaster of Rancagua, and speedily learned from them that the collapse of the revolution was due to the incapacity of Carrera, and to see in O'Higgins the man of the future. He and the Mendocinos received these fugitives with open arms and with generous hospitality; but Carrera, though an exile on foreign soil, arrogated to himself a position as chief of an independent nation, and as such issued decrees from the barracks where he and his suite were quartered.

San Martin asserted his authority with firmness and

with great prudence, but these Chilians introduced an element of disorder into the Province. Conflicts were frequent between the police and the dispersed soldiery, who refused obedience to any but their own officers, and continued the internecine dispute which had resulted so fatally on the plains of Maipó.

San Martin put a summary end to this disorder, by surrounding the barracks where Carrera and his partisans were lodged, with the troops of Las Heras and O'Higgins. Carrera was forced to retire to San Luis, whence he afterwards proceeded to Buenos Ayres, and his adherents dispersed. At the same time a commission of Chilians was appointed to collect the remnant of the treasure brought from Santiago, which was lodged in the coffers of the Province until such time as it might be employed for the liberation of Chile. Thus was Carrera crushed by the man of iron, and his insensate ambition no more troubled the destinies of his native country. Nevertheless he was well received in Buenos Ayres by Alvear, who about that time became Supreme Director of the United Provinces. He and Carrera were kindred spirits. Together they had served in Spain, and together they had dreamed dreams of power and dominion in their own land; now jealousy of San Martin became a further tie between them.

In January, 1815, San Martin, alleging the state of his health as a reason, sent in his resignation to the Supreme Director, who at once accepted it and named Don Gregorio Perdriel as his successor. Perdriel proceeded at once to Mendoza, but the leading men of the city assembled in open Cabildo and, supported by the mass of the people, refused to accept this new Governor, and insisted upon the withdrawal of his resignation by San Martin. Perdriel was recalled to Buenos Ayres, and Alvear was himself deposed in April by a mutiny of the troops in the capital. General Rondeau, who was at that time in command of the army of Peru, was named by the Cabildo as his successor. Alvear in his fall dragged with him the Assembly of the year 1813, and the Cabildo instructed the new Government to call at once a National Congress elected by universal suffrage. The men of Mendoza applauded the deposition of Alvear, and declared that they would not, in future, recognise any National authority save one based upon the will of the entire people. In logical pursuance of which declaration they decreed that the nomination of their Governor by the central power was null and void, and by acclamation named San Martin as the Governor elected by themselves. The Cabildos of San Luis and San Juan confirmed this declaration and decree, so that the Province of Cuyo became for the time an independent State, ruled by a Governor of its own selection.

The problem now before San Martin was one of extreme difficulty. From this small society he proposed to raise an army and to replenish an empty treasury without exhausting the sources of production and without waste, by innoculating all with his own ideas, and so leading them, each man in his own station, and according to his capacity, to work zealously together for one end. He turned the whole Province of Cuyo into an association of workers and fighters, whose co-operation should result in the reconquest of Chile.

He commenced by the invocation of the war-spirit among them, organizing their militia, and forming even the children into regiments, doing military exercise and carrying their own flags. He invited foreign residents to enlist, among whom the most forward were the English, who raised at their own cost a free company of light infantry, having the right to name their own officers. But the nucleus of his army he formed of well-disciplined troops. This spirit he kept alive by exaggerated reports of the strength of the enemy in Chile, and by alarms of an imminent invasion. The people seconded his efforts by voluntary contributions for the public service. They lent mules, horses, and harness, whenever they were required, sure of receiving them back when the need had passed over; cartmen and muleteers carried ammunition and supplies, and the landowners pastured his troop-horses, free of charge, seeking no other payment than general approbation. Punishment for minor offences was inflicted in fines, which were paid into the public treasury, the ordinary taxes were rigidly enforced. Cuyo bled money at every pore for the redemption of South America.

To give to his exactions the character of legal contributions, authorized by the will of the people, he used the Cabildos as his agents, their authority, as a sort of Parliament, giving a moral support to measures which were in reality arbitrary decrees; and he was well supported by the Lieutenant-Governors of San Luis and San Juan, men of inflexible will in everything relating to the public service.

In 1814, the general revenues of the Province, raised by customs duties and municipal taxes, amounted to nearly 180,000 dollars. The reconquest of Chile by the Spaniards, which put an end to the trans-Andine trade, cut off two-thirds of this revenue, so that in 1815 it was insufficient to meet current expenses. Voluntary subscriptions failed to supply the deficiency; a forced loan was levied upon the Spanish residents. But these were mere expedients. Export duties were imposed, a monthly war contribution was established, the tithes and the fund for the redemption of Indian captives, and the intestate estates of deceased Spaniards, were sequestered; a general property tax was levied, and forced loans from Spaniards and Portuguese were frequently exacted. Unpaid volunteers were never wanting when assistance was required in preparing the outfit of the army.

News was received that an expedition of 10,000 men had left Spain for the River Plate under the command of Morillo. San Martin called for a public subscription in aid of the general government. The ladies of Mendoza, headed by his own wife, set a noble example by throwing their jewels into the public chest. The fall of Monte Video diverted the course of the expedition, but the funds collected remained in the treasury.

Amid all the din of military preparation the material interests of the Province were not neglected. Education was studiously fomented, vaccination was introduced, much attention was bestowed upon the public promenades and upon the system of irrigation, and the most rigid economy was enforced in every branch of the administration. The people saw in San Martin a father whom they loved, and a ruler whom they respected. His manners contributed to his authority and to the popularity gained by his deeds. His austere figure aptly symbolised the paternal despotism he established, and gave him a certain mysterious prestige. Alone among many friends, but without one confidant, nor even a councillor, he looked after everything himself, with no more help than that of one secretary and two clerks. His want of education has caused some historians to decry his talents. It was the same with William of Orange and with Washington. They shone not by their intellect, but by their deeds and by their personal character. As Macaulay says of Cromwell, he spoke folly and did great things. Or, as Pascal says, the heart has reason of which reason knows nothing.

In San Martin the will was the dominant characteristic. He worked not by inspiration but by calculation, searching carefully first for the thing necessary to be done, and then doing it. It has been said of him that he was not a person but a system. He wore almost constantly the plain uniform of the mounted grenadiers, with the Argentine cockade on his cocked hat. He was an early riser, and usually spent all the morning at his desk. At mid-day he went to the kitchen, chose two plates of the food prepared, and frequently ate it there standing, washing it down with two glasses of wine. In the winter he would afterwards take a short walk and smoke a cigarette of black tobacco; in summer he would sleep for two hours on a skin stretched in the verandah. All the year round he drank coffee which he prepared himself; then, after another spell at his desk, would spend the afternoon inspecting the public offices. In the evening his house was open to visitors, who were forbidden to talk politics, but if invited to a game at chess found him a doughty adversary. At ten o'clock he wished them good-night and, after a light supper, retired to his couch. But if illness prevented him from sleeping he would rise and repair to his desk.

The system of government followed by San Martin in Cuyo somewhat resembled that of Sancho Panza in his island of Barrataria, or that of the legendary King Zafadola, who visited his taxpayers in their houses, asking them how they could expect him to govern if they did not pay the taxes?

An officer presented a petition for extra rations, as his salary was not enough to live on.

"All officers are in the same case," was the answer.

A man of San Juan, who had been made prisoner by the Spaniards in Chile and released on parole, claimed exemption from service in the army on that account.

"The Governor takes that responsibility upon himself, you are at liberty to attack the enemy. But if your hands are tied by a ridiculous prejudice they shall be untied by a platoon."

The wife of a sergeant asked pardon for some neglect of duty by her husband.

"I have nothing to do with women, but with soldiers subject to military discipline."

A prisoner applied for his release in the name of the patron saint of the army.

"He did enough for you in saving your life."

A farmer being accused of speaking against "La Patria," he annulled the sentence on condition that the accused should send ten dozen pumpkins for the supply of the troops.

To try the temper of his officers he got up a bull-fight and sent them into the ring as "torreadores." As he applauded their courage he turned to O'Higgins, who was beside him, and said :—

"These lunatics are the men we want to smash up the Spaniards."

One day he went to the powder factory in full uniform, booted and spurred, and was refused admission by the sentry. He came back in a linen suit with slippers on, and was admitted. After which he gave orders that the sentry should be relieved, and with great formality presented him with an ounce of gold.

One day an officer presented himself, asking for the citizen Don José de San Martin, and being admitted, confessed to him that he had lost at play regimental money which had been entrusted to him. San Martin opened a cabinet, took out gold coins to the amount named, and gave them to him, saying :—

"Pay this money into the regimental chest, and keep the secret; for if General San Martin ever hears that you have told of it, he will have you shot upon the spot."

Two Franciscan friars who, according to him, had shown themselves unfriendly to " political regeneration," were forbidden by him to confess or to preach, and were put under arrest in their convent until further orders. He instructed the parish priests to preach of "the justice with which America had adopted the system of liberty"; and seeing that they failed to do so, he further warned them that severe measures would be adopted if they neglected "so sacred a duty."

Among his contemporaries there were, at that time, but few who estimated him at his real value. He himself indulged in no illusions on the matter, but stoically trusted to time and patience to give him his true place among them. As he wrote to Godoy Cruz, concerning reports which were in circulation : "You will say that I was vexed. Yes, my friend, somewhat; but, after reflection, I followed the example of Diogenes, I dived into a butt of philosophy. A public man must suffer anything in order that the vessel may reach her port."

At that time he suffered from chronic disease, and could only sleep for a few minutes at once seated on a chair, and was compelled to take opium to gain needful rest.

On the 29th November, 1815, the army under Rondeau was completely defeated by Pezuela at Sipe-Sipe in Upper Peru. Morillo's expedition was triumphant in Columbia, and the Royalists sang *Te Deums* both in Europe and in America. In these days of despair San Martin invited his officers to a banquet. Never did he appear in better spirits. When the dessert was placed on the board he rose to his feet and in a loud voice proposed a toast:—

"To the first shot fired beyond the Andes against the oppressors of Chile."

His words found echo in every heart. Confidence revived. From that moment the passage of the Andes and the reconquest of Chile ceased to be a vague idea, it became a plan of campaign which was to change the aspect of the war.

CHAPTER X.

THE SPY SYSTEM OF THE PATRIOTS.

1815—1816.

THE restoration of royalty in Chile was attended with such excesses as might have been expected had some foreign power triumphed over the country. A system of blood and fire was established for its pacification, which had the natural result of reanimating the spirit of resistance. The great majority of the people were tired of war, and failed to see that revolutionary anarchy was any improvement on colonial despotism; they were anxious only for peace, and welcomed their conqueror as a liberator. A moderate policy might have consolidated Spanish power in Chile for a considerable time, but these excesses fanned into a blaze the embers of the old patriotic spirit, which was buried under the ashes of Rancagua.

Osorio was by nature inclined to clemency, but the instructions of Viceroy Abascal prohibited him from adopting any such course, and the Spaniards who surrounded him urged upon him the necessity of the most severe measures of repression. Yielding to these influences he became the instrument of a pitiless persecution, the result of which was to arouse the spirit of insurrection in every Chilian heart.

Forced loans and arbitrary contributions formed the sources of his revenue, and so crushed all industry that soon even these sources dried up, and supplies could only be obtained by confiscations. All the civilizing reforms of the revolutionary epoch were abolished, and the old monopolies were re-established. The most distinguished patriots were exiled to the island of Juan Fernandez; all the native inhabitants were classified as "suspects," and many were murdered in the prisons by the soldiery. A new spirit of patriotism was engendered by misery and despair. Spaniards again became a privileged class, they occupied all the public offices, they alone were allowed to carry arms, their testimony only was received in the courts. Every native Chilian had to be in his own house at nine o'clock at night, and could not travel even the shortest distance without a permit. Fights between the soldiery and the "rotos," as the men of the labouring class are called, were of daily occurrence. Many men of the Talavera regiment, which was particularly obnoxious, were murdered by the populace. Even the Chilian troops, which had done such good service under Sanchez and other leaders, were most thanklessly treated. Commissions won by their officers on the field of battle were not recognised, their pay was scanty, and the pensions of their widows were not paid at all.

At the commencement of 1815 Osorio had 5,000 men, perfectly armed and equipped, under his orders. His instructions were, as soon as he had pacified the country, to cross the Andes with 3,000 men, and to act in Cuyo and Cordoba in combination with Pezuela. Abascal had the converse of the same idea, which was later on carried out by San Martin. Small bodies of armed men had frequently crossed the Andes, but it is not the number of the troops employed, nor the power of the peoples in conflict, which constitutes the fame of such achievements, that fame lies in their motives and results. In this lay the importance of the passage of the Alps by Hannibal and by Napoleon; and the passage of the Andes by San Martin and by Bolívar, are famous as parts of a great scheme for the emancipation of a continent. Osorio was not the man for such an enterprise, and his force was so weakened by detachments in aid of Pezuela, that he never attempted it.

The disasters suffered by the Patriots in this year were not fruitless; time was gained, in which San Martin perfected his preparations, and this he lengthened by entering into a correspondence with Osorio, proposing some arrangement for the prevention of further bloodshed. He also took advantage of the correspondence so established to set on foot an extensive system of spies and secret agents all over Chile, by whose means he propagated false intelligence of such great military preparations in Mendoza as filled Osorio with fears of an immediate invasion, and had still more effect upon the feebler spirit of Marcó del Pont, who relieved him of the command in December.

The secret agents, who rendered the greatest service to San Martin, he found among the Chilian refugees in Mendoza. When the talents or social position of any of these men inspired him with confidence, he put them under arrest on some charge of treachery, from which he aided them to escape and fly across the Andes, "from his tyranny." Their alleged sufferings disarmed the suspicions of the Spanish rulers of Chile to the extent that some of them were actually employed by them to procure information from the eastern side of the Andes. By their help San Martin discovered that several Spaniards in Mendoza held secret communications with Osorio. He arrested them, and by threats of immediate execution, compelled them to show him all the letters they received, and to return answers dictated by him. His principal care was to persuade the Spaniards that the projected expedition would attack the south of Chile, in order to induce them to relax their vigilance in the quarter which was really menaced, and to concentrate their troops in positions where they could be of no service.

His agents were incessantly occupied in furnishing him with details concerning the number, armament, and posi tions of the Royalist forces, and in stirring up the Chilian people to co-operate with the invading army. Thus the whole country was soon on the watch for the moment when their liberators would pass the Andes. The name of San Martin became so popular, that his agents had no difficulty in obtaining all the help they needed; horses were always to be had when they wanted them, and they were warned in time of any danger which threatened them.

Chilian patriots, among whom the most active was Manuel Rodriguez, also secretly organised bands of volunteers, who waited but the signal to rise in arms. Some of them gave their lives for the cause on the gallows. Marcó del Pont adopted the most severe measures of repression, which only served to fan the flame of discontent.

In September, 1816, Rodriguez imprudently raised the flag of insurrection in the south of Chile. His raw troops were speedily dispersed, but San Martin made good use of his mistake by writing him an angry despatch, telling him that he had ruined his plans by drawing the Royalist forces to the south and causing them to occupy the passes by which he had hoped to cross the Cordillera. This despatch he caused to fall into the hands of Marcó del Pont, whose attention was thus again diverted from the real point of danger.

At this time Brown, the gallant Irishman who had driven the Spanish naval forces from the River Plate, and had been rewarded by the gift of his flagship, the *Hercules*, again offered his ship and his services to the Argentine Government. He was well supplied with guns, small arms, and ammunition, and was granted letters of marque as a privateer. On the 15th October, 1815, he sailed from Buenos Ayres for the Pacific with Captain Buchardo, a Frenchman, as his second in command. His squadron consisted of four vessels—the *Hercules* of 20 guns, commanded by Michael Brown; the *Trinidad* of 16 guns, commanded by Walter Chitty; the *Halcon*, commanded by Buchardo, which three vessels were brigs; and the armed quetch *Uribe*, named after its commander, a Chilian, who had been a colleague of Carrera in the late revolution. The crews of the two first were almost entirely English. The *Halcon* had a mixed crew of Chilians and Argentines, and her marines were commanded by Ramon Freyre. The crew of the quetch were all Chilians, and she carried a black flag as a sign of no quarter. It was stipulated that any prizes they might make should be sold in Buenos Ayres, one-ninth the prize money to go to Government, two-ninths to the Commodore, and the rest was to be divided among the officers and crews.

San Martin took care to inform Marcó of this expedition by means of his secret agents, and at the same time spread through Chile a rumour that an army from 4,000 to 7,000 men was assembled in Mendoza for the passage of the Andes. Marcó, terrified at the idea of being attacked both by land and sea, issued the most injudicious orders to his subordinates, scattered his forces, and applied to the Viceroy for naval support.

The *Hercules* and the *Trinidad*, in the attempt to double Cape Horn, were driven into the Straits of Magellan by a tempest, where they both received serious injury from sunken rocks, but, being repaired, reached the barren island of Mocha in the Southern Sea, where they were joined by the *Halcon*. The quetch was wrecked, the captain and master being drowned. Brown with his two ships, and Buchardo with his one, then sailed by different courses to Callao, where they reunited to blockade the port, and captured two large prizes, one of which, the *Consequencia*, was armed and added to the squadron. On the 21st January, 1816, they sailed boldly into the harbour, and forced the Spanish ships to take refuge under the guns of the batteries.

On the night of the 22nd the gallant Commodore attacked the Royalist flotilla with five armed boats, but was beaten off with a loss of thirty killed and wounded. After maintaining the blockade for three weeks, they sailed for Guayaquil. The fort at the entrance to this port was taken by assault by Freyre with the crew of the *Halcon*, who effected a landing under the fire of the guns of the squadron. The Commodore then entered the port with the *Trinidad*, captured a schooner carrying marines, and took the first battery with four brass guns, which were transferred to the schooner. He then attacked another battery, but a sudden squall drove the *Trinidad* ashore, and he was forced to haul down his flag to prevent the massacre of his men by the Spanish infantry. He himself stripped off his clothes and sprang overboard intending to swim to the schooner, but seeing that the Spaniards were commencing to kill their prisoners, he climbed on board again, seized a lighted match, ran down to the magazine, and threatened to blow up the ship with all on board unless the laws of war were respected. This daring action brought the Spaniards to their senses, the slaughter was stopped, and Brown, with no other clothing than the Argentine flag which he wrapped round him, was led a prisoner on shore.

Buchardo, with the rest of the squadron, attacked another battery in the hope of rescuing his comrades, but was beaten off. One of the prisoners taken on the *Consequencia* off Callao was Mendiburo, the Governor of this province, and the commandant of Guayaquil was so eager to get rid of his enemies that he proposed an exchange of prisoners, which was at once accepted. The three remaining vessels with the schooner then left the port.

On the open sea the jealousy latent in the hearts of the two commanders broke into an open flame. Each of these two adventurers considered that the other deserved hanging at the yardarm; but in times of danger they had most nobly supported each other. Now they agreed to separate, dividing the plunder between them, and Buchardo returned with the *Consequencia* to Buenos Ayres. Brown sailed on to Santa Fé in New Granada, but, finding that city occupied by Royalist troops, he followed his late comrade to the Atlantic.

The Argentine Government had hoped great things from this expedition, and had written to San Martin to hold himself ready to take advantage of any movement it might occasion in Chile; but the astute general replied that a naval force, to be of any effective aid to an invading general, must consist of ships of war, not ot privateers, and must be under his orders. The result showed that it was but of slight service to the cause, and was a waste of material which might have been much more usefully employed.

CHAPTER XI.

THE IDEA OF THE PASSAGE OF THE ANDES.

1815—1816.

The plans of San Martin were not in accordance with the ideas which prevailed in the military circles of the United Provinces. The many disasters which had befallen Argentine armies in Upper Peru had failed to show either the leaders of those armies or Government that the true road to Lima did not lie through those mountain passes. He did not obtrude his opinions upon any one, still his idea at times leaked out in despatches, and after the fate of Alvear, met with a somewhat better reception at headquarters. Carrera had made a proposal to Government for a foolhardy attempt upon Coquimbo, which was rejected after a consultation with San Martin, but his application for permission to assume the offensive had also been refused. He then caused a report to be circulated in Chile that he was about to march his army to the north, to reinforce the routed forces of Rondeau, in the hope that Marcó might be induced to cross the Andes and attack Mendoza, and by representing this danger to Government, he succeeded in persuading them to send him some light field guns and other war material, of which he was in need; and also to grant him power to assume the offensive in spring. He also prevailed upon them to unite the scattered squadrons of the mounted grenadiers, and to place them under his orders, as the nucleus of a cavalry brigade.

In March, 1816, a detachment of the grenadiers, under Aldao, made a successful reconnaissance by the Uspallata Pass, of the Royalist positions on the western slopes of the Andes, and brought back much useful information; but true to his principle of concealing his plans, San Martin reported to Government that the central passes were so well defended that the only practical course was by those to the south of Mendoza; and also that advanced field works were necessary about Uspallata, in order to secure the Province of Cuyo as the base of operations. This procured him a further much needed supply of guns.

In April General Balcarce, the hero of Suipacha, succeeded Alvarez as Provisional Director, and San Martin was thenceforward much better supported by the central power; military supplies were sent to him on a much more liberal scale than under the previous administration.

The power of the Lautaro Lodge had fallen with Alvear, but the society still existed, and San Martin now established a branch in Mendoza, in which the principal leaders of the Chilian refugees, and many of the foremost men of Cuyo, were affiliated.

At this time he received most efficient assistance from his friend Don Tomas Guido, who had first met him in London, and who had afterwards in Tucuman learned from him something of his ideas in regard to the conduct of the war. Guido drew up a memorial and presented it to the Supreme Director, in which he warmly supported the idea of attacking Peru by way of Chile; and his aid became still more efficacious when the meeting of the Congress of Tucuman, a few weeks later on, placed the administration of affairs in new hands.

CHAPTER XII.

THE ARMY OF THE ANDES.

1816—1817.

THE organization of the Army of the Andes is one of the most extraordinary feats recorded in military history. It was a war machine, composed of men filled with the spirit of the Argentine Revolution and with a passion for things American, without which spirit and without which passion it could never have achieved the task before it. Never was the military automaton more thoroughly endued with human energy.

The auxiliary corps of Las Heras formed the nucleus of this army, to which was soon added two companies of the 8th Regiment from Buenos Ayres, with four field guns. In 1815 Colonel Zapiola joined it with two squadrons of the Grenadiers. These corps were greatly strengthened by volunteers, who joined them in Cuyo.

In 1816 the new Government appointed by the Congress of Tucuman, constituted it formally as THE ARMY OF THE ANDES, under the command of San Martin as Captain-General, with General Soler as chief of the Staff, and further strengthened it with the 7th Regiment of Infantry from Buenos Ayres, and additions to the 8th; Colonel Conde being placed in command of the 8th, and Colonel Cramer, a Frenchman, who had served under Napoleon, in command of the 7th. The 11th, under Las Heras, was divided into two battalions, of which the second became the 1st Light Infantry under Lieutenant-Colonel Alvarado. A fifth squadron under Necochea was added to the Grenadiers. Thus early in September the army numbered 2,300 men with the flags, a force still insufficient for the work, but recruiting went on briskly.

The question of giving freedom to all slaves who would enlist being under discussion at Tucuman, San Martin spread the report in Cuyo that the idea was to be carried out, and advised the Cabildos to prevail upon the slave-owners to set their slaves free before the project became law. There was much unwillingness to accede to this proposition, but at length it was resolved to set two-thirds of the slaves free, the manumission not to be effective until the army crossed the Andes. This gave a further reinforcement of 710 men to the infantry. Before the end of the year the army numbered 4,000 men, almost all of whom were Argentines. The Chilian emigrants were organized into a reserve as the nucleus for the future army of Chile. This reserve was placed under command of O'Higgins, who received a commission as a General of the United Provinces, but within it were many partizans of Carrera, upon whom San Martin looked with suspicion.

This army was sustained by a combination of patriotic subscriptions, gratuitous services, and of regular and arbitrary taxes. Some carried arms, others gave money or labour, all the inhabitants of Cuyo contributed in some way or another to the great work. For the furnishing of arms, powder and equipments, special measures were adopted. San Martin found the man he wanted for this work in a mendicant friar named Luis Beltran. This Beltran was a native of Mendoza, and being in Chile at the time of the revolution had joined the Patriots and served as an artilleryman at the siege of Chillán. After Rancagua he returned on foot to his own country, with a bag of tools of his own making on his shoulders. Self-taught, he was at once a mathematician and a chemist, an artilleryman and a maker of watches or of fireworks, a carpenter, an architect, a blacksmith, a draughtsman, a cobbler, and a physician. In addition he was of a robust constitution and of soldierly bearing. He became one of the chaplains of the new army. San Martin soon discovered his extraordinary talents, and entrusted him with the establishment of an arsenal. Soon he had three hundred workmen under his orders, all of whom were taught by himself. He cast cannon, shot, and shell, melting down the church bells when other metal was not to be had; he made limbers for the guns, saddles for the cavalry, knapsacks and shoes for the infantry, and all other kinds of necessary equipment; forged horse-shoes and bayonets, repaired damaged muskets, and in his leisure moments drew on the walls of his grimy workshop designs for carriages specially adapted for the conveyance of war material over the steep passes of the Andes. In 1816, he took off his friar's frock, donned the uniform of a lieutenant of artillery, with a monthly salary of 25 dollars, and became the Archimedes of the Army of the Andes.

In addition to this arsenal, San Martin established a laboratory of saltpetre and a powder factory, in charge of his aide-de-camp Major Condarco, using water power to work the machines. This factory produced excellent gunpowder, sufficient for the supply of the army, at very small cost. He also set up a manufactory of army cloth, which cloth was dyed blue, and uniforms for the troops were made of it by the women of Mendoza, free of charge. A military tribunal was created, and the medical staff was organized under Dr. Paroissien, a naturalised Englishman. The commissariat and treasury were also placed under the strictest regulations. Everything was prepared for an offensive war, and for distant operations.

In May, 1816, the scheme was almost upset by the persistence of the Central Government in prosecuting the war in Upper Peru. San Martin had taken great interest in the projected Congress of Tucuman since the idea was first mooted, looking upon it as the last hope of the revolution. Four deputies were sent from Cuyo, who were all friends of his, and who took deep interest in his plan. One of them, Don Juan Martin Pueyrredon, was elected President.

The majority of this Congress were in favour of the establishment of a constitutional monarchy. San Martin and Belgrano, who commanded the armies of Cuyo and the North, were the pillars of the State edifice, and, though San Martin was in theory a Republican, they both shared in this opinion, but both were equally convinced that the first step should be a Declaration of Independence, in order to put an end to the present anomalous position, in which they, still nominally subject to the King of Spain, made war upon Spain under a flag of their own. Thus the Declaration of Independence on the 9th July was welcomed by San Martin as a master stroke of policy.

Don Juan Martin Pueyrredon, now President of the United Provinces, had already so far adopted the military ideas of San Martin, that on the 16th June he had given orders for the despatch of men and arms to Cuyo, but San Martin was not content with mere acquiescence in his plans, he wanted the hearty approval and concurrence of the Chief of the State. He accordingly left Mendoza for Cordoba on the 15th July, and there met the President. The conference lasted three days and resulted in a complete understanding between them.

Then as no maps existed of the passes of the Andes, he sent his aide-de-camp Condarco, who was a skilful engineer, with a copy of the Declaration of Independence to the Governor of Chile.

"But," he said to him as he gave him his instructions, "your real errand is to reconnoitre for me the roads by Los Patos and Uspallata. Without making a note, you must bring back in your head a plan of them both. I shall send you by Los Patos which is the longest road,

K

and as they are certain to send you back at once, if they don't hang you, you will return by Uspallata, which is the nearest way."

As San Martin had anticipated, the copy of the declaration which Condarco presented to Marcó del Pont, was burned by the public hangman of Santiago, and the messenger was sent back at once with scant courtesy, but in his receptive brain he brought with him plans of both roads, which he drew out on paper at his leisure, and these plans so obtained, became the chart of the first operations of the Army of the Andes.

In the early spring, San Martin brought the various corps of his army from their cantonments, and encamped them on an open plain about a league to the north of Mendoza, where the recruits were thoroughly drilled, and the whole force was taught to act in concert. Every hour of the day had its allotted work, and in the evening the officers attended classes for instruction in tactics. To complete its organization, a printing press was added to the stores, from which bulletins of victory were to issue to the world, teaching to the liberated people the principles of the Argentine revolution, which the soldiery supported with their bayonets.

On the 17th January, 1817, there was high holiday in the city of Mendoza. The streets and plaza were decorated with flags and streamers. The whole army marched in to salute the Virgen del Carmen as its patron saint, and to receive a special army flag embroidered by the ladies of the city. When the usual formalities were over, San Martin ascended a platform in the great square with the flag in his hand, and waving it over his head, said in a voice which could be heard by all:—

"Soldiers! This is the first independent flag which has been blessed in America."

One great shout of "Viva la Patria!" rose from the people and the troops in answer.

Then he added—

"Soldiers! Swear to sustain it and to die in defence of it, as I swear to do."

"We swear!" was the answer from four thousand throats. A triple discharge of musketry and twenty-five guns, then saluted this new flag, the flag of redemption for one-half of South America, which passed the Cordillera, waved in triumph along the Pacific Coast, floated over the foundations of two new Republics, aided in the liberation of another, and after sixty-four years, served as a funeral pall to the body of the hero, who thus delivered it to the care of the immortal Army of the Andes.

CHAPTER XIII.

THE PASSAGE OF THE ANDES.

1817.

"WHAT spoils my sleep is not the strength of the enemy, but how to pass those immense mountains," said San Martin, as from Mendoza he gazed upon the snow-clad summits of the Andes, which as a mighty barrier separate the wide plains of the Argentine Pampa from the smiling valleys of Chili, through twenty-two degrees of latitude, from the desert of Atacama to Cape Horn.

These mountains at 33° south latitude divide into two parallel ranges, one running southward along the borders of the Pacific Ocean, the other forming the grand Cordillera upon which San Martin gazed from Mendoza. The coast range is a succession of granite hills with rounded summits and gentle slopes, like to the waves of a petrified sea. The great Cordillera is in its centre composed of three or four ranges of conical and sharply-defined peaks which rise one over the other to a height of 21,000 feet above the level of the sea, crowned with perpetual snow. At its feet lie deep valleys, from which perpendicular precipices rise up to the clouds, and the mighty condors wheeling in airy circles at that dizzy height are the only living things to be seen. There are also lakes fed by torrents of melted snow which, pouring down the mountain sides into these valleys, find at times no exit, their path being closed by immense heaps of débris hurled from the lofty summits by the force of ice and water. These immense groups of mountains are traversed by rugged defiles, and narrow paths, the result of volcanic action, wind along the edges of precipices, while below roar the mountain streams carrying great rocks along with them, tossing them about as though they were straws. Here nature displays her giant strength as an artificer, decking herself with no other ornaments than the cactus, mosses, and thorny plants; everywhere are seen traces of the world in embryo, as it emerged from chaos in the process of creation.

Between the Cordillera and the coast range stretches a great central valley, cut across in places by spurs from the higher mountains, which take an oblique line to the south till they lose themselves in the ocean, or reappear as solitary islands or as clusters of islands, which are the summits of mountains springing from the bed of the sea.

The great Cordillera can only be crossed at certain passes. Those which have connection with our history are: in the centre, those of Uspallata and Los Patos, in front of Mendoza and San Juan; to the north, those of La Ramada and Come-Caballos, by which the Argentine province of La Rioja communicates with Coquimbo and Copiapó; and to the south, that of the Planchon, which gives access to the valley of Talca, and that of the Portillo which leads to the plain of Maipó and to the capital of Chile. These passes, from 9,000 feet to 12,000 feet above the level of the sea, are covered with snow in winter, and are practicable only in the height of summer. Until then they had been crossed only by small detachments of soldiery, or by troops of mules, the paths being in many places so narrow as only to give room for one mounted man at a time. The passage of a numerous army with guns and baggage was held to be impossible and had never been thought of till the feat was accomplished by San Martin. Food and forage for men, mules, and horses had to be carried with them, and it was necessary to reach the other side in force sufficient to overcome a watchful enemy; to concentrate the different columns upon his weak points; and to make all the preparations secretly, so that the army might rush like a thunderbolt from the western slopes of the mountains and do battle in the open plain.

San Martin, by his complex spy system, had deluded the enemy into the belief that the invasion would come from the passes of the south; his real intentions he had kept from friends and enemies alike. In September, 1816, he invited the Pehuenche Indians, who occupied the eastern slopes of the Andes commanding the entrances to the passes of the Planchon and Portillo, to a conference at the fort of San Carlos to the south of Mendoza. With the invitation he sent them many mules laden with spirits and wine, with sweetmeats, cloth, and glass beads for the women, horse gear and clothes for the men. In savage pomp they came; the warriors, followed by their women, rode up to the fort on the day appointed in full war costume, flourishing their long lances, and commenced proceedings by a sham fight in the Indian fashion, dashing at full speed round the fort, from whose walls a gun was fired every five minutes and was answered by Indian yells. Then the chiefs entered the fort and were told by San Martin that the Spaniards were foreigners who intended to rob them of their lands, their cattle, their women, and children; and that he desired to pass through their country with an army, to go by the Planchon and Portillo Passes to the country the other side of the mountains, there to destroy these Spaniards. The Indian chiefs listened to his request and granted him the permission he required, after which they, with their warriors, gave themselves up to an orgy which lasted eight days.

On the sixth day San Martin returned to Mendoza satisfied that the Indians, with their usual perfidy, would at once inform Marcó of his project, and took care that their information was confirmed by the agents of Marcó in Mendoza, who sent him despatches to the same purport, dictated by San Martin. At the same time San Martin advised the Government and his friend Guido that he had arranged with the Indians for supplies of cattle and horses, and for help in his expedition, without in any case giving a hint of his real intentions.

Marcó, harassed by the alarming news sent him by his supposed spies in Mendoza, and annoyed by the guerillas under Martin Rodriguez, who infested the country between the Maule and the Maipó, and sacked villages even in the vicinity of the capital itself, adopted most ill-conceived and contradictory measures. He fortified the ports and organised a flotilla to act against an imaginary naval force, which his spies in Cuyo informed him had already left Buenos Ayres. He cut trenches in the pass of Uspallata; made a map of the southern provinces, and a survey of the mouths of the passes in that district; strengthened the guards at all the passes; after concentrating his troops, scattered them again all over the country; and followed the example of San Martin by holding a great conference with the Indians of Arauco.

The policy of San Martin was successful; the Captain-General of Chile attempted to defend the whole of his frontier and had no idea where the real attack was to come from. One only of his many councillors advised him to concentrate the army on the capital, and there make ready for whatever might happen. Instead of that, he increased the general discontent by arbitrary exactions, till all classes of the people longed for the appearance of San Martin and made ready to help him as best they could. Small parties of troops were on several occasions attacked and routed by armed bands of the peasantry, and the bandit Neyra made himself famous by similar exploits.

In the encampment at Mendoza matters were far different; there methodical activity and automatic obedience blended with intelligent enthusiasm; there one far-seeing will reigned supreme. There everything was known that Marcó either thought or did, each man worked diligently at his appointed task, and all trusted blindly in their chief. The forges blazed day and night, the arsenal turned out cartridges by the hundred thousand. Fray Beltran made special carriages for the artillery, adapted to the mountain passes, the guns themselves were to be carried on the backs of mules; slings were prepared for carrying them over dangerous places, and sleds of raw hide in which they might be hauled up by men when the gradients were too steep for the mules.

The General-in-Chief, silent and reserved, thought for all, inspected everything, and provided for every contingency. Large provision was made of *charquicán*, a food much in vogue among the muleteers, composed of beef dried in the sun, roasted, and ground to powder, then mixed with fat and Chile pepper and pounded into small compass. A soldier could carry enough of this in his knapsack to last him eight days. Mixed up with hot water and maize meal ready roasted, it formed a soup at once nutritious and appetising. San Luis alone furnished 2,000 arrobas, and the total provision amounted to 3,500 arrobas (87,200 lbs.). The soldiers made for themselves closed sandals of raw hide called *tamangos*, which were lined with fragments of old clothes collected for that purpose from all the province. Water-bottles were made from the horns of the animals slaughtered in the encampment, and slings were made for them out of the rough edges of the cloth from which their uniforms were made. The sabres of the cavalry were carefully sharpened, but they had only three trumpets till Government sent them two more. Thirty thousand horseshoes were prepared, which was a great innovation, as the Argentines were not accustomed to shoe their horses; without them the hoofs of the cavalry horses would have been worn down in the transit over the stony passes. Four cables, each 170 feet long, and two anchors formed a portable bridge. Cuyo alone furnished 13,000 mules, but the promises of Government to replenish the exhausted treasury were not fulfilled. A rebellion had broken out in Cordoba which taxed the

ORGANIZATION OF THE ARMY.

resources of Pueyrredon to the utmost to repress; but he aided San Martin in every way he possibly could, with clothes, saddles, tents, and arms, and wrote him :—" Don't ask me for anything more unless you wish to hear that I have hung myself to a beam in the fort." And also : " You may well say that among us there has never been seen an army so well fitted out; but neither has there been seen a Director who had equal confidence in a general, and, it must be added, never a general who so well merited that confidence as yourself. After all, my mind would be easier if you had another thousand good soldiers with you."

Everything was ready. The army consisted of 3,000 infantry in four battalions, led by Alvarado, Cramer, Conde and Las Heras; five squadrons of the mounted grenadiers, 700 sabres, led by Zapiola, Melian, Ramallo, Escalada, and Necochea; and 250 artillery, with ten 6-pounders, two howitzers, and nine 4-pounder mountain guns, under command of La Plaza. Twelve hundred mounted militia from Cuyo accompanied the army, besides muleteers and artisans.

The army was arranged in three divisions, each entirely independent of the others. The vanguard under Soler, and the reserve under O'Higgins, marched by the pass of Los Patos. Las Heras with the artillery marched by that of Uspallata, which was the only one practicable for guns and ammunition. All the food necessary for fifteen days they took with them, also 600 bullocks for slaughter, and a special supply of onions and garlic, very necessary at high levels both for man and beast.

As flankers to the main army, a detachment of militia and Chilian emigrants left San Juan under Cabot, by the pass of La Ramada, marching upon Coquimbo, and another left Rioja by the pass of Vinchina, marching on Copiapó and Huasco. To the south another detachment, composed of mounted infantry, grenadiers, and Chilians, marched under the Chilian Captain Freyre, by the Planchon pass, in support of the Chilian guerillas, and were aided by a party of thirty dragoons under Captain Lemos, who went by the Portillo Pass.

Both the main body and the detachments had orders to debouch on Chilian territory from the 6th to the 8th February, 1817. Each general of division was given by San Martin himself a pen-and-ink plan of the route he was to follow, with notes and written instructions. San Martin himself went by the pass of Los Patos, but had arranged a system of flag-signals by which Las Heras could communicate with him across the intervening valleys.

His last instructions from Government were :—

"The consolidation of the independence of America from the Kings of Spain and their successors, and the glory of the United Provinces of the South, are the only motives of this campaign. This you will make public in your proclamations, by your agents in the cities, and by all possible means. The army must be impressed with this principle, and shall have no thought of pillage, oppression, or of conquest, or that there is any idea of holding the country of those we help."

He was also authorized to raise a national army in Chile, which should remain under his orders even when a new Government was established; was prohibited from capitulating with the enemy under any circumstances; and was charged to avoid any interference in party questions among the Chilians. He was also authorized, after the re-establishment of the municipality of Santiago, to preside over the free election of a provisional president. He was instructed to use his influence to postpone the election of a Congress until Chile was entirely free from the enemy, and to persuade the Chilians to send deputies to the Congress of the United Provinces, in order to establish a perpetual alliance between the two countries.

As the leading files of the army entered the passes, San Martin, on the 24th January, 1817, wrote to Godoy Cruz :—

"This afternoon I leave to join the army. God grant me success in this great enterprise."

The plan of the campaign, as drawn up by San Martin on the 15th June, 1816, was to cross the Cordillera by the passes of Uspallata and Los Patos, to re-unite his forces in the plain beyond, there to beat the principal force of the enemy and to seize the capital.

The principal spur from the main range which cuts the central valley of Chile is that which springs from the great peak of Aconcagua. From this spur a smaller one branches off, which is called the Sierra of Chacabuco, and runs parallel to the main spur, enclosing between them the parallel valleys of Putaendo and Aconcagua, watered by two streams bearing the same names, which ultimately unite to form the river Aconcagua, which empties itself in the ocean beyond the coast range of hills. The road by Uspallata passes to the south of the great peak and through the valley of Aconcagua to the frontier town of Santa Rosa. The road by Los Patos is much longer, and, passing to the north of Aconcagua, leads by the valley of Putaendo to the narrow pass of Achupallas, which lies to the west of Santa Rosa. Thus any force stationed at this point would be placed between two fires by the convergence of the two divisions, and if it retreated to the Sierra of Chacabuco which lay to the south, would leave the plain of Chacabuco available for the concentration of the army. Chacabuco was thus the strategic point upon the occupation of which depended the issue of the whole campaign.

Meantime Cabot had left San Juan on the 12th January, and on the 8th February issued from the northern passes. The whole province of Coquimbo rose in arms to welcome him. Captain Ceballos, detached by him, routed a Royalist force of a hundred men on the plains of Salala, capturing two small guns and forty prisoners. By the 12th Cabot was master of the entire province. On the same day Davila, with the detachment from Rioja, took the city of

Copiapó. The whole of the north of Chile was in the power of the invaders.

On that same 12th February Freyre, at the other extreme of the line of operations, occupied the city of Talca, after a skirmish on the plains, cutting all communication between the capital and the south. He represented himself to be the vanguard of the main army, and was joined at once by the Chilian guerillas and by Neyra.

It was only on the eve of departure that San Martin explained his plan in its entirety to his generals. On the 18th January Las Heras marched with a flying column by Uspallata, with instructions to entrench himself at Chacabuco, but to retreat if attacked by superior forces. Two days in his rear marched Beltran with the artillery. The main body marched on the 19th by Los Patos; the vanguard was commanded by Soler, and one day's march in his rear came the reserve under O'Higgins. Groups of pioneers preceded the columns, clearing the way for them. Soler had instructions to debouch on the 8th February into the valley of Putaendo, to seize the bridge which crosses the river Aconcagua in front of the town of San Felipe, to occupy that position, thence to open communications with Las Heras, and, if possible, to attack the enemy in the rear at Santa Rosa.

All the troops were mounted on mules, and marched in single file along the narrow paths, each twenty men being in care of a muleteer, the length of each day's march being decided by the facilities for grass and water at the halting-places. Not only was the road itself by Los Patos more difficult than that by Uspallata, but on account of the greater elevation, and of its vicinity to the eternal snow of the higher peaks, the cold was very much more intense; it freezes hard there every night, even at midsummer, and the rarefaction of the air caused many of the men to drop from the ranks.

Marcó had despatched 1,000 men under Colonel Atero to reconnoitre the pass of Uspallata, and on the 24th January the advanced posts of Las Heras were attacked by the enemy at Pichueta, on the eastern slope of the Cordillera. A reinforcement under Major Martinez drove the Royalists, after two hours' fighting, across the summit. San Martin, on hearing of this, at once despatched Major Arcos with 200 men to seize the pass of Achupallas. On the 4th February Arcos found the guard there strongly reinforced; he attacked at once, and the day was decided by Lieutenant Juan Lavalle, of the mounted grenadiers, who here led the first of those desperate charges of cavalry for which he was afterwards so renowned.

At three in the morning of the 2nd February Las Heras crossed the summit of the Cordillera, and on the 4th, at sundown, an advanced post of the Royalists at Guardia Vieja was attacked by Major Martinez, and carried at the point of the bayonet; after which Las Heras, in obedience to express orders from San Martin, retired upon his reserve. On the 5th the alarm was given in the valleys of Putaendo and Aconcagua by the fugitives from Guardia Vieja and Achupallas, but Atero, deceived by the countermarch of Las Heras into the idea that he was in full retreat, left the pass of Uspallata open, and marched with 700 men to meet the invaders at Achupallas. Thus, without further trouble, Las Heras debouched on the 8th on to the plain and occupied Santa Rosa.

Soler, with the escort and two squadrons of grenadiers, had hurried on to the assistance of the small force at Achupallas, and thence on the 6th descended into the valley of Putaendo with all his cavalry. Necochea was then detached with 100 men of the escort against the town of San Felipe. On the morning of the 7th he was met by Atero, and, by feigning to retreat in the face of such superior numbers, induced the Royalist leader to follow him up the valley with 300 horsemen, leaving his guns and infantry in a strong position on high ground behind him. When he had drawn him well away from his reserve, Necochea suddenly wheeled his men into line and charged, breaking up the enemy completely, and driving him back to the shelter of his guns, with a loss of 30 killed and 4 prisoners. Atero, after this repulse, retreated with all speed to San Felipe, destroying the bridge over the Aconcagua river. The fugitives reported that the enemy were tall men armed with very long swords, whose charge no cavalry in Chile could resist. On the 8th the two divisions encamped in the valley of Putaendo, and were welcomed with enthusiasm by the inhabitants.

On the 9th the broken bridge was repaired by the sappers, and while the whole army crossed, a squadron of grenadiers under Melian advanced to the hill of Chacabuco, and were there met by advanced parties of the column under Las Heras. Beltran had lost 6,000 mules out of 10,000, and two-thirds of his horses, but he brought all his guns with him.

Thus the preliminary operations were crowned with success. A strategic combination of movements over a frontage of 1,300 miles was completed in every point on the day prefixed by the author of the plan. He had reason to be proud of the exploit, but neither then or at any later date was he ever known to boast of it. He had at that time much else to think of, his cavalry horses were for the most part foundered by the passage of the rugged defiles, and he had no time to lose if he was to fight a decisive battle on the 15th as he had promised.

The judgment of posterity is unanimous in respect to the importance of the passage of the Andes by San Martin, not alone as a great military feat, but also for the influence it had upon the final result of the struggle for emancipation. Spanish historians speak of it as the turning-point of the contest between Spain and her colonies. In German military schools it is cited as an example of the importance of discipline in an army, and of the value of foresight and attention to details on the part of a general.

The passage of the Andes by San Martin was a feat requiring greater strategy and skill than the passages of the Alps by Hannibal and by Napoleon; it was unequalled till Bolívar repeated the exploit on the equator. If compared with the two former, it is seen to be a much greater achievement than either of them from its effects upon the destinies of the human race. In place of vengeance, greed, or of ambition, San Martin was animated by the hope of giving liberty and independence to a new world. The passage of the Andes by San Martin resulted in Maipó; the passage of the Andes by Bolívar resulted in Boyacá; two decisive victories which liberated entire peoples from the slavery of foreign despotism; the passages of the Alps by Hannibal and by Napoleon resulted only in the sterile victories of Trebia and of Marengo.

CHAPTER XIV.

CHACABUCO.

1817.

FROM San Felipe, San Martin sent off a trusty spy to Santiago with instructions to bring him back, on the third day, information of the movements of the enemy. He then set himself to work to prepare for battle, mounting his artillery and concentrating the different divisions. On the 10th February all the army was united on the open plain at the foot of the slope of Chacabuco.

On the 10th and 11th the engineers, protected by skirmishers, reconnoitred the roads and passes leading across the Sierra. On the 11th the spy returned, bringing answers to San Martin from his agents in the capital, and copies of the secret orders of Marcó. The spy had visited the barracks of the Royalist troops, and had counted those on the march for Chacabuco. San Martin then summoned a council of war.

The Sierra of Chacabuco rises to a height of 4,300 feet above the level of the sea. About three miles before reaching the summit, the main road from Santa Rosa to Santiago divides into two paths. That to the left, which is the shortest but also the steeper of the two, is still only a bridle-path; the other is now the main road, but was at that time little known. Both lead to the plain of Chacabuco, but the points at which they descend from the heights are nearly two miles distant one from the other. The left-hand path first reaches the lower ground near the head of a valley about three miles long, down which it winds until it joins the other path at the farmhouse of Chacabuco, which stands at the head of the plain.

From the summit of the Sierra the whole country is seen spreading out as a beautiful panorama. The plain at the foot, extending southwards some seven miles in the direction of Santiago, is shut in by the hills of Colina, through which there is a path. Behind lie the great masses of the Cordillera, to the west the spur runs on till it joins the coast range, as yet unseen.

San Martin informed his officers that he had determined to advance without waiting for the rest of his artillery, and to fight the decisive battle before the enemy had time to concentrate his forces. The army was to march in two columns by the diverging paths, which columns should debouch simultaneously upon the plain beyond, and attack the Royalist position in front and on the flank. The column of the right was put under command of Soler, and consisted of 2,100 men, with seven light guns. That of the left, under command of O'Higgins, consisted of 1,500 men, with two guns. The latter was to engage the attention of the enemy in front, without attacking the position, while Soler marched upon his left flank and rear, when a general advance would decide the day.

Atero, after the skirmish in the valley of Putaendo, had retreated to Chacabuco, and Marcó hurriedly sent reinforcements, offering the soldiery a reward of twenty dollars for each one of the enemy killed, and twelve for each prisoner; but, at the same time, he secretly sent off his baggage to Valparaiso, and not until the 10th did he appoint a commander for the army assembling at Chacabuco. He then selected Colonel Maroto of the Talavera regiment, who reached the headquarters at the farmhouse on the evening of the 11th. Maroto found under his orders 1,500 infantry, 500 cavalry, and five guns, a force far inferior in numbers to that of the invaders, and depressed in

L

spirit, but they were the flower of the Spanish army. All that he had time to do that evening was to strengthen an outpost which was stationed on the summit in a position which commanded the eastern pass, purposing to occupy the heights with his entire force on the following day.

At two in the morning of the 12th February, under a bright moon, the Argentine army commenced their advance, the infantry leaving their knapsacks behind them. Flanking parties from Soler's division were the first to meet the enemy, but had barely time to exchange a few shots when the position was attacked by O'Higgins, who drove this advanced guard before him over the summit. The Royalists retreated in good order upon the main body, which had advanced three miles up the valley at dawn of day.

Maroto, believing that the whole force of the Patriots was in pursuit of his vanguard by the main road, withdrew his army across the valley, which was intersected by a muddy stream, and took up a strong position on the opposite slope, placing two of his guns so as to command the mouth of the pass, and extending his line to a hill on his extreme left, where he established a strong force of infantry, with the cavalry in the rear.

Zapiola, with three squadrons of the grenadiers, harassed the retreat of the Royalist vanguard, but could make no impression upon it, the ground being unfavourable for cavalry, but he succeeded in preventing the enemy from occupying two hills at the mouth of the pass, where they might have seriously hindered the advance of O'Higgins; and advanced into the valley till forced to retire by the fire of the two guns in position in front.

At 11 A.M. O'Higgins debouched from the pass, and drew up his infantry in line on the open ground under fire of the enemy. For an hour he contented himself with returning their fire and beating off their skirmishers, till, as he afterwards said himself, his blood was boiling to be at them. In his excitement he forgot the positive orders of San Martin to wait for Soler before attacking the enemy, and gave the word to charge. His men advanced with alacrity, but were soon entangled in the muddy stream, which they in vain attempted to cross under the fire of the enemy, and finally retreated in disorder to the mouth of the pass.

San Martin, sitting on his war-horse, saw from the heights above the repulse of his lieutenant. At once he sent off his aide-de-camp Condarco to hasten the march of Soler. This is the incident in his life which is commemorated in the equestrian statue which now graces the Plaza San Martin in Buenos Ayres.

He then galloped down the slope and joined O'Higgins. As he reached the lower ground, he noticed an extraordinary movement in the ranks of the enemy, and then descried the head of Soler's column advancing rapidly on his flank.

O'Higgins again advanced, while the grenadiers under Zapiola charged the centre of the enemy, and sabred his artillerymen at their guns. The position was carried by the bayonet, and the Royalist infantry formed square on their centre. Colonel Alvarado, with the vanguard of the right wing, at the same time captured the hill on the left flank of the Royalists, while Necochea and Escalada charged the cavalry in the rear. The victors then fell simultaneously upon the square, which was speedily broken. Some of the fugitives made for the farmhouse in their rear, but found their retreat cut off by Soler, and were forced to surrender at discretion; others tried to escape by the valley, and there fell under the sabres of the grenadiers.

The Royalists lost in this action 500 killed, 600 prisoners, all their artillery, a standard, and two flags; while the loss of the Patriots was 12 killed and 120 wounded. But the moral effects of the victory were still greater; the disaster of Chacabuco spread panic among the adherents of the Royal cause all over Chile. Only three men were undismayed—Barañao, Ordoñez, and Sanchez.

Barañao, on the march with his hussars to join the army, was met at the entrance to the plain of Chacabuco by news of the disaster. He countermarched to Santiago, and offered Marcó to take up an infantry soldier behind each of his horsemen, and to fall upon the Patriot camp by night; but Marcó thought of nothing but his own safety, and fled to Valparaiso, leaving the capital in the hands of the populace.

On the 13th the Patriot army was in full march upon Santiago, Necochea, with his squadron of grenadiers, being sent in advance to maintain order in the city; where the next day the army entered amid the enthusiastic plaudits of the inhabitants. As a Chilian historian says:

"San Martin, occupied in carrying out his vast plans, cared little for these futile manifestations. He thought only of the resources for carrying on the work which he had gained by the victory."

On the 15th he issued a proclamation convoking an assembly of notables, who should name three electors for each of the provinces of Santiago, Concepcion, and Coquimbo, in order that they might appoint a chief for the State.

The Assembly, to the number of one hundred, met under the presidency of Don Francisco Ruiz Tagle, the provisional Governor, and declared that—

"They were unanimous in naming Don José de San Martin as Governor of Chile with full powers."

San Martin refused to accept the appointment, and summoned another Assembly, to the number of two hundred and ten, which by acclamation named General O'Higgins Supreme Director of the State, which was what San Martin desired. The new Director appointed Don Miguel Zañartu his Minister of the Interior, and Lieutenant-Colonel Zenteno, San Martin's secretary, Minister of War and Marine; and then issued a proclamation to the people and addressed a note to the foreign Powers.

When Marcó left the capital, his troops at once dispersed. Some of them, with Maroto at their head, reached Valparaiso, and at once embarked. The rest were made prisoners, among them Marcó himself, who had not even energy sufficient for a rapid flight. San Martin received the late Governor-General with great affability.

"Give me that white hand," said he, with bluff sarcasm; and, leading him to an inner room, he conversed privately with him for two hours, and then dismissed him.

San Bruno, who had murdered prisoners in the public jail, was also taken prisoner, and, being sent at once for trial, was quickly sentenced, and shot in the great square, which was an act of simple justice.

News of the victory of Chacabuco was received in Buenos Ayres on the 24th February. All day shouts of triumph echoed through the streets, while cannon roared from the fort and from the ships of the squadron anchored in the roadstead. The captured flags were hung out from the balconies of the Cabildo, grouped round a portrait of the victorious general. Medals were decreed to the soldiers who had fought under him, and to himself a special badge of honour, while his daughter, Maria Mercedes, received a life-pension of 600 dollars per annum, which her father devoted to her education.

Government also sent San Martin his commission as Brigadier-General, the highest military grade in the Argentine service. He, in accordance with his previously expressed determination, declined the honour, but asked for further supplies of men, arms, and money, to carry on the campaign, and appointed himself General-in-Chief of the united Argentine and Chilian armies.

After arranging with the Chilian authorities for the formation of a naval squadron, and establishing in Santiago a Supreme Council of the Lautaro Lodge, half Chilians and half Argentines, he announced his intention of returning to Buenos Ayres to concert measures with Government for the prosecution of the war.

The Cabildo of Santiago offered him ten thousand ounces of gold for the expenses of his journey, which he declined to accept for himself, but devoted it to the establishment of a public library in that city.

One month after the battle he passed by the scene of his late victory, and saw there a mound of earth, under which lay the dead of the 12th February of the Patriot army, most of them negroes from Cuyo, liberated slaves. This mound was the first landmark of the War of Emancipation.

CHAPTER XV.

THE FIRST CAMPAIGN IN THE SOUTH OF CHILE.

1817.

AFTER the victory of Chacabuco, San Martin made three mistakes, two of mere detail, but one of importance, which had an evil influence upon his later operations. The campaign which ought to have finished immediately was thus prolonged, and he was compelled to fight four more battles to accomplish the reconquest of Chile, retarding by three years the prosecution of his great enterprise.

On the 12th February he remained encamped on the field of battle instead of pursuing the enemy at least to the end of the plain of Chacabuco. The following day, instead of marching upon the capital he ought to have pursued the fugitives to Valparaiso. By this mistake 1,600 veteran troops escaped to Peru, to act against him later on. But his great mistake consisted in his neglect to secure the fruits of his victory by an immediate campaign in the South. The military strength of Chile lay in the South—the people were warlike, the royal cause had there many partisans, and the country was full of strong military positions, in especial the fortress of Valdivia, backed by the islands of Chiloe, a sea-port by which reinforcements from Peru could be poured into the country. Looking far ahead, the victor of Chacabuco overlooked that which was close at hand.

Ordoñez was an officer of great talent, who up to that

time had had no opportunity of distinguishing himself. He and San Martin had fought side by side against Napoleon. At the close of the war he was a colonel, and with this rank he came to America in 1815 as Governor of Concepcion. He was there still and now came forward as the most doughty opponent of his old comrade. He had no regular troops with him; but ably seconded by Sanchez, he summoned the militia, collected the soldiery dispersed to the north of the Maule, garrisoned the frontier of Arauco, fortified the Peninsula of Talcahuano, aided by the royal squadron, made large provision of supplies, and scoured the country from the Bio-Bio to the Maule with his light troops. For two months he was unmolested, and had time to organize a division of 1,000 men, and to receive a reinforcement from Lima of 1,600 regulars.

Freyre, after his success at Talca, had contented himself with intercepting communications, and his force was weakened by Rodriguez, who marched his guerillas to the North, while his instructions from San Martin to collect horses and cattle for the main army were neglected. At the same time several smaller parties of the Patriots were cut up by the Royalists.

San Martin did not totally neglect the South. On the 18th February a column of 1,000 men under Las Heras, left Santiago, and on the 4th March crossed the Maule and joined Freyre at Diguillin, but he marched so slowly that the enemy had plenty of time to prepare for him. O'Higgins, who was left in supreme command by San Martin, was greatly irritated at this delay, and in April marched himself to his assistance, with 800 men. But his progress was just as slow as that of Las Heras, who in the meantime, after calling a council of his officers to attest the meagreness of his equipment for such an expedition, marched resolutely on Concepcion, encamping on the 4th April at a farmhouse near to that city.

Ordoñez, who had been watching his movements, fell

upon him at night with 700 light troops, but was beaten off with the loss of two guns; and the next day Las Heras occupied Concepcion.

Concepcion lies on the northern bank of the Bio-Bio, at the head of the peninsula of Talcahuano, and about five miles distant from the fortified town of the same name. Las Heras was thus in a critical position; he dare not retreat, and his force was insufficient to attack Ordoñez in his entrenchments. He built a small fort on the Gavilán Hill, to the south-west of Concepcion, and waited for O'Higgins. On the 1st May four Spanish vessels anchored in the Bay of Talcahuano, bringing the 1,600 fugitives from Chacabuco, who had been sent back from Peru to reinforce the garrison, and Ordoñez thought himself strong enough to resume the offensive. On the night of the 4th he sallied out with 700 men and four guns to attack the left flank of the position held by Las Heras, while Colonel Morgado, with 400 men and two guns attacked on the right, and a small force in boats rowed up the Bio-Bio to menace the city from the river. The action commenced at daybreak and was hotly contested for three hours, until Freyre, who commanded on the right of the position, having routed Morgado and captured his two guns, came to the assistance of Las Heras, and Ordoñez was compelled to retreat, hotly pursued by the grenadiers under Medina, who captured one of his guns. The flotilla was beaten off by two companies of the 7th Regiment, which arrived during the action. The loss of the Royalists in this smart affair was 192 killed and 80 prisoners. The Patriots had 6 killed and 62 wounded.

When all was over O'Higgins arrived upon the scene, and in his satisfaction at the victory forgot all his displeasure. He took the command, and at once commenced operations against Talcahuano. Ordoñez having command of the sea and the Bio-Bio, had easy communication with the ports of Arauco, which both furnished supplies and harassed the left flank of the Patriots. Freyre, with a flying column of 300 men, was detached to capture these forts. On the 12th May, Captain Cienfuegos, with sixty men, crossed the Bio-Bio and took the fort of El Nacimiento, after which two other forts nearer to Concepcion surrendered. The key of this line was the fortress of Arauco, situate at its western extremity on the sea-coast. Freyre incorporated the detachment under Cienfuegos, and on the 26th May encamped on the River Carampague in the vicinity of this fort. The garrison, to the number of 200 men, sallied out to dispute the passage of the river. Freyre, with 50 grenadiers and 50 infantry mounted *en croupe*, crossed the river lower down, and fell upon the Royalists with such impetuosity, while the rest of his force attacked them in front, that he completely routed them, and the following day captured the fort, with eleven guns and large stores of ammunition, having lost eleven men drowned in the passage of the river, and one man wounded.

A militia captain named Diaz rallied the dispersed soldiery, and adding to them some 400 Indians, returned to the attack. Cienfuegos, who had been left in command, met this new foe on the open, but was completely beaten, and Arauco was reoccupied by the Royalists on the 3rd June, to be retaken by Freyre on the 17th July. O'Higgins then made a treaty with the Indians of Arauco, and so secured their neutrality.

Meantime an advanced post had been established in the vicinity of Talcahuano, and frequent skirmishes took place with the garrison, in which the Patriots had always the advantage. On the 22nd July the army advanced within cannon shot of the line of forts which crossed the peninsula, but was compelled by heavy rain to retire on the 24th. Ordoñez kept his main force within the line of his entrenchments, but officers of his raised bodies of guerillas in the rear of the Patriots, cutting off supplies, while detachments in boats made frequent descents on the coast line of Arauco, losing many men, but greatly harassing the Patriots.

Talcahuano was by nature a strong position, but was made stronger still by art. The garrison consisted of 1,700 men and seventy heavy guns were mounted on the forts, while a frigate, a brig of war, and five gunboats in the bay, and a boat with one heavy gun on the western side of the peninsula, enfiladed the approach from the South. It was called by O'Higgins the Chilian Gibraltar, and here it was that Ordoñez by far-seeing prudence, held the united forces of Chile and the United Provinces in check for three years.

During the winter O'Higgins had strengthened his army with several battalions of Chilian recruits; in October he had nearly 4,000 men under his immediate command, and was also joined by two French officers of distinction. The first, General Brayer, came with a great military reputation, gained in the wars of the French Republic and under Napoleon; but his arrogance soon lost him the sympathy and confidence of his new comrades. The other, Alberto D'Albe, Captain of Engineers, was also a man of great experience, and being of a more modest character, rendered great service to the American cause.

Heavy rains paralysed operations until spring was well advanced; but on the 25th November, O'Higgins again moved forward to some high ground within cannon shot of the line of entrenchments. The plan of attack was drawn up by General Brayer. On the extreme left of the Royalist position was an outwork called the Morro, against this the main attack was to be directed, while the attention of the enemy was diverted by false attacks on the rest of the line. O'Higgins and most of his officers were in favour of an attack upon the other flank; but San Martin being consulted, gave his opinion in favour of Brayer's plan, which was accordingly adopted. A desultory cannonade was maintained for several days, when a north wind springing up, which prevented the Spanish men-of-war from aiding in the defence of the line, the columns marched to the attack in the early morning of the

6th December. The attack on the Morro was led by Major Beauchef and Captain Videla, with a mixed force of Chilians and Argentines. Mounting on the shoulders of their men they scaled the outer wall, and tore down a portion of the stockade behind, when such a heavy fire was poured upon them that Videla being killed and Beauchef severely wounded, the column could advance no farther, till Las Heras brought up the supports, when the position was carried by the bayonet. At the same time a Spanish gunboat on the Bio-Bio was captured by some boats led by an Englishman named Manning, and an unauthorised attack by Conde on the centre was repulsed.

At daybreak Las Heras found to his dismay that the Morro was merely an advanced work, and that he was still outside of the line of entrenchments. Colonel Boedo fell in attempting to force his way beyond; the guns of two forts on the heights, those of the frigate *Venganza*, and those of some gunboats converged their fire upon the conquered outwork, causing heavy losses; in spite of which Las Heras maintained his position till O'Higgins sent him orders to retire, which he did in good order, after spiking the guns he had captured, and carrying with him his wounded and prisoners. The loss of the Patriots was 150 killed and 280 wounded.

This disaster put an end for the time to all offensive operations, and on the day of the assault another strong reinforcement of Royalist troops embarked at Callao for Talcahuano.

CHAPTER XVI.

ARGENTINE-CHILENO ALLIANCE.

1817.

THE alliance between Argentina and Chile, sealed with the blood of her soldiers in the assault on Talcahuano, is the most important factor of this epoch in the struggle for the emancipation of America, whether the objects of the alliance be spoken of or whether its results be summed up. This alliance, the first celebrated in the New World between independent nations, was no artificial combination; it arose from the natural tendencies, and from the reciprocal interests of two peoples, and its effects were felt from Cape Horn to the Equator. Never did two allied nations work more cordially together for one end, never were greater deeds accomplished with such feeble resources. Without this alliance the struggle for independence would either have failed or would have been indefinitely retarded. It originated in the help given by each country to the other in the first years of the struggle, from 1811 to 1814. The fall of Chile in the latter year only strengthened the bond; it was then seen to be an absolute necessity to both. Chile alone could not free herself from her oppressors, and Argentina without her had no military road by which she could reach her enemy, while she herself lay open to assault.

The Argentine Republic undertook the conquest of Chile for three reasons: first, as a measure of self-defence;

second, to secure the dominion of the Pacific; as a means to the complete emancipation of South America, which was the third reason for, and the final object of, the undertaking. San Martin was the soul of the alliance, O'Higgins was the connecting link, the Army of the Andes the muscle and sinew, and the Lautaro Lodge the secret mechanism. It was to establish this alliance that San Martin had so hurriedly left for Buenos Ayres after the victory of Chacabuco.

San Martin recrossed the Andes without other company than his favourite aide-de-camp O'Brien, and a guide. As he left Mendoza on the 19th March, he received a letter from Pueyrredon, telling him that a war was imminent with the Portuguese of the Banda Oriental, for which arms and money would be required from Chile, and that in a few days he expected five armed ships, which Carrera was bringing from North America, which he would send on to Valparaiso and place at his orders.

The Portuguese had occupied the Banda Oriental in 1816, with the tacit connivance of the Argentine Government, and Pueyrredon was at that time striving to avoid a rupture by diplomacy. But a war with the Portuguese formed no part of the plans of San Martin, who, at the end of March, reached Buenos Ayres, and avoiding a triumphal entry, which was preparing for him, went to business at once.

Fifteen days afterwards he commenced his return journey, having made such arrangements as he could for the equipment and support of a naval squadron on the Pacific, promising, as General-in-Chief, help from Chile to the extent of 300,000 dollars.

Don José Miguel Carrera had in the year 1815 managed to raise 20,000 dollars among his personal friends in Buenos Ayres, and with this, had gone off to the United States to raise a naval squadron for an expedition to Chile. By lavish promises he had prevailed upon some merchants in New York and Baltimore to sell him five ships, fully equipped. In one of these, the corvette *Clifton*, he reached Buenos Ayres on the 9th February, 1817. Pueyrredon not only refused to pay for the ships, but also prohibited the further progress of the expedition, knowing that the presence of the Carreras in Chile would be most prejudicial to the cause of the alliance. A few days afterwards the brig *Savage* arrived from Baltimore, and Carrera formed a plan for escaping with the two ships, but his intention being denounced to Pueyrredon by one of the French adventurers who had come with him, he was arrested as a conspirator, and confined in the Retiro Barracks, where San Martin visited him on the 12th April. Carrera haughtily refused to shake hands with him, and rejected his repeated offers to arrange matters for him with Pueyrredon. They never met again.

San Martin and Pueyrredon both wrote to O'Higgins, proposing that Chile should pension the three brothers Carrera, in recognition of their former services. But O'Higgins considered that such a measure would offer a reward to crime. Carrera soon afterwards escaped from prison and fled to Monte Video; later on he became conspicuous in the ranks of the enemies of Buenos Ayres.

On the 11th May San Martin was again in Chile, and was received in triumph at the capital, the enthusiasm of the people being increased by the news received the same day of the victory of Las Heras at Gavilán.

The same day he sent his friend and aide-de-camp, Alvarez Condarco, off, by way of Buenos Ayres, to London, with money to purchase another ship of war. Condarco had also another mission, which is enveloped in mystery, and is pointed to as a stain on the reputation of San Martin and O'Higgins. A certain sum was to be left in deposit in London for their private account. The documents relating to this matter are written in cypher, and have remained secret for more than sixty years. Only three persons have read them, of whom two are dead, the third is the author of this history.* The amount cannot have exceeded 29,500 dollars, a sum which San Martin had most certainly earned, while the rigid exactness of all his dealings with public money placed in his hands is unquestioned. He steadily refused all recompense for his services; he did accept the hospitality of the city of Santiago when there, but the yearly expenses of his establishment did not exceed 3,000 dollars.

In pursuance of the Alliance, the Government of Chile remitted 40,000 dollars to Buenos Ayres for the army of Upper Peru, and the Argentine Government sent a thousand new muskets for the use of the Chilian army. The maintenance of the Army of the Andes, and the filling up of death vacancies, was assumed by Chile, and there was no further question on either side of pecuniary responsibility.

When O'Higgins in April went to take command of the Army of the South, he left Colonel Don Hilarion de la Quintana as his deputy at Santiago. Quintana was an Argentine, a family connection and an aide-de-camp of San Martin. Thus the supreme power in the State was made subject to Argentine influence under the direction of the Lautaro Lodge. This appointment wounded the national susceptibilities of the people, was contrary to the policy adopted by the Argentine government, and provoked open declarations that "Chile owed nothing to the Army of the Andes."

To destroy this impression, government, on establishing a military school, reserved twelve nominations of cadets for natives of the Province of Cuyo, professing "eternal

* It appears that Condarco, when in London, purchased the ship *Cumberland*, mounting sixty guns, for 160,000 dols., giving an order for that amount on the Government of Chile, and paying as a deposit 25,000 dols., which sum, being returned to him on payment of his draft, he placed in the hands of someone in whom he had confidence, on account of O'Higgins and San Martin. His confidence was misplaced, his English friend lost the money in gambling on the Stock Exchange, and San Martin found himself penniless when he landed in England in 1824.—TR.

gratitude to the illustrious peoples of the Rio de la Plata."

But international gratitude is always a burden, and the Chilians saw in it no reason for confiding the highest post in the State to a foreigner.

Such was the position of affairs when San Martin returned from Buenos Ayres. Quintana and O'Higgins then both wished him to take charge of the administration. He refused, and advised O'Higgins to appoint a Chilian in place of Quintana.

One of the chief administrative acts of Quintana was to commence the coinage of Chilian money, with an appropriate inscription indicative of the establishment of Chile as a sovereign State. One thousand dollars of this coinage were given to San Martin and Belgrano for distribution as medals among the Argentine troops.

At this time Pueyrredon appointed Don Tomas Guido Argentine representative in Chile, and his official reception at Santiago on the 17th May was one of the great events of the year. Quintana, as one result of these renewed relations, sent Irizarri to Europe as the diplomatic agent of Chile, with instructions to act in conjunction with the diplomatic agent of the United Provinces, wherever he might be. Rivadavia was at that time Argentine representative in Europe, and to him were sent fresh powers and instructions to treat for the establishment of an independent monarchy in America.

O'Higgins, from his headquarters at Concepcion, issued a decree creating a "Legion of Merit," in imitation of the Legion of Honour created by Napoleon. This institution had an aristocratic tendency, as its members enjoyed special privileges; it was, therefore, unpopular, and the Argentine Government would permit no privileges to such Argentine citizens as received the distinction. San Martin looked more favourably upon it, as it responded to his idea of creating a special military class independent of local influences.

One of the results of the restoration of Chile by Argentine arms was to give preponderance to one of the parties into which the country was divided. The Argentines, while recognizing the independence of the country and establishing a national government, had imposed a dictator upon the country, postponing indefinitely its constitutional organization. The Government of O'Higgins had against it not only its old adversaries, but also a large number of Chilians who were jealous of foreign influence. They took Carrera as their chief, and National Autonomy as their watchword, while they were animated only by personal ambition.

Doña Javiera de Valdés, sister of the Carreras, resided at that time in Buenos Ayres. At her house there were daily meetings of Chilian emigrants who were hostile to O'Higgins. Among them a plot was hatched. She herself was the life and soul of the conspiracy. It was decided that several of the conspirators should cross the Andes to prepare their friends in Chile for an outbreak, and should be followed by Don Luis and by Don Juan José Carrera, who should keep quiet until joined by Don José Miguel, who would go round Cape Horn from Monte Video, in the ship *General Scott*, which he was expecting from New York. They thought they had only to land in the country to be received with acclamation and placed in charge of her destinies. All that they feared was the Argentine army, which was to be expelled, O'Higgins was to be banished from the country as a traitor, San Martin was to be tried by court-martial as a criminal, and all who resisted them were to be put to death. It was an absurd and criminal project which, if only partially successful, would have ruined Chile for the second time.

The first party of the conspirators crossed the Andes in July. Luis Carrera, disguised as a peon, was arrested at Mendoza for robbing the mails. Juan José, travelling under a false name and accompanied by a post-boy, was caught in a hailstorm during the night near San Luis;

the boy died, he was arrested on suspicion of murder, and afterwards sent on to Mendoza and imprisoned with his brother. Luzuriaga, Governor of Mendoza, sent full accounts of these occurrences to Santiago. Meantime the other conspirators had arrived at a farmhouse belonging to the Carrera family, and had been put under arrest as a measure of precaution, in consequence of warnings from Buenos Ayres. These news from Mendoza made it certain that some conspiracy was on foot. Numerous arrests among the partisans of Carrera followed, the most notable among the prisoners being Dr. Don Manuel Rodriguez. Some said that the Government was the author of the conspiracy. The general excitement was so great that Quintana could no longer maintain his position, and eventually Don Luis de la Cruz, a native Chilian, chosen by the Lautaro Lodge, was appointed Deputy Director.

San Martin, the guest of the Chilian people, residing in a palace, still continued the simple, hard-working manner of life he had adopted in Mendoza. He dined alone at 1 P.M., but at 4 P.M. a state dinner was served at which Guido presided. At dessert he joined the company and took coffee with them. In the evening his saloon was a favourite resort of the best society of the city, the soirée being invariably opened by singing the Argentine National Hymn, after which San Martin led off the first minuet. These " tertulias " were celebrated in the society annals of the day; and not a few of the Argentine officers fell captive to the beauty and grace of the girls of Santiago, Las Heras and Guido among the number.

San Martin had small sympathy for the Chilian people; their manners and character did not please his austere mind, and he was not the sort of man to make many friends. In his own country he had but three, Belgrano, Pueyrredon, and Godoy Cruz; in Chile he had but one, O'Higgins. He also suffered much at this time from neuralgia and rheumatism, and could only sleep by an immoderate use of morphia. He thought that he could not live much longer; those about him thought the same and sent notice of their fears to Buenos Ayres, in consequence of which General Antonio Gonzalez Balcarce, the hero of Suipacha, was sent to join him as his second in command.

In spite of his forebodings San Martin did not falter in the prosecution of his great enterprise, and taking advantage of his friendship with Captain Bowles, Commodore of the British Pacific squadron, he sent, under his care, a trusty agent to Lima with letters to the Viceroy proposing an exchange of prisoners. This he was anxious to effect, not only for the sake of the prisoners and their friends in both countries, but also for the purpose of procuring an official recognition of Chile as a belligerent power. But under these was a third purpose, to him of more importance than either of the others. His messenger was a confidential agent, who might thus have a pretext for meeting the leaders of society in Lima, and opportunity for sounding them, and for spreading among them the Argentine ideas of which he was the champion.

CHAPTER XVII.

CANCHA-RAYADA.

1817—1818.

THE year 1817 had commenced with a victory and ended with a defeat, the year 1818 was to commence with a defeat to be followed by a victory which would decide the fate of Chile. From that moment all the forces of the revolution in South America would converge from the extremities towards the centre, shutting up the colonial power of Spain in its last stronghold, Peru, where the two great liberators of the South and the North, San Martin and Bolívar, would join hands.

In the epoch at which we have now arrived, Chile had as yet no definite form, but possessed all the elements of a vigorous nationality, patriotism, energy, and a pronounced tendency to independence; a democracy yet in embryo, combined with an aristocracy at once territorial and political. The instincts of the masses decided them for the cause of independence, while their political organization assumed the most elemental form, that of a people become an army, under the direction of a class and under a military dictatorship to which all were subject. The revolution and the leveling pressure of despotic rule, had destroyed provincialism and the social inequalities which stood in the way of national unity; common misfortunes and common efforts had created public spirit. Independence thus became a fact, and the establishment of a republic the necessary sequence. With the assent of all the convocation of a Congress was still postponed, but the political situation was compact. Yet there was some resistance to this system of government; the educated classes accepted it only as a transient necessity, and there were still some partisans of the royal cause in the South. Among the rulers themselves there were still some who clung to the fallen party of the Carreras; but for the presence of Argentine bayonets and the influence of San Martin the intestine dispute would have broken out afresh.

Viceroy Abascal, who had crushed the revolution in Upper Peru, in Quito, and in Chile, had in 1815 been replaced by General Pezuela, and the army of Upper Peru was put under the command of General La Serna. Pezuela lacked the talents of his predecessor but he continued his policy. Seeing Chile threatened by an invasion from Mendoza, he ordered La Serna to effect a diversion by marching on Tucuman. But La Serna was held in check by the Gauchos of Salta and Jujui under Martin Güemes, and the successful passage of the Andes by San Martin forced upon him a disastrous retreat.

Pezuela did not fully appreciate the importance of the victory of Chacabuco, and contented himself with sending back the fugitives, in the belief that the Royalist army was still able to hold the country unaided. The defeat of Ordoñez at Gavilán opened his eyes to the danger, and the arrival of reinforcements from Spain enabled him to fit out a fourth expedition. While busied in these preparations, the British ship of war *Amphion*, Captain Bowles, anchored at Callao, bringing Don Domingo Torres as special envoy from San Martin. So far as its ostensible object was concerned the mission was a complete failure, but Torres succeeded in communicating with the Patriots of Peru, and took back with him in January, 1818, full particulars of the expedition which followed close upon his heels.

Three thousand four hundred well equipped men reached Talcahuano early in January, in four ships mounting 234 guns. Most of these were veteran troops, and were commanded by General Osorio, the conqueror of Chile in 1814, who was sent to supersede Ordoñez. His instructions were, after driving the Patriot army to the north of the Maule, to re-embark his entire force, land in the neighbourhood of Valparaiso, and march on the capital, The plan was apparently a good one, but was drawn out in ignorance of the strength of the Patriots. The losses in the army of the Andes had all been made up, and the new Chilian army by this time almost equalled it in number. The united army now consisted of 9,000 men, of whom three-fourths were well drilled troops, while the total force collected at Talcahuano did not much exceed 5,000 men with twelve guns.

The cannon which roared a welcome to the Spanish squadron at Talcahuano, were heard by the Patriot army then in full retreat upon the capital. Osorio saw at once that he had failed to surprise the enemy, and that all chance of an easy landing in the neighbourhood of Valparaiso was at an end. He despatched the squadron to blockade that port, and after fifteen days spent in organizing his forces at Concepcion, he marched for the North, stimulated to activity by Ordoñez. On the 12th February his advanced posts on the Maule heard the salute fired by O'Higgins at Talca, in celebration of the first anniversary of Chacabuco.

The rôles were now changed; the general of the Army of the Andes, instead of choosing the place of invasion on a line of 1,300 miles of Cordillera, had now to defend 1,300 miles of coast. He expected the enemy to land near Valparaiso, and in December had written to O'Higgins to make every preparation for a rapid retreat, leaving the country behind him destitute of horses and supplies. O'Higgins commenced his retreat on the 1st January, 1818. and on the 20th reached Talca, accompanied by more than

50,000 people with their cattle and horses, and there proclaimed triumphantly the Independence of the Chilian Republic, which, in default of a Congress, had been decreed by a general vote of the Chilian people on the 17th November previous.

At Santiago, Don Luis de la Cruz, Deputy Director, presided at a solemn ceremony in the great square. Guido was the bearer of the standard of the new Nation; beside it the President of the Municipality carried that of the United Provinces. The Declaration of Independence being read, De la Cruz was the first to swear to maintain it, he was followed by the Bishop and by San Martin; then the people kneeling down, repeated the oath, and commemorative medals were distributed among them.

Meantime San Martin had drawn the greater part of his troops from the city and had established an encampment at Las Tablas near the coast, in readiness to meet the enemy at any point, giving the command there to Balcarce, and looking himself to the construction of bridges over the rivers to the south of Santiago, to facilitate the concentration of the different corps when requisite.

By the end of February he was no longer in doubt as to the intentions of the enemy. O'Higgins was directed to evacuate Talca and retreat sixty miles to the north. Early in March the concentration was complete, and San Martin had under his command 4,500 infantry, 1,500 cavalry and thirty-three guns.

On the 4th March, Osorio crossed the Maule and encamped at Talca. On the 14th the united army broke up from quarters and marched against him. The same day the Royalist army left Talca, and Primo de Rivera, chief of the staff, crossed the river Lontué with a strong detachment of infantry and cavalry to reconnoitre the position and force of the Patriots, of which Osorio as yet knew nothing, recrossing the river the same night. On the 15th, Freyre, supported by Brayer with the bulk of the cavalry and eight guns, crossed the river with 200 light horse, advanced to Quecheraguas, where the Royalist vanguard was quartered, and summoned Primo de Rivera to surrender, but receiving no support from Brayer, who did not even cross the river, he was forced to retire with the loss of seventeen men. Rivera after this success retreated upon his reserves at Camarico.

On the 16th, the entire Patriot army crossed the Lontué and encamped at Quecheraguas, while Osorio retired precipitately. San Martin, afraid that he would repass the Maule, marched inland to cut him off. The two armies marched on parallel lines at a distance of only seven miles one from the other; both crossed the Lircay on the 19th. On the afternoon of the same day, Osorio, whose rear was greatly harassed by the Patriot cavalry under Balcarce, wheeled into line in an excellent position, his right resting on the suburbs of Talca, his left on the Claro River, and his front defended by a stretch of broken ground known as the Cancha-Rayada, which he occupied with 500 horse. Balcarce, ignorant of the nature of the ground, charged this advanced corps, and coming under fire of the Royalist artillery, was compelled to retire in disorder. O'Higgins, with twenty guns, forced back the enemy's right wing into the suburbs of Talca, but as darkness came on, decisive action had to be postponed till next day.

In the twilight the Royalist generals, after gazing upon the Patriot army from the church towers of Talca, held a council of war. Before them was an enemy greatly superior in numbers, behind them flowed a deep and rapid river. Osorio talked of continuing the retreat to Talcahuano, but was overruled by Ordoñez, who said that the attempt could only result in the total destruction of the army, and advised a night attack upon the Patriot position. Most of the officers supported him, and Osorio retired to a convent, leaving him in command. At 8 P.M., under a cloudy sky, Ordoñez drew up his army in line of battle, with cavalry on the wings and guns in the intervals between the different battalions. He himself took charge of the centre, Primo de Rivera led the right wing and Colonel Latorre the left; so, in deep silence, they marched across the Cancha-Rayada, straight upon the watch-fires of the Patriot vanguard.

Meantime San Martin, warned by a spy of what was going forward in the Royalist camp, and seeing that his troops were in the worst possible position to resist a night attack, had marched several battalions and the Chilian artillery from his front to a strong position on his extreme right. The broken nature of the ground much retarded the manœuvre, and the rest of the army had not moved at all when the cavalry outposts gave warning of the approach of the enemy.

The right of the Royalist army, having the least distance to march, was the first to come into action, and was received by O'Higgins with so heavy a fire, whilst at the same time a detached company under Captain Dehesa opened fire on their left, that for a moment the advance was checked, till Ordoñez in person led them again to the charge. O'Higgins had his horse killed under him and received a ball in the elbow. From this moment all was confusion in the Patriot camp. The artillery was abandoned and the grenadiers on the extreme left, roused from sleep by the firing, fled in a panic. The cavalry of the right retired upon the reserves, and were received by a volley of musketry under the belief that they were Spaniards. Alvarado, with the 1st Light Infantry, passed behind the Royalist line and joined the right wing, being also taken for a Spanish corps and losing twenty-one men by the fire of his own friends before the mistake was discovered. The 2nd Chilian infantry, under command of an Italian officer, moved to the rear, and also reached the right wing in safety.

Ordoñez pushed on to a hill in the rear of the Patriot position, then halted and opened fire in every direction. One of these chance shots killed an aide-de-camp of San Martin at his side, and after some fruitless efforts to restore order he was forced to repass the Lircay with the fugitives, and was followed by O'Higgins with the remains of his division and the reserve artillery. All seemed lost.

It was eleven o'clock, and the autumn moon shone down through the heavy clouds upon the plain so lately occupied by an army. In the distance were heard occasional shots and the gallop of Spanish horse in pursuit, while the right wing in its secure position listened in silence, receiving no orders and knowing nothing of what had happened. The commander, Colonel Quintana, had gone off for orders and had not returned. The officers held a council of war and put themselves under command of Las Heras. He found himself with 3,500 men, but had no ammunition for his guns and no cavalry. He placed his guns in front, and, forming his infantry into one compact column, commenced his retreat soon after midnight, pursued by a squadron of Royalist horse, which did not dare to attack him. At daybreak he was sixteen miles from the field of battle. He rested for an hour, and found that 500 men had deserted during the night. At 10 A.M. he continued his march, and at five in the afternoon reached Quecheraguas, where he remained till midnight, when he crossed the Lontué, and, resuming his march next morning, reached Chimbarongo at midday, where he received news that San Martin and O'Higgins were at San Fernando with the 8th battalion, occupied in collecting the dispersed cavalry.

San Martin came to meet him, and praised the soldiers for their steady behaviour. He was by no means cast down, and directed Las Heras to continue his march to Santiago. O'Higgins suffered much from his wound, but was more determined than ever.

By the dispersion of Cancha-Rayada the Patriots lost 120 killed, 22 guns, and 4 flags, but the nucleus of the army was saved, and with it the independence of America. The Royalists had more than 200 killed and wounded, and had so many missing that they could not at once follow up their victory.

News of the disaster reached Santiago on the afternoon of the 21st, carried there by some of the principal officers, among them being Brayer. According to them everything was lost, San Martin killed, and O'Higgins mortally wounded. Consternation spread over the city, and shouts of "Viva el Rey!" were heard occasionally in the streets. Some talked of flying to Mendoza, or to the ships at Valparaiso. The Royalists and some of the leading citizens opened communications with the conqueror. One of them even had a horse shod with silver to present to him on his arrival. No one slept that night in Santiago.

Government hastily resolved to erect a fort on the southern road, and to send the public treasure to the North for safety, while they called in outlying detachments of troops and summoned the National Guard. The next day news was received that San Martin was at San Fernando.

Brayer, interrogated by the Deputy Director, affirmed that the country could never recover from such a defeat, an opinion which was warmly disputed by Guido. On the 23rd April a despatch was received from San Martin announcing the safe retreat of Las Heras, and stating that he had 4,000 men under his orders. Still the panic was not allayed, and Dr. Rodriguez, taking advantage of the circumstances, rode on horseback through the streets, haranguing the people till he induced them to meet in an open Cabildo and appoint him coadjutor to La Cruz. His fantastic measures were of no real use, but they served the temporary purpose of raising the spirits of the people till the real leaders arrived upon the scene.

Early the next morning O'Higgins reached the city. He soon put an end to disorder, purchased horses, and prepared supplies of ammunition. On the 25th he was joined by San Martin, who, worn out by fatigue and want of sleep, yet found strength as he drew rein at the gate of his palace to make the one speech of his life, in which he assured the excited people that the cause of Chile would yet triumph, and promised them soon a day of glory for America. On the same day a council of war was held in his apartments, at which O'Higgins was present, when it was resolved to establish a camp on the plain of Maipó about seven miles to the south of the city, there to await the approach of the enemy. On the 28th Las Heras joined the army with his division, and day and night were spent in active preparation.

Public confidence revived, but San Martin trusted nothing to fortune, he prepared for any contingency, gave secret orders for concentration on Coquimbo in case of a second reverse, established stores of supplies on the way there, and despatched Colonel de la Cruz to organize the northern provinces. He also established guards at the entrances to the passes of the Andes, and a park at Santa Rosa, so as to secure his retreat to the east. Further, he stationed a strong corps of cavalry at Rancagua, fifteen miles to the south of his camp.

Ten days after the dispersion the united army was reorganized and ready for the fray. It consisted of five battalions of Chilian and four of Argentine infantry, in all nearly 4,000 strong, two regiments of Argentine and one of Chilian cavalry with 1,000 sabres and twenty-two guns, in all more than 5,000 men.

CHAPTER XVIII.

MAIPO.

1818.

AT daybreak on the 20th March the Royalist army, although triumphant, was in utter confusion. Only one battalion, that of Arequipa, under Rodil, had not dispersed. Osorio, leaving his convent, rode over the field of battle, endeavouring to estimate the value of the victory he had done nothing to win. The orderly retreat of Las Heras filled him with apprehension, and his own cavalry was worn out. He crossed the Lircay and advanced to Pangue, from whence he despatched Ordoñez with a flying column in pursuit, and returned with the rest of his force to Talca to reorganize. Ordoñez reached Quecheraguas the next day, when Las Heras had already crossed the Lontué. On the 24th he was joined by Osorio with the rest of the army.

The country was a desert; the roads were inundated by the waters from the irrigating ditches which the Patriots had cut as they retreated; the Royalist general could learn nothing of the position or condition of the Patriot army. Marching blindly on, he reached San Fernando on the 28th, and sent forward a detachment of 200 horse, which, being attacked and dispersed by sixty grenadiers under Captain Cajaravilla on the 30th, were the first to give him certain information that there still remained an enemy in front of him.

On the 31st the Royal army, 5,500 strong, crossed the

Cachapoal, and advanced so cautiously that only on the afternoon of the 2nd April did it encamp on the left bank of the Maipó. Leaving the main road, Osorio crossed by a ford lower down, and encamped at Calera on the 3rd, moving on in the afternoon to the farmhouse of Espejo, where he established his headquarters, with the Patriot army close at hand. On the 4th he held a council of war, and proposed to retire on Valparaiso. Ordoñez, Rivera, and the principal officers opposed this idea, so it was resolved to fight the next day.

The scene of the decisive battle of the 5th April, 1818, is a plain bounded on the east by the river Mapocho, which divides the city of Santiago, on the north by a range of hills which separates it from the valley of Aconcagua, and on the south by the river Maipó,* which gives it its name. The west of this plain consists of a series of downs, with some low hills, covered with natural grasses and occasional clumps of thorny trees. From Santiago there runs in this direction a stretch of high land called the "Loma Blanca," from the chalky nature of the soil. On the crest of this Loma the Patriot army was encamped. In front of the western extremity of this Loma rose another of triangular form, beyond the south-western angle of which stood the farmhouse of Espejo, communicating with the higher ground by a sloping road of about twenty-five yards in width, shut in by vineyards and by the mud walls of enclosures, and crossed at the foot by a ditch. This Loma was occupied by the Royalist army. Between the two Lomas lay a stretch of low ground, varying in width from 300 to 1,250 yards, which was shut in on the west by a hillock which formed a sort of advanced work on the left of the Royalist position.

The position held by the Patriot army commanded the three roads from the capital to the passes of the Maipó, and the road to Valparaiso. For its further security San

* This word *Maipó* is commonly spelt in Buenos Ayres *Maipú*, which is the Pehuenche way of pronouncing it.

Martin had entrenched the city, and garrisoned it with 1,000 militia and one battalion of infantry, under command of O'Higgins, whose wound precluded him from service in the field. The army was in three divisions: the first, under Las Heras, on the right; the second, under Alvarado, on the left; and a reserve in a second line, under Quintana. Balcarce was in general command of the infantry, San Martin keeping the cavalry and the reserve under his own orders. San Martin issued the most precise orders for the regulation of the troops in action, especially enjoining upon every corps, whether cavalry or infantry, that they should never await a charge from the enemy, but that, when fifty paces distant, they should rush forward with sabre or bayonet.

During the whole day of the 4th April skirmishers of the Patriot army were constantly engaged with the enemy advancing from the fords of the Maipó. Early on the morning of the 5th San Martin, attended by O'Brien and D'Albe, with a small escort, rode to the edge of the Loma to watch for himself the movements of the foe. He feared that they would go far to the west and secure the road to Valparaiso for retreat in case of a reverse. As he saw them occupy the high ground in front of him with their left only extending to the road, he exclaimed:—

"What brutes these Spaniards are! Osorio is a greater fool than I thought him. I take the sun for witness that the day is ours."

At that moment the sun shone forth over the snowy crests of the Andes from a cloudless sky upon him.

At half-past ten the Patriot army advanced by the crest of the Loma from its camping-ground. On the march, Marshal Brayer presented himself to San Martin, asking permission to retire to the Baths of Colina.

"You have the same permission you took on the field of Talca," replied San Martin. "But as half an hour will decide the fate of Chile, as the enemy is in sight, and the baths are thirteen leagues off, you may stay if you can."

The Marshal answered that he could not "because of an old wound in the leg."

"Señor General," replied San Martin, "the lowest drummer in the united army has more honour than you." And, turning rein, he gave orders to Balcarce to announce to the army that the general of twenty years of warfare was cashiered for unworthy conduct.

On reaching the edge of the Loma, the army was drawn up in order of battle, four heavy guns in the centre, the light pieces and the cavalry on the wings, and the reserve two hundred yards in the rear.

The first movement of the Royalist general was to detach Primo de Rivera with eight companies of infantry and four guns to occupy the detached hill on his left, threatening the right of the Patriots, taking them in flank if they crossed the low ground, and securing, as he thought, the road to Valparaiso; Morgado, with some cavalry, keeping up the connection with the main body. The crest of the Loma was occupied by the infantry in two divisions with four guns each, the rest of the cavalry being stationed on the extreme right. Both armies were in such excellent positions that neither could attack except at a disadvantage.

San Martin, uncertain of the whereabouts of the enemy's artillery, was the first to open fire with his four heavy guns from the centre. The reply gave him the information he required, and he at once ordered the two divisions to attack the enemy. Las Heras advanced resolutely with the 11th battalion, under the fire of the four guns on the hill, to another hill to the right of Primo de Rivera, while the grenadiers, under Escalada, Medina, and Zapiola, drove Morgado and his horsemen in confusion from the field. Rivera was thus cut off from the main body. At the same time the left wing crossed the hollow, ascended the slope in front of them, and reached the high ground without seeing an enemy, but were then vigorously charged by the bulk of the Royalist infantry, under Ordoñez and Morla, and driven back with heavy loss; but the Royalists pursuing them down the slope were in their turn forced to retire by a withering fire from the Chilian guns, under Borgoño, which had remained on the crest of the Loma Blanca.

San Martin now sent orders to the reserve to advance at once, in support of the left wing, by an oblique movement across the low ground, so as to fall upon the flank of the Spanish infantry. On his way Quintana was joined by three battalions of those that had been driven back, and fell with great impetuosity upon the Royalists, who, however, held their ground most tenaciously. Meantime Freyre, with the Chilian cavalry, had charged and put to flight the Royalist cavalry on the right, and now came back upon the other flank of the Spanish infantry. Alvarado, having rallied his broken division, came to the assistance of Quintana with Borgoño and his eight guns.

Osorio, after sending orders to Rivera to withdraw from his advanced position, fled, leaving Ordoñez in command, who at once commenced to retreat in excellent order upon the farmhouse of Espejo.

At this moment O'Higgins, wounded as he was, appeared upon the field, and, meeting San Martin, greeted him as the saviour of Chile; but it was already five o'clock, and the battle was not yet won. Ordoñez, with heavy loss, had made good his retreat to the farmhouse, where he made the most active preparations for defence.

Las Heras, in pursuit of the left wing, was the first to arrive there, but found several detached corps there before him. He immediately ordered the occupation of the high grounds around it, which commanded the position, but Balcarce coming up ordered an immediate attack by the road. Colonel Thompson, with a battalion of Chilian light infantry, led the assault, but was beaten back with grape and musketry, losing 250 killed, and all his officers wounded. Borgoño and Blanco Encalada from the high ground then opened fire with seventeen guns, and soon drove the enemy from his outer defences into the houses and vineyards. Then the 11th battalion, supported by pickets of the 7th and 8th, broke their way through the mud walls and took the houses by assault. The carnage was frightful till Las Heras succeeded in putting a stop to it.

Ordoñez and all his principal officers, with the exception of Rodil, who escaped, gave up their swords to Las Heras, and the victory was complete. This was the hardest fought battle in all the War of Independence. The Royalists lost 1,000 killed, twelve guns, four flags, and a great quantity of small arms, ammunition, and baggage captured; and one general, four colonels, seven lieutenant-colonels, 150 officers, and 2,200 men were made prisoners. The Patriots lost more than 1,000 men killed and wounded, the greatest sufferers being the freed negroes of Cuyo, of whom more than half remained upon the field.

Great tactical skill was displayed by San Martin in this battle. The victory was achieved by the opportune attack of the reserve upon the weakest flank of the enemy. Like Epaminondas, he won only two great battles, and both by the oblique movement invented by the Greek general. Its importance was only equalled by that of Boyacá and that of Ayacucho; and without Maipó neither the one nor the other would have been fought. Maipó crushed the spirit of the Spanish army in America, and that of all adherents to the cause of royalty from Mexico to Peru. It had, further, the singular merit of being won by a beaten army fifteen days after its defeat.

The Arequipa battalion retreated in good order, under Rodil, but dispersed after crossing the Maule. This battalion and the dispersed cavalry were all who escaped from the field. San Martin had witnessed the flight of Osorio, and sent O'Brien after him with a party of cavalry. However, he escaped by the coast, leaving his carriage, with all his correspondence, in the hands of his pursuer, and reached Talcahuano on the 14th April with fourteen men. There he was joined by 600 more of the fugitives —all that remained of the victors of Cancha-Rayada.

San Martin made small use of his victory. He at once despatched Freyre in pursuit with a party of cavalry, but not until the guerillas began to commit depredations did he send Zapiola with 250 grenadiers to maintain order in the South. Osorio made use of this respite to strengthen himself in Concepcion and Talcahuano, and, by calling in outlying detachments, succeeded in collecting 1,200 men by the middle of May.

Pezuela, who fully appreciated the magnitude of the disaster, wrote to the Viceroy of New Granada and Venezuela for reinforcements. Sámano sent him the Numancia battalion, 1,200 strong, weakening himself at the time that he was threatened by Bolívar; but Morillo could send him none from Venezuela, and he confined his efforts to making preparations against invasion, leaving Osorio unaided to sustain himself in Chile as he could.

On the 21st May Osorio sent two detachments across the Nuble, one of which surprised the town of Parrol. Zapiola sent off Captain Cajaravilla with 200 horse to retake the town, which task he gallantly accomplished, capturing 70 prisoners; while Lieutenant Rodriguez of the grenadiers cut the other detachment to pieces at Quirihue. This put a stop to the efforts of the Royalists for that time, and Zapiola, being reinforced, determined to attack Chillán, where Colonel Lantaño was in command with a garrison of 500 men. The expedition was confided to Cajaravilla, who attempted to carry the place by assault, but was beaten off and compelled to retire.

Osorio, fearing that he would be attacked in the spring by the whole united army, resolved to evacuate Talcahuano, and to return to Peru. Accordingly, on the 5th September, he left Colonel Sanchez in command of the Chilian Royalists, and, after dismantling the fortifications, sailed for Callao on the 8th with thirty-five heavy guns, a great quantity of war material, and 700 Spanish troops —all that remained of the strong reinforcement he had brought with him.

CHAPTER XIX.

AFTER MAIPO.

1818.

THE same day on which the despatch announcing the victory of Maipó reached Mendoza, Don Luis and Don Juan José Carrera were shot in that city. The suit against them had been carried on in a most irregular manner, both in Mendoza and in Santiago. Don Luis was accused and convicted of having violated a mail bag; Don Juan José was accused of the murder of a boy, of which there was no proof. Both were indicted for conspiracy against Chile in Argentine territory, and in Chile for high treason. It was at once an international, criminal, and political case, and was tried by two courts of different nationalities, and totally independent of one another. The Argentine Government was by accident, and San Martin indirectly mixed up in it. Questions of jurisdiction arose, and the case was still pending when, in February, 1818, Don Luis was discovered to be engaged in a conspiracy against the Government of Cuyo.

After the disaster of Cancha-Rayada fugitives from Chile spread panic through the province, and Luzuriaga, the Governor, asked permission to send the accused to Buenos Ayres; he was apprehensive of what might happen should another defeat bring upon him a flood of Chilian emigrants, but the municipality called upon him in the name of the people to finish the case at once. He then appointed three judges to try the case, of whom one was Dr. Monteagudo, who was one of the fugitives from Chile. On the 8th April at 3 P.M. both the accused were sentenced to death; at 5 P.M. they were shot. They fell not so much in expiation of crimes committed as in sacrifice to the necessities of the Argentine-Chileno Alliance.

San Martin, writing of this affair, says:—

"After the action of Maipó, I used all my influence with the Government of Chile in favour of the Carreras, and I procured a pardon for them, but it was then too late." O'Higgins had acceded to his request when they were no longer dangerous.

Now that the victory of Maipó had secured the independence of Chile, the latent spirit of opposition to the dictatorial government of O'Higgins again broke out. The most moderate desired the establishment of a constitutional régime; the more extreme deemed that the time had come for a radical reform. Among these were the old adherents of the Carreras, who from local patriotism were inimical to the Argentine-Chileno Alliance, and to the influence of San Martin. Dr. Rodriguez was one of them, and aspired to be their leader. During the forty-eight hours of his rule, in the confusion which followed the disaster of Cancha-Rayada, he had raised a squadron of horse, which he styled the Hussars of Death, entirely composed of men disaffected to the Government. He now declared that they would bring the rulers of the people to order.

O'Higgins saw in this corps a focus of sedition, and ordered it to be disbanded. Rodriguez protested but was compelled to submit. Rodriguez was at once a guerilla chief and a demagogue; he was a lawyer who wore the epaulets of a colonel. He was a true patriot, but had neither judgment nor foresight, and infused his own disorderly spirit into the agitation.

The municipality of the capital called upon the Director to convene an open Cabildo. It met on the 17th April. Rodriguez called upon the Assembly to declare itself a representative body until the convocation of a Congress, and as such superior in authority to the actual rulers of the State. The motion was carried. O'Higgins ordered the arrest of Rodriguez, and the ferment subsided. O'Higgins then decreed the appointment of seven principal citizens as a committee to draw up a plan of a provisional constitution, which "should define the powers of each authority and should establish on a solid basis the rights of citizens." A constitution was accordingly drawn up and promulgated.

Rodriguez was sent under arrest to the barracks of Alvarado's battalion under charge of a Spanish officer named Navarro, who was told by Alvarado and Monteagudo that Government desired "the extermination of Rodriguez," for the sake of public tranquillity and the existence of the army. On the 23rd May the battalion left Santiago for Quillota, where Rodriguez was to be tried by court-martial as a disturber of public order. On the march an officer presented Rodriguez with a cigarette on which was written, "It would be well for you to fly."* On the evening of the 24th the party encamped on the banks of a stream. As night fell Navarro, with a corporal and two men carrying carbines, walked with Rodriguez into a gorge near by. Soon after a shot was fired. "Rodriguez is dead," said some officers in the encampment. Next morning his body was found covered with stones and twigs; his escort said he had tried to escape, and the affair was hushed up.

Of all the trophies of the victory of Maipó, San Martin had reserved only one for himself; this was the portfolio containing the secret correspondence of Osorio, which was found in his carriage when it was captured by O'Brien. On the morning of Sunday, the 12th April, San Martin, attended only by O'Brien, and taking the portfolio with him, rode out from Santiago some seven miles to a secluded spot called "El Salto." Procuring a chair from a house close by he seated himself under the shade of a tree, opened the portfolio and read the contents carefully. They were letters written by several of the leading citizens of Santiago to Osorio after the affair of Cancha-Rayada, declarations of their loyalty. Then asking for a small fire of sticks to be lighted in front of him, he burned them one

* Huya que le conviene.

by one, the wind carrying away their ashes; proofs of treachery which arose only from panic, were buried in oblivion. No one but himself ever knew who were the writers of these letters.

The next day he left for Buenos Ayres, on the same errand which had caused his sudden journey after Chacabuco, to concert measures for an expedition to Peru. On the 11th May, again avoiding a triumphal entry, he quietly took up his residence in his own house in the Argentine capital. Again the Argentine Government decreed him a commission as Brigadier-General; again he declined all promotion, but Congress insisted upon giving him a public vote of thanks, and a crowd of Argentine poets celebrated his victory in verse.

San Martin spent the whole of June in consultation with the members of the Lautaro Lodge, upon the means of fitting out a squadron for the Pacific. In July it was resolved that 500,000 dollars should be raised by a loan for that object, and soon afterwards Don Miguel Zañartu was officially received in Buenos Ayres as the representative of Chile.

San Martin then returned to Mendoza and made two attempts to cross the Cordillera, but was driven back by snowstorms, and remained there all the winter, nothing loth, for he found himself much more at home among the simple, bluff-spoken Cuyanos than in the more polished society of Santiago.

About the end of July he received a letter from Pueyrredon telling him not to draw upon the treasury as he had been authorized to do, for it was found impossible to raise the projected loan. San Martin at once sent in his resignation, which caused such consternation in official circles that he was again authorized to draw for the full amount specified. At that time there arrived in Mendoza various remittances of coin from Chile to merchants in Buenos Ayres. San Martin seized this money on the pretext that transit was not safe, which was quite true, and gave the owners drafts on the national treasury in exchange.

Pueyrredon, with great difficulty managed to pay these drafts on presentation, but he wrote to San Martin :—
" If you do that again, I am bankrupt, and we are lost."

With these resources and other remittances which followed, San Martin replenished the empty chest of the Army of the Andes with 200,000 dollars, and the situation was saved.

His spare time in Mendoza he filled up by making elaborate calculations concerning the men, arms, and equipment necessary for his projected expedition to Peru, while Pueyrredon and the diplomatic corps were as fully occupied in the construction of a scheme which was to render the expedition unnecessary. It was proposed that a conference of European powers should nominate a sovereign who should unite all the Spanish colonies south of the Equator under his sway. Of this monarchy San Martin and his army was to be the right arm. Of all this San Martin was fully informed, and to the scheme he made no opposition, but went on all the same with his calculations, till he crossed the Andes in October, and on the 29th of that month dismounted at the gate of his palace in Santiago full of hope, for his last letter from Pueyrredon announced the despatch of two vessels of war for service on the Pacific.

Bolívar, victorious in Venezuela and encouraged by the victory of Maipó, was at this time preparing for another passage of the Andes.

Spain in eight years of warfare had sent sixteen expeditions to America, with more than 40,000 veteran troops, had expended seventy-five millions of dollars, and seemed in no way as yet inclined to relinquish the attempt to subdue her rebellious colonies. She had yet 100,000 soldiers and militia in America, and was preparing a fresh expedition of 20,000 men for despatch to the River Plate.

Thus while diplomatists amused themselves and the world with visionary schemes for securing the independence of America, those more nearly interested in the question thought only of settling it by fire and sword.

CHAPTER XX.

THE FIRST NAVAL CAMPAIGN ON THE PACIFIC.

1818.

WHEN San Martin in 1814 at Tucuman first made a sketch of his continental campaign, he saw that the true road from Chile to Lima was by sea. At that time both oceans, from California on the Pacific to the Gulf of Mexico on the Atlantic, were dominated by the Spanish navy. Chile had but a few fishing-boats among the islands of the South Pacific, yet from the extent of her sea-line, from the number of her ports, and by her geographical position, shut in on a narrow strip of land between the Andes and the sea, Chile was eminently fitted to be a great naval power. Travelling by land was so difficult, that the sea was the natural road of communication between the different districts. In the forests of Arauco the pine and the oak tree flourished luxuriantly, her valleys produced hemp and flax in abundance. In the bowels of the earth were stored up vast supplies of copper, iron, and coal. Chacabuco and Maipó had secured the independence of Chile, but without a fleet further progress was impossible.

After Chacabuco the Spanish flag was still kept flying on the forts of Valparaiso. Deceived by this stratagem, the Spanish brig *Aguila* entered the harbour and was captured. She was armed with 16 guns and named the *Pueyrredon*, and an Irishman named Morris was put in command. His first exploit was to sail to the island of

Juan Fernandez to the rescue of the Patriots there imprisoned by Marcó and by Osorio.

Some months afterwards the *Wyndham* frigate of 44 guns anchored at Valparaiso. She belonged to the East India Company, and at the suggestion of Alvarez Condarco, then in London, had been sent there for sale. Guido raised a loan among the merchants of Valparaiso, and gave the guarantee of the Argentine Government for 50,000 dollars, so that the Government of Chile, in spite of the exhausted state of the treasury just before Maipó, purchased the ship for 180,000 dollars, and named her the *Lautaro*. She shipped a crew of 100 sailors of various nationalities, and 250 Chilians, soldiers, boatmen, and fishermen. The marines were placed under the command of Captain MILLER, an Englishman, and command of the ship was given to Captain O'Brien,* who had served in the English navy, with Turner as lieutenant. All the officers were either English or North Americans, except Miller; not one of them could give orders in Spanish. "Nevertheless," says Miller, in his Memoirs, "ten hours after sailing she fought and fought well."

The Spanish Pacific squadron at this time consisted of 17 ships, mounting 331 guns. After the victory of Maipó, O'Higgins ordered his two ships to put to sea in search of the Spanish ships which had been blockading Valparaiso. They sailed on the afternoon of the 26th April. At daybreak on the 27th the *Lautaro* sighted the 44-gun frigate *Esmeralda* making for the port, followed at some miles distance by the 18-gun brig *Pezuela*. O'Brien hoisted the English flag and sailed straight for her, till off her quarter and to windward, when he hauled down the English flag, hoisted the Chilian, and ran into her, exchanging a broadside. Followed by thirty or forty men, he then leaped on board, driving the Spaniards from the upper deck, and hauling down her flag. A shot from the lower deck killed

* No relation to O'Brien the aide-de-camp.

him, and he fell, shouting, "Stick to her, boys! The ship's ours."

But while the fighting went on the ships had separated. Turner, thinking the enemy was captured, sent off a boat with eighteen men to assist, and sailed off in the *Lautaro* against the *Pezuela*, which hauled down her flag without firing a shot. Meantime Coig, commander of the *Esmeralda*, had rallied his men, recaptured the upper deck, drove the rest of the assailants overboard, and on the return of the *Lautaro* made off, accompanied by the *Pezuela*, for Talcahuano, both of them being swifter ships than the *Lautaro*. On their way back to port the Chilian vessels captured a Spanish brig, whose value more than covered the cost of the *Lautaro*.

Government then bought an American privateer mounting 20 guns, and named her the *Chacabuco*. Soon afterwards an American brig mounting 16 guns was purchased, and named the *Araucano*. In August the ship *Cumberland*, purchased by Condarco in London, arrived, and was named the *San Martin*.

Chile had thus rapidly acquired a small fleet of her own, and, looking about for an admiral, she chose Don Manuel Blanco Encalada, a young officer of artillery. Born in Buenos Ayres of a Chilian mother, Encalada had adopted Chile as his country; he had held a separate command before the disaster of Rancagua, was among the Patriot prisoners rescued by the *Pueyrredon* from the island of Juan Fernandez, was present at Cancha-Rayada, and had distinguished himself at Maipó. He had previously served in the Spanish navy as a junior officer, and was at this time twenty-eight years of age.

On the 21st May a Spanish expedition of eleven transports, two of which were armed vessels, under convoy of the 50-gun ship *Maria Isabel*, sailed from Cadiz for the Pacific, carrying two battalions of the regiment of Cantabria, 1,600 strong, a regiment of cavalry of 300 sabres, 180 artillerymen and pioneers, with 8,000 spare muskets.

One of the transports was in such bad condition that they were forced to leave her at Teneriffe, and distribute her men among the other ships. Five degrees north of the equator the convoy was dispersed by adverse winds. On the 25th July the British brig *Lady Warren* reached Buenos Ayres, and reported having seen them about a month before. In consequence of this information the Argentine Government sent off the brig *Lucy*, flying the Chilian flag, and the brig *Intrepido*, flying the Argentine flag, each carrying 18 guns, with orders to double Cape Horn and join the Chilian squadron. At the same time word was sent to San Martin to invite the Chilian Government to despatch all their squadron against the expedition.

On the 26th August one of the transports named the *Trinidad*, with 180 soldiers on board, cast anchor at Ensenada, a port on the River Plate, some forty miles to the south of Buenos Ayres. She had separated from the convoy to the north of the equator, when the troops, headed by two sergeants and a corporal, had mutinied, shot their officers, and had compelled the master to sail for Buenos Ayres. The Argentine Government thus came to know the signals and the point of reunion of the expedition, which information they at once sent on to Chile.

Soon after this the 36-gun frigate *Horacio*, which had been purchased in the United States by Aguirre, the Argentine commissioner, reached Buenos Ayres, and announced that she was followed by the *Curacio* of the same armament.

On the 19th October the *San Martin*, Captain Wilkinson, the *Lautaro*, Captain Wooster, the *Chacabuco*, Captain Diaz, and the *Araucano*, Lieutenant Morris, sailed from Valparaiso. The squadron mounted 142 guns, and was manned by 1,100 men, most of whom were Chilians. The officers were nearly all English or North Americans. As O'Higgins, who had gone to the port to hurry on their departure, rode up the hill on his return to Santiago, he looked upon the four ships spreading their sails to a fresh sou'-wester, while the Chilian flag fluttered in the breeze from their mast-heads, and exclaimed,—

"Four ships gave the western continent to Spain; these four will take it from her."

On losing sight of land, Blanco Encalada opened the sealed instructions which had been given him, and found that he was ordered to the island of Mocha to await the Spanish convoy. The native Chilians were for the most part quite fresh to the service, but Miller, who sailed with the squadron, writes of them :—

"The native marines and sailors showed their good qualities, both as soldiers and sailors, by ready obedience; soon afterwards they showed bravery also."

A strong wind separated the *Chacabuco* from her consorts, who cast anchor on the 26th October at the Island of Santa Maria to await her, while the *Araucano* was sent back to reconnoitre the bay of Talcahuano, about forty miles to the north.

As the ships flew the Spanish flag a boat came off bringing a letter from the Admiral of the Spanish convoy to any transport that might touch there. This letter confirmed information already received from a whaler that the *Maria Isabel* had been there five days before accompanied by four transports, and had gone on to Talcahuano, while the rest of the convoy with crews sick and out of provisions had been unable to double Cape Horn.

Blanco Encalada sailed at once for Talcahuano. On the night of the 27th he arrived there with two ships, and learned that the *Maria Isabel* was alone in the bay; the transports, after landing 800 men, had gone on to Callao. On the morning of the 28th, with a fresh breeze, the two Chilian ships entered the bay and saw the Spanish ship at anchor under the batteries.

The *Maria Isabel* fired a blank cartridge and hoisted her flag. The *San Martin* replied with another blank cartridge and hoisted the English flag. When within musket shot both the Chilian ships hoisted their own flag with loud cheers, which immediately produced a broadside from the Spaniard. The *San Martin* replied with another and cast anchor within pistol-shot of the enemy, on which the Spaniard cut his cables and ran aground. Part of the crew landed in boats while the rest kept up a fire from the poop. The Chilian ships continued to fire till her flag was hauled down, when two boats put off to her with fifty men under Lieutenants Compton and Bélez, and took prisoners seventy men and five officers of the Cantabria regiment.

Encalada then landed two companies of marines to dislodge the Royalist troops on shore, who kept up a fire on the prize from behind walls on the beach; but Sanchez coming up with a strong force from Concepcion, compelled them to re-embark. In spite of the fire from shore every effort was made to set the prize afloat, but without success on account of the wind which blew from the sea.

During the following night preparations were made by both parties to continue the struggle next day. Sanchez placed four guns in battery on the beach, while Encalada swung the *Lautaro* round by an anchor from the poop, and brought her guns to bear on this battery and on the fort of San Agustin, which commanded the entrance of the bay.

At daybreak on the 29th both sides opened fire within pistol-shot of each other. About eleven o'clock a stiff breeze came up from the south, a cable was passed from the *San Martin* to the prize, the anchor was weighed, the sails spread with great rapidity, and she was towed off amid shouts of "Viva la Patria!" from the Chilians, mingled with loud "hurrahs" from the English sailors. The Chilian squadron celebrated their victory by a salute of twenty-one guns, and sailed out of the bay in triumph with their prize, which they at once named the *O'Higgins*.

The four ships of the Chilian squadron met again at the island of Santa Maria and were there joined by the Argentine brig *Intrepido*, Captain Carter, and the *Galvarino* under Captains Guise and Spry, who had both served in the English navy. The squadron now consisted of nine vessels, including the *O'Higgins*, with 234 guns.

One after another the rest of the transports fell into the hands of the Patriots to the number of five, with 700 prisoners. Four only, with 800 men, had reached Callao. From that date Spain lost for ever the dominion of the Pacific. The road for the expedition to Peru lay open.

Thirty-eight days after the four ships had sailed from Valparaiso, thirteen vessels carrying the Chilian flag anchored in line in the bay, amid the enthusiastic acclamations of the people.

On the 28th November, 1818, there anchored in the bay of Valparaiso a ship bringing as passenger one of the first sailors of Great Britain, who was yet to increase his fame by exploits in the New World. His name was THOMAS ALEXANDER COCHRANE, a name made famous by extraordinary deeds of derring-do. Born in Scotland of noble family, and lately a member of the British Parliament, he had been conspicuous among the Radical opposition, and was both hated and feared by the ruling party. Mixed up in Stock Exchange transactions of a doubtful character, he was condemned to a heavy fine and to exposure in the pillory, and was expelled from the House of Commons. The people paid his fine by subscription, Government remitted the degrading part of the sentence, and he was re-elected by the county he had represented. But he had had enough and more than enough of political life; he preferred exile and heroic adventures, and accepted the offers which were made him by Condarco and Alvarez Jonte, the agents of Chile and of San Martin in London. He decided to devote his services to the cause of independence in South America. Ere leaving his native country a farewell banquet was given to him by his admirers, at which he boldly proclaimed his radical principles in impassioned words, which give the key to his character—extreme in everything, in heroism, in hatred, or in love. The Chilian Vice-Admiral, in no way vainglorious of his recent triumph, acknowledged at once the superiority of Cochrane. He resigned the command of the squadron, and Cochrane was appointed Vice-Admiral in his stead.

Blanco Encalada was married to one of the most beautiful women in Chile; the wife of Cochrane, who came with him, was a most worthy type of British beauty, and was idolized by her husband. These two young wives became the stars of Chilian society on shore, whilst on the ocean the two Admirals sustained in honour the star of the young Republic which was emblazoned on the flag floating from the mast-heads of the fleet which now dominated the Pacific.

CHAPTER XXI.

THE REPASSAGE OF THE ANDES.

1818—1819.

WHILE in the years 1818 and 1819 the independence of Chile became firmly established, and in the north of the continent the revolution crossed the Andes and invaded New Granada, the prospects of the United Provinces clouded over; civil war blazed on the coasts of La Plata, and public opinion in Chile turned against the American policy of San Martin, while a fresh expedition of 20,000 men was assembling at Cadiz, destined for the River Plate.

In the South of Chile Chillán and Talcahuano were the strongholds of the Royalists. Concepcion was the centre of the reaction, while Valdivia and Chiloe gave them access to the sea. San Martin saw that no expedition to Peru was possible while this enemy remained in his rear. In September, 1818, Zapiola was strongly reinforced and was instructed to commence operations, but his force was still unequal to the task. In November Balcarce was sent south with an army of 3,400 men and eight light fieldpieces. In order to avoid useless bloodshed, San Martin proposed an arrangement to Sanchez for the evacuation of the territory. Sanchez referred him to the Viceroy of Peru.

In December Freyre crossed the Nuble with the vanguard and occupied Chillán, which was evacuated on his approach. In January Balcarce arrived with the bulk of the army, but Sanchez had already retreated from Concepcion and Talcahuano, and in spite of an active pursuit by Escalada and Alvarado crossed the Bio-Bio with small loss, and shut himself up in the fortress of Valdivia. This is spoken of as the last campaign in Chile, but bands of Indians and banditti still for three years infested the southern provinces.

José Miguel Carrera, still in Monte Video, fulminating vows of vengeance against Pueyrredon, San Martin, and O'Higgins, there met some French adventurers whom he succeeded in interesting in his cause. They went on to Buenos Ayres, and, after many secret consultations at the house of Doña Javiera, three of them left for Chile in November with a troop of bullock carts. Pueyrredon received secret information that another conspiracy was on foot, and sent a party after them to arrest them. One of them, named Young, attempting to resist, was shot. The other two, with some of their accomplices who had remained in Buenos Ayres, were tried by court-martial on a charge of conspiracy to assassinate. Three were acquitted, the other two, Robert and Lagresse, were shot on the Plaza del Retiro on the 3rd April, 1819, protesting their innocence to the last.

San Martin, on his return to Chile, found that the successes of the Chilian fleet had greatly relaxed the eagerness of the Government for the projected expedition. Now that they had command of the sea they were safe from invasion, and the treasury was so exhausted that the pay of his soldiers was very irregular. The people also murmured against a Government which relied for support upon Argentine bayonets. Nevertheless, he and O'Higgins both issued proclamations to the Peruvian people, announcing an expedition for the purpose of giving liberty to Peru: "So that they would become a nation with a Government established by themselves, in accordance with their own customs, with their situation, and with their inclinations."

Further, the Chilian envoy Irizarri, passing through Buenos Ayres on his way to England, there signed a treaty of alliance with the Argentine Government:—"To put an end to Spanish domination in Peru by means of a combined expedition."

In June, 1818, Bolívar stretched out the right hand of fellowship to the Argentine people by an official letter to the Government, and by a proclamation to "the inhabitants of the River Plate," in which he sets forth his favourite policy of a union of all the peoples of South America. Some months later on O'Higgins wrote to Bolívar, proposing to him an alliance based upon the continental ideas of San Martin.

San Martin had written from Mendoza to the Government of Chile and to Balcarce, informing them of his plans for the expedition to Peru, giving three months for collecting the necessary supplies. When he reached Santiago nothing had been done, and the revenues were mortgaged for months to come. He then wrote to the Argentine Government, giving a most miserable account of the financial state of Chile, and the consequent inefficiency of the Army of the Andes, which he suggested should be withdrawn from Chile as the projected expedition was for the time impossible. He also wrote to the Government of Chile, expressing his fears of the speedy dissolution of the united army, and proposed that a part of it should be employed in desultory attacks on the coasts of Peru, while he himself resigned the command.

On receiving no satisfactory reply, he concentrated the Army of the Andes at the upper part of the valley of Aconcagua, crossed over himself with a small detachment to Mendoza, and was soon after followed by a division of 1,200 men, by which operation he brought pressure to bear on the Chilian Government by leaving them to their own resources, while he recruited his cavalry in their own country, and preserved Cuyo from being drawn into the vortex of anarchy which at that time desolated the United

Provinces. In this internecine strife he took no part whatever, but the presence of a portion of his army in Mendoza strengthened the hands of Government and aided greatly in bringing about a truce.

The first news which San Martin heard on his arrival in Mendoza was an account of a terrible tragedy which had just occurred in San Luis. This city was the prison of the principal captives of Maipó and Chacabuco. They were well treated by Dupuy, the Deputy-Governor, who had only a picket of militia under his orders, and who trusted more to the wide Pampa which surrounded them than to prison walls for their security. The officers were not confined in the public prison, but lived in houses and mixed freely with the people. They were so many that they thought they would have no difficulty in overpowering the small garrison. A plan of escape had been for months discussed among them, when, on the 1st February, 1819, Dupuy, on account of the disturbed state of the country round, issued an order that they were not to leave their houses after sundown. Captain Carretero of the Burgos regiment was the head of the conspirators. On the evening of the 7th he invited a number of his comrades to breakfast with him the next morning, proposing to spend the day killing vermin in his orchard. At six o'clock next morning twenty officers met at his house; he led them into the orchard and gave them a light breakfast of bread and cheese washed down with brandy; then, drawing a poniard, he told them that in an hour they would all be free or dead, and distributed ten knives among them, telling the rest to arm themselves with sticks. Captain La Madrid was sent with ten men to seize the barracks, Captain Salvador, with six, to capture the prison and set the prisoners at liberty; while he went off to join Ordoñez, Primo de Rivera, and Morla, who, with their orderlies, would make sure of the Deputy-Governor.

The first party reached the barracks, disarmed the sentry, and overpowered the guard. In an inner yard were a number of Gaucho rebels under arrest, among them being one who afterwards acquired terrible notoriety as a Gaucho chieftain—Juan Facundo Quiroga. Quiroga led his fellow-prisoners to the assistance of the soldiers, and, armed only with the broken shaft of a lance, fought so fiercely that all the assailants except one were killed, and he was badly wounded.

The party sent against the prison on crossing the great square were met by the officer in command of the militia, who was galloping about with his sabre drawn, calling the people to arms. Armed men poured out of the houses upon them; only one escaped, the rest being killed.

Meantime Carretero, Morgado, and Morla had gone to Dupuy's house and asked to see him. Being admitted, they set upon him, and after a short struggle threw him down, when Ordoñez and Primo de Rivera entered with their orderlies, bringing the sentry with them, after shutting the outer door. But a militia captain and a doctor who were with Dupuy, had escaped and gave the alarm. A number of the townspeople, headed by a young officer named Pringles, surrounded the house with shouts of "Death to the Goths." Dupuy rushed to the door and opened it, the crowd poured in. Ordoñez, Morla, Carretero, and Morgado were killed. Primo de Rivera, finding a loaded carbine in an ante-room, shot himself through the head.

Of forty conspirators twenty-four were killed, the rest were tried by a court-martial, of which Dr. Monteagudo was President. Eight were acquitted, seven were shot, but young Ordoñez, a nephew of the General, was spared, partly on account of his youth, and partly because he was engaged to a young lady of the city, whose relatives interfered on his behalf. He was afterwards set at liberty by San Martin, who also gave Quiroga his freedom as a reward for his bravery, a favour which Quiroga never forgot.

Marcó del Pont, ex-Governor of Chile, was also at that

time a prisoner in San Luis, but took no part in the conspiracy and was not molested.

The repassage of the Andes by a portion of the army had the effect San Martin expected upon the Government of Chile. On his return from San Luis to Mendoza he found despatches awaiting him from Guido, from O'Higgins, and from the Lautaro Lodge, informing him that all were convinced that the safety of the country depended upon the despatch of the expedition to Peru. At the end of March Major Borgoño arrived as the representative of the Lodge, fully authorised to arrange all the details with him.

San Martin required an army of from 4,000 to 6,000 men, and a supply of 500,000 dols., of which he would provide 200,000 dols., furnished by the Argentine Government. He also accepted the rank of Brigadier-General in the Chilian army, which was again offered to him.

By return of post he received the ratification by the Lodge of the arrangement made with Borgoño, and an order to proceed at once to Chile to superintend the preparations.

It was in these circumstances, when he gave himself up entirely to the great work of his life, that he separated from his wife for the last time. She returned to Buenos Ayres never to see him again in this world. When he again saw his native land she was dead, leaving him one only daughter, who went with him into exile.

On the 19th June, 1819, Pueyrredon retired from public life into that obscurity which is the fate of great men when their appointed task is accomplished.

CHAPTER XXII.

COCHRANE—CALLAO—VALDIVIA.

1819—1820.

THE new Admiral when hoisting his pennant on the *O'Higgins* might, after the manner of the old Dutch admirals, have nailed a broom to his masthead; his commission was to sweep the Spanish fleet from the Pacific.

This ideal hero was one of the first sailors of the first navy of the world, and became indisputably the first in the naval annals of three Nations of South America, yet he never was master of his own destiny, he founded no school which should endue posterity with his spirit. With great faculties, both moral and intellectual, he had no political talent, there was no method in what he did. His exploits were performed under many flags, and in both the Old and in the New World, but he made no country his own. He left his native land with curses, he parted from Chile, from Peru, from Brazil, and from Greece in anger, stigmatizing them as ungrateful. He valued his deeds in gold as though they had been merchandize. Yet, in the abstract he was a lover of liberty; he placed his sword and his genius only at the service of some noble cause.

On the 14th January, 1819, he sailed from Valparaiso with four ships, the *San Martin*, *O'Higgins*, *Lautaro*, and *Chacabuco*, leaving Rear-Admiral Blanco Encalada to follow him. On the 10th February he was off Callao.

The bay of Callao is one of the largest on the South

Pacific. Near its centre stands the city of Callao, on the shore at the foot of the coast range of the Cordillera, three miles from the pass through it, which gives access to the beautiful valley of Rimac, in which stands the city of Lima. The port of Callao is a roadstead shut in by two islands. One of them, named San Lorenzo, is seven miles in length, and shelters the roadstead from all winds except those which blow from the west. Off its southern point lies a smaller island called the Fronton. The open water between the two islands is the main entrance to the inner bay, but between the Fronton and the land there is a much narrower passage, called the Boqueron, in which there are only five fathoms of water and many rocks. To the north of the island of San Lorenzo lies a sandbank, off the mouth of the river Rimac, which is called the Bocanegra.

The old walls of the city of Callao were destroyed by an earthquake in 1746. In their place three great circular castles were erected, crowned with lofty towers. Between them stretched the batteries of the arsenal and of San Joaquin, mounted with 165 heavy guns, which swept the whole of the roadstead. Under their fire the Spanish squadron lay at anchor, consisting of the *Esmeralda* and *Venganza*, 44 gun frigates; the corvette *Sebastiana*, of 36 guns; the brigs *Pezuela*, *Maipo*, and *Potrillo*, each of 18 guns; the schooner *Montezuma*, of 7 guns; the *Aranzazu* of 5 guns; and twenty-six gunboats, besides six armed merchant vessels.

The 28th February was the day fixed upon by Cochrane for the attack; the same day Pezuela had arranged for a review of the squadron and a sham fight. At daybreak a thick fog covered the bay, and the Viceroy embarked on the brig *Maipo*, the better to watch the manœuvres. At eleven o'clock, as the fog commenced to lift, the sailors of the *Maipo*, then near to the island of San Lorenzo, saw a fine ship flying the Spanish flag skirting the sandbank of the Bocanegra. The Viceroy wished to speak her, but the commander of the brig refused to go nearer as he would lose the wind. Pezuela was thus saved from falling a prisoner to Cochrane. The strange ship was the *O'Higgins*, which sailed on into the bay and captured a gunboat, followed only by the *Lautaro*, the other two ships being unable to enter the harbour for want of wind.

Favoured by the fog the two ships anchored within range of the batteries, hoisted the Chilian flag, and opened fire, but at nightfall slowly retired, with a few killed and wounded, and some damage to spars and rigging.

The next day the two ships again approached and drove the gunboats under shelter of the batteries, the Spaniards not daring to do more than remain on the defensive when they heard who was in command.

Cochrane had hoped to take the enemy by surprise, but having failed to do so he now tried to repeat his exploit of the Basque Roads, for which purpose he took possession of the island of San Lorenzo, and set to work to make two fire-ships. On the night of the 22nd March he engaged the attention of the batteries with his four ships while one of his fire-ships drifted down on to the Spanish squadron. But the fire-ship ran aground and was struck by a shot from the batteries, when the wind dying away he was forced to leave her to sink.

On the 24th he again attacked, and succeeded in capturing the schooner *Montezuma* and some merchant vessels and gunboats. The *O'Higgins*, at some distance from her consorts, was becalmed in a fog, and the Spaniards put off from shore in boats with the intention of boarding her. Fortunately a light wind sprang up before they reached her, and they were seen in time and beaten off.

Cochrane then retired to the neighbouring port of Huacho in search of fresh water, and was there joined by Blanco Encalada with the *Galvarino* and the *Pucyrredon*. Leaving the Rear-Admiral with four ships to blockade Callao, Cochrane sailed northwards, distributing proclamations from O'Higgins and San Martin, and also one from himself, among the people along the coast. At one place he landed and captured some brass cannon; then returning to Callao he found that Blanco Encalada had gone south in search of provisions, and seeing nothing more was to be done at present, he followed him.

Cochrane had brought with him from England a mechanic who had worked with Congreve at the Arsenal at Woolwich. He now set him at work to make rockets, and made trial of them in the bay of Valparaiso, expressing himself as perfectly satisfied with them. Government also furnished him with a nine inch mortar which had been sent from Buenos Ayres, and a 28-gun frigate, purchased in the United States and named the *Independencia*, was added to the squadron. A brigade of 400 marines was also organized under the command of an English officer of experience named Charles, with Major Miller as his second.

The *Pueyrredon*, the *Intrepido*, and the *Montezuma*, were sent southward on a cruise in search of some Spanish ships which were reported to be on the way from Europe, and, on the 12th September, Cochrane and Blanco Encalada again sailed from Valparaiso with six ships of war, and two of the transports which had been captured by Blanco Encalada on his first cruise, and which were intended for fire-ships.

Cochrane had such faith in the terrible power of his new rockets that he was confident of success, and wrote to O'Higgins that at eight o'clock on the night of the 24th, the Spanish squadron at Callao would be in flames.

On the 28th September he anchored off the island of San Lorenzo, and on the 30th sent a challenge on shore to the enemy to come out and fight ship to ship. The Spaniards, who had in the meantime greatly strengthened their defences, by surrounding their ships with a boom, and had prepared furnaces to heat shot, returned a laconic refusal.

This time the attack was to be made by four pontoon batteries, one carrying the mortar, two carrying rocket-tubes, and the other the ammunition. On the night of the 2nd October, Miller led the van in the *Galvarino*, with the mortar in tow, the *Pueyrredon* followed, towing the ammunition. Then came the other two pontoons towed by the *Araucano*, Captain Hind, and the *Independencia*, Captain Charles. All the crews of the pontoons wore life belts.

The action was commenced by the mortar, which opened fire at less than eight hundred yards distance from the boom, and sunk a gunboat. But after throwing several shells into the batteries, the mortar bed broke away from its bearings, and no more could be done. The distance was too great for the rockets which fell harmlessly into the water, and under the heavy fire from the batteries it was impossible to run closer in. A red-hot shot struck the pontoon commanded by Hind, and caused an explosion by which twelve men were badly burned. The *Galvarino* was struck several times, and Lieutenant Bayley was cut in two by a shot. At dawn the pontoons were recalled. In a subsequent attack an attempt was made to destroy the boom by a fire-ship, but the wind dying away, she became a target for the enemy's guns; she was already sinking when the match was lighted by Lieutenant Morgall, and she blew up before reaching the boom.

The rockets were found to be so inefficient, that Cochrane desisted for the time from any further attempt.*

The day after the last attack, a large ship was seen making for the port, which on sighting the Chilian squadron sheered off again. Cochrane followed, but taking her for a whaler, he returned to his anchorage and afterwards sailed to Arica. On his return he again saw the same ship, which sent a boat on shore. This ship was the 50-gun frigate *Prucba*, one of the vesssls which had been reported to be on the way from Europe. Three had left Spain in company bound for Callao, but one being found to be unseaworthy, had put back on

* See Appendix III.

reaching the line, and the other had foundered off Cape Horn.

Cochrane decided upon pursuing the *Prueba*, but as he had many sick he first sent Blanco Encalada with them to Valparaiso in the *San Martin* and *Independencia*, and despatched Captain Guise with the *Lautaro*, the *Galvarino*, and a transport with 350 marines on board, to Pisco, with orders to land there and procure a supply of fresh provisions. He then with the other three ships sailed for Guayaquil, where he captured two transports, each of which mounted twenty guns. From his prisoners he learned that the *Prueba* had been there, but after sending her guns on shore to lighten her, had gone up the river, and was now at anchor in shallow water under the protection of some shore batteries.

Soon after this he was rejoined by Guise, who had successfully accomplished the task allotted to him, but with some loss. He had found Pisco garrisoned by a force of 800 men, who were driven out by the marines at the point of the bayonet after some hard fighting, in which Colonel Charles was killed and Miller received three wounds. After holding the town for four days, he re-embarked the marines and sailed for Guayaquil.

Cochrane then sent the *Lautaro* to Valparaiso in charge of the prizes, and leaving the *Pueyrredon* and the *Galvarino* at the island of Puna, which commands the Gulf of Guayaquil, to keep watch over the *Prueba*, he sailed for the port of Santa, which lies to the north of Callao. Here he was soon joined by other ships of the squadron, which he sent back to Valparaiso, and sailed away south by himself in the *O'Higgins*. He was sorely disappointed with the ill-success of his attempts on Callao, and would not return to Valparaiso till he could return in triumph. He was turning over in his mind a daring scheme, equal to any that he had so far accomplished.

Pacing to and fro one day on his quarter-deck, as the good ship sailed steadily on towards the colder regions of the South, he met Miller, who, in spite of his wounds, had taken command of the marines on the *O'Higgins*, and asked him—

"What would they say if with this one ship I took Valdivia?"

As Miller made no answer, he added—

"They would call me a lunatic."

Lunatic or not, this was the exploit he had determined on attempting, and he further explained himself.

"Operations which the enemy does not expect are almost certain to succeed if well carried out. Victory is always an answer to a charge of rashness."

Valdivia from its fortifications and from its natural strength, was looked upon as the Gibraltar of America. The bay of Valdivia is an estuary into which the river Valdivia falls by two channels, forming an island known as the Isla del Rey. This estuary, which runs nearly due east and west, is about seven miles long, and its width at the mouth is about three miles, gradually diminishing until the width is little more than one mile, when the bay itself opens out in a magnificent sheet of water. In the centre of this bay and in front of the western point of the Isla del Rey stands a small island called the Mancera. On this bay there are several landing-places, but only one port, the Corral, and the coasts on both sides are fringed with steep or perpendicular rocks, and covered with dense brushwood. The bay has thus two coasts, one to the south the other to the north, which are separated by a wide space of open water, by the river Valdivia, and by the Isla del Rey. The northern part is inaccessible from the ocean, but at the western extremity of the southern part there is a landing-place where ships were accustomed to take in water.

At this time Valdivia was defended by nine forts and batteries, distributed on both sides of the bay, and armed with 128 guns. Two of these forts stood on the islands, and commanded both mouths of the river. On the north the entrance to the bay was guarded by an impregnable castle, called the Niebla, cut out of the solid rock, and by a battery, called Fort Piojo. On the south were the English fort, which commanded the watering-place, the fort of San Carlos, on a small peninsula, and Fort Amargos, whose fire crossed that of the Niebla. The entrance was further defended by the Chorocomayo redoubt and by the Castle of the Corral. Both these forts were masked by a dense forest, and the ground about them is so broken that their only communication by land was by a narrow path winding among the rocks and through the forest, and crossing a gulley which was commanded by the guns of both forts. Valdivia was ordinarily garrisoned by 800 troops and by as many militia, but at this time the militia were absent.

On the 18th January, 1820, the *O'Higgins* sailed into the bay, flying the Spanish flag. The Spaniards believed her to be the *Prueba*. Cochrane signalled for a pilot, who was sent off to him with a guard of honour, whom he made prisoners, and learned from them that the *Potrillo* was expected with money to pay the troops. He then proceeded in his gig to inspect the entrance to the river, under fire of the forts, for by this time his true character was discovered. Two days afterwards he captured the *Potrillo*, which had 20,000 dollars on board, but seeing that he had not men enough for an attack upon the place, he then went off for Talcahuano in search of more.

On the 22nd the *O'Higgins* reached Talcahuano, and was fortunate enough to find there the *Intrepido* and the *Montezuma*. Colonel Freyre, who was then in command of the fortress, eagerly entered into Cochrane's plans, and gave him 250 men under command of Major Beauchef. With this reinforcement he sailed again for Valdivia. On leaving the harbour the *O'Higgins* struck on a rock and commenced to make water rapidly, but the leak was patched up, Cochrane infusing his own spirit into his men, and declaring that she would float as far as Valdivia.

When out of sight of land he transhipped the marines from his flag-ship to the other two vessels, and went on with them, flying the Spanish flag till he arrived off the bay of Valdivia on the 3rd February, and signalled to the English fort for a pilot. But his ruse was discovered and the fort opened fire on him. Then, in spite of a heavy sea running, he determined to effect a landing in two long boats and a gig in which he went himself.

At the sound of the cannonade reinforcements had come up from the other forts, so that the garrison now numbered 360 men, of whom a detachment of 65 was thrown forward to protect the landing-place. At sundown Miller landed with 75 marines and drove in this detachment. He was followed by Beauchef with his 250 infantry, who pushed on up a narrow path and drew on himself the fire of the garrison, while Sub-Lieutenant Vidal skirted the wall of the fort, and finding a side entrance fired a volley in their rear, which so alarmed the defenders that they fled in panic, carrying with them the reserve who were drawn up on an open space behind.

Beauchef vigorously pursued the fugitives from fort to fort along the narrow path, till at daybreak the English fort, San Carlos, Amargos, Chorocomayo, and Corral were all in the hands of the Patriots, who had only nine men killed and 34 wounded. One hundred of the enemy escaped in boats, as many more were killed, the rest were either prisoners or dispersed.

At daybreak on the 4th the *Montezuma* and *Intrepido* sailed into the bay under the fire of the northern forts. To dislodge the enemy from these positions, 200 men were re-embarked, but the *Intrepido* ran on a sandbank off the Island of Mancera and sank; thus ended the career of the only Argentine ship which figured in the celebrated Chilian squadron of the Pacific.

Soon afterwards the *O'Higgins* appeared, and the Spaniards, abandoning the northern forts and the islands, fled to the city. The *O'Higgins* was leaking so badly that she was run aground in the mud to keep her from sinking. The next day the city was taken without resistance. Spain lost her last base of operations in the south of Chile, and Chile was now in possession of all her own territory except the islands of Chiloe.

Cochrane thought to finish his cruise by the capture of these islands, but Colonel Quintanilla, who was in command, was better prepared than was the garrison of Valdivia. A landing was effected on the 17th; a body of infantry was driven back and a battery was captured, but Miller, who led the assault on the principal fort, was again wounded, and the attack was repulsed. But the dominion of the Pacific was secured, and Cochrane returned in triumph. At Santiago he met San Martin, who, leaving Mendoza on the 20th January, had again crossed the Andes in pursuit of his great enterprise, and now found the road to Peru opened for him by the heroism of the great Admiral.

CHAPTER XXIII.

THE DISOBEDIENCE OF SAN MARTIN.

1819—1820.

THREE great duties pressed upon San Martin when he withdrew a part of his army to the east of the Andes. First, the prosecution of his plans for the liberation of America; second, his duty as a soldier to support the constituted authorities of his country in a time of civil war; and third, his duty as an Argentine in view of the expected expedition from Spain against the River Plate.

His opinion was in respect to the first, "that if the expedition to Peru is not carried out, everything will go to the devil;" in regard to the second, he had an invincible repugnance to mix himself up in internecine strife; in regard to the third, he could fight against Spain just as well on the West coast as on the East.

Thus, when he had procured through the Lodge authority from the central government to proceed with his plans, he thought only of how to carry them out, but fears of the expedition from Spain for some time yet perturbed all his combinations.

The Court of Spain thought with this new expedition of 20,000 men against Buenos Ayres to strike a mortal blow at the heart of the revolution in South America; but matters had changed considerably since the year 1815, when the last great expedition under Morillo, originally intended for Buenos Ayres, had been diverted to Venezuela. The insurrection had made great progress, and above all, Portugal was no longer the ally of Spain, and had seized Monte Video, which was the necessary base of any operations against Buenos Ayres. Further, the war against the colonies was very unpopular in Spain, not only among the people but in the army.

In spite of all this, the preparations were pushed forward. Six ships of the line, thirteen frigates, three corvettes, ten brigs, three schooners, twenty-nine gunboats, and forty transports, with from 18,000 to 20,000 troops, were under orders to rendezvous at Cadiz, under command of the Count of Abisbal, better known to history as José O'Donnell.

The Argentine Government had secret agents in Cadiz, who kept them well informed of all that went on. These men reported great discontent among the troops in cantonments on the island of Leon, and that there was a conspiracy on foot to proclaim the Constitution of the year XII., in which most of the superior officers were implicated.

General O'Donnell, aided by General Sarsfield, affected to join the conspiracy in order to discover the plan of it, but when it was on the eve of breaking out, issued a proclamation to the troops, calling upon them to adhere to their allegiance, and promising them, among other rewards for their loyalty, that they should not be sent to America. The leaders of the conspiracy were without difficulty arrested, but the projected expedition was thus prevented from sailing. In July, 1819, yellow fever broke out in the army; but in spite of all this, Government was still resolved to send off the expedition. The Count of Calderon was put in command, and the Minister of Marine was instructed, in September, to embark the troops at once.

In July of this same year 1819, General Rondeau was, by the influence of the Lautaro Lodge, appointed Supreme Director of the United Provinces in place of Pueyrredon. This was merely a change of names, the reins of power remained as before in the hands of the oligarchy which had ruled for so many years. One of the first acts of the new

Government was to send for San Martin to come to Buenos Ayres, to consult on the measures to be adopted in view of the threatened expedition from Spain. San Martin was himself full of apprehension, but without consulting his own Government, he proposed to O'Higgins that the Chilian squadron, under Cochrane, and in the pay of the Argentine Government, should sail to meet the expedition on the Atlantic and destroy it in the open sea, offering to pay at once 50,000 dollars towards the expenses.

This scheme would, he thought, have great attraction for the enterprising spirit of the Admiral, but Cochrane, bent upon destroying the Spanish fleet at Callao, would not listen to it until the business in hand was accomplished, when there would, he said, be ample time yet to meet the new fleet on the Atlantic and blow them to pieces with his Congreve rockets.

In answer to a second letter from Rondeau in August. San Martin offered to march with 4,000 men, of whom 3,000 would be cavalry, to drive the Spaniards into the river, as he had done before at San Lorenzo; "with sixteen squadrons and thirty light field pieces we can be sure of victory."

In October news was received in Buenos Ayres that O'Donnell had rebelled against the Spanish Government, and had marched with the army of Cadiz upon Madrid. This news was false, but it had the effect of causing Rondeau to countermand the orders for the concentration of the army.

Meantime the truce between the central Government and the Gaucho chieftains of the interior had come to an end. Ramirez from Entre Rios, and Artigas from the Banda Oriental, had joined hands with Lopez of Santa Fé, and war had again broken out on the northern frontier of Buenos Ayres. For the third time Government looked to San Martin for help, and ordered him to Buenos Ayres, with the division quartered at Mendoza. Just at the same time he received advices from Chile that all was ready for the proposed expedition to Peru. San Martin hesitated, but wrote to Government that he was about to march to Buenos Ayres with 2,000 cavalry and eight guns, but should leave his infantry in Mendoza. One battalion of infantry was quartered in San Juan, the grenadiers were in San Luis, and his total force of regular troops in Cuyo was now raised by recruiting to 2,200 men, besides which he had called out the militia of San Luis to the number of 2,000 men.

The idea of Government was to concentrate the whole army in the Province of Buenos Ayres to the number of 8,000 or 10,000 men, ready to act either against the Spaniards or against the Gaucho hordes, but as the latter numbered only 1,500, it was a most cowardly measure to abandon the northern frontier, menaced by the Royalists of Upper Peru, and to break the terms of the alliance with Chile, and could only have ended in the isolation of Buenos Ayres from the rest of the provinces. The civil war was a spontaneous effervescence of the people, and could not be cured by the sabre. It arose not only from the semi-barbarous instincts of the masses, but also from the discontent of the more educated classes with a political system which was not in accordance with the principles of the Revolution, and this discontent permeated the ranks of the army itself.

Rondeau, in pursuance of his plan, took the field with the Army of Buenos Ayres, and marched to the northern frontier of the Province, against the Gaucho hordes, seeking a junction with the Army of the North, coming from Cordoba. His army alone was superior in number to the enemy. Why, then, did he send for another army from Cuyo?

The real object of this concentration was that Gomez, the Argentine envoy in Paris, had entered into an arrangement with the French Government to crown the Duke of Luca, a Prince of the House of Bourbon, King of the United Provinces; France engaging on her part to divert the projected expedition from the River Plate, and to secure the acquiescence of Portugal and the evacuation of the Banda Oriental by marrying the future king to a Brazilian Princess. Congress, setting at naught the Republican constitution so lately sworn, and without any attempt to consult the will of the people, sanctioned this arrangement in secret session, and on the 12th November authorised their agent to conclude the treaty. As the Spanish expedition would thus be set free to act against Mexico, Venezuela, or New Granada, or to reinforce the Government of Peru, this was an act of treachery to the programme of the revolution and a desertion of the cause of America.

Rondeau was the last weak representative of the centralized system of government, which had so far led the revolution; now the Argentine people took the matter into their own hands, and by civil strife crushed out the last remnant of the colonial system. Now was heard for the first time among them the word FEDERATION. The people, groaning under a load of taxation to supply revenues in the disposal of which they had no voice, found the domination of Buenos Ayres equally oppressive with that of Spain, and gave a new interpretation to the word liberty: they now construed it to mean provincial independence.

At the close of the year 1819 the Army of the Andes was the only Argentine representative of the American propaganda. Stationed on foreign soil, it had escaped the contagion of party spirit, which had infected all the other armies of the Republic, and was ready to follow its great captain whithersoever he should choose to lead it.

Still San Martin hesitated. To obey Rondeau was to plunge into civil strife, to the destruction of his great plan; his regard for discipline impelled him to obey at any cost. He had already given orders to march, when news reached him that the Province of Tucuman had declared itself independent; that the army under Belgrano had mutinied and imprisoned its general; and that there was a similar conspiracy on foot in Cordoba among the officers of the army there, which had ramifications even in Cuyo.

He was suffering severely at the time from rheumatism, and leaving Alvarado in command of the division in Cuyo, he retired to the baths of Cauquenes in Chile, after writing to Rondeau that in view of these complications he had postponed the departure of the army until further orders; but before that he had written to O'Higgins asking him to collect mules in the valley of Aconcagua, in readiness for the day when he should recross the Andes.

Neither Rondeau nor Congress seem to have had any idea of the true state of affairs; they still thought that they could control public opinion by force, and the answer to the despatch from San Martin was a fresh order to him to march at once with all his army to Buenos Ayres. To this San Martin replied by sending in his resignation for the third time. Government refused to accept it, but gave him leave of absence until his health was restored.

The conduct of San Martin at this time has been very severely criticised, but there is no question that his 2,000 men would have been of no real assistance to Government, which fell a victim to its own errors and incapacity; and it is equally unquestionable that without him the expedition to Peru would never have set out. Without his co-operation the success of Bolívar in Columbia is highly problematical, and it is certain that had the Royalists been able to send another expedition from Upper Peru, they would have met no effective resistance in the northern provinces of what is now the Argentine Republic.

San Martin took upon himself the "terrible responsibility" of this disobedience, an act by which the accomplishment of the mission of emancipation which the Argentine people had undertaken was finally secured. Condemned by his contemporaries, he appeals to the judgment of posterity.

CHAPTER XXIV.

THE CONVENTION OF RANCAGUA.

1820

THE army of Cadiz, decimated by yellow fever, was for sanitary reasons dispersed. On the 1st January, 1820, Don Rafael del Riego, Colonel of the regiment of Asturias, then in quarters at the village Cabezas de San Juan, proclaimed in front of his regiment the constitution of the year XII., opening an era of liberty for his own country, and putting an end to an era of war in America. The revolution triumphed, the King was forced to swear the constitution, and, by common accord between the people and the government, a new policy was inaugurated in regard to the insurgent colonies, one that sought to solve peacefully the question which the appeal to arms had only made more complicated.

It was at this juncture that San Martin by his disobedience saved from destruction in the vortex of civil war the one army which could secure the emancipation of America. San Martin crossed the Andes carried in a litter, but it was not in mineral baths that he sought the cure for his rheumatism and neuralgia; that cure he sought and found in the active prosecution of the plan which lay at his heart.

Immediately on his arrival in Chile, he proceeded to concert measures with O'Higgins for the despatch of the expedition. He offered to bring over from Mendoza 2,000 men and ten guns, but terrible news soon reached him. The mutiny of the Army of the North had been followed two days after by a similar mutiny in the 1st battalion light infantry of his own army, then in quarters at San Juan.

San Martin thought he had secured Cuyo from the anarchy that prevailed by the presence of his disciplined troops, but when distinguished officers of his own army and of that of Belgrano headed mutineers and joined hands with Gaucho chieftains, he saw that the elements of order were dissolved. The Army of the North, under command of General Cruz, was on the march to join Rondeau, when in the Province of Santa Fé it made a truce with the Gaucho levies, styled "montoneras," and retreated to Cordoba, and there established a new system of military rule, withdrawing itself both from the civil war and from the war of emancipation.

The battalion quartered at San Juan was in reality a small *corps d'armée*, having both artillery and cavalry attached to it. It numbered 900 men and was under the command of Colonel Sequeira, a gallant officer, but a martinet who was greatly disliked by his men. At daybreak on the 9th January the men, headed by their sergeants, silently left their barracks, occupied the Plaza, and made a party of the civic guard prisoners, killing the officer; while the Colonel and some of his officers were left in the barracks under guard of a company. Some disaffected officers then took command, shouting, "Viva la Federacion!" and "Down with the tyrant!" but they had no plan of action, and soon quarrelled amongst themselves, and the Colonel and the officers who were with him were murdered. Alvarado marched against them from Mendoza, but fearing to trust his own men went back again. San Martin sent offers of pardon, which were rejected; the spirit of anarchy prevailed everywhere. The Governor of Cuyo and his deputy both resigned. The mutinous battalion soon after dispersed, and the

Province of San Juan declared itself an independent state. Alvarado then, in obedience to orders from San Martin, joined him in Chile with 1,000 cavalry and two guns, leaving Godoy Cruz as Governor of Mendoza.

On the 1st February, 1820, the Army of Buenos Ayres was totally defeated at Cepeda by the Montonera horsemen. Congress was soon after dissolved, and the nation split up into fragments, of which each one was a small republic, and most of them fell under the rule of petty chieftains. From this chaos was presently to rise up a new people, with well-defined divisions and with one national spirit. For a time the Army of the Andes obeyed no superior authority, but it still upheld the Argentine flag on foreign soil, and followed the lead of its own General.

Such being the state of affairs, San Martin, on the 28th January, wrote officially to O'Higgins, asking him if he could still dispose of 6,000 men for the expedition, but stating that 4,000 were absolutely necessary. O'Higgins replied that he could promise 4,000 only, fully equipped. San Martin agreed that they should march under the Chilian flag, but stipulated that the Army of the Andes should carry its own, as representing the United Provinces.

Thus San Martin took upon himself the "terrible responsibility" of disposing of Argentine troops and military stores, without any authority so to do from his own government. In order to relieve himself in some measure of this responsibility, he convened a meeting of the officers of the Army of the Andes, then in cantonments at Rancagua, under the Presidency of Las Heras. He himself was not present, but a letter from him was read, which showed that as the Government from which he derived his commission no longer existed, the army was *de facto* without a General, and called upon them to appoint one, to whom he offered his services in any capacity.

San Martin had requested them to vote without discussion, but Colonel Martinez and several officers opposed this, on the ground that the commission of General-in-Chief was granted for a specific purpose which was not yet accomplished, and was therefore not cancelled by the fall of the Government by which it had been conferred. In these terms a document was drawn up and signed by all the officers.

Las Heras, in writing to San Martin an account of the result of the meeting, expressed his great surprise that he should have given him such a task, and said that many of his best friends felt themselves greatly aggrieved at the proposition, as the commissions of all of them were derived from the same authority as that of the General-in-Chief. Thus the army endorsed the disobedience of their General, an act which under any other leader would have had a most evil effect upon its discipline.

While the preparations of the Chilian Government went slowly forward a new difficulty arose. Cochrane, proud of his recent triumph in Valdivia, aspired to the command-in-chief of the expedition to Peru. Devoid as he was of all political talent, a more unfit leader for such an enterprise it would have been difficult to find. Peru was not to be conquered, it was to be liberated; he thought only of conquest. He might have won a battle, but he would never have founded a nation. His dream seems to have been inspired by the examples of Drake and Anson, who made great profit by gallant feats of arms; he purposed to enrich himself and his sailors by plundering the coasts of Peru. San Martin was an American, and thought only of his great purpose, nothing of its results to himself. On the 6th May, 1820, San Martin was appointed by the Senate and by the popular vote, Generalissimo of the expedition.

Still Cochrane insisted, and several times sent in his resignation. Government was about to appoint Guise to the command of the fleet, as Spry and many others of the English officers preferred him to Cochrane, but this was prevented by the intervention of San Martin, and the proud sailor at last submitted, though with a bad grace, after another fruitless attempt to supplant San Martin by Freyre. The Chilian Government was not to be led astray by national susceptibility, and knew that no Chilian officer could compare with San Martin in military capacity.

San Martin knew the importance of a thorough understanding between himself and the Admiral, and went to visit him at Valparaiso, but in spite of his friendly overtures there was never much cordiality between them.

The presence of San Martin and his army was not only a great burden to the Chilian treasury, but it was also a political peril, of which Government was well aware. Party spirit was only kept in check by the danger which menaced the country from Peru, and personal ambition would impel party leaders to seek the aid of so powerful an auxiliary so long as it was at hand. The Government of Chile in sending off the expedition, thus performed a deed of heroism which was not only conducive to their own security as a nation, and was worthy of the gratitude of America, but was also one that saved the political situation in their own country.

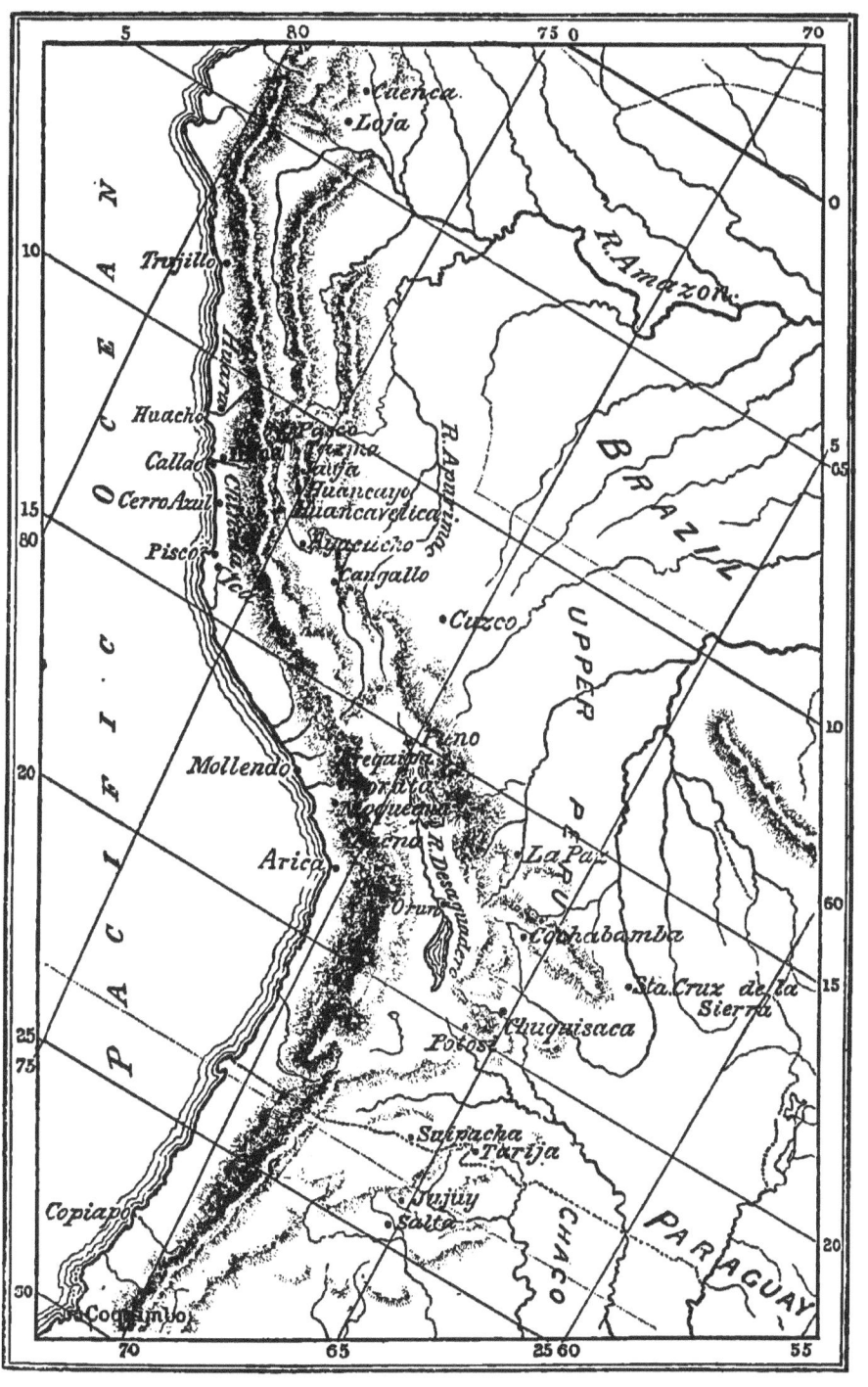

II.—MAP OF THE VICEROYALTY OF PERU, INCLUDING UPPER PERU.

CHAPTER XXV.

PERU.

1820.

PERU was the first of the American colonies in which, at the era of the Conquest, the spirit of rebellion against the Mother Country broke out. During the Colonial epoch the mixed races frequently rebelled against their Spanish masters. At the end of the eighteenth century Tupac-Amaru, who came of the old royal race of the Incas, made an attempt to restore the kingdom of his forefathers. But these insurrections had no root in the soil, they were but the convulsive efforts of a conquered race reduced to slavery. When they were quelled the country remained at peace for many long years. Peru, like to one of the tracts of perennial calm upon the ocean, felt nothing of the currents which ebbed and flowed around her; she was isolated from the world; the movements which convulsed America in 1809 and 1810 were hardly felt there. The instinct of nationality, which is the germ of independence, was not entirely wanting; but there was no cohesion among the masses of the people, whose inertness presented a dead weight against the progress of the revolutionary idea.

Peru was at the Conquest truly an imperial colony, embracing all the Spanish possessions in South America, from Cape Horn to the Equator. The word Peru became synonymous with wealth. After the creation of the Viceroyalties of New Granada and La Plata, that of Peru still stretched over a vast area, extending 25 degrees south of the Equator, and from the Pacific to the frontiers of Brazil, while its central position gave it a paramount influence over all its neighbours.

Lima was the capital of this imperial colony. This city stands not far from the sea, in a beautiful valley, at the foot of the Western Cordillera, where rain never falls, and where the thunder is heard to roll and the lightning is seen to flash but once in a century. A transparent veil of clouds tempers the fiery rays of the sun, while the moist southern breeze imparts a softness to the atmosphere which has its reflex in the temperament of the people.

Lima rivalled Mexico in wealth, and was the seat of a viceregal court, with its privileges, its pomps, and its enervating vices. It was also surrounded with walls, and Callao, with its castles and batteries, was but the port of the great city. She had also an official Church, a corrupt clergy, and an inquisition, the only one which had burnt heretics in America. Three-fifths of her population, like to that of ancient Rome, was composed of slaves, freedmen, and tributary Indians, with a passion for bull-fights they had learnt from the Spaniards, and for chicha,* which they inherited from the Incas. Her women were celebrated for beauty and grace, and she was the natal city of the patron saint of America, Santa Rosa de Lima, among whose relics are shown the dice with which she played with her Divine spouse.

Situate in the tropic of Capricorn Peru has every climate known in the world, ranging from the torrid zone at the sea level to the eternal snow of her Cordillera. The Creoles of Peru were by nature intelligent, and cultivated science and the arts. They had also a literature of their own. The *Mercurio Peruano*, published in the eighteenth century, was the first periodical printed in South America.

* An intoxicating drink made from maize.

The University of Lima was as famous in America as that of Salamanca in Spain; the skill of her physicians was renowned all over the continent. Peru was also the centre of the Royalist reaction; for ten years she had held the revolution in check. Thus it was when the emancipating armies from the north and from the south closed in upon her in the year 1820. She was the Carthage of San Martin.

At the outbreak of the revolution Peru proper had a population of about a million and a half, and Upper Peru had nearly half a million. Of these the indigenous races formed about half, mixed races a fifth, negro slaves about fifty thousand, and Spaniards hardly a seventh, the remainder being Creoles, the descendants of Europeans born in America. The North and the South of Peru were two separate countries, which looked with jealousy one on the other, even for many years after they became one nation. The highlands of the interior and the lowlands of the coast were also two entirely different regions. The inhabitants of the lowlands were enervated by the climate, but the mixed races which inhabited the hills were very athletic, and made excellent infantry.

Spaniards and Creoles dwelt in cities on the coast, or in fertile valleys among the mountains. The indigenous races, who were serfs, were almost entirely confined to the hills; the mixed races and free negroes formed the working classes of the cities; the farms were cultivated by African slaves. The Peruvians were thus a people who had no cohesion among them, and were easily dominated by the powerful military clique which ruled the colony, while their passive inertness was a formidable barrier to the spread of revolutionary ideas among them.

In 1810 General Abascal was Viceroy of Peru; he was already old, but was possessed of great talents, both political and military. He was one in whom prudence was blended with decision and with perseverance. The flames of insurrection blazed around him, but he showed a bold front to the storm, and made Peru the citadel of the colonial power. If it had been possible to conquer the revolution he would have conquered it; as it was he greatly retarded its progress.

To counteract the contagion of the revolutionary spirit, he inspired the Peruvians with a spirit of devoted loyalty to the mother country, and to her exiled King. On the basis of the few Spanish troops he had with him, he raised a native army, recruited in the Highlands and officered by Peruvians. Their own generals led them to victory, till the struggle, from being a revolt against the domination of Spain assumed the aspect of a civil war, in which Americans fought against Americans in defence of American ideas.

Thus Abascal quelled the rebellion in Quito, stemmed the tide of Argentine invasion, and reconquered Chile. He was then reinforced by troops from Spain, led by generals who had proved their skill in the War of the Peninsula. The revolution was crushed wherever it had broken out, save only in the United Provinces and in a part of Venezuela. In 1817 the passage of the Andes by San Martin put a stop to his success. Chacabuco and Maipó turned the tide of victory against him, and the Royalist reaction was shut up in the Highlands of Peru, where the principle of loyalty to the flag of Spain had taken deep root in the hearts of the people.

Meantime Abascal had retired from the scene, full of years and of glory, and left Pezuela, the hero of Upper Peru, as Viceroy in his place. In 1816 General José de La Serna had arrived from Spain with reinforcements, and with a commission as General-in-Chief of the armies of Upper Peru. He was an experienced soldier, but was characterized by a moderation which made him at times irresolute. In politics he professed Liberal principles, and soon acquired a great ascendency over the army, introducing a new influence which later on had very important effects.

Although Peru was the centre of the Royalist reaction, nevertheless the American sentiment of independence was still latent within her, but the want of cohesion among the various races which formed her people rendered her helpless to work out her own destiny. All nations have passed through these periods of impotence. Chile and New Granada, under much better conditions, would never have redeemed themselves without Argentine and Columbian intervention.

The revolutionary movements of the year 1809 found an echo in Lima, and a young lawyer named Mateo Silva fell a victim to his patriotic ardour, dying in the casemates of Callao, after six years of imprisonment. In 1810 another conspiracy was discovered, and was also crushed; but the progress of Liberal opinion in Spain had its effect in Peru. From the mother country came liberty of the press in 1811, and in 1812 the establishment of Cabildos was decreed by the Regency of Spain, when Peruvians for the first time made use of the right of election. But when the Spanish Constitution fell in 1814, liberty of speech fell with it in the capital of Peru.

In 1811, 1812, and 1813, various insurrectionary movements, fomented by Argentine emissaries, broke out in Upper Peru, but were promptly crushed with great severity. In 1814 a much more formidable insurrection broke out in Cuzco, the ancient capital of the Incas, in which the clergy took a prominent part. In August a Junta was formed under the auspices of the Cabildos, General Pumacahua, a pure Indian, being named President, and José Angulo Captain-General. The new Government erected two gibbets in the principal square as a sign of their authority, devised a flag, raised an army, cast small cannon, and despatched emissaries to enter into alliance with the Argentine Provinces. Their first operations were crowned with success. Arequipa fell into their hands, and an expedition to the east captured the city of La Paz; but their hordes of half-naked Indians, armed with pikes and slings, were totally routed in two battles with great slaughter by troops from Lima, supported by militia. General Ramirez, being detached from the army of operations in Salta with 1,200 men and four guns, speedily retook La Paz and Arequipa, and in March, 1815, marched against the insurgents under Pumacahua, 20,000 strong with thirty-seven guns, cut them to pieces, and put an end to the insurrection. The head of Pumacahua was stuck on a post in the great square of Cuzco. Angulo and other leaders were shot.

From that time the Patriots of Peru thought no more of achieving liberty by their own efforts, but they continued their propaganda among the people by means of secret societies, which had their head-quarters in Lima. In 1817 these societies opened communication with San Martin, who responded to their overtures by sending Torres on a special mission to Lima, as is recorded in Chapter XVII. Torres in his secret interview received very valuable information from the Patriot leaders concerning the plans of the Viceroy and the forces at his disposal, and concerted with them the means of regular communication. The subsequent appearance of the Chilian squadron on the coast, and the proclamations of O'Higgins, San Martin, and Cochrane, greatly raised their hopes, and information furnished by them was of great service to the admiral in his operations. He was accompanied by Alvarez Jonte, who acted as intermediary between him and the Patriots of Peru, and was the bearer of special instructions to them from San Martin, who directed them to make no insurrectionary movement until he was in a position to support them, when local outbreaks might be of service in distracting the attention of the enemy.

San Martin also sent off to Peru three young officers of his, who were Peruvians by birth, one of whom betrayed his trust, and caused the arrest of several of the Patriots; but the other two fulfilled their mission with great skill, so that even in the army the revolutionary spirit made great progress. Colonel Gamarra, who was in command of troops drawn from Upper Peru, was discovered to have secret correspondence with Belgrano, but the Viceroy dared not prosecute him from fear of arousing a mutiny among his men.

Pezuela was fully alive to the dangers of his position, and wrote earnestly to Spain for support. At the same time he instructed his successor in command of the Army of Upper Peru, to advance into Argentine territory. La Serna was driven back by Martin Güemes and his gauchos, but in this campaign saw such evidence of the superior quality of his troops that he thought it necessary to take precautions against possible disloyalty among them. He accordingly put an end to their independent organization, and drafted them into his Spanish regiments, a measure which was eventually productive of great evil to the Royalist cause.

The American officers were all staunch Royalists, but the Spanish officers were more or less infected with the new ideas. Thus, the *morale* of the Army of Upper Peru became greatly deteriorated. A part of it was soon after withdrawn to Lower Peru to reinforce the army there, in preparation for meeting the threatened invasion from Chile, upon which La Serna, alleging that he held his commission direct from the King, and had the right to dispose of his troops as he chose, threw up his command. Olañeta, a Peruvian and an ardent Royalist, was appointed to succeed him, and La Serna retired to Lima.

The Royalist army was at this time led by many distinguished officers, among them being Camba, the historian, and Valdés, who was held by Americans to be the most skilful and the most noble of all their adversaries. The army which held Lima was more than 8,000 strong, that of Upper Peru was more than 7,000. The total force, including detached garrisons, consisted of 23,000 men, against whom San Martin matched himself with 4,000 men in the last struggle for the independence of America.

CHAPTER XXVI.

THE EXPEDITION TO PERU.

1820.

From Valparaiso, on the 22nd July, 1820, when on the eve of sailing on his daring enterprise, San Martin addressed a proclamation to his fellow-countrymen in justification of his refusal to enter into their civil discords, showing how the intervention of his army could only have added to their miseries, prophesying that when tired of anarchy they would seek refuge in oppression, and concluding:—

"Whatever be my lot in the campaign of Peru, I shall prove that ever since I returned to my native land her independence has occupied my every thought, and that I have never had other ambition than to merit the hatred of the ungrateful and the esteem of the virtuous."

Later on he wrote to the Cabildo of Buenos Ayres, announcing the departure of the expedition, and declaring that:—

"From the moment a central authority is established the Army of the Andes will hold itself subject to its orders."

The expedition took the name of "The Liberating Army of Peru." It consisted of six battalions of infantry and two regiments of cavalry, in all 4,430 officers and men, of which more than half belonged to the Army of the Andes, with thirty-one guns, two howitzers, and two mortars, and also spare arms and equipment for 15,000 men. General Las Heras was chief of the staff, having with him Arenales and Luzuriaga; Guido also went with his friend the general-in-chief as aide-de-camp, with the rank of colonel.

The squadron consisted of eight ships-of-war, mounting 247 guns, victualled for six months, and carrying 1,600 seamen and marines, of whom 600 were foreigners, chiefly English; also of sixteen transports, with four months' provisions for the troops, and eleven gunboats. The military chest contained 180,392 dollars in coin and in letters of credit.

On the 20th August the expedition sailed from Valparaiso, Cochrane leading the way in the *O'Higgins*, San Martin and his staff bringing up the rear in the *San Martin*. The Chilian Congress had drawn up most implicit instructions for San Martin for the regulation of his policy in establishing an independent Government in Peru. O'Higgins had issued a proclamation to the Peruvian people, telling them that the object of the expedition was simply to liberate them from Spanish domination, and that they should be perfectly free to adopt any form of government they thought best; he knew also that in the face of a foe greatly superior in strength no general could afford to tie himself down to one fixed line of conduct; he therefore never delivered these instructions to San Martin, but left him perfectly free to carry out his own plan as he might deem it best. To Cochrane his instructions were very explicit, absolute obedience in everything to the orders of the commander-in-chief.

San Martin had thought of landing in the south of Peru, and effecting a junction with Belgrano; recent events rendered this impossible. His object now was to avoid coming into contact with the Royalist forces and to prevent their concentration, while he won over the people to act in concert with him, and arranged a combined plan of action with Bolívar, who was now master of New Granada.

With these ends in view he effected a landing at Pisco, after a pleasant voyage of eighteen days, with the idea of drawing the attention of the enemy to the south and away from the real base of his operations, which he purposed establishing in the northernmost province of Trujillo. Cochrane tried in vain to persuade him to land near to Callao and march at once upon Lima.

The beach of Pisco is a long stretch of sand, lying at the foot of the Cordillera, about 160 miles south of Lima. In it the sea has cut out the bay of Paracas, seven miles to the north of which stands the town of Pisco, close to fertile valleys running up between spurs from the great mountain range.

The first division, under Las Heras, disembarked in the bay on the 8th September, and the same evening occupied the town without resistance. On the 13th the whole army was on shore and encamped in the valley of Chincha, while scouting parties scoured the country.

The Viceroy had scattered his forces all along the coast from Guayaquil to Arica. A detachment of 500 infantry, 100 horse, and two guns, under Colonel Quimper, was stationed at Pisco, but fled precipitately when the squadron anchored in the bay.

On landing San Martin issued a proclamation to his army:—

"Remember that you are come, not to conquer but to liberate a people; the Peruvians are our brothers."

He denounced the most severe penalties on any found plundering or maltreating the inhabitants, and also issued a proclamation to the Peruvians, telling them that the new constitution established in Spain had in no way changed her colonial system:—

"*The last Viceroy of Peru* endeavours to maintain his decrepid authority. I come to put an end to this epoch of sorrow and humiliation."

The invaders drew plentiful supplies from the surrounding country, mounted their cavalry and recruited their infantry with 600 slaves, giving freedom to all who would join their ranks.

Pezuela, very much against his will but in obedience to orders received from the Home Government, was at this time preparing for the public swearing of the new constitution, when, on the 11th September, he received news of the landing at Pisco. He at once sent a squadron of militia to reinforce Quimper, and stationed Colonel Camba with 2,000 horse on the high road from Lima to Pisco, and, in accordance with his instructions, proposed peace to San Martin, on condition that Chile should send representatives to the Spanish Cortes to arrange their differences. Similar proposals he also sent off to the United Provinces. By this measure he recognised Chile and the United Provinces as belligerent powers, but without directly acknowledging their independence.

San Martin appointed Guido and Garcia del Rio commissioners to treat with those of the Viceroy, who were the Count Villar de Fuente and Captain Capaz, late commander of the *Maria Isabel.* These commissioners met at the town of Miraflores, seven miles from Lima, and at once arranged an armistice.

The Chilian commissioners declined to accept the Spanish Constitution, and rejected the proposal to send Chilian deputies to the Cortes, on which the Royalist commissioners proposed that the invading army should return to Chile, and that everything should remain in *statu quo*, whilst Chilian representatives went to Spain and there arranged matters with the Home Government. The others acceded to the proposition that Chile should send representatives to Spain, but proposed that the army should occupy the provinces of Potosí, Cochabamba, Chuquisaca, and La Paz, considered to be the Argentine section of Upper Peru; that the Spanish garrison of Chiloe should be included in the armistice; and that in case Bolívar should conclude a similar armistice with Morillo, the Viceroy of Peru should not reinforce the garrison of Quito.

Neither party would consent to any modification of the terms proposed by them, so the conference came to an end on the 1st October. In a private interview with the Viceroy the Chilian commissioners had insisted upon the independence of Peru as a preliminary step to any arrangement, but had expressed their willingness to accept a Prince of the Royal House of Spain as monarch of Spanish America.

The Viceroy and his commissioners threw the blame of the rupture of the negotiations upon San Martin, which accusation he answered in a dignified address to the Peruvian people.

The armistice came to an end on the 5th October, and on the same day Arenales left the encampment in the valley of Chincha, at the head of a strong detachment of the Patriot army, for the Highlands, while San Martin masked the movement by manœuvring with the rest of his army on the road to Lima.

On the 24th October, San Martin issued a decree establishing the flag and escutcheon of the new Republic of Peru, the flag white and scarlet, the escutcheon a sun rising over mountains with a tranquil sea at their feet. On the following day he re-embarked his army and sailed off for the North, apparently leaving Arenales behind him, but in reality going off to meet him.

Cochrane in his Memoirs severely criticises the disembarkation and delay at Pisco, but Camba, who was better able to judge, speaks of this measure as the first step in the destruction of the military power of Peru. The same opinion was expressed by Pezuela in his report to Government. Cochrane seems to have been anxious only to conquer the country; the object of San Martin was to revolutionize it by winning the confidence of the Peruvian people, and so securing their concurrence in founding a republic of their own, which concurrence as yet only a minority of them were prepared to give.

CHAPTER XXVII.

THE OPENING OF THE CAMPAIGN.

1820—1821.

THE Generalissimo of the Liberating Army of Peru had two campaigns before him—one military, of which he carried the plans in his own head; the other political, the secret ramifications of which were in his own hands. The first described a circle, one half of which was drawn along the coast by the keels of Cochrane's ships; the other half was drawn through the Highlands of Peru by the feet of the flying column under Arenales. These two halves separated at Pisco to reunite in the north, enclosing Lima between them.

The second was more complicated. The idea was to raise into activity the moral force of public opinion, stirring up a spirit of insurrection among the Peruvian people, without the aid of which his military force was inadequate to the task before it. From Pisco he flooded the country with proclamations, and organized secret agencies in Lima and throughout the interior.

On the 29th October the squadron sighted the island of San Lorenzo, and, passing it, entered the Bay of Callao, sailing in regular order beyond the range of the batteries, a glorious pageant. The ships of war came first, with their crews at quarters and the guns run out. Then came the long line of transports, their decks crowded with troops in all the varied uniforms of the Liberating Army, including those of the division left behind under Arenales. The walls of the city and the heights behind were crowded with spectators. One of these spectators, who has described the scene, says: "The Liberating expedition and the capital of Peru were on mutual exhibition."

A part of the squadron remained to blockade Callao, the rest, with the transports, sailed on to the Bay of Ancon, twenty-two miles to the north of Lima. Two hundred infantry and forty of the grenadiers, under Captain Brandzen, landed, under command of Major Reyes, a Peruvian, with the object of occupying the village of Chancay, and collecting horses and provisions.

The Royalist army, encamped at Asnapuquio, six miles from Lima, sent against them a column of 600 men, under Colonel Valdés, upon which Reyes retired. Brandzen, who brought up the rear with his forty horsemen, turned upon the enemy as they passed a narrow defile, and charged with such impetuosity that he drove their cavalry back in confusion upon the infantry, and gained time for Reyes to make good his retreat with all the cattle he had collected.

Meantime two important events had occurred. Guayaquil had pronounced in favour of the Revolution, and Cochrane had cut out the frigate *Esmeralda* from under the guns of Callao.

The province of Guayaquil, once a dependency of Peru, now formed part of the Viceroyalty of New Granada, being attached to the district governed by the Captain-General of Quito, but from the exigencies of the moment was for a time again under the rule of the Viceroy of Peru. The port of Guayaquil was the arsenal of Spain on the Pacific, and, Callao being blockaded, was now the last refuge of the navy dispersed by Cochrane, and was garrisoned by a strong battalion of Spanish infantry.

Quito had remained quiet since the outbreak of 1809, but the advance of Bolívar on the north, the invasion of Peru by San Martin, and the victories of Cochrane on the

Pacific, aroused a dangerous excitement among the people. On the 9th October a part of the garrison of Guayaquil rose in arms, and was supported by the people. The Province joined the movement, declared itself independent, appointed a Junta, and placed itself under the protection of San Martin and Bolívar. Melchor Aymerich, an experienced officer, was at this time Captain-General of Quito, and had 5,000 men under his command, exclusive of the garrison of Guayaquil.

The active spirit of Cochrane found nothing more to do upon the ocean. The Spanish fleet was reduced to three frigates, the *Prueba*, the *Venganza*, and the *Esmeralda*. The two first, after bringing from the southern ports a division of the army of Upper Peru, had taken refuge at Guayaquil. Cochrane boldly determined to capture the other frigate by cutting her and some smaller vessels out from under the fire of the 250 guns mounted on the batteries of Callao, a feat which would increase his renown, and might induce San Martin to adopt more active operations against Lima, for the Admiral had no sympathy for his dilatory proceedings. He informed San Martin of his intention, and the Generalissimo accepted the idea with enthusiasm.

Anchored near to the *Esmeralda* were the corvette *Sebastiana*, two brigs, two schooners, and three armed merchant vessels, within a semicircular line of twenty gunboats, all shut in by a boom, through which there was only one narrow entrance. Cochrane asked for volunteers. The whole of his crews offered themselves. From them he selected 160 seamen and 80 marines. Three days he employed in preparing fourteen boats, and in instructing the men. On the night of the 4th November the flotilla assembled alongside the flag-ship, under lee of the island of San Lorenzo, where they could not be seen from shore. On the 5th the three other vessels of the blockading squadron were sent for a cruise outside. The Spaniards, thinking the blockade was raised, celebrated the occasion by a banquet on the *Esmeralda*. After sundown, amid complete silence, an address from the Admiral was passed round the boats :—

"The moment of glory is approaching. I hope that the Chilians will fight as they have been accustomed to do, and that the English will act as they have ever done at home and abroad."

Men and officers were all dressed in white, Cochrane himself wearing a blue band round his arm. At half-past ten the fourteen boats pulled with muffled oars silently away in two parallel lines, one led by Captain Crosbie, the other by Captain Guise. Cochrane went himself in another boat ahead of the rest. The British frigate *Hyperion*, and the United States frigate *Macedonia*, lay at anchor outside the boom. As the boats passed by the latter ship, her officers, in low voices, wished the crews good luck; but an officer of the *Hyperion*, who shouted "Hurrah!" as he saw them, was put under arrest, for Cochrane was not popular with the commanders of British ships, whatever sympathies he might have among the men. The last boat of the flotilla remained alongside the *Maccdonia*, and Cochrane, knowing nothing of the desertion, went on, followed by only thirteen boats.

It was very dark when at midnight they reached the passage through the boom. It was guarded by a gunboat. Cochrane, pistol in hand, sprang on board, threatening instant death to any man who spoke. The crew surrendered, and the boats rowed on unperceived straight for the *Esmeralda*, where Captain Coig and his officers, after their banquet, were playing cards in the cabin. Cochrane, leaping into the chains, was the first on board, but was knocked back into the boat by the sentry on the poop. In a moment he was up again, followed by his crew. The sentry fired, but was immediately cut down.

"Up, my lads! she's ours!" shouted Cochrane to the other boats, and then hailed the tops, which were already occupied by men previously told off for the purpose. The sails of the ship were at his orders, but the deck was yet held by the Spanish marines, who had seized their arms on hearing the shot fired by the sentry.

Cochrane, with the boats led by Crosbie, had boarded on the starboard quarter; now Guise and his division boarded on the port side. The two parties met on the quarter-deck, Guise and Cochrane shaking hands in the enthusiasm of the moment. From the forecastle the marines opened fire upon them. Cochrane was shot through the thigh. Seating himself on a gun, he bound up the wound with his handkerchief, and ordered a charge on the enemy. Twice the assailants were beaten back, and Guise was wounded; but again he led on the boarders, and the crew of the *Esmeralda* were either forced overboard or driven below the hatches.

The alarm-gun roared from the castle of Real Felipe; a gunboat opened fire on the frigate, by which Captain Coig was severely wounded, and one Chilian and two English seamen were killed. The other ships beat to quarters. Guise, who was now in command, saw the imprudence of attempting any further captures. He ordered the cables to be cut, the sails were set, and the *Esmeralda* sailed away in the hands of her captors. The ships and the shore batteries opened a heavy fire upon her. Some of the shot passing over the *Hyperion* and *Macedonia*, these vessels hung out distinguishing lights. This contingency Cochrane had foreseen. Immediately similar lights were displayed on the *Esmeralda*, and at half-past two she anchored off the island of San Lorenzo. The boats followed her with two gunboats in tow which they captured as she sailed off.

The loss of the expedition was eleven killed and thirty wounded. The Spaniards lost about 160 men killed or drowned, and 200 prisoners.

The Royalists on shore accused the neutral ships of complicity in this shameful defeat, more especially the men of the *Macedonia*, whose sympathy for the cause of South American Independence was well known. Next day, when one of her boats was sent ashore as usual for provisions, the crew was barbarously massacred by the infuriated populace.

Cochrane sent a flag of truce on shore proposing an exchange of prisoners, to which the Viceroy acceded. About 200 Chilians and Argentines, who had languished for years in the casemates of Callao, thus recovered their liberty.

The *Esmeralda* was renamed the *Valdivia*, in honour of Cochrane's victory of the year before.

The moral effects of the capture of the *Esmeralda* were very great, but from a political point of view the revolution in Guayaquil was of yet more importance. Still San Martin turned a deaf ear to the counsels of Cochrane, who advised an immediate advance upon Lima, and on the 9th the convoy weighed anchor at Ancon, and sailed to the port of Huacho, which lies ninety miles to the north of Callao. On the 10th the disembarkation commenced, and D'Albe, the French engineer, threw up three redoubts to secure the place. He also improvised a mole to facilitate communication with the squadron.

The army marched inland, and on the 17th encamped in the beautiful valley of Huara, which is well watered, and abounds in trees, and was reputed healthy; but fevers are endemical along the coast in the summer, and dysentery in the autumn.

This valley is seven miles broad by fifty-two miles in length, and is intersected by a river of the same name which flows from the Cordillera to the sea. This river is fordable at several points, but offers many strong positions for defence against superior forces, of which San Martin took advantage, and established himself solidly on its bank, ready to act either on the defensive or on the offensive, as occasion might require. In his front stretched a sandy desert, while one of his flanks rested on Huacho, and the other on the Sierra. In this position he held Lima in check, cut off all communication between the northern provinces and the capital, could either advance or retreat at his pleasure, and was ready to effect a junction with Arenales when he should make his appearance.

Pezuela occupied the entrenched camp at Asnapuquio with nearly 7,000 men. He had sent off a small division against Arenales, and now threw out a vanguard of about 2,000 men to keep watch over the movements of San Martin. With this vanguard was the battalion of Numancia, the men of which were for the most part natives of Venezuela, and the officers were all Americans. The emissaries of San Martin had been actively at work with this battalion, and both officers and men now only waited for an opportunity to join the army of the Patriots. San Martin determined to give them this opportunity.

The cavalry being now well mounted, he detached Alvarado with 700 horse against the enemy's vanguard. Alvarado marched away along the coast on the 24th November, sending Lieutenant Pringles in advance with eighteen grenadiers, as escort to a messenger who carried a missive to inform the disaffected regiment of the approach of the Patriot cavalry, and was charged to concert measures with them for their evasion. Pringles had strict orders not to fight on any account, but, after marching all night, he found himself at daybreak on the 27th close to the entire vanguard. In front was an advance party consisting of a squadron of dragoons led by Valdés. Upon them he charged impetuously with his eighteen men, but was beaten back. Finding his retreat cut off by another squadron, he attempted to cut his way through it, but lost three men killed and eleven wounded. Seeing escape was impossible, he then plunged into the sea with such of his men as could follow him, but, when Valdés galloped forward promising quarter, he surrendered.

The fifteen prisoners were paraded in triumph through the streets of Lima, where the account of this skirmish excited great enthusiasm. They were afterwards exchanged, and Pringles was tried by court-martial. He was censured for disobedience to orders, but both he and his companions received a badge of honour bearing the words, "Glory to the vanquished in Chancay."

The skirmish with Pringles disclosed to Valdés the proximity of the Patriot cavalry, on which he retired from the coast into the valley of Chancay, placing the Numancia battalion on guard in the pass. Alvarado found his way into the valley by another pass; but his men and horses were so fatigued by the rapid march that he was forced to withdraw to a neighbouring farm in search of rest and forage. On the 1st December he again came up with the enemy, who retreated through a rugged defile, the Numancia battalion being left seven miles to the rear of the main body. On the 3rd this battalion took advantage of its position to join the Patriot column unmolested, a welcome contingent of 650 bayonets.

San Martin declared that "the battalion belongs to the army of Columbia, but shall remain incorporated with the army of Peru till the close of the war." He showed his confidence in his new troops by confiding the flag of the Liberating army to their care.

These events encouraged the spirit of insurrection throughout Peru, which extended even into the ranks of the army. Hardly a day passed without some desertions being reported. On the 8th December thirty-eight officers and a cadet fled from Lima, and the leaders began to lose confidence in each other. Some of the principal citizens of Lima presented an address to the Viceroy, urging upon him the necessity of an honourable capitulation with San Martin. He was generally blamed for the untoward progress of the war, but was, in reality, powerless, his authority being undermined by a conspiracy which existed in the army to supplant him by La Serna.

On the 29th November San Martin drove the Royalists out of the populous department of Huaylas, which lay in his rear. The people, to the number of 70,000, swore the independence of Peru, immediately after which the whole of the Northern Provinces pronounced spontaneously in favour of the Revolution.

These were the producing provinces of Peru, and the chief source of the wealth of the Viceroyalty. They were almost entirely included in the Intendency of Trujillo, and had a mixed population of some 300,000 souls.

A Peruvian general, known as the Marquis of Torre-Tagle, was at that time Governor of Trujillo, and had been in secret correspondence with San Martin since he landed at Pisco. On the 24th December Torre-Tagle convened an open Cabildo at Trujillo, when, after showing the hopelessness of resistance to the superior force of San Martin, he advised submission. The Royalists, headed by the Bishop, stoutly opposed the proposition. He answered their arguments by shutting them up in prison, and on the 29th raised the banner invented at Pisco, and, with the mass of the people, swore to maintain the independence of Peru. In memory of this event, Trujillo bears to this day the name of "Departamento de la Libertad."

Torre-Tagle then called upon the city of Piura to join the movement. This city was garrisoned by a Royalist battalion, and the people were unarmed; but the attitude of the Patriot leaders was so determined that the soldiery disbanded. In this way the whole of the North of Peru, from Chancay to Guayaquil, fell into the hands of the Patriots, and San Martin secured a safe base of operations, from which he could draw supplies and horses, and which gave him at once a reinforcement of 430 infantry and 200 cavalry.

On the 5th January, 1821, San Martin advanced with his whole army to Retes, seeking a junction with Arenales. La Serna, who was now in command of the Royalist army, with Canterac as chief of the staff, immediately prepared to attack him in a most disadvantageous position, but lost so many days in these preparations in consequence of the inefficient state of the army, that the friends of San Martin in Lima had time to advise him of his danger. Meantime he was joined by Arenales, and at once retired to his former position in the valley of Huara. The opportunity thus lost greatly increased the unpopularity of the Viceroy with the army. The effects of the blockade of Callao by Cochrane began now to be severely felt in Lima, and were greatly aggravated by the operations of bands of guerillas which San Martin had organized among the country-people. An Argentine from Salta named Villar, who had been a prisoner in the casemates of Callao, was the commander of these guerillas. They infested all the roads leading to the capital, and frequently destroyed small detached parties of troops or outposts of the Royalist army.

From Huara San Martin decreed a "Provisional Regulation," by which the territory occupied by the Patriots was divided into four departments, each under a President, who had under him governors of districts, while a Court of Appeal was established at Trujillo. This was the first attempt at Constitutional administration in Peru, and prepared the way for a National Government.

In three months San Martin had achieved success as great as the winning of a pitched battle could have given him, a result which amply falsifies the accusations of inactivity or timidity which have been brought against him, for these successes were gained by an army of 4,000 men opposed to one of 23,000.

CHAPTER XXVIII.

THE FIRST CAMPAIGN IN THE HIGHLANDS.

1820—1821.

PERU may be looked upon as a conglomeration of mountains, enclosed within a sort of triangle, whose base on the third degree of south latitude measures about eight hundred miles, from which it extends southward for about fifteen hundred miles to the southern frontier of Upper Peru on the eighteenth degree of south latitude, where the width of the triangle is reduced to about sixty miles. This territory comprises three zones; the coast zone, the highland zone, and the mountain zone. Along the shores of the Pacific ocean lies a belt of sand, never more than sixty miles in width, cut by twenty-three rivers, which flow from the Highlands to the sea through fertile valleys, separated by deserts of sand-hills, moved to and fro by the winds; on which sand-hills there is no sign of vegetation, neither are there birds in the air, nor reptiles on the earth; a far-stretching series of deserts on which rain never falls. This is the region now in part occupied by San Martin and his army.

On the east of this "Tierra Caliente" rises abruptly the western range of the Andes; further still to the east stretches the huge line of the true Cordillera. Between these ranges there lies in Upper Peru a vast tableland, but in Lower Peru the intervening space is intersected by numerous valleys and by the Andine lakes, which are sometimes as much as 16,000 feet above the level of the sea.

Under the Viceroys, Lower Peru was divided into eight

"Intendencias": the most northern of these was that of Trujillo, which was also the largest in extent, and by geographical position formed a distinct country. Those of Lima and Arequipa extended along the coast, those of Cuzco and Puno lay further inland to the South, bordering upon Upper Peru; while in the centre lay the Intendencias of Huancavelica, Huamanga, and Tarma. These three form the Highlands of Peru, and are intersected in every direction by foaming torrents, passable only by suspension bridges hanging from cables of raw hide.* The only roads from the coast into this region pass by deep gorges through the coast range of the Cordillera, and wind round the higher mountains along the edge of precipices, ever ascending till they reach the tableland lying between the range and the main Cordillera.

General Arenales had already distinguished himself in mountain warfare, as is set forth in Chapter V., and was thus selected by San Martin at Pisco to command the flying column, which was to make its way through the Highlands and rejoin the main army in the North, which went by sea. The chief object of this expedition was to spread the revolutionary propaganda through the interior of the country, but it would also distract the attention of the enemy, and possibly prevent the concentration of his forces at Lima.

The column consisted of two battalions of infantry under Major Dehesa and Colonel Aldunate; one squadron of cavalry under Major Lavalle, and two guns. Colonel Rojas was chief of the staff. On the night of the 5th October Arenales marched in a south-easterly direction upon Ica, where Colonel Quimper was stationed with 800 men. At his approach two companies of infantry passed over to him, and Quimper hastily retreated along the coast. He was pursued by Rojas with 250 men, and overtaken at the village of Nasca. The Patriot cavalry, led by Lavalle, charged at once, and taking the Royalists by surprise, utterly routed them, with a loss of 41 killed and 86

* For a description of a similar bridge in Chile, see Appendix IV.

prisoners. On the following day, the 16th October, Lieutenant Suarez, with thirty light horse, captured the baggage, so that the first force detached from the army of Lima against the expedition was totally destroyed.

The movements of Arenales were so well masked by the manœuvres of the main army, that the Viceroy knew nothing of them until the 30th October, and then allowed several days to pass before he sent off reinforcements into the menaced district. Thus Arenales ascended the mountain passes unopposed, and on the 31st October occupied the city of Huamanga, after a march of 255 miles in ten days. Here he gave his troops some rest, but sent out detachments under Lavalle and Rojas, who routed several parties of the enemy very superior in number, and captured the city of Tarma, so that by the 21st November he was in complete possession of the valley of Jauja, which is watered by the Rio Grande.

After arming the militia and giving some political organization to the liberated districts, he marched on Pasco, which O'Reilly had occupied with a division of 1,000 men, sent from Lima. On the morning of the 6th December, during a heavy fall of snow, he occupied a hill in front of the town but separated from it by a small lake and by marshes. O'Reilly on perceiving him, drew up his men in front of the town, but the Patriot infantry led by Aldunate and Dehesa, advanced resolutely under fire of the artillery, and drove them back into the town at the point of the bayonet, where they dispersed, while Lavalle, wading through the marshes, charged the enemy's cavalry and put them to flight.

The trophies of this smart action were 343 prisoners, including General O'Reilly and Colonel Santa Cruz, a regimental flag, and two guns; but the most important effect of the victory was to open the road for communication with San Martin at Huara.

Arenales had left a strong rear-guard at Ica under two officers named Bermudez and Aldao, who being attacked by very superior forces, were compelled to follow the main body up the mountain passes to Huancayo, and were much harassed on their way by hordes of Indian slingers.

Meantime the Spanish General, Ricafort, who was on the march from Arequipa to Lima with a detachment of the reserve, heard of the doings of Arenales and ascended from the coast into the Highlands, where he was joined by a reinforcement from Cuzco, and having collected 1,300 men marched upon Huamanga. Here he was met by a horde of Indians, who had broken out in insurrection, and having got possession of some guns and a few muskets, opened fire upon him from the high ground in front of their city. He had no great difficulty in defeating them and gave no quarter. The fugitives being joined by other parties of insurgents, then occupied the village of Cangallo with about 4,000 men. Ricafort marched against them with 400 infantry and 200 horse, and again routed them on the 2nd December, killing a thousand of them without losing one man. The village was sacked and burnt.

Ricafort then returned to Huamanga, and then learning that Bermudez and Aldao had put themselves at the head of the insurgents of Huancayo, marched against them with his whole force, dispersed the raw Indian levies, captured the town and sacked it. Aldao, who with a small body of horse, had greatly distinguished himself in this affair, retired to Jauja, where, quarrelling with Bermudez, he put himself at the head of the insurrection in conjunction with Otero, an Argentine, who had been appointed Governor by the Patriots. Then learning that Arenales had marched to the coast, he retreated to Reyes, but afterwards hearing that Ricafort had withdrawn his force from the Highlands and gone to Lima, he returned, re-occupied Huancayo, and raised an army of 5,000 Indians, to which he gave some rough sort of military organization.

Arenales rejoined the main army on the 8th January, 1821, after a triumphant march of 840 miles through the centre of the enemy's territory, with a hostile army on each side of him.

CHAPTER XXIX.

THE ARMISTICE OF PUNCHAUCA.

1821.

AT the commencement of the year 1821 the Royalist cause appeared completely lost in Peru. Pezuela, at a council of general officers, declared, without reserve, "the impossibility of continuing the defence of the country."

This speaks highly for the political and military talents of San Martin, who in four short months had achieved this result. That the Spanish leaders, abandoned by the mother country, should raise up the fallen standard of the King, and with resources drawn from the country itself should maintain the struggle for yet another four years, speaks quite as highly for their talents and energy.

When Badajoz was besieged by the French in 1811, Colonel Menacho, who was San Martin's first chief, was in command of the garrison. He died, and in a council of war then held, one officer only voted for holding out. The city surrendered. The following year the Regency, with the approval of the Cortes, declared that in such a case, "if one officer voted for resistance, even though he was a subaltern, the garrison should not capitulate, and the said officer should take the command." The leaders of the Spanish forces in Peru maintained that this decision gave them the right to refuse to surrender. The Liberal ideas brought by late reinforcements from Spain, while they weakened political authority, strengthened the power of the military element.

The ill-concerted measures adopted by the Viceroy to meet invasion, the timid prosecution of the war, and the successes of the Patriots, deepened the antagonism of the different parties into which the Royalist camp was divided. The idea of treachery on the part of the Viceroy became general; it was believed that he contemplated a shameful capitulation. Before adopting extreme measures, the Liberal leaders, headed by La Serna and Valdés, prevailed upon Pezuela to create a "Junta of War," which worked like a fifth wheel in a coach; and the inactivity of the Viceroy on the occasion when San Martin advanced to Retes, precipitated matters. It was resolved to depose him.

On the night of 28th January, 1821, La Serna withdrew from the encampment at Asnapuquio. The next day Canterac and Valdés paraded the army, and the officers being convened to a council of war, summoned the Viceroy to lay down the supreme command in four hours, "as the only means of preventing disturbances and preserving Peru to Spain." Pezuela resigned, and the power fell into the hands of the Spanish Constitutionalists, who were thus forced, in defence of the rights of the mother country, to fight in the cause of an absolute King, against their own principles as upheld by the Patriots of America.

The first act of La Serna, now Viceroy, was to invite San Martin to send Commissioners to a conference, for the purpose of putting an end to the disputes between Spaniards and Americans. San Martin joyfully acceded, and named Guido and Alvarado representatives of the Patriot cause. La Serna on his side appointed Colonels Valdés and Loriga.

The Commissioners met at a farm-house near Retes, when the Spanish officers presented a modification of the proposals of Miraflores, on the basis of the acceptance of the Spanish Constitution. The others declined to negotiate on any other basis than the recognition of the independence of Peru.

Alvarado then asked Loriga to walk out with him, leaving the other two to discuss the question. The Spanish officer accepted the invitation, and during their promenade informed Alvarado that they thought of abandoning Lima and retiring to the more healthy Highlands, where, with abundant supplies at command, they could easily beat off any attack of the Patriots. This information was the only immediate result of the conference, but it gave rise to further negotiations, on the basis of the establishment of an independent monarchy in Peru.

The change of Viceroys in no way improved the position of the Royalists; on the contrary, fresh disasters befell the army of Lima, and the new general fell into the same errors as his predecessor. The scarcity of provisions became worse in the city, and yellow fever broke out in the army, while the arrival of a royal commissioner from Spain prevented La Serna from taking any decided step.

The condition of the Patriot army at Huara was not much better. It also suffered greatly from fever, so that barely a thousand men were fit for service. San Martin himself fell ill, but his guerillas cut off supplies from Lima, and expeditions along the coast or into the Highlands kept the enemy in continual alarm.

On the 25th March the envoy from the new Government of Spain, a naval officer named Abreu, arrived at Huara, where he was well received. Four days he remained there, holding long conversations with San Martin, for whom he conceived a great admiration. At his instigation La Serna attempted to negotiate privately with San Martin, but San Martin replied that he would listen to nothing which was not proposed officially, and about the same time sent a column of his sickly troops, commanded by Miller, to act under Cochrane's orders against Callao, and another under Arenales into the Highlands. Then leaving a strong rear-guard in charge of the hospitals and park at Huara, he embarked the rest of his troops in transports, and dropped down the coast to Ancon, whence his cavalry, aided by guerillas, scoured the country, and shut up the Royalists within a small triangle formed by the encampment at Asnapuquio, Lima, and Callao, and there awaited the opening of a formal negotiation.

After the Liberal movement in Spain in 1820 the revolusionists of South America were no longer spoken of as rebels or insurgents, but were recognized by the Home Government as belligerents, and were now invited by King Ferdinand, by a proclamation, to treat for peace with their brethren of the old country, "as their equals," but they were offered only the Constitution of 1812, which they had already rejected by declaring themselves independent, and were threatened with forcible compulsion in case of refusal. This olive-branch of peace, wafted across the seas, only supplied fresh fuel to the flames of war.

Envoys from Spain bearing this message of peace had reached the northern part of the continent in December, 1820, during an armistice between Bolívar and Morillo. They had persuaded Bolívar to send Columbian commissioners to Spain, but in April, 1821, before anything could be known as to their prospects of success, hostilities recommenced, and there were no further attempts at negotiation.

To Mexico also the same message was sent, a message apparently one of peace and conciliation, which, when looked into, was seen to mean submission or war, and to which, in Mexico as elsewhere, answer was given in one formula, independence or war.

When in 1820 the revolution broke out in Spain the revolution in Mexico was crushed. General Vicente Guerrero, with a handful of men, alone upheld the flag of insurrection in the rough country to the south. In Mexico the movement was chiefly the work of the indigenous element of the population, and assumed the character of a rising of the proletariat against the superior classes, thus arousing a spirit of resistance in the country itself, which powerfully aided the efforts of the Royalist troops for its suppression. But amid this discord of opinions a sentiment for independence was latent in the hearts of all, so that the defeat of the insurrection combined with the Liberal movement in Spain to bring about a pacific evolution.

The proclamation of a Liberal *régime* in the mother country produced in Mexico a split among the various parties who had upheld the colonial system. While Spaniards became Absolutists or Constitutionalists, the natives became Republicans or Monarchists. Apodaca was at that time Viceroy. He put himself at the head of a reaction, and is said to have been incited thereto by the King, who, fearful of the fate of Louis XVI., proposed withdrawing from Europe to Mexico, there to reign with absolute power, free from the trammels of a Constitution. This reaction could not triumph without the aid of the native Monarchists.

Among the Creoles who had served in the Royalist ranks, and had distinguished himself by cruelties to his own countrymen, was a man named Agustin Iturbide, then thirty-seven years of age. Unscrupulous in the pursuit of wealth, of life either dissolute or ascetic as best served his interests, and with some natural talent, he was possessed by a secret ambition, in which race-patriotism had a place. His sleep was broken by envious dreams of the laurels gained by Bolívar and San Martin, and though lacking the great qualities of either of them, he aspired to be the liberator of Central America. This was the man selected by Apodaca to aid his plan of reaction, by leading the natives to support his policy. He appointed him Commandant-General of the South, and sent him with a division of native troops to stamp out the embers of insurrection kept alive by Guerrero. Iturbide soon came to an understanding with Guerrero and threw off the mask.

On the 24th February, 1820, in the town of Iguala, one hundred and twenty-seven miles from the city of Mexico,

Iturbide published a document known to history as the "Plan of Iguala." In it he proclaimed the independence of Mexico, and at the same time hoisted a flag symbolic of the new revolution, a tri-colour, white, red, and green; white signifying religious purity, red signifying friendship with Spain, and green signifying the hope of emancipation. The plan was in three parts, from which it took the name of the plan of the "three guarantees," a name which was also applied to the army which upheld it. The first part stipulated the establishment of the Catholic religion to the exclusion of every other; the second part declared Mexico an independent state, under a monarchical government tempered by a constitution; the third part stipulated the union of Americans and Europeans. King Ferdinand was recognized as Emperor of Mexico, if he would come and swear to the constitution, and after him his brothers in natural succession; in default of whom, Congress should name a prince of one of the royal houses of Europe. Further, the equality of all the races—indigenous, African, and European—was proclaimed, without other distinction between them than that given by individual merit or virtue.

The leaders of the insurrection, with Guerrero, abjuring for the moment their Republican principles, placed themselves under the orders of Iturbide for the sake of national independence. The Creoles who had opposed the revolution gave in their adhesion to the new "Plan." The clergy adopted it in hatred of the reforms of the Spanish Liberals; the Spanish Absolutists in hatred of the Constitution; and the Constitutionalists for the sake of peace. The whole country pronounced in favour of the "Plan of Iguala." The Royalists, conquered without fighting, held only the capital, the port of Vera Cruz, and the fortress of San Juan de Ulua. In July, 1821, Iturbide was acclaimed Liberator of the country.

By this means a solution was found for the dilemma—submission, or independence and war. The bond with the mother country was untied but was not broken. Thus was it understood by O'Donoju, the successor to Apodaca, who subscribed to the "Plan of Iguala" by treaty, in August, 1821.

In Brazil, about this time, took place an evolution similar to the plan proposed by Iturbide, while in Columbia the armistice was broken, and in Peru negotiations, based on ideas similar to those enunciated in the "Plan of Iguala," came to an end.

We have nothing more to do with the history of Mexico. Suffice it that the Spanish Government rejected the treaty signed by O'Donoju; that Mexico was lost for ever to Spain; that Iturbide seated himself on the vacant throne and was crowned Emperor, only to be deposed soon afterwards and banished. On attempting to recover his dignity he was shot.

The negotiations initiated confidentially by the Viceroy in Peru were more formally carried forward by an official invitation from him. La Serna appointed Don Manuel de Llano y Najera and Don Mariano Galdiano, both of whom were Americans, as colleagues to Abreu. San Martin appointed Guido, Garcia del Rio, and José Ignacio de la Rosa, formerly Governor of San Juan, to represent the Patriots. The farm-house of Punchauca, fifteen miles from Lima, was made the meeting place of the Commissioners. Neither party made any preliminary stipulation, both professed to be anxious for peace and union.

The Royalist Commissioners were instructed to propose the acceptance of the Spanish Constitution, with some concessions in detail, in accordance with the spirit of the proclamation of King Ferdinand. Those of the Patriots were instructed by San Martin to reject the Spanish Constitution as a bond of union, and to insist upon the recognition of the independence of Chile, of the Provinces of the River Plate, and of Peru, without consenting to any armistice, except on this basis. In case it were proposed that the Patriots should send Commissioners to Spain to treat of this matter, they were to demand, as a preliminary, the evacuation of Lima, and were to refuse to enter into any treaty for the conduct of the war, which had been spoken of, as it had up to then been carried on in accordance with the law of Nations.

The Royalist Commissioners opened the discussion by presenting a note, on the 4th May, 1821, stating that in regard to the suggestion made by San Martin at Miraflores, that independence should be secured by the establishment of a monarchy with a sovereign from the royal house of Spain, they had no power to make any such arrangement, and recommended the adoption of the Spanish Constitution since it was a proof of the liberal sentiments of the Spanish Government and of their desire for reconciliation. Further, they proposed an armistice, while commissioners were sent by both parties to Spain, as had been done by Bolívar in Columbia. To this the Patriot Commissioners replied, on the day following, that no negotiations could be entertained except on the basis of the recognition of independence, but in view of the inability of the Spanish Commanders to make this recognition, they were willing to consent to a suspension of arms, with some guarantee, and that they hoped no further mention would be made of the Spanish Constitution, the very name being obnoxious to the liberties of the New World.

To this no answer was given, but an armistice of sixteen months was proposed by the Royalist Commissioners. Then the Patriots demanded that the fortifications of Callao should be handed over to them intact, as a guarantee, to be delivered up if hostilities should again break out, and their note concluded as follows :—

"If Don José de San Martin be determined to achieve the independence of America by arms or by negotiation, he is no less desirous of uniting this part of the New World to the mother country by those bonds of friendship and commerce which would redound to the prosperity of both."

To the surprise of the Patriot Commissioners themselves, the Viceroy acceded to the terms of the proposed armistice, only stipulating that he should withdraw twelve heavy guns from Callao. It then became easy to arrange the terms of a provisional armistice of twenty days, during which it was stipulated that La Serna and San Martin, accompanied by their respective commissioners, should meet on the 23rd May.

Neither party seems to have acted in good faith on this occasion. La Serna had written, on the 7th April, to his generals in the Highlands, that he did not believe that the negotiation would lead to any result, and instructed them to occupy advantageous positions which they might hold during a possible suspension of hostilities. San Martin afterwards declared, in a confidential letter to O'Higgins, that the division of Arenales required a rest after passing through the Highlands, and that he himself had twelve hundred sick. He knew very well that arrogant Spain would never admit a recognition of independence which was forced upon her.

On the 2nd June, the interview between San Martin and La Serna took place at Punchauca. The two leaders met very cordially, with expressions of mutual esteem. San Martin proposed the appointment of a regency for the independent government of Peru, until the arrival of a prince of the Royal House of Spain; the said regency to consist of La Serna as President, with two colleagues, one named by the Royalists, the other by the Patriots, and offered to go himself to Spain as a commissioner to arrange matters with the Home Government.

Abreu expressed himself warmly in favour of the proposition, and the Viceroy appeared willing to accept it, but desired to consult the various corporations of the Viceroyalty before concluding so important an arrangement, and promised an answer in two days. They then discussed, informally, the mode in which the troops of both armies should unite in the public square of Lima to

S

solemnise the declaration of the independence of Peru. To the interview succeeded a banquet, at which the most friendly toasts were exchanged.

In all this the policy of San Martin was fundamentally wrong. He had no authority to make any such proposition. It was not in accordance with the principles for which he fought, and the applause with which it was received by the Monarchists of the Holy Alliance, implies its condemnation by the Republicans of America.

La Serna was more clear-sighted. Instead of consulting the corporations he consulted his officers, who, without absolutely rejecting the proposition, declined to accept it immediately, as it was in direct contravention of their orders, which forbade them to treat on the basis of colonial independence. On this, La Serna sent Valdés and Camba to arrange, if possible, with San Martin for a suspension of hostilities, until he had time to consult the Home Government. On the refusal of San Martin to listen to this proposal the commissioners again met at Miraflores, and, as neither party was ready to resume hostilities, the armistice was prolonged for twelve days, and San Martin consented to relax the blockade of Lima so as to permit the entrance of supplies sufficient for the daily wants of the citizens, "as he did not make war upon the people." This measure greatly increased the power of the partisans of the Patriot cause in the capital, and they prevailed upon the Cabildo to make a representation to the Viceroy in favour of peace, to which representation he paid no attention, and it produced great irritation in the army.

At this time San Martin received a visit from Captain Basil Hall, of the British navy, who, in his Journal, has given a very graphic account of the policy of the great General.*

During the rest of the armistice the Commissioners kept up appearances by still continuing to meet, while both parties actively prepared for the resumption of hostilities. La Serna detached Canterac with the most healthy of his

* See Appendix V.

troops, to occupy Huancavelica, thus to be ready to meet the advance of Arenales into the Highlands. San Martin returned with all his army to Huacho.

On the 4th July, the armistice having run out, La Serna publicly announced his determination to abandon Lima, and delegated the supreme authority to the Marquis of Montemira. He left a garrison of 2,000 men in the fortifications of Callao, 1,000 sick in the hospitals, and, on the morning of the 6th, marched off with barely 2,000 men, by the valley of Cañete.

The city was panic struck. The leading Spaniards fled with their families to Callao. The women rushed to the monasteries. San Martin hastened to reassure the people by a letter to the Archbishop, and, faithful to his declared policy, made no attempt to occupy the city. A deputation of the inhabitants waited upon him, asking his protection: whereupon he ordered the guerillas, of whom they were most afraid, to retire from the neighbourhood, and surrounded the city with a cordon of regular troops, placing them under the orders of the civil governor. Still the citizens could not believe that he was acting in good faith till an order from the Governor to a regiment of cavalry, which had encamped a mile and a half from the city, to retire to a greater distance, was at once obeyed, when confidence was restored, and, at the invitation of the authorities, at sundown on the 9th, a division of the army entered the city amid the shouts of the populace.

The next day, after sundown, San Martin, accompanied only by an aide-de-camp, rode quietly through the streets of the city to the palace of the Viceroys, where the citizens thronged to give him welcome, and the members of the Cabildo, hurriedly convened, presented him with an address. He soon wearied of their enthusiastic protestations of regard, and, remounting his horse at half past ten, he rode out to the village of Mirones, half-way to Callao, where he had established the headquarters of his army, as a preliminary step to laying siege to the fortress.

On the 11th he issued various proclamations to the citizens, and the royal arms were torn down from over the doors of the public offices, the escutcheon of Peru being put in their place, with the inscription *Lima Indcpendiente*.

San Martin also issued a proclamation to the inhabitants of the liberated departments, calling them to arms, and promising, with their assistance, to finish the campaign in forty days. But he took no active measures in furtherance of this project. Apparently he attached too much importance to the possession of Lima, for, with the exception of Trujillo, the country had as yet made no effort to second him, and remained passively watching the course of events.

The Viceroy, with his dispirited army, was allowed to retreat almost unmolested, though his loss by desertion was very great. Canterac was already securely established in the Highlands. San Martin here repeated the mistake he was guilty of after Chacabuco. Again he showed want of energy in following up a victory. He attached too much importance to the success which had so far attended his political combinations.

CHAPTER XXX.

THE SECOND CAMPAIGN IN THE HIGHLANDS.

1821.

WHEN Arenales rejoined the main army at Huara, and Ricafort descended by the mountain passes to Lima, Aldao and his Indian hordes were left in possession of the greater part of the Highlands, opposed only by a division under Carratala, who held Huancavelica and Huamanga. Aldao had given his Indians some sort of organization, styling the cavalry "The Mounted Grenadiers of Peru," and the infantry, "The Loyalists of Peru," under which names they figured as the two first Peruvian regiments on the muster roll of the liberating army. San Martin had small faith in such troops, nevertheless, as a step towards forming a native army, he appointed Colonel Gamarra, a Peruvian, Commandant-General of the Highlands, and in February sent him, with a number of officers of all ranks, to take the command.

About the same time Ricafort returned to Huancavelica, and one of the first measures of La Serna after he became Viceroy, was to send Valdés with 1,200 men to support him. The united forces of the Royalists numbered 2,500 men, but on advancing against Aldao, they found that the suspension bridges over the Rio Grande had been cut by the Indians. Nevertheless they found a place at which they could ford the stream and easily put to flight the raw levies opposed to them.

Before they could reach Gamarra, he had retreated from Jauja and Pasco with 600 of Aldao's men, by the pass of Oyuna, where his men dispersed. Carratala remained watching the pass, while Valdés and Ricafort returned by Canta to Lima; but were so harassed on the march by Vidal's guerillas, that an entire company of light infantry were taken prisoners, and Ricafort, badly wounded, was carried into Lima on a stretcher.

It was then that Arenales marched from Huara on his second expedition to the Highlands. The purpose of this expedition was to hasten the evacuation of Lima and to occupy such positions as would prevent the Royalists from re-establishing themselves in the Highlands; then to open communications at Ica with another expedition, which was sent along the coast southwards under Miller. For the first of these purposes the guerillas, guarding the passes from Lima, were instructed to obey all orders received from Arenales. In case of disaster, Arenales was instructed to retire on the reserve stationed at Huaylas.

The division of Arenales consisted of 2,200 men, the column under Miller of 600, thus San Martin was left with about 3,000 sick and convalescent in front of the Royalist Army of 7,000.

The troops sent with Arenales, worn out by the endemic fevers of the coast, were more like spectres than men, so that the first movements of the expedition were very slow. The Cordillera was crossed by the Oyon Pass on the 6th May. The heights were covered with snow and the cold was intense. Aldao with the remnants of his division led the van. Pasco was occupied on the 11th, and Carratala retired precipitately. Tarma and Jauja were taken on the 20th and 23rd, and Carratala continuing to retreat, the valley of Huancayo lay open to the Patriots on the 25th.

Arenales now prepared for a vigorous attack upon Carratala, when advice reached him of the signing of the armistice of Punchauca, which put a stop to operations for the present, retired to Jauja and employed himself in reorganizing his force, now swelled by recruiting to over 4,000 men.

Arenales was a peculiar character. Austere and subtile, his military ideas were as conspicuous for foresight as for audacity, while his every act was inspired by a sense ot justice and duty. He was very strict with his subordinates, who both feared and respected him. He went about attended only by an orderly, had only one spare charger and one baggage mule. He himself saddled and unsaddled his horse, and shod him himself also. He mended his own boots and uniform, and was so careless of dress that San Martin at times had his valise replenished for him, unknown to him. On the march he carried his own provisions in his saddle-bags—a cheese and a piece of cold beef. San Martin styled him " Mi compañero," and was more familiar with him than with any one else. He responded by exact obedience to orders, but did not scruple to criticise them whenever he thought proper.

From Jauja Arenales wrote San Martin, earnestly impressing upon him the advisability of transferring his whole force to the Highlands, leaving Lima to be watched by the fleet, but at the conclusion of the armistice he resumed operations by marching against Canterac, who had passed the Cordillera, when, on the 12th July, he received a despatch from San Martin, ordering him to retire on Pasco or on Lima, if menaced by the enemy.

Arenales saw clearly that this movement would entail the destruction of his division; he had heard of the evacuation of Lima, but knew nothing of the movements of La Serna. In his perplexity he called a council of war, at which it was decided to retire to Huancayo.

This movement was the salvation of Canterac, who had lost so heavily on the march from Lima, that he reached Huancavelica with only 1,500 starving men. La Serna, marching on Jauja, found the passes occupied by the mountaineers, who rolled great rocks down the mountain slopes upon his troops, so that, after heavy loss, he was forced to retreat, after throwing several guns into the river. Then following the route previously taken by Canterac, he joined him on the 4th August, the united force numbering barely 4,000 men, of whom many were sick.

At Huancayo Arenales found that Vidal and his guerillas had withdrawn to Lima, on which he continued his retreat to Jauja. Thence he wrote again to San Martin, showing him how the occupation of Lima would be as disastrous to the Patriot as it had been to the Royalist army, but in obedience to orders continued his retreat, losing hundreds of his new recruits by desertion.

Again he wrote to San Martin, proposing a new plan of campaign, which would compensate for the loss of the Highlands. The answer he received was an order to continue his retreat to Lima.

The division entered the capital in triumph on the day set apart for the celebration of the Independence of Peru, which by these mistaken measures was virtually postponed for another four years.

CHAPTER XXXI.

THE EXPEDITION TO THE SOUTH.

1821.

COCHRANE, having failed to persuade San Martin to undertake active operations against Lima, and not content with the rôle imposed upon him of simply blockading Callao, set his fertile brain to work to devise some means of capturing these fortifications.

San Martin entered heartily into his plans, and by means of his secret agents opened communications with some of the subordinate officers of the fortress, and placed Miller with 550 men under the orders of the Admiral.

Nails, made in Lima for the purpose, were distributed among the conspirators, who were to spike the guns when an attack was made on the northern forts; a part of the garrison was bought over, and false keys were made to open the gates; but the Viceroy, who seemed to be quite as well served by his spies as San Martin was by his, took measures to circumvent these plans, so nothing was attempted.

Cochrane then proposed, with a small force of infantry moved rapidly by sea from place to place, to wear out the Royalist army by continual marchings to and fro; and San Martin at last resolved to send an expedition to the South, to co-operate with the movements of Arenales in the Highlands. Six hundred picked infantry and eighty horse under Miller, were placed at the disposal of Cochrane for this purpose.

On the 22nd March Miller and his troops landed at Pisco, and took possession of the town of Chincha, under protection of the guns of the *San Martin*, *O'Higgins*, and *Valdivia*, an attack on an advanced party by Colonel Loriga being beaten off by Captain Videla.

On the same day an insurrectionary movement took place in Cuzco, headed by Colonel Lavin, an Argentine, formerly an ardent Royalist, but at this time under arrest in that city on account of an abortive conspiracy at Arequipa. The insurrection was put down, all the insurgents, including Lavin, being killed.

Leaving Miller at Chincha, the Admiral then sailed off to Cerro Azul, but being unable to effect a landing on account of the heavy sea, he wrote to San Martin again, advising an attack on Lima, and later on asked for a further reinforcement of infantry for an attack on Cerro Azul, which was the key to the provinces of the south. San Martin could spare no more men, whereupon he wrote to O'Higgins, asking for a contingent which would enable Miller to penetrate into Upper Peru. San Martin also wrote in support of this suggestion, but the Chilian Government replied that they could do no more, which was the simple truth. Meantime the Spaniards at Pisco and their adherents suffered heavily from forced contributions, to the great discredit of the expedition.

The Viceroy, on hearing of the landing at Pisco, despatched a division, under Camba, to watch the movements of the Patriots. Inland from Pisco lay two beautiful valleys, the Chincha Alta and the Chincha Baja. Camba encamped in the first of these valleys, while Miller moved up from the town and encamped in the second. For a month the two parties sat watching, each the other, nothing doing, then an enemy more to be feared than either came down on both of them, the endemic fever of the coast, the tertian ague. Both those beautiful valleys became hospitals, where officers and men alike lay prostrate. Cochrane's idea of wearing out the Royalist army by fruitless marchings to and fro was by no means easy of accomplishment, yet still he persevered. On the 22nd April the expedition was re-embarked, Miller being carried on board, while most of his men were barely able to hold their muskets.

Cochrane then sailed away for Arica, where there was a six-gun battery and a garrison of 300 men. After a fruitless cannonade, 250 men were landed higher up the coast in two divisions, one of which, led by Miller, marched on the city of Tacna ; while Major Soler of the grenadiers marched with the other upon Arica, which is the port of Tacna. Arica was evacuated by the enemy on his approach, and Soler, starting in pursuit, captured a string of mules on the road to Lima, which were laden with 120,000 dollars in specie. Effects to the value of 300,000 dollars, the property of Spaniards resident in Lima, were also confiscated in the town and shipped on board the *San Martin*.

Miller was received with enthusiasm at Tacna, and was joined by many volunteers. The garrisons of both the city and the port passed over to him, and were embodied in a new battalion styled " The Loyalists of Peru." Cochrane presented the new corps with a flag, a golden sun on a blue ground.

One of the volunteers was a Peruvian named Landa, a man of gigantic stature, and well acquainted with the country, who had served in the ranks of the Royalists. To the service which he subsequently rendered to the Patriots much of the success of the expedition may be attributed. Another of the volunteers was Colonel Portocarrero, also a Peruvian, who was one of the secret agents of San Martin.

Miller had now 900 men under his orders, of whom 400 were drilled troops, and determined to enter upon a formal campaign. Rumour had greatly exaggerated the number of his forces, and all the country about was in a ferment.

General Ramirez, who was stationed at Puno, directed

several detached corps to concentrate on the river Ilo, under Colonel Santos la Hera, to resist the invasion. Miller, who was kept well informed by Portocarrero and Landa, started to prevent this concentration of the Royalists. He reached the river Samba on the 20th May, and at midnight, after a forced march of eighteen hours across a desert, reached the Ilo, opposite to the village of Mirave, where La Hera was encamped. An advanced picket gave the alarm, but two Englishmen, named Hill and Hunn, with twenty men, forded the river, and drew off the attention of the enemy, while Miller and the bulk of his force crossed unmolested in the darkness. At daybreak Miller attacked the village, and carried it after a sharp struggle, in which young Welsh, Cochrane's physician, who accompanied the expedition as a volunteer, was killed.

Hardly had the last fugitives of La Hera's party disappeared when Colonel Rivero came in sight, with another detachment from Puno, mounted on mules. A few rockets put them to flight.

The same afternoon Miller started in pursuit, and on the 24th reached the city of Moquegua, where Portocarrero was Deputy Governor, who at once passed over to him. The remains of La Hera's force had been overtaken and made prisoners by Soler, and on the 26th Miller overtook Rivero, and either killed or made prisoners nearly all his party. In fifteen days from landing Miller with his small force had put more then a thousand of the enemy hors de combat, and Cochrane wrote to San Martin, telling him that in eight days more they would have Arequipa.

La Hera, having met in his flight with other parties on the march to join him, now turned upon Miller and tried to cut off his retreat, but Miller reached Tacna in safety, and was there met by the news of the armistice of Punchauca.

During the suspension of hostilities Miller employed his time in drilling his raw troops, while Ramirez collected

2,000 men to oppose him; Cochrane returned to Callao, leaving only three small transports at Arica, which very soon followed him.

Miller, left to himself, was at the expiration of the armistice compelled to retreat to Arica, where he seized four merchant vessels and embarked with those of his partisans who were most seriously compromised, leaving his sick to the care of La Hera, who, grateful for kindness shown by Miller to his prisoners, gave them every possible attention. A great contrast to the general procedure of the Royalist leaders.

Miller, now raised to the rank of colonel, sailed from Arica on the 22nd July, and, being unable by reason of the heavy sea to land near Islay for an attempt on Arequipa, turned north and landed at Pisco. After destroying a Royalist force under Santalla, he established himself at Ica and assumed command of the district.

As a diversion this expedition was more successful than could have been expected from the small force employed, thanks to the brilliant qualities displayed by Miller in separate command. Greater results might have been achieved by the employment of a larger force, but without reinforcements from Chile, that could only have been accomplished at the expense of more important objects.

This campaign concluded with a disaster. The *San Martin*, already laden with booty, had, in defiance of the armistice, seized a cargo of wheat at Mollendo, and went to the bottom when discharging at Chorillos; a fate ominous of that which was soon to overtake her great namesake.

CHAPTER XXXII.

PERU INDEPENDENT.

1821.

On the 6th July, 1821, the Patriots entered Lima; on the 24th June was fought the battle of Carabobo, the Waterloo of the Royalists of Columbia. San Martin's plan of a continental campaign was on the point of realization; he from the south, and Bolívar from the north, converged to a common centre. The only troops which now upheld the standard of the King, were those which still held the Highlands of Peru, the province of Quito, and one isolated fortress, soon about to surrender. On the ocean, only three vessels, the remnant of the naval power of Spain, crushed by Cochrane on the Pacific, wandered to and fro like phantom ships. The definitive triumph was but a question of time. Never before was plan on so vast a scale carried out with such mathematical precision—a plan, nevertheless, sketched out in accordance with the designs of inevitable fate.

As was said by the first captain of the age and as was recorded by an American thinker, "All the great captains who have undertaken great emprises have carried them out in conformity with the rules of art, adapting the force employed to the obstacle to be overcome, knowing that events are not the work of chance, but obey those laws which rule the destinies of men."

When the two liberators of South America violated these laws, one straying from the path, the other blinded by ambition, both fell; one deliberately, as he found himself wanting in strength to complete his mission; the other cast down by the irresistible forces which he had arrayed against himself.

The emancipation of America was no longer in question, the independence of Peru was assured, whatever might be the errors of men or the vicissitudes of the struggle. But this, though clear to the superior minds which presided over the scene, was not perceived by those more immediately concerned. This was more especially the case in Peru, where the idea of the revolution had as yet taken no deep root; that spirit of nationality which would secure the triumph at any cost was not yet aroused. San Martin sought to awaken this spirit by a solemn declaration of independence.

The position of San Martin was complex; before America he stood as a liberator, he was the arbiter of the destinies of Peru; he was a general of two republics who had confided their armies to his care; and as a great leader he was responsible to his conscience. As he entered the "City of the Kings" in triumph he was at the apogee of his glory, but as Rothschild the banker said, it requires ten times more skill and prudence to keep a fortune than to make one.

San Martin wrote to O'Higgins:—

"At last, by patience, we have compelled the enemy to abandon the capital of the Pizarros; at last our labours are crowned by seeing the independence of America secure —Peru is free—I now see before me the end of my public life, and watch how I can leave this heavy charge in safe hands, so that I may retire into some quiet corner and live as a man should live."

His public declarations were also grave and moderate, but the exaggerated importance he gave to the possession of Lima, led him to abandon the Highlands, where lay the decision of the question, and showed that, to some extent, his judgment was warped by success.

At the time of the occupation of Lima, San Martin published in his camp a bulletin written by Monteagudo, which is a declaration of political principles, and gives a reason for the policy which he pursued. Treating of the war as almost at an end, he offers a restricted liberty for the establishment of order, but makes no profession of political faith, national independence being the only point which is definitely established.

On the 14th July, San Martin convened a meeting of the principal citizens of Lima, nominated by the Cabildo. At this meeting the following resolution was carried:—

"The general will is decided for the independence of Peru of Spanish domination, or of that of any other foreign power."

Which declaration was sanctioned by the applause of the people.

On the 28th July the independence of Peru was solemnly proclaimed with imposing ceremony in the great square of Lima, San Martin displaying the new flag of Peru, amid the roar of cannon and the acclamations of the people who, as the procession passed through the main streets of the city, showered flowers and perfumes upon it. Cochrane, who looked on from a balcony of the viceregal palace, was singled out for a special ovation by the populace. Medals commemorative of the occasion were afterwards distributed among the people.

San Martin sent back to Chile the flags captured at Rancagua, and to Buenos Ayres five flags and two Spanish standards, as trophies of the victories of the united army.

While these pompous ceremonies went on, the siege of Callao was vigorously prosecuted by Las Heras, who repulsed several sorties of the garrison, but as e had no siege train, he could not venture an assault. Cochrane offered to land guns from the fleet, but as the garrison had only provisions for two months, more reliance was placed on a strict blockade.

The garrison seeing their situation desperate, resolved

to scuttle their ships, and commenced by the corvette *San Sebastiano*, on which Cochrane wrote again to San Martin urging an immediate assault; then perceiving a gap in the boom which surrounded the remaining ships, he on the night of the 24th July, sent eight boats under Captain Crosbie, who cut out from under the batteries the 34-gun corvette *Resolucion*, two smaller vessels and sundry boats, without any loss on his part.

On the 14th August Las Heras made an attempt to capture the fortress by surprise. He had noticed that the gates of the Castle Real Felipe were frequently left open, and the drawbridges lowered. The distance from his line to the walls was about 3,000 yards, which cavalry could cross at a gallop in ten or twelve minutes. A body of horse supported by infantry made a sudden rush from Bella Vista, the centre of his line, but in spite of their speed, the enemy perceived them in time to raise the bridge leading to the inner fortifications. The cavalry galloped through the streets of the town, sabred stragglers and made several prisoners, among the latter being the wounded general Ricafort.

On the same day, Cochrane made overtures to the governor, La Mar, very unworthy of his high renown. He had an idea that silver bullion to the value of thirty millions of dollars was stored up in Callao, besides much other property belonging to the wealthy Spaniards of Lima. He proposed that La Mar should surrender the fortress to him and give him up one-third the treasure, engaging in return to furnish ships in which he, and any he chose to take with him, might escape with the rest of the treasure.

Cochrane states in his Memoirs, that he required the money to pay his crews, and denies that he had any ulterior object, but he himself acknowledges that if he had gained possession of the forts, he would have forced San Martin to keep his promise to leave the Peruvians free to choose their own government.

T

The logical sequence of the Declaration of Independence, was the establishment of a National Government in Peru, but it was of prime necessity that the new government should not only govern but should carry on the war. There was great difficulty in organizing any such government, as there was no social nucleus round which the heterogeneous population might gather, and Peru had not one citizen who possessed either prestige or moral authority. A deputation from the Cabildo of Lima waited upon San Martin, praying him to take the reins of government into his own hands. He answered somewhat enigmatically, that circumstances had already given him the supreme power, and he should keep it so long as he considered it necessary for the public welfare. The Lautaro Lodge, in which the majority were officers of the united army, then addressed him to the same effect, declaring that the public safety required him to place himself at the head of an administration.

On the 3rd August, 1821, he issued a decree, whereby he gave himself the title of " Protector of Peru," uniting in his own person the supreme administrative authority, both military and political. No one in the world, except Cromwell, had ever taken upon himself this title with this authority. America alarmed, thought he had done so from ambition, and saw in him a future despot, but she thought wrong; a dictatorship was necessary, and in taking it he ensured the speedy loss of all his power.

The Protector named Dr. Unanue, a Peruvian of great reputed wisdom but of no experience, his Minister of Finance; Garcia del Rio, Minister of Foreign Affairs; and Monteagudo, Minister of War and Marine. Riva Aguero was named President of the department of Lima, and Las Heras took command of the army.

La Serna, on receiving official notification of this step, wrote to San Martin, telling him with some irony that he thought the title of Liberator suited him better than that of Protector, and that the people who had so spontaneously sworn to uphold the independence of Peru, would just as readily swear to uphold the new Spanish constitution. O'Higgins enthusiastically approved of it, seeing in it the only means of carrying the great work they had both at heart to a successful termination.

The first official act of the Protector was to issue a decree against the Spaniards, drawn up by Monteagudo, and showing evidence of his intemperate spirit, but it was also in accordance with the calculating spirit of San Martin.

On leaving Valparaiso, San Martin had published a proclamation to "The Spanish Europeans resident in Peru," declaring that he wished to behave generously to them, providing they made no opposition to the independence of the country. During the negotiations at Miraflores and Punchauca, he had endeavoured to propitiate the Spanish civilians, but when hostilities had again broken out and he was master of Lima, the splenetic behaviour of the Spanish residents, made him resolve to crush them.

He now declared that the persons and properties of all Spaniards who would live in peace and swear the independence of the country, should be respected; that those who would not trust to this promise, should ask for passports and should leave the country with their movable goods; but that those who submitted to the Government and secretly worked against it, would be prosecuted with the utmost rigour of the law, and their estates confiscated; and wound up by saying :—

"I know what passes in the most secret corner of your houses. Tremble, if you abuse my indulgence. Let this be the last time that I have to remind you that your destiny is irrevocable and you must submit to it."

Public safety in no way justified such rigour, which was a violation of promises given. But there was more in this decree than excessive severity and intemperance of language, it formed part of a financial plan. War is war, and the independence of South America was in great part paid for by Spanish fortunes, wrested from their owners by forced loans and by confiscations. It was now the turn of the Spaniards of Peru to contribute their share. San Martin had made use of this system in Mendoza, he had recommended it in Chile. Sentimental characters do not lead great causes to victory in the struggle of life. All the same, the measure was unjustifiable in the absence of any overt act on the part of the Spaniards.

One result of this new system of persecution, was the banishment of the Archbishop of Lima, a man of eminent piety and eighty years of age, who, though a Royalist, had aided San Martin in quieting the city on his arrival; he had authorized with his presence the municipal council which had declared the country independent; he had assisted at the *Te Deum* which celebrated the declaration. Most of the Peruvian clergy were ardent Patriots, but not so the high dignitaries of the church. San Martin took advantage of a mere pretext to send him his passport and an order to leave the country in twenty-four hours.

On the 4th September, 1821, when San Martin was, as Protector of Peru, in the apogee of his power, his old enemy José Miguel Carrera, died cursing him in Mendoza. Associated with Artigas, Ramirez, Bustos, and others of the Gaucho chieftains of the Argentine Provinces, Carrera had distinguished himself among them for rancorous hatred of Buenos Ayres. Unfortunate in all his enterprises, he was at length captured, and shot as a bandit, upon the same bench where his brothers had perished before him.

CHAPTER XXXIII.

THE PROTECTORATE OF PERU.

1821—1822.

PERU was independent, but she had not achieved independence for herself; neither did she know how to organize a Government when she had one of her own; for everything she was indebted to outside help—principally to San Martin, who was now Protector of Peru, but whose power depended upon the help of Peru, and upon the support of the two armies he had brought with him. But in Peru the national spirit which he had awakened had a latent tendency to turn against him as a stranger, and in the armies the spirit of discipline was relaxed in direct consequence of that act of disobedience of his own which had placed him at their head. The bond of union which still gave strength to these discordant elements was the Lautaro Lodge, over which his influence was still supreme.

As Arenales had foreseen, Lima became the Capua of the liberating army; everything appeared to be left to the slow action of time. The military officers murmured and conspired, while Cochrane strove in every way he could to preserve the fleet from the enervation which was Peruvianising the army.

Far otherwise passed their time the Royalist leaders in the Highlands. Masters of a healthy country abounding in resources, a reaction had set in in their favour, when the people found themselves deserted and bethought them of the sacrifices they had made. In fifty days La Serna was ready to assume the offensive. At Callao there was great provision of arms much needed in the Highlands; the garrison, if left alone, must soon succumb to hunger. A carefully selected division of 2,500 infantry and 900 horse, with seven guns, was put under command of Canterac, with Valdés as chief of the staff, and sent to the relief of the beleaguered stronghold, while La Serna remained with the rest of the army at Jauja.

Canterac marched on the 25th August, crossed the Cordillera, and descended by the pass of San Mateo towards Lima without meeting a single foe. At Santiago de Tuna, fifty miles from the capital, he divided his force into two columns, with orders to concentrate at Cienaguilla, eighteen miles to the south of Lima. Loriga, with the left column and nearly all the cavalry, went by the defile of Espiritu Santo, cutting to pieces a small Patriot force on his way.

The main column, under Canterac himself, kept straight on for the valley of Rimac, to give the Patriots the idea that he was marching straight on the capital; but during the following night he turned off to the left, seeking the other road by Espiritu Santo. The way was across the slopes of the mountains, over an unknown country where there was no water, and which was so cut up by abrupt descents that horsemen and infantry alike lost their footing and fell over precipices. The unpopularity of the Spaniards was so great that they could not find one guide in all the transit. On the 4th September they reached a barren stretch of sand over which, dying of thirst under a tropical sun, they plodded wearily along; two companies could have destroyed them all. The soldiers threw themselves on the ground utterly prostrate; immediate promotion was offered to the first who should find water; not a man stirred. Yet they were little more than a mile from the river Lurin. At last Canterac himself found water; and those who were strong enough to move filled flasks and carried the precious liquid to their dying comrades, only just in time to save the life of Valdés, who commanded the rear-guard. On the 5th they rejoined Loriga's column at Cienaguilla.

San Martin was in the theatre when news of this invasion reached him on the 4th September. From his box he called the people to arms; the new national hymn was sung by the officers present, the audience joining in the chorus, and the greatest enthusiasm prevailed.

San Martin was ill-prepared to meet such an emergency, and was equally ill-informed. On the 5th he knew nothing of the concentration of the enemy in the valley of Lurin, and announced that 200 or 300 men were descending by the pass of San Mateo; but he calmly made such arrangements as he could. The unarmed militia flocked to their barracks, the walls were manned by volunteers, the gates were entrusted to the civic guard. These precautions sufficed to keep Canterac from attacking the city; his chief object was Callao.

The united army was superior in number to the invaders, but was of very inferior quality. It consisted of 5,830 men, of whom 2,095 paraded under the Argentine standard, 1,595 under the Chilian, the rest were Peruvians. San Martin drew up his forces a mile and a half to the south of the city, on the banks of the river Surco an affluent of the Rimac, which was crossed by three bridges. The position was a very strong one, and commanded the roads to the south and east of Lima. The cavalry was stationed on the right flank, and skirmishers were thrown out on the roads in front.

Canterac did not dare to attack him, but drew up his army on the 9th in three parallel columns—cavalry, infantry, and baggage—with a squadron of cavalry in the rear, and marched by his left flank to the plain of San Borja, flanking the position occupied by the Patriots. San Martin drew back his right wing and took up a fresh position; then, as the enemy remained quiet, he moved further to the right, in his turn outflanking the enemy. Canterac then took up a fresh position, at right angles to the former and facing towards the city. During the night San Martin again moved forward his right wing. The next day Canterac retired under the guns of Callao, and San Martin, rubbing his hands, exclaimed to Las Heras :—

"They are lost! They have not food for fifteen days!"

Soon after this Cochrane rode up. Las Heras asked him to persuade the General to attack at once, which Cochrane attempted. San Martin answered him curtly:—

"My measures are taken."

By-and-by, as San Martin was listening to the report of a countryman, Cochrane ordered the man away, saying :—

"The General has no time to listen to follies."

San Martin frowned, and, turning rein, rode off to his quarters. Cochrane followed him and again urged him to attack, offering to lead the cavalry himself. The answer of the Protector was :—

"I only am responsible for the welfare of Peru."

San Martin and Cochrane never met again.

The Patriot army then advanced half way on the main road from Lima to Callao, and a field battery was thrown up at La Legua, mounting six guns and two howitzers.

The only way for the Royalists to save Callao was to supply the garrison with provisions, which were only to be obtained by taking Lima, or by occupying the suburbs, neither of which was possible. Canterac could only retreat, leaving Callao to its fate. The joy of the garrison on welcoming the reinforcement was short-lived, they were only so many more mouths to feed. Canterac had instructions from the Viceroy in this case to destroy the fortifications and bring away the garrison, with as much of the armament as he could carry off, but La Mar refused to abandon the Spanish families which had taken refuge with him. Some English merchants offered to supply provisions by water for 100,000 dols. in cash, and an order for 400,000 dols. on the Treasury of Arequipa. The Treasury was almost empty, but the amount was made up by the private resources of the refugees, and by the officers and men of Canterac's division, who contributed the pay they had received.

Instead of being able to bring away arms, Canterac found it necessary to leave behind five out of the seven light guns he had brought with him. The situation of the Royalists was very critical; in two days eight officers and 200 men had deserted, the rest were eating their horses. Three days more of this, and even retreat would be impossible.

On the 16th, at four o'clock in the afternoon, the division marched from Callao on the main road to Lima. Canterac, with some light troops and his two guns, made a feint against the battery of La Legua to hide his real intention, while the bulk of his force moved to the left, crossed the Rimac, and turned north, Canterac, with his detachment, covering the retreat under the fire of a Chilian brig-of-war, which caused some loss.

Protected by the darkness, Canterac marched all night along the coast, and next day occupied the valley of Carabaillo, nine miles to the north of Lima, from which a road passes through the Cordillera to Jauja. Here he halted to rest and feed his weary troops.

San Martin, in spite of the eagerness of his army, had watched the retreat in silence, and only on the 17th despatched Las Heras with a strong force in pursuit. But the inactivity of San Martin seems to have been communicated to Las Heras; he showed little of his wonted energy, and on the 19th gave up the pursuit to Miller, with a detachment of 700 infantry, 125 horse, and 500 guerillas.

Meantime the Royalist division was falling to pieces—hundreds of the men and even some officers deserted. Miller was not dilatory in his movements, but erred on the side of rashness; he outmarched the enemy, trying to cut off his retreat, and was on two occasions dislodged with heavy loss from positions he had taken up. After that he contented himself with attacks on the rear-guard, and followed right through the Cordillera, where, on the 27th, he found in a hut, abandoned by his comrades, the body of Colonel Sanchez, the hero of San Carlos and Chillán.

On the 1st March Canterac reached Jauja; he had lost one-third of his force, but had sustained his reputation as a gallant soldier and an able tactician.

San Martin, after the retreat of Canterac, summoned La Mar to surrender, offering honourable terms of capitulation, to which, after some delay, La Mar acceded. The troops were permitted to march out with their arms and standards, the Spaniards being allowed to retire to Arequipa, while the militia dispersed to their homes. Three months were given to the officers and the civil employés in which to find the means of leaving the country if they did not choose to remain.

On the 21st September the Peruvian flag was hoisted on the castles of Callao. La Mar, who as a Peruvian sympathised with the Patriot cause, resigned his rank and honours into the hands of the Viceroy and retired into private life.

San Martin thus won another victory without risking his army. As a Peruvian historian says:—" He overcame a powerful army by the simple force of public opinion and by skilful tactics." The strongest fortress in South America was now in his power, with several hundred guns of all calibres, thousands of muskets, and great stores of ammunition. He was now free to turn his arms to the north for the liberation of Quito in answer to a request from Bolívar, and could then return with reinforcements to put an end to the war. But the rôle of Fabius is one not generally appreciated; prudence is often mistaken for timidity; the general who prefers the shield to the sword offends the pride of his soldiers. San Martin gained by his policy great fame as a tactician, but he lowered his renown as a resolute soldier.

In the first six months of the Protectorate of San Martin

the foundations were laid of the administrative organization and the political constitution of Peru. One of his first measures was to create a national army. Under the name of the "Peruvian Legion" he organized a division, recruited among the natives, composed of a regiment of infantry under Miller, one of cavalry under Brandzen, and a company of artillery with four guns. He reorganized the finances and reformed the commercial system. He abolished the personal service of the indigenous races, the poll-tax, and other oppressive customs. He manumitted all slaves who would join the army, and declared free all who might in future be born of slave parents. Corporal punishment was forbidden in the public schools; a national library was founded; the press was set free from all unnecessary restrictions; torture and excessive punishments were abolished. All which reforms and many others were carried out in pursuance of ideas brought by Monteagudo from the River Plate.

San Martin also issued a decree defining his own powers, and recognised such debts of the late authorities as had not been contracted for war purposes; but he did not draw up any plan for the political organization of the country, leaving that question for future solution.

The Peruvian nobility were left with their titles and escutcheons; San Martin looked upon them as a social influence of which good use might be made. He also instituted a new order, the "Order of the Sun," in imitation of the "Legion of Honour," instituted by Napoleon, as had previously been done in Chile by the institution of "The Legion of Merit"; and also a special decoration for women who distinguished themselves by services in the Patriot cause, a gold medal with a suitable inscription, which, however, was distributed with more gallantry than discretion, and gave rise to much scandal, some of which has not even yet died out. All this was in preparation for the establishment of that monarchy, the idea of which was still in the air.

San Martin also decreed to himself an annual salary of 30,000 dols., of which he spent the greater part in presents and in public displays; but even so, this brought much adverse criticism upon him, and contributed to give currency to a report then commonly circulated about him, that he entertained the inane project of crowning himself King. The people in their ballads sang of him as their future Emperor, and it became a habit among the officers of the army to speak of him as " King Joseph."

Up to that time the American spirit of independence and the love of glory had sufficed to bind together the units of the army; the alloy of gold had not yet destroyed the temper of their swords. Badly fed, badly dressed, with only half their pay when they had any, suffering from all sorts of privation and disease, they had never received any pecuniary reward for their services. The Government of Chile had promised to give the victors of Maipó the land on which they had achieved that crowning triumph, but the promise was never fulfilled. The municipality of Lima now gave to San Martin 500,000 dols., arising from the sale of the properties of Spanish residents which had been confiscated, for distribution among his principal officers, and offered to the rest who should continue in the service grants of land in the provinces yet to be conquered. San Martin distributed the half million dollars among twenty officers—25,000 dols. to each one—which was in those days a fortune; but this, instead of binding them to his cause, produced resentments and jealousies, as is ever the case when self-interest enters into the relations between man and man, of which he was soon to have sad proof.

In October he received information that a conspiracy to depose him existed among the higher officers of the army. He summoned them to a secret council and disclosed the matter to them, but received very unsatisfactory replies.

That such a conspiracy existed appears certain, but it was not yet mature, and the inquiry was sufficient to dissipate it. Colonel Heres, of the Numancia battalion, was removed from his command, with many thanks for his distinguished services, and retired to Columbia, his native land. Las Heras and several other officers resigned their commands, and Alvarado, who appears to have been also one of the conspirators, was named General-in-Chief. San Martin had thus the sad certainty that although the disaffection had not spread among the junior officers, nor among the rank and file, the sympathies of the army were no longer with him as they had been at Rancagua.

The chief cause of the general discontent was his advocacy of monarchical principles; he sacrificed his own principles in favour of what he considered the most practicable system. In his own words:—

"The evils which afflict the new States of America arise not from the people, but from the Constitutions under which they live. These Constitutions should harmonise with their instruction, education, and habits of life. They should not have the best laws, but those most suited to their character, maintaining the barriers which separate the different classes of society, so that the most intelligent class may preserve its natural preponderance."

His ideal of legislation was based upon the precepts of Solon, an oligarchy of intelligence counterbalanced by a Conservative plutocracy. He forgot that in his own country he had seen safety only in the establishment of a sovereign Congress, and that the advocacy of monarchical ideas had there only fanned the flames of anarchy; that he himself had been forced to disobey when he was called upon to support a monarch elected by a secret committee; he forgot that he himself had founded a republic in Chile, and had sketched out a republican constitution for Peru, and that, with the exception of Mexico, every one of these new States had adopted the Democratic Republican system as a necessity of the age.

San Martin also failed to see that he must work in harmony with Bolívar, who had just established the Republic of Columbia, and with the great Democratic Republic of the United States. He also failed to see that it was in sympathy with these views that England had withdrawn from the Holy Alliance, and looked upon the republican form of government as the *sine quâ non* of independence in America. He was led astray by his Minister, Monteagudo, who was just as blind as himself to the inevitable tendency of the age.

In order to educate public opinion Monteagudo had established in Lima a literary society, styled " The Patriotic Society of Lima," for the discussion of political questions, in which he openly advocated the establishment of a monarchy.

The Protectorate of San Martin was based upon the express condition "that he should give place to the government which the Peruvian people should select"; but before he had held office five months he and his Council decided to send a mission to Europe to negotiate an alliance with Great Britain, and to accept a prince of the reigning family as a Constitutional monarch. In case this proposition was rejected, they were then to make a similar proposal to the Government of Russia; and that failing, then to any European prince; last of all, to the Prince of Luca, the imaginary sovereign of the River Plate.

This mission was confided to Garcia del Rio, who proceeded to Europe accompanied by Dr. Paroissiens; but, better instructed by subsequent events, Garcia took no step in prosecution of the ostensible object of his journey, contenting himself with a general advocacy in the European press of the cause of the Patriots in America.

CHAPTER XXXIV.

SAN MARTIN AND COCHRANE.

1821—1822.

HISTORY seeks in vain to blot from her pages the invectives hurled at each other by the two heroes of the liberating expedition to Peru. They themselves have perpetuated them in documents, in which each appeals to the judgment of the world.

Cochrane has insulted and calumniated San Martin by calling him a sanguinary tyrant, an incompetent general, a hypocrite, a thief, a drunkard, &c., &c.

San Martin, through his ministers, accused Cochrane of depredations akin to piracy, and of being an embezzler of public property, who made traffic with the naval force placed under his command.

The Admiral, who thought nothing great but his own deeds and his own hatred, extreme in everything, who had spoken of his own country as a degraded nation, ruled by a parliament of scoundrels, looked upon the South American revolution as a commercial transaction, carried on by a set of intriguing, cowardly rascals.

San Martin, more prudent, returned him insult for insult by other hands, but he did not descend to calumny, and when the angry moment had passed, troubled himself no more about him.

The antecedents of this quarrel we have already sketched. Though seeking to make common cause with him, San Martin never confided in Cochrane, had a very low idea of his merits as a leader of troops on land, and found reason to repent of such trust as he did place in him on such service. This the Admiral attributed to jealousy.

In the squadron itself there was a party inimical to Cochrane. Guise and Spry drew up a protest against the new name given to the *Esmeralda*, and were tried by court-martial for breach of discipline, but San Martin, who saw in Guise a future admiral, took him under his protection, and made Spry one of his aides-de-camp.

In the inscription on the medals struck in celebration of the Declaration of Independence, no mention was made of the fleet. At this Cochrane took umbrage and would accept no excuse. From this time he became very pressing in his demands for the arrears of pay due to his crews, speaking clearly of the danger of a mutiny. These arrears dated from before the sailing of the expedition; the foreigners were only kept on board by an express promise from San Martin to pay everything and a year's pay as bounty, when he took Lima. He also decreed a donation of 50,000 dollars to the captors of the *Esmeralda*. Neither of these promises were fulfilled.

On the 4th August, 1821, Cochrane went himself to the palace to urge these claims, and alleges that San Martin refused any money except as part of the purchase money of the ships which should be sold to Peru. This is denied by Monteagudo and Garcia del Rio, who were present. It was then that he was informed by San Martin himself that he had assumed the title of Protector of Peru, upon which Cochrane, now looking upon himself as the representative of Chile, reiterated his claims. San Martin acknowledged his responsibility for the year's pay he had promised as bounty, and for the 50,000 dollars promised to the captors of the *Esmeralda*, but denied that he was in any way responsible for the pay of crews in the service of Chile, and told Cochrane he might take his ships and go where he pleased, but regretting his hasty words, he then stretched out his hand to the Admiral, asking him to forget what had passed.

"I will forget when I can," replied Cochrane.

The Admiral seems also to have regretted his haste, for on returning on board he wrote to San Martin a letter in English, full of profuse compliments, to which San Martin replied in similar terms, but neither of them touched at all upon the question between them. The correspondence continued, but no money was paid, and Cochrane wrote to O'Higgins that he could not answer for the loyalty of his crews, who were in want of common necessaries, and hinted his fears that they would seize the ships and turn pirates.

When Cochrane returned on board, after the refusal of San Martin to attack Canterac (see last chapter), he found his men on the verge of mutiny. On the approach of Canterac, San Martin had, as a measure of precaution, sent the coin and bullion from the mint and treasury on board a ship at anchor at Ancon, and had given permission to private individuals to embark their valuables on the transports, or on board of neutral vessels. When Cochrane heard of this, he seized the whole of this treasure, under pretext that they were contraband shipments, but gave receipts for the packages. He received a peremptory order to return them to their owners, but wrote to San Martin that he could not obey the order, as he had no other means of preventing a mutiny, than by paying his men with whatever money he could lay hands on.

If the blockade were raised Callao could not be captured, so San Martin was forced to temporise, and insisted only on the restitution of private property, to which Cochrane acceded.

When Callao surrendered, the Peruvian Government ordered Cochrane to give up the rest of the treasure to an official of the War Office. Cochrane regretted that his duty to Chile obliged him to prevent by any means in his power insubordination and rebellion in the Chilian fleet. San

Martin then gave way, and Cochrane distributed one year's pay to all his crews, but kept the rest of the money for the general use of the squadron. After this, many of the seamen deserted to spend their money on shore, which occasioned so much disorder, that San Martin ordered Cochrane to return to Chile and report to his own government.

Cochrane denied the right of the Protector of Peru to give any such order, but some days after weighed anchor and left the harbour.

San Martin then wrote to O'Higgins, proposing to declare Cochrane an outlaw, but O'Higgins was too clear-sighted to commit any such folly, and acknowledged that they themselves were much to blame for what had occurred. Besides which Cochrane's conduct gave great satisfaction to the Chilian people, and he himself had sent a despatch to the Chilian Government, informing them that he was sailing to Guayaquil to careen the *O'Higgins*, and to look for the two Spanish frigates *Prueba* and *Venganza*.

Cochrane was incapable of treachery to the cause he had adopted, he was the same hero as before, with all his defects and all his great qualities. His intention on leaving Callao was to complete his great work, by driving the last vestiges of Spanish domination from the Pacific. He sent the *Lautaro* and the *Galvarino* back to Chile, and with the rest of his ships reached Guayaquil on the 18th October, where he spent six weeks in repairing them.

On the 3rd December he sailed again, looking into every bay and inlet along the coast as far as California for his prey. The two frigates had been employed on transport service, by various Spanish authorities on the Pacific coast, and on the 4th December had left Panama for Guayaquil, where they capitulated to Salazar and La Mar, who were there at the time as representatives of Peru.

The *Prueba* was sent off by them to Callao to give herself up to the Peruvian Government, but the *Venganza* remained at Guayaquil to make some necessary repairs, and she was still there when Cochrane returned on the 3rd March. The Admiral sent an armed boat to seize her and hoist the Chilian flag; the people manned the batteries and threatened to sink her; upon which he consented to leave her with them, until the question of ownership was decided by the governments of Chile and Peru.

Cochrane then sailed South, and touching at one of the northern ports of Peru, was refused either provisions or water by the authorities, who had special orders to that effect from the Protector. In great dudgeon he went on to Callao, where the appearance of his ships caused great alarm. The *Prueba*, now the *Protector*, under command of Captain Guise, was manned by troops from shore, and anchored under the batteries.

Cochrane sent an angry missive to the Minister of Marine, complaining of the treatment he had met with, and again demanded payment of the debts owing to him. The Minister went off to see him, invited him ashore and offered him the command of an expedition against the Philippine Islands. Cochrane was not to be appeased by words. A few days after that, the schooner *Montezuma* sailed close past him without saluting. He threatened to fire on her and compelled her to cast anchor, then boarding her he hauled down the Peruvian flag and hoisted the Chilian. It seemed as though the quarrel would culminate in actual fighting, till on the 10th May Cochrane sailed for Valparaiso, where he was welcomed in triumph, and his conduct received official approbation.

Soon after, Cochrane left for ever the shores of the Pacific, whose waves will murmur the record of his glorious deeds to the end of time.

Having now one ship of war, the Peruvian Government commenced to organize a navy, which they placed under the command of Blanco Encalada.

CHAPTER XXXV.

THE DISASTER AT ICA.

1821—1822.

AFTER the return of the expedition from Callao, La Serna removed his head-quarters to Cuzco, leaving the bulk of the army behind him in the valley of Jauja, under Canterac. He strengthened the garrisons of Puno, Arequipa, and Tacna, and entrusted the defence of the southern coast to the army of Upper Peru.

Canterac detached two light columns under Loriga against Pasco, where the insurrection had still a footing under Otero, who had 200 regulars with him and 5,000 Indians. On the approach of Loriga, Otero marched out to attack him, and fell upon him suddenly, in the early morning of the 7th December, at the village of El Cerro, where the Royalists had halted to collect supplies. In the confusion a part of the ammunition blew up, and the troops in the darkness were seized with panic, but Loriga succeeded in rallying them, occupied the church and some neighbouring houses, and waited for daylight, when he in his turn attacked the Patriots, and completely routed them, killing 700 Indians.

In Upper Peru, Lanza, the guerilla chief, maintained himself in the mountains between Cochabamba and La Paz.

In Potosí a mutiny broke out among the troops, which was quelled by General Maroto.

The Indians of Cangallo and Huamanga again rose in arms; but the former town was burned by Carratala, and the Viceroy issued a decree forbidding any attempt to rebuild it. The Government of Peru erected a monument to the memory of the unfortunate town, and Buenos Ayres named one of her principal streets Cangallo, as a lasting record of this barbarous deed.

But these transitory events had no effect upon the war itself, the Cordillera formed a barrier between the opposing forces which neither of them could pass. The Royalists still outnumbered the Patriots, two to one, but the territory occupied by them, extending from Pasco to the Argentine frontier, was so enormous, that they were nowhere strong.

Bolívar was on the march against Quito; success would enable him to assist San Martin to crush the Royalist forces in Peru, but no cordial alliance was possible with Bolívar until all these new nations had agreed upon one common form of government, and the unsettled state of Guayaquil, which was claimed as a province by both Columbia and Peru, threatened to produce discord between them.

San Martin rose to the emergency. He sent a contingent of 1,500 men from Peru to assist Bolívar in his operations against Quito, and so secured his success. Then, setting on one side his monarchical ideas, he, on the 27th December, 1821, issued a decree summoning a Congress:—

"To establish a definitive form of government, and to give to the country the constitution best adapted to it."

He at the same time appointed the Marquis of Torre-Tagle Deputy-Protector, while he himself went off to Guayaquil in the hope of obtaining an interview with Bolívar.

Not daring to leave La Serna unmolested while he arranged with the Liberator of the North the plans for united and decisive action, he despatched General Tristan and Colonel Gamarra, both Peruvians, with 2,000 men, to occupy the valley of Ica, and spread a false report that Arenales was about to return with another expedition to the Highlands. La Serna was too well informed to trouble himself about reports, and knew well the quality of the two Patriots now in command at Ica.

Early in April Canterac, with 2,000 men and three guns, marched from Jauja, and Valdés with 500 from Arequipa. The Patriot army evacuated Ica at their approach, but their retreat by night was intercepted, they were thrown into disorder and cut to pieces. The Royalists made more than 1,000 prisoners, including fifty officers, took four guns and two flags, and returned in triumph, after shooting one in every five of the officers of the Numancia battalion, whom they had made prisoners.

Tristan and Gamarra were tried by court-martial, and shown to be utterly incompetent for such a command; but the chief blame of the disaster fell upon San Martin himself, who had appointed them.

This defeat was in some measure compensated the following month by the fall of Quito, which terminated the war in the North, and San Martin not having been able to effect his proposed interview with Bolívar, who did not come to Guayaquil when expected, when he returned to Lima left the civil administration in the hands of Torre-Tagle, and devoted his attention exclusively to the army. He issued a proclamation in which he promised the Peruvian people that the war should be concluded in the year 1822, then current, and on the 4th July signed a provisional treaty with Columbia.

At the same time he applied for help to the Government of Chile, and to the governors of the various Argentine Provinces, bordering the eastern slopes of the Andes, now *de facto* independent States, an endeavour to unite all Spanish America in one grand effort to crush the Royalist cause in its last stronghold, the Highlands of Peru.

Still harping on the ideas he had disclosed at Punchauca and Miraflores, he also wrote to La Serna, proposing a cessation of hostilities, on the basis of the recognition of the independence of Peru. To this the Viceroy returned a curt answer, "That however beneficial independence might be to Peru, it could only be hoped for or established by decree of the nation (Spain)."

San Martin also wrote to the same effect to Bolívar, but found that their ideas did not at all coincide. And wrote to O'Higgins proposing a naval expedition to the coasts of Spain.

Torre-Tagle was but the nominal head of the civil Administration, the real ruler was his Minister, Monteagudo, an inveterate enemy of all Spaniards, who thought the true way to victory was to make the struggle one of race. On the 31st December he issued a decree, that all Spaniards who had not been naturalised should leave the country; in January, that they should also forfeit half their property; and in February, that the infraction of these decrees should entail banishment and confiscation. After the disaster of Ica still more barbarous decrees were issued, and a commission was appointed to enforce them.

Two great forces from the South and from the North were about to join hands in the great work in which they were both engaged. We have sketched the progress of the revolution from the banks of La Plata, across the Cordillera, and by the Pacific to Peru; it is now time to turn our attention to its progress from the Spanish Main through New Granada and Columbia to the frontiers of Peru at Quito.

CHAPTER XXXVI.

THE REVOLUTIONS IN QUITO AND VENEZUELA.

1809—1812.

SPANISH AMERICA on the Southern Continent, is divided geographically and socially into two great systems, which are nevertheless analogous, having the same origin and the same language. Simultaneously they felt the same impulse, simultaneously arose in both sections the spirit of independence. In each section one man took the lead, devoting his life to the cause which was at once his own and that of his race; yet were these two men of character wholly different. The one, cool and calculating, was devoid of personal ambition; the other, whose dreams were of glory and of power, was its slave. Yet in each glowed the passion for emancipation, and each in his own way accomplished the task before him. The one, San Martin, gave liberty to the South, the other, Bolívar, gave liberty to the North. They joined, and the social equilibrium was established.

The northern zone of the Continent extends about twenty degrees north of the Equator, from the frontiers of Peru to Panama and the Carribean sea. In 1810 this zone comprehended the Viceroyalty of New Granada, the Captain-Generalcy of Venezuela, and the Presidency of Quito; three political divisions marked out by geographical lines, and peopled by several heterogeneous races. At that date New Granada had 1,400,000 inhabitants, Venezuela 900,000, and Quito 600,000. Of these, 1,234,000 were

III.—Map of the Viceroyalty of New Granada, including Venezuela and Quito.

white, Europeans and Creoles, 913,000 were of indigenous races, 615,000 of mixed races, and 138,000 were negro slaves. Santa Fé de Bogotá was the capital of New Granada, Caracas was the capital of Venezuela. The City of Quito, situate high above the level of the sea, had been the centre of pre-Columbian civilization; during the colonial epoch it was at times attached to the Viceroyalty of New Granada, at times to that of Peru. The district of which this city was the capital has been styled the Thibet of the New World.

The two parallel ranges of the Andes, which form the valley of Chile, unite to the north of Argentine territory, but again separate in Peru, and running northward enclose Quito and the valley of Popayán, which forms the extreme south of New Granada. They then again diverge, this time into three branches, one of which forms the isthmus of Panama, while the others extend to the northeast as far as the Gulf of Mexico, wide valleys interposing between each range.

To the east of the most easterly of these ranges lies a vast plain, drained by the great river Orinoco and its tributaries. Situate under the tropic of Cancer summer and winter are there unknown, but the season from March to September is one of constant rain. During the intervening months, the rivers leave their beds and convert the vast plain into as vast a sea. When the waters retire, the plains are covered with luxuriant pasturage, giving sustenance to millions of cattle and horses, which are herded by a semi-civilized race of horsemen, known as the "llaneros" of Columbia, a race similar to the "gauchos" of the Argentine pampa. The llaneros live in lonely huts, and pass their days in the saddle. Inured to fatigue and danger, they are sober and abstemious, dress in the most simple manner, are dexterous in the use of the lance, and are splendid swimmers. Endowed with such qualities, and led by men of their own race, their deeds eclipse those of the most renowned heroes of antiquity.

The Columbian revolution broke out separately, in each of the three great sections. The first outbreak took place at Quito in August, 1809, almost simultaneously with similar movements in Mexico and in Upper Peru. The Captain-General, Ruiz de Castillo, was deposed, and a Junta was appointed. The movement was crushed by the combined forces of New Granada and Peru, and the leaders were put to death in prison in August, 1810. They were the first martyrs in the cause of independence in South America.

These outbreaks, simultaneous but unconnected, proceeded from identical causes; these causes not being removed, the consequent effects were naturally reproduced, and found echo all over the Continent.

On the 25th May, 1810, the star of liberty arose in Buenos Ayres, but previous to that date, on the 19th April of the same year, the municipality of Caracas, joined by deputies from the people, deposed Emparán, the Captain-General, denied the authority of the Regency of Cadiz, and appointed a Junta to rule over the " United Provinces of Venezuela," in the name of the King. The leader of this movement was a canon of the church, named Madariaga, by birth a Chilian, and a member of the Secret Society established by Miranda, whom he had met in London. His associates were Roscio and Ponte, men of noble character, whose political knowledge was more theoretical than practical. Most of the Provinces answered the call of the capital by deposing their governors and appointing Juntas.

The Central Junta issued a Manifesto to the other colonies of Spanish America, inviting them to form a continental league, for mutual protection. No such league was formed, but the example was everywhere followed. The first act of the Junta was to summon a Congress, elected by the people, into whose hands they proposed to surrender their provisional authority.

The northern provinces of Maracaibo and Coro had not

deposed their governors, Generals Miyares and Ceballos. These two officers denounced the movement, and commenced to raise troops to oppose it. The Junta took precautionary measures so as to be prepared against any attack, and meantime sent envoys to the United States and to England; looking to the latter power for protection in the event of an invasion of Venezuela by the French. Don Luis Mendez, Don Andrés Bello, and Don SIMON BOLÍVAR, a colonel of militia, were selected for this mission.

Bolívar was at that time twenty-seven years of age. There was nothing heroic in his appearance; he was short in stature, thin and narrow-chested, but his rugged, irregular features, gave a look of energy to his sallow countenance. His hair was black and curly; his high narrow forehead was deeply seamed with horizontal lines; he had thick, sensual lips, and beautiful teeth; his large black eyes were sunk deep in their orbits, and sparkled with an unsteady light, indicative of his character. He looked like one possessed by a latent fire, a man of feverish activity, combined with duplicity and arrogance; his profile was that of a deep thinker. Altogether his aspect was that of a man of great ideas, but of small judgment; his deeds do not belie that impression.

At the age of three years he was left an orphan, heir to a rich patrimony, with hundreds of slaves. His tutor was a philosopher of the school of the Cynics; the ideas he learned from him were so extravagant as to verge on lunacy, but he carried them with him throughout his life, and they moulded his career. From him he learned to dream of an ideal form of government, neither monarchical nor republican, in which all offices should be held for life. This tutor was named Simon Rodriguez, and was born in Caracas, the natural son of a priest.

Before he was seventeen years of age, Bolívar went to Europe; he was in Paris when Bonaparte was named First Consul, and professed enthusiastic admiration for his character. In Europe he married a daughter of the noble Venezuelan family of Del Toro, and then returned to Caracas. In the third year after his marriage, he lost his wife, and made a second voyage to Europe, where he again met his tutor. In his company he visited the scenes made immortal by Rousseau, whose "Nouvelle Heloïse" was his favourite book, and saw Napoleon crowned King of Italy at Milan. They went on to Rome, and from Mount Aventine looked over the ruins of the great city of the Cæsars. In a moment of enthusiasm the Acolyte seized the hands of his master, and swore to liberate his native land.

Six more years passed, and the revolution broke out in Venezuela, without any open help from him. He was then leading the life of a feudal lord, in wealth and in luxury, produced by the toil of slaves; yet though he took no open part in this revolution, he had done something to prepare it. He was on intimate terms with the Captain-General and had betrayed his secrets to the conspirators.

Soon after their arrival in London, the three envoys obtained a private audience with the Marquis of Wellesley, who was at that time Minister of Foreign Affairs. Bolívar, who talked French fluently, was the spokesman. Forgetting his *rôle* as a diplomatist, he made a speech in which he spoke harshly of Spain, and of his desire and of his hopes for the absolute independence of Venezuela; and most indiscreetly presented, not only the credentials of the envoys, but their instructions also.

The British Minister listened coldly, and glancing his eye over the papers, replied that the ideas he had heard expressed were in open contradiction to the documents. These credentials were conferred by a Junta ruling in the name of King Ferdinand, and the object of the mission was stated to be an arrangement with the Regency of Cadiz in order to prevent a rupture. Bolívar had read neither the credentials nor the instructions. As they retired, he candidly confessed his negligence to his companions, and agreed that the instructions showed both foresight and wisdom.

This is a true sample of Bolívar's character, both as a politician and as a soldier; ever pre-occupied by some idea of his own, he took no thought of the obstacles in his way, and gave no heed to the opinions of others; he blindly pursued his own dreams and his own designs. Victor or vanquished he always persevered, reading with "his mind's eye," as he said himself, no other documents than those written on his brain by his master Simon Rodriguez. His ruling idea at this moment was independence, and he went straight for it.

In spite of this diplomatic slip, the British Government answered the envoys according to the tenor of their instructions, and replied that they could not interfere in any question concerning the government of any country which recognised the King of Spain as its sovereign, but they offered their mediation for the reconciliation of the Colonies of Spain with the mother country. They had previously forwarded instructions to the governors of the British West Indies to protect the new governments in South America against French aggression. They now issued fresh circulars to the same effect, more especially recommending them to cultivate amicable relations with these new governments, whether or no they recognised the authority of the Regency of Cadiz.

This was satisfactory, but the result was owing to British policy, not to the skill of the envoys.

In London Bolívar became acquainted with General Miranda, and being initiated as a member of his Secret Society, renewed the oath he had made on the sacred hill of Rome, to work for the independence and liberty of South America. Contact with the ardent spirit of the Apostle of emancipation blew into a flame the embers lighted by the teachings of Rodriguez; again Bolívar forgot his instructions, which forbade him to have anything to do with the plans of Miranda. He thought that his presence would give fresh impulse to the idea of independence, and invited him to accompany the envoys on their return. Miranda accepted the invitation, and they landed at Caracas in December.

When news of the revolution in Venezuela reached Cadiz, the Regency proclaimed the leaders of the movement rebels, and, declining the mediation of Great Britain, declared war against them, and ordered a blockade of the coast. Cortabarria, a member of the Council of the Indies, was charged with the task of subduing them, [and Miyares was appointed captain-general in place of Emparán. In the Spanish West India Islands preparation was made to sustain the decrees of the Regency by force. Thus the first link in the chain which bound the colonies of the Spanish Main to the mother country was broken.

The Central Junta of Caracas responded by raising an army of 2,500 men; placed the Marquis Del Toro in command, and sent him against Coro, the head-quarters of the Royalist reaction. On the 28th November the army attacked the town, but was beaten off. Its retreat was intercepted by a division of 800 men, but it forced its way on and reached Caracas with heavy loss, harassed on the way by a hostile population.

When Miranda again landed on American soil he was sixty years of age. The people received him with ovations; Government appointed him lieutenant-general of their army; youthful citizens looked to him as the oracle of their future destinies; the soldiery regarded him as the herald of victory; yet at first his influence was not felt in public affairs.

Grave, taciturn, and dogmatic, with unflinching opinions formed in solitude, Miranda discussed nothing, though he sought to make proselytes. Government appointed him, with Roscio and Ustariz, republicans of the North American school, to draw up a plan for a Constitution on the basis of the federation of the Provinces. The old dreamer, who mixed up classic traditions with modern theories, sought to combine them with the worn-out institutions of the colonial epoch. According to his plan, the administration should be entrusted to two Incas (Roman consuls), appointed for ten years; the rest of the plan was modelled on the municipal institutions of the colonies. He was far behind the day in which he lived. To propagate his doctrines, and to foment the spirit of independence, he with Bolívar organized a political club on the model of that of the Girondins, of which he had been a conspicuous member.

The first Congress of Venezuela was convened on the 2nd March, 1811; thirty deputies from various Provinces were present, Miranda was one of them. This Congress appointed an Executive Junta of three members, created a High Court of Justice in place of the Audiencia; and named Roscio, Ustariz, and Tobar commissioners to draw up a Constitution. The question of independence was then discussed. Miranda, who was the leading advocate of an immediate declaration, carried the measure, by a majority, on the 5th July. The same day the flag raised by Miranda in 1806, stripes of yellow, blue, and red, was adopted as the national ensign of Venezuela. Thus Venezuela was the first independent republic in South America.

Many of the inhabitants of Caracas were natives of the Canary Islands. Among them the agents of Cortabarria found the leaders for a reactionary movement, which broke out on the 11th July. The insurgents were quickly surrounded by the populace, aided by a part of the garrison, and compelled to surrender. The greater part of those taken in arms were banished, but the leaders were put to death and their heads were exposed on the public roads; sad presage of the war of extermination which was to deluge the soil of Venezuela with blood.

On the same day a more formidable outbreak took place at Valencia. The inhabitants armed, as they said, in the cause of religion, and entrenched the city. An army corps under Del Toro marched against them, but was beaten off, on which Miranda was placed in command. A strong outwork was carried by assault, but the army was again repulsed in an attack on the great square. Bolívar and Del Toro were both present in this affair.

Miranda, after receiving a reinforcement, again attacked the city. Proceeding more cautiously, he gradually shut up the Royalists in the great square, where want of water soon compelled them to surrender at discretion. This short campaign cost the Patriots 800 men in killed alone, but Miranda did not sully his victory by bloodshed, and Congress released all the prisoners, an act of clemency which was severely blamed, in view of the severity with which the Canarians of Caracas had been treated.

The debate on the Constitution produced a lengthy discussion in Congress. A plan drawn up by Ustariz, which was an adaptation of the Constitution of the United States, was adopted almost unanimously, but Miranda voted against it, alleging that a Federal Constitution was not suited to the country.

Valencia was declared the capital of the new Republic.

Congress being in want of funds, had issued a paper currency for the payment of their employés of all classes; its rapid depreciation in value brought about a state of misery and discontent which enervated the spirit of the revolution.

Cortabarria recruited 1,000 men in Puerto Rico and sent them, under Cajigal, to reinforce the Royalists of the Western Provinces, where the reaction gained ground every day.

Popular leaders rose up on every side in defence of the cause of Spain; their successes served to display the strength of the country itself, and to prepare weapons for the revolution when its principles were understood and adopted by the people.

In February, 1812, a small detachment of 230 men, under a naval officer named Monteverde, marched from Coro, raised all the country as far as Barquisimeto, and at Carora defeated a Patriot force of 700 men. The town of

Carora was sacked, and many Patriots were shot without trial.

In the east of Venezuela, Spanish Guayana had declared against the revolution. Colonel Moreno marched with 1,400 men to rescue the Province from the Royalists, and being joined by various scattered detachments of the Patriots, collected a flotilla of twenty-eight gunboats on the Orinoco, and threatened the town of Angostura, which stands on the northern bank near to the mouth of that river.

On the 25th March, 1812, the Royalists, with nine schooners and eight gunboats, attacked the Patriot flotilla in the bay of Lorondo, and after two days' fighting completely destroyed it. Moreno retreated, and eventually fled, while the remnant of his force capitulated at the town of Maturin.

On the 26th March, 1812, in the afternoon of a calm day, a great roar was heard under the hills of Mérida. The ground commenced to rock to and fro in violent oscillations. In less than a minute the cities of Mérida, Barquisimeto, San Felipe, La Guayra, and Caracas were nothing more than heaps of ruins, under which 20,000 people lay entombed. In the capital almost all the garrison perished. At Barquisimeto the greater part of a division of 1,000 men which was on the march to arrest the progress of Monteverde, with a large amount of military stores, were buried. Under these ruins the first Republic of Venezuela found a grave.

This earthquake was felt only in territory occupied by the revolutionists; the Provinces of Coro, Maracaibo, and Guayana, which were faithful to the King, suffered nothing. The clergy, who were for the most part Royalists, made use of the fact, pointing to it as a chastisement of Heaven upon impious men and upon rebels. Fear entered into the hearts of the people, and dismay into those of the Patriots.

Monteverde dug seven guns and much war material from

beneath the ruins of Barquisimeto, armed the people, and raised his force to 1,000 men. At San José a division of 1,300 raw recruits sallied out to meet him; one squadron passed over to him, the rest were cut to pieces. The prisoners were butchered, and the neighbouring town of San Carlos was sacked and burned. The cities of Mérida and Trujillo declared for the King. The common people, and deserters from the Patriot armies, flocked to Monteverde; he marched upon Valencia. Forty-five days after his departure from Coro he entered the Federal capital in triumph.

Affairs were now in so critical a state that Miranda was appointed Dictator. He established his head-quarters at Victoria, between Valencia and Caracas, and advanced with 4,000 men against the former city. During a skirmish between outposts an entire company passed over to the Royalists, and Miranda retreated to a position which he strengthened with field-works. The hero of Valmy and Jemappes, whose name is inscribed on the Triumphal Arch at the Barrière d'Etoile, seems to have disappeared under the cloak of the Dictator, and the irresolute General of Maestrich and Nerwinde reappeared on a new scene.

Colonel Antoñanzas, detached by Monteverde to the plains of Caracas, took the town of Calabozo by assault, and put the garrison to the sword. Then being joined by a Spaniard named TOMAS BOVES, he attacked San Juan de los Morros, where not only the fighting men, but the old men, women, and children, were butchered.

The Province of Barinas declared for the King, and Monteverde, being now secure in his rear, twice attacked Miranda in his entrenchments, but was each time repulsed with heavy loss. Having received reinforcements from Coro, he made a third attack, and was again repulsed, but, undismayed, he made a flank movement and turned the position of the Patriots, whereupon Miranda, though with a force greatly superior in number to his adversary, set fire to his stores, and retired precipitately, on the night of the 17th June, to Victoria. Monteverde, at the head of a small detachment, again attacked him in his new position, and caused great confusion in the encampment, but was eventually beaten off.

The Royalist leader had now more than 3,000 men under his orders, and, being joined by Antoñanzas, made a general attack on the entrenchments thrown up by Miranda at Victoria on the 29th June, but was repulsed with heavy loss after expending all his ammunition.

Miranda made no attempt to pursue him, and in a council of war it was decided to retreat to Valencia. A Spaniard prevailed upon Monteverde to disregard the decision of the council, and to remain where he was for three days. These three days were the last of this revolution.

On the 24th June a general insurrection of the slaves broke out in the valleys to the south-east of Caracas. Miranda had decreed liberty to all slaves who would join the Patriot armies. Their Spanish owners preferred to arm them themselves to fight against the Patriots. The negroes committed all manner of excesses, attacked several towns, maltreated the white inhabitants, and came so near to Caracas that Miranda was compelled to detach troops against them.

Bolívar had been placed in command of the city of Puerto Cabello. During a temporary absence of his, the Spanish prisoners, who were numerous, gained over the garrison of the citadel, and took possession of it. Bolívar attempted to retake it with the troops quartered in the city; his advance posts went over to the enemy. On the 4th July Monteverde approached; Bolívar sent out 200 men against him. They were beaten, and only seven men with one officer returned. On this the rest of his troops disbanded, and, with seven officers, he fled by sea to La Guayra. When Miranda heard of this he exclaimed, " Venezuela is stricken to the heart."

The Royalists had now the whole of the west and the plains; they dominated both banks of the Orinoco and the sea coast; the Patriots held barely a third of the territory of Venezuela. The army still numbered 5,000 men, mostly recruits, but the general had no confidence in them, nor had his subordinates any longer faith in him. Every one accused Miranda of having caused the miseries they suffered: some called him a traitor. In despair he summoned a council, and by their advice opened negotiations with the enemy.

In order to be in a better position to treat, Miranda made an attack upon the enemy's lines, and routed several detached parties of the Royalist troops, after which he proposed a suspension of hostilities. The proposition was accepted by Monteverde, on condition that the Royalist troops should be permitted to advance on Caracas.

Miranda then made further proposals, and authorised his commissioners to sign a capitulation, which should guarantee the freedom and properties of the insurgents. Some of his officers protested against this, and advised him to risk everything on the chance of a battle, but in reality all wished for peace, and he knew it. A capitulation, though a defeat, would do more for Venezuela than would a passing victory; public opinion had veered round and was master of the situation. It was necessary that Venezuela should suffer the yoke of the victorious reaction, in order that she might know what it meant, and might gather up her forces for the decisive struggle.

The capitulation was agreed to by Monteverde, and by the commissioners appointed by Miranda, on the basis of the complete submission of the Patriots and a general amnesty. Miranda, after some hesitation, acceded to these terms, and withdrew to Caracas. The troops either joined the Royalist forces or dispersed.

On the 30th July Monteverde entered Caracas in triumph, while Miranda, with Bolívar and several of his principal officers, trusting not at all to the capitulation, left for La Guayra, intending to fly by sea. The captain of an English ship had offered a passage to Miranda, and urged him to embark at once. Bolívar and the others prevented him from going on board, saying that he required rest. They dined together, and after Miranda had retired, twelve officers formed themselves into a sort of secret tribunal, and decided that he, as the author of the capitulation, ought to share the fate of the rest. Bolívar accused him of receiving bribes from the Spaniards, and voted for his death as a traitor to the cause of independence, but it was resolved to detain him. Before dawn Bolívar went to his room, removed his sword and pistols, and then awoke him. He was made prisoner by his own friends and shut up in the castle of San Carlos.

Monteverde paid no attention whatever to the terms of the capitulation. The prisons were filled with citizens; Bolívar hid himself, but all except two of the other members of the secret tribunal were among the prisoners. Many died in the dungeons, and the Canarians had their revenge in the open plunder of all who had taken part against them.

Miranda was sent to Puerto Cabello and loaded with chains. From his dungeon he addressed a memorial to the Supreme Court, demanding, in the name of the new Spanish Constitution, the liberty of his comrades as guaranteed by the capitulation, but he asked nothing for himself. His protest was unheeded, and he, being sent to Spain, languished for three years in a dungeon at Cadiz, where he died miserably on the 14th July, 1816, and was buried in the mud banks, over which the waters of the Mediterranean ebb and flow, in front of that city.

Bolívar, after remaining for some days in hiding, was presented by a Spanish friend of his to Monteverde, who gave him a passport " in recompense for his service to the King in the imprisonment of Miranda."

CHAPTER XXXVII.

THE REVOLUTIONS IN NEW GRANADA AND QUITO.

1809—1813.

THE events in Spain in the year 1808 produced great excitement in New Granada, which was increased in the following year by receipt of advices of the revolution in Quito, mentioned in the last chapter. On the 9th September, 1809, Amar, the Viceroy, summoned an assembly of the Corporations and of leading citizens of the capital, and sought counsel from them. Men of American birth, who were members of this assembly, not only spoke in favour of the Junta of Quito, but asked for the establishment of a similar government at Santa Fé de Bogotá. Spaniards advised the immediate dissolution of the revolutionary government. Amar followed the counsel of the latter, and sent a column of 300 men to dissolve the Junta; at the same time the Viceroy of Peru sent 800 men on the same errand.

The Junta of Quito had already raised three battalions of infantry, and sent two companies with three guns against the detachment from New Granada, but these troops, while on the march, were completely routed by the inhabitants of the Province of Pasto on the 16th October. The revolutionists, dismayed at this disaster, on receiving promise of an amnesty, replaced Castillo, the late captain-general, in command.

When the two expeditions reached Quito the amnesty was set aside. The leaders of the revolution were arrested, some were sentenced to death, others to penal servitude. The indignant populace attacked and captured one of the barracks, but were promptly driven out again by the soldiery and dispersed. The soldiers then proceeded to the public gaol, where the prisoners were confined, and killed twenty-five of them; after which they spread about the streets, and killed eighty citizens, among the victims being three women and three children. The butchery was only stopped by the intercession of the Bishop.

Castillo, horrified at these excesses, hastily convened an assembly of the civil and ecclesiastical authorities and of leading citizens. With their concurrence he proclaimed a general pardon, and sent the Peruvian troops, who had taken the lead in the massacres, back to Lima.

Word of these atrocities reached New Granada at the same time that news arrived of the revolution in Venezuela, and produced an immediate effervescence throughout the country.

In New Granada, according to one of their own writers, "all the races of the world had come together to mingle their blood, their traditions, their strength, and their character, and united in the work of civilization."

Two-thirds of the population were white, residing mostly in the towns and cities, hence the revolution took here a civic form, and was greatly hampered by local jealousies and by divergencies of opinion among the leaders.

The first revolutionary movement occurred at Cartagena, where the people, headed by their Cabildo, demanded a Junta. With the intervention of an agent of the Regency of Cadiz, then in the city, a Junta of three was appointed, of whom the actual governor was one; but as he openly showed his dissatisfaction with this arrangement, he was banished to Havana on the 11th June, 1810.

To the east of the most easterly range of the Cordillera lie the wide plains of Casanare; here two youths raised the standard of insurrection. They were joined by some small groups of the country people, which were dispersed by troops sent against them by the Viceroy. The leaders were put to death, and their heads were sent to the capital.

On the 4th July a Junta was set up by the Cabildo of Pamplona.

At Socorro two companies of the line and some militia were quartered. In a moment of false alarm they fired upon an assemblage of the people. Eight thousand citizens arose in arms and besieged them in their barracks. A Junta was formed of eight deputies elected by the people, and the government was placed in their hands.

At Bogotá everything was ripe for a revolution. Several attempts had been made without result, but the news from Venezuela and from the provinces, and above all the expectation of the speedy arrival of commissioners from the Regency of Cadiz, decided the Patriots to make another attempt, which was precipitated by an incident. On the 20th July a Spaniard spoke contemptuously of Americans; the people rushed tumultuously to the great square, demanding an open Cabildo and a Junta. They were supported by the municipal authorities. The Viceroy declined to accede to their wish. The bells of the churches were rung, and six or seven thousand armed men assembled in front of the public offices. The Viceroy had a thousand troops. A conflict seemed imminent, when at last he gave way, and sanctioned the summoning of a special Cabildo.

At six o'clock the same evening the Cabildo met. The debate was stormy, Dr. Camilo Torres taking the lead. The Patriots demanded a Junta, the Spaniards sought to gain time by resisting the proposition. One of the popular orators declared that any man who left his place before a Junta was appointed, was a traitor to his country. The speech was applauded by the people outside. A Junta was named, with the Viceroy, who was very popular, as President, and was installed in office at three in the morning of the 21st July.

The Junta drew up a constitution, on the basis of a federal union of the various provinces. The sovereignty of King Ferdinand was recognised, and also the authority of the Regency of Cadiz, so long as it should exist. This was a compromise on all sides, and the Junta being overawed by the popular leaders, had no real power. Later on the Viceroy was deposed, and the Junta was instructed to govern in the name of the King in complete independence of any other authority in Spain. Two days afterwards Montufar and Villavicencio arrived as commissioners from Spain, but were powerless to do more than accept what was already done. Montufar, who was entrusted with a special mission to Quito, continued his journey to that city, where we shall presently find him at the head of the revolutionists.

Anarchy and reaction were not slow to follow on these hasty steps. Local jealousies, which had been kept in check by the colonial system; divergence of opinion between the leaders of the movement; the antagonistic interests of Americans and Spaniards, and the instincts of the masses who grouped themselves on geographical lines, all combined to bring on complications in which the strength of the country was wasted without any good result.

The Junta sent a circular to the provinces inviting them to send deputies to a Congress. Nearly every province followed the example of the capital by appointing a Junta, but some of them refused to send deputies to a Congress, preferring to consider themselves independent republics.

Cartagena refused to acknowledge in any way the authority of the Junta of the capital, and invited the other provinces to send deputies to a Congress in that city. One province only acceded to this proposition, but it sufficed to prevent the assemblage of the Congress at Bogotá, and postponed the formation of a central government, which was the urgent necessity of the moment.

The revolutionary leaders in the capital then tried a new plan. They formed the Province of Santa Fé, of which Bogotá was the chief city, into a monarchical republic, which they called "The State of Cundinamarca," its ancient name, with a legislature of two chambers, and Dr. Lozano was named President during the captivity of the King.

Lozano, after several fruitless attempts to bring about a general understanding, succeeded at last in assembling a Congress, but the want of a central government had produced such anarchy that the people, inflamed by the writings of Don Antonio Nariño, who advocated a centralized government, deposed Lozano, and on the 19th September, 1811, appointed Nariño Dictator.

Congress continued the debate on the Constitution, and adopted the federal system by a majority, but had no power to establish it, and withdrew from the capital, where it was overawed by the popular leaders, to the small town of Ibague, in the Province of Mariquita.

On the 11th November, 1811, the Province of Cartagena declared itself an independent State, and the Eastern Provinces endeavoured to join the Confederation of Venezuela.

Meantime the Royalists made no attempt to oppose the revolution in the great centres of population, but secured all the country to the south of the Province of Santa Fé, and established their base of operations at Quito, with Guayaquil as their port on the Pacific. To the north they held the Provinces of the Isthmus of Panama, with the fortress of Portobello, and also the city and Province of Santa Marta on the western bank of the Magdalena, and the Province of Rio Hacha, also on the Magdalena, but further inland. The insurgent Province of Cartagena, lying on the coast, was thus isolated from the other provinces which had declared for the revolution.

The Royalists established a second base of operations at Santa Marta, where they raised an army of 1,500 men, besides militia, and were reinforced by a battalion of Spanish troops from Cuba, while three Spanish ships-of-war guarded the coast, and either sunk or captured a Patriot flotilla sent against them from Cartagena in March, 1812.

Dr. Torices, a young man, twenty-four years of age, being named Dictator by the Constituent Convention of Cartagena, fitted out another flotilla, which he placed under the command of a French adventurer named Labatut, and sent it against the Royalists, who had crossed the Magdalena. Labatut drove them from the lower part of the river, and then returned and captured the city of Santa Marta in January, 1813.

At this time Don José Domingo Perez, who had been appointed Viceroy of New Granada by the Regency of Cadiz, reached Portobello, but his authority was not recognised by the insurgent provinces.

On the outbreak of the revolution Colonel Tacon was Governor of Popayán. By his energy he prevented the installation of a Junta in that city, but the Patriots set one up in the small town of Cali. The Governor sent troops against them. Santa Fé sent 300 men, under Colonel Baraya, to their assistance, on which basis they raised an army of 1,100 men, mostly Indians, armed with lances. Tacon led another army, 1,500 strong, against them, but was attacked and defeated by Baraya on the 28th March, 1811. This was the first victory gained by the Patriots of New Granada, and Tacon was forced to retire to the valley of Pasto, where he stood at bay in the passes leading to Quito, while Popayán fell into the hands of the revolutionists.

Meantime a fresh insurrection had taken place at Quito, and Tacon, after raising the Royalist population of the valleys, marched upon that city with 600 men. The new Government sent against him Don Pedro Montufar, the envoy from the Regency of Cadiz, and Tacon, being deserted by the greater part of his men, retreated to the coast, where he received help from Guayaquil, but was again defeated and withdrew to Peru.

Montufar easily dispersed the Royalist levies in the valley of Pasto, and returned to Quito, but the Royalists soon reassembled, and, incited by the priests, attacked the city of Popayán, but were beaten off, and were totally dispersed on the night following by a sortie of the garrison, which was headed by a young North American named Macaulay. A portion of them, aided by fresh levies, captured the city of Pasto before Macaulay could reach the place, but he prevailed upon them to give up their prisoners, and then marched away by night to join a column advancing from Quito. Being again attacked by these men of the valleys, he arranged a truce with them, which they made use of to surprise his camp, killing 200 men and making 400 prisoners, he himself being among these latter, with Caicedo, the late commandant of Pasto.

These valleys of Pasto and Patia were the Vendée of the revolution of New Granada, and the reaction was now there triumphant.

Don Pedro Montufar, in the capacity of commissioner from the Regency of Cadiz, had reached Bogotá after the pacific triumph of the revolution in that city. He had acceded to the new state of affairs, and had afterwards gone on to Quito, where he was received with enthusiasm. Under his auspices a Junta was there installed on the 19th September, 1810, under the presidency of Ruiz de Castillo, the late captain-general, but the authority of this Junta was not recognised by the Southern Provinces, where Peruvian influence was supreme. The Junta then raised an army of 2,000 men, which it placed under the command of Montufar, with orders to reduce these provinces to submission.

At the same time Molina, who had been appointed by the Viceroy of Peru captain-general of Quito in place of Ruiz de Castillo, reached Guayaquil, where he raised an army for the defence of these provinces. Neither Molina nor Montufar had much confidence in their troops, and confined their operations to desultory skirmishes, until, on the 11th December, the citizens of Quito deposed Ruiz de Castillo from his post as President of the Junta, summoned a Congress, and declared Quito to be an independent State. Ruiz retired to a convent, from which he was dragged by a mob and brutally murdered.

In the following year Marshal Montes arrived from Peru to take command of the Royalist forces, and on the 2nd September, 1812, defeated the Patriots at Mocha, giving no quarter. Montufar raised a new army, and took up a position on some precipices which covered the road to the capital, but Montes, marching for nine days by a circuitous route over the rugged slopes of Chimborazo, gained his rear and obliged him to retreat.

The Patriots then fortified the city of Quito, and declared they would hold out to the last extremity, but it was taken by assault on the 3rd November. Montufar retired northwards with the remnant of his force, but was pursued by Colonel Sámano, who beat him twice and captured all his guns. Sámano following out his instructions, shot all superior officers who fell into his hands, and, going on to Pasto where the prisoners of Popayán were confined, he shot one in every five of the officers and one in every ten of the soldiers, the victims being chosen by lot. Caicedo and Macaulay were among them. Thus was crushed the second revolution in Quito.

While the reaction closed in upon New Granada, the interior of the country was a prey to anarchy. Federalism struggled against centralization, Cundinamarca against the provinces, Nariño against Congress, till all was chaos.

Nariño pursued his policy of centralization by sending troops into the districts around the capital and annexing them to what he called "the legal province." Congress protested from its retreat at Ibague. Baraya, with the district of Tunja, pronounced in favour of Congress, and defeated a force sent by Nariño to reduce the Province of Socorro. Nariño was forced to come to terms, and resigned, but was reinstated by the citizens of the capital, who, on the 11th September, again proclaimed him Dictator, with absolute powers.

Congress, with eleven deputies who represented seven provinces, met soon after at Leiva and named Dr. Torres President. Torres, who was an enemy of Nariño's, soon found a pretext for an open rupture with him. Civil war broke out; Baraya, in command of the Federal troops, defeated Nariño and laid siege to Bogotá, but was repulsed and totally defeated in an ill-planned attack upon the city.

At this time Marshal Montalvo, a Cuban by birth, arrived as Viceroy in place of Perez. Patriotism, enervated by civil strife, revived. On the 16th July, 1813, Cundinamarca declared itself an independent State, and the Province of Antioquia followed the example. Nariño came to an arrangement with Congress, and offered troops to reinforce the army which was sent against the Royalists now advancing from the south.

General Sámano had occupied the city of Popayán with 2,000 men, and now menaced the Province of Antioquia. Congress placed the Federal army under the command of Nariño, giving him the rank of lieutenant-general. Nariño then abdicated the dictatorship and marched against the enemy. His first operations were successful; he defeated the main body under Sámano, occupied Popayán on the 31st December, and on the 13th January, 1813, again defeated the Royalist army, which fled to Pasto, but he made no attempt to follow up his victories. General Aymerich, who then replaced Sámano in command, was allowed two months in which to reorganize his scattered forces. Then Nariño again advanced with 1,400 men, and made his way through the guerillas, who swarmed in the valley of Patia, to the Juanambu river, where he found that the fords were defended by batteries. He forced a passage by one ford, but was driven back by Aymerich, who afterwards retreated.

This river Juanambu is an impetuous torrent, rushing

westward between precipitous cliffs from the slopes of the eastern Cordillera. The few fords are only occasionally passable, and the river is generally crossed by means of baskets or troughs of raw hide slung upon cables stretched from bank to bank, which are called "taravitas." The Patriot army was delayed twenty days in crossing by means of taravitas established by themselves, and then advancing again encountered the enemy strongly posted on the hills of Chacabamba.

The position was carried, with heavy loss, after four hours of desperate fighting. Again the Royalist army retreated, but the country people rose *en masse* in defence of their homes and drove back the Patriot vanguard, which was led by Nariño in person. Fugitives from this skirmish reported that he was taken prisoner; the main body was seized with panic, spiked their guns, and fled precipitately; only 900 reached Popayán. Nariño, returning with thirteen men to his encampment, found himself without an army. Deserted by his men he wandered alone for some days on the mountains, living on such wild fruits as he could find, then giving himself up he was sent in irons to Spain.

Bolívar, after leaving Caracas, resided for some time at Curaçoa, and then offered his services to the independent Government of Cartagena. He was appointed military commandant of the district of Barrancas, on the Upper Magdalena, and resolved to make a campaign of his own against the Royalists of Santa Marta, who obstructed the navigation of the river. Here the future Liberator first showed his genius for enterprise.

At the head of a small party of militia, he attacked the fortified town of Teneriffe, drove out the garrison, capturing their guns and boats, and then took the town of Mompox. Labatut, who commanded the Patriot flotilla acting against Santa Marta, complained of this to the Dictator as an intrusion upon his sphere of operations; but Torices reinforced Bolívar with some regular troops and fifteen armed boats, with which he ascended the river, and after sundry successful skirmishes entered the city of Ocaña in triumph in January, 1813.

In March, Labatut was driven from Santa Marta, and the coast line was occupied by the Royalists. Torices himself then led an expedition against them by sea, but was defeated with the loss of his artillery on the 13th May, Colonel Chatillon, who commanded the infantry, being killed.

The Royalists, being reinforced from Venezuela, then collected an army of 2,600 men in the Province of Barinas, under command of a naval officer named Tiscar, sent Colonel Correa with 1,000 men against Pamplona, and 700 men by another route to co-operate with him.

Colonel Castillo Rada, an officer of New Granada, who was raising troops in the Province of Pamplona, applied to Bolívar for help. Bolívar then conceived the daring plan of attempting the reconquest of Venezuela, and wrote to Torices and to Dr. Torres, showing them the advisability of carrying the war into the enemy's territory. Without waiting for an answer from either of them, he marched with 400 men by a stony pass across the mountain range in front of Ocaña, drove in the outposts of the enemy, and, spreading the report that he was followed by a large army, crossed the river Zulia in one canoe, and on the 28th February fell upon Correa. After four hours' sharp firing, the fight was decided by a furious charge with the bayonet; the Royalists were totally defeated, with the loss of all their artillery, and Bolívar was soon after joined by Castillo Rada with the troops he had raised in Pamplona.

Bolvíar's idea of reconquering Venezuela was looked upon as folly, just as San Martin's idea of reconquering Chile was when he first broached it. Happily, Bolívar also found a Pueyrredon to believe in him. He had published a memorial which produced a profound sensation in New Granada. In it he disclosed for the first time his peculiar ideas on the organization of a Republican Government, and on the proper mode of conducting the war. Explaining the causes of the fall of the Republic of Venezuela, he said:—

"Our rulers did not consult codes which would teach them the practical science of government, but those drawn up by dreamers who built republics in the air on the basis of the perfectability of human nature. We had philosophers as leaders, philanthropy for legislation, arguments instead of tactics, and sophists for soldiers."

He also denounced the federal form of government as contrary to the interests of young societies in face of a foreign war, and the folly of placing trust in raw levies in place of devoting all their energy to the organization of regular troops, and wound up by insisting that the safety of New Granada lay in the reconquest of Venezuela.

President Torres read this memorial with great attention, and though it clashed with his ideas as a federal, he saw that it was the work of a deep thinker who was also a man of action, and the language used appealed both to his reason and to his heart. The successes achieved by Bolívar in his first daring attempt decided him. He resolved upon the reconquest of Venezuela.

CHAPTER XXXVIII.

THE RECONQUEST OF VENEZUELA.

1813.

By the surrender of Miranda Monteverde was left unopposed in Venezuela, and was made Captain-General, with the title of "Pacificator." He commenced his work of pacification by deeds from which the warmest partisans of Spain now turn away their eyes in horror. He violated the capitulation by imprisoning so many citizens that the gaols could not hold them; many died of hunger and suffocation in filthy dungeons. In the provinces his reign of terror assumed forms still more barbarous; the whole country seemed given up to hordes of banditti.

Colonel Cervéris, pro-consul of Cumaná, acted with such inhumanity as even disgusted the hard hearts of his superiors, who replaced him by Antoñanzas, and the Audiencia complained of his misconduct to the Home Government. All this was but the prelude to a war of extermination, which was provoked by the Royalists by murders, by mutilations and by torture.

The people, cowed in spirit by their sufferings, by their political calamities, and by the natural catastrophes which had befallen them, were only too anxious for rest on any terms under the domination of the colonial system. Clemency would have kept them peaceful, but the reign of terror drove superstitious fears from their minds, and changed weakness into strength. They fled from their persecutors into the woods and mountains; the leaders emigrated. Misery and despair created a desire for vengeance in the breasts of the most timid.

A handful of exiles gave the signal from a rock in the Antilles, and the whole of the eastern part of the territory rose in rebellion.

Famous in the history of the New World is the gulf called "Triste," discovered by Columbus on his third voyage, when he, without knowing it, landed for the first time on the Continent of which he was in search. At its mouth, between the eastern extremity of the Peninsula of Paria and the island of Trinidad, there lies a smaller island called Chacachacare; on it the fugitives from Cumaná took refuge. Though only forty-five in number, they resolved to renew the war and to raise the country against the Spaniards. A gallant youth of good family, from the island of Margarita, Santiago Mariño by name, put himself at their head. Manuel Piar, a handsome mulatto, two brothers, José Francisco and Bernardo Bermudez, and the engineer Ascue, formed his staff. With no other arms than six muskets and some pistols, they landed on the coast on the 13th March, 1813, surprised a guard, captured twenty-three muskets, and marched resolutely on the fortified town of Güiria. The garrison, who were all natives, joined them; on the 16th March they had 200 well-armed men.

With seventy-five men Bernardo Bermudez took the town of Maturin, where there was a deposit of military stores; his brother fortified Irapa on the Gulf, and Mariño made this place his head-quarters.

Cervéris had a small flotilla on the Gulf and 400 men, but did not dare to act on the offensive until, being reinforced by a Basque named Zuazola with 300 men, he sent him to retake Maturin. Zuazola easily overcame a small Patriot force which opposed his march, slaughtered them without mercy, and sent boxes full of human ears to Cumaná as trophies of his victory. He then tried to induce those of the country people who had fled to the woods to return to their homes, by giving them assurances of safety, but all who presented themselves were either killed or mutilated, men, women and children.

Some were flayed alive, some were tied two and two together by the shoulders and thrown into a lake.

Colonel Fernandez de la Hoz, governor of Barcelona, having joined Zuazola, they attacked Maturin with 1,500 men. In the absence of Bermudez, Piar was in command, and had 500 men with him. By a sudden attack upon them with his cavalry, he threw the Royalists into such disorder that they were forced to retreat. In April they again advanced and were this time completely routed.

Monteverde, who had looked upon the invasion as the escapade of a wild boy, now became alarmed and marched on Maturin with 2,000 men, but his troops were thrown into disorder by the heavy fire of cannon and musketry which was poured upon them from the town, and a charge of cavalry led by Piar completed the rout. Monteverde escaped with difficulty, leaving 400 dead upon the field, and lost all his guns and baggage. Marshal Cajigal, who was now placed in command of the district, remained strictly on the defensive at Barcelona, while the Patriots threatened Cumaná.

The island of Margarita lies in the Carribean Sea, off the mouth of the Gulf of Cariaco, on which the city of Cumaná is situate, and is about thirty-five miles from the mainland. It is divided by a range of mountains which run down the centre from east to west; the north and south coasts are thus completely separate, the only communication between them being by a narrow defile, easy of defence. Asuncion, the capital, lies inland on the south side, and is dominated by the fortress of Santa Rosa, but has a port on the coast, which is defended by the castle of Pampatar. The north side of the island is known as the district of Juan Griego, and has a good port on the Carribean Sea, which is defended by a blockhouse. The possession of Margarita was of great importance to both parties, not only by reason of its situation, but also because the inhabitants, being mostly sailors and fishermen, would be of great assistance in naval operations along the coast.

At that time Colonel Pascual Martinez, a petty tyrant of the Cervéris type, was governor of Margarita. The Audiencia reproved him for his conduct, and ordered certain prisoners on the mainland who had been accused by him, to be set at liberty. Furious at this, he declared that if any one of these men set foot on the island he would shoot him. Among the prisoners so set at liberty was a man of mixed race, who from being a fisherman had risen to be one of the largest proprietors on the island. This man, Juan Bauptista Arismendi by name, was a sort of chieftain among his fellows, a rude hero of the people, a man of vehement passions combined with innate sagacity, and of an adventurous spirit. On the fall of Miranda he was accused of treason and hid himself. Governor Martinez seized his wife and children and threatened to shoot them if they did not disclose his hiding-place. Arismendi gave himself up, his property was confiscated, his family reduced to poverty, and he himself was sent as a prisoner to La Guayra. He swore vengeance.

Being released, he returned to the island and was thrown into a dungeon. The populace rose *en masse*. Martinez shut himself up with a garrison in the castle of Pampatar, but was forced to surrender; Arismendi was made governor and kept his vow of vengeance. Martinez and twenty-nine Spaniards who were with him were shot.

Arismendi immediately opened communications with Mariño, offering to assist him in any way in his power. Mariño, who was now besieging Cumaná, asked for a flotilla to blockade the place. Arismendi sent him three armed schooners and eleven boats under an Italian named Bianchi, with a supply of arms and ammunition for the Patriot forces. Cumaná was thus speedily invested both by land and sea.

Cumaná was well fortified and was defended by a garrison of 800 men with forty guns, under command of Governor Antoñanzas. The Patriots dared not attempt an assault, but their blockade soon reduced the city to extremities. Antoñanzas, taking advantage of the careless watch kept by the Patriot flotilla, shipped a portion of his force on some small craft, and sailed away, as he said, in search of help, leaving the fortress in charge of a subordinate officer. This officer, seeing his position hopeless, entered into arrangements for a capitulation, but while the negotiation was in progress, spiked his guns, embarked the remainder of the garrison in such boats as they could lay hold of, and followed Antoñanzas, who had not succeeded in escaping from the Gulf. After rejoining him a fresh breeze sprang up, and the fugitives again set sail in eight small vessels, but were attacked by Bianchi as they left the Gulf. Only three vessels escaped, on one of which was Antoñanzas, who soon after died of a wound received in the action.

The city was occupied by the Patriots, and twenty-five prisoners of distinction were shot, at the instigation of José Bermudez.

Mariño then marched against Cervéris, who retreated, after shooting Bernardo Bermudez, who was lying in a hospital dangerously wounded.

Piar, with a strong column, occupied Barcelona, which was evacuated on his approach by Cajigal, who retired to Guayana. When he reached the Orinoco, a man named José Tomas Boves, who had served under Antoñanzas and Zuazola, and a Canarian named Morales, asked to be left behind, in order that they might raise the Llaneros against the Patriots. Cajigal gave them permission to make the attempt, and also left with them one hundred men and some supplies. This small force became the nucleus of a powerful army, which was destined to crush the Republic of Venezuela for the second time.

José Bermudez, with another column, captured several towns on the coast of the Gulf of Paria, and furious at the death of his brother, killed every Royalist who fell into his hands.

In eight months all the eastern part of Venezuela was thus reconquered by the Patriots, who named Mariño Dictator of the Provinces of Cumaná and Barcelona, and of the island of Margarita, with Piar as his second in command, at the same time that Bolívar entered Caracas in triumph and was acclaimed Dictator of the West after one of the most extraordinary campaigns of the epoch, which in some respects resembles the first campaign of Buonaparte in Italy.

While Bolívar, after his victory over Correa, was awaiting due authorization from the Government of New Granada to proceed with his scheme of reconquest, a young lawyer named Briceño, who had been a member of the Congress of Caracas, maddened at the excesses of Monteverde, presented to him a plan he had published in Cartagena, which he with others had sworn to carry out. His design was to make a general massacre of "the cursed race of European Spaniards and of the Canarians."

Bolívar and Castillo Rada, who shared the command with him, assented to it with the proviso "those found with arms in their hands."

Briceño started off on his campaign of murder with one hundred and forty sworn assassins, and a few days after sent back two heads as a trophy, a present which excited the horror of the two commanders. Briceño was soon after defeated and made prisoner by a very superior force, and was shot at Barinas, which execution was afterwards used by Bolívar as a pretext for cruel reprisals.

The Government of New Granada adopted the idea of Bolivar; the Republic of Venezuela should be restored under its auspices, and the federal form of government should be re-established under the previous authorities. The invading army was to be a liberating army only, and should take no part in the internal affairs of the sister republic, which should be called upon to pay the expenses of the expedition. Bolívar accepted these conditions, and swore to carry them out faithfully.

His first step was to detach Castillo Rada with 800 men against Correa. Castillo defeated the Royalist army in a sharply contested action, and drove it back to Trujillo, but then withdrew his forces and resigned his command through jealousy of Bolívar, thinking that his fellow-countrymen would prefer him as a leader to a Venezuelan. But Torres did not hesitate, he chose Bolívar to command the Granadian contingent, conferred the rank of brigadier upon him, and ordered him at once to drive the Royalists out of the Provinces of Mérida and Trujillo, after which he was to await instructions, which would be conveyed to him by commissioners from Congress, who would accompany him in all his future operations as those of the Convention accompanied the armies of Revolutionary France.

Bolívar had barely 600 men, while he was opposed by 6,000, who were so posted that wherever he attacked them they were always two to one. The first invasion of Bolívar along the western slopes of the eastern range of the Cordillera which crosses the territory of Venezuela, was a series of flashes of lightning which ended in a thunderbolt. On the 30th May he took Mérida unopposed. The city raised a battalion of 500 infantry and a squadron of cavalry to reinforce his army. His vanguard, under Girardot, then occupied Trujillo, and a strong detachment under D'Eluyar forced Correa to take refuge in Maracaibo.

The garrison of Trujillo retreated to Carache, a town devoted to the Royalist cause, but were driven out by Girardot, who shot all the Spaniards who were taken prisoners, and the town was declared "infamous" by Bolívar in a proclamation. In fifty days there was not an enemy left in either province.

From this time Bolívar assumed a new attitude, as the independent representative of the Republic of Venezuela, and became a sort of Dictator. In contravention of the express orders of the Government of New Granada, he on the 15th June fulminated in a proclamation an order for the extermination of all Royalists, which he established by decree on the 6th September as a fundamental law of Venezuela. The atrocities committed by Monteverde and his myrmidons produced their natural effect.

"Every Spaniard who does not conspire against tyranny in favour of the just cause, in the most active and efficacious manner, shall be held to be an enemy, shall be punished as a traitor, and shall be put to death."

A new system of dates was also adopted by him:— "Third year of Independence and first of the War to the Death."

This decree of extermination has found many apologists; with the exception of some Spaniards no one has condemned it as an act of personal atrocity. Only two men have utterly censured it. One of them, an historian of Venezuela named Gonzalez, says :—

"It created thousands of enemies to the Republic in the interior, and alienated exterior sympathy. It was the fury of a storm, a stain upon our history."

The other who condemned it was Bolívar himself, who in his last days spoke of it as a "delirium."

This struggle did not assume a ferocious character until the indigenous races took part in it. The Spanish leaders, Miyares, Ceballos and Cajigal, always acted with humanity and repressed the excesses of their subordinates, as also did Cortabarria, the agent of the Regency. Nothing that the Royalists had yet done could in any way justify this decree as a measure of retaliation.

At Trujillo Bolívar received orders from the Government of New Granada to proceed no further. As his ambition was to encircle his brow with the civic crown as liberator of his native land, to pause was to endanger the advantage he had already gained. From the east came echoes of the success achieved by Mariño and his comrades, but he aspired to be the man who should rescue the ruins of Caracas, the city of his birth, from the enemy. They might forestall him. On his own responsibility he went on.

Tiscar, the Spanish general, who occupied Barinas with 1,300 men, had done nothing to prevent the capture of Mérida and Trujillo, but at last determined to cut off the retreat of the invaders, and detached Colonel Marti with 700 men for that purpose. Bolívar at once crossed the mountains in his front with a strong vanguard, after detaching Rivas and Urdaneta with 500 men, by a more southerly route, in the same direction. On the 1st July Rivas found himself confronted by the entire column under Marti in a very strong position, from which he drove the Royalists to another stronger still, where he on the next day completely defeated them after five hours fighting, capturing a gun and 400 prisoners, all the Spaniards among whom were at once shot.

Tiscar retreated on the approach of Bolívar, who occupied Barinas on the 6th July, taking 13 guns and a large quantity of military stores, while Tiscar was so actively pursued by Girardot, that his men dispersed, and he fled to Guayana.

At Barinas, Bolívar raised some new battalions and several squadrons of cavalry, and separated this increased force into three divisions under Urdaneta, Girardot, and Rivas, which he dispersed in such a manner as must have ensured defeat in the face of an active enemy, but his manœuvres, imprudent as they were, resulted in the most brilliant success. Rivas, with 600 men, totally defeated 1,000 Royalists under Colonel Oberto on the 22nd July, and then recrossing the mountains for the third time in one month, rejoined Bolívar and Girardot.

Bolívar, who had now 1,500 men, marched rapidly against Colonel Izquierdo, who was encamped on the plain of Taguanes. Izquierdo, who had only 1,000 men, retreated in close column on Valencia, hotly pursued by the Patriots. After six hours marching, the Patriot cavalry headed the column, which was at once charged by the infantry and totally destroyed, Izquierdo himself falling mortally wounded.

Monteverde on hearing of the fall of Barinas, had gone to Valencia, but seemed perfectly bewildered by the rapid movements of Bolívar, and did nothing to assist his scattered divisions. Tardily, he left Valencia with some infantry and cavalry to support Izquierdo, but was met by the news of his defeat, and fled to Puerto Cabello, while

Bolívar entered Valencia unopposed, capturing thirty heavy guns and large quantities of military stores.

The garrison of Caracas, composed of civic guards and volunteers, for the most part dispersed, and General Fierro, who was in command, made overtures to Bolívar for a capitulation. Bolívar granted honourable terms, guaranteeing the lives and properties of the inhabitants, on condition that all the Province, including the fortress of Puerto Cabello, was given up. Fierro, without waiting to make a formal surrender, fled to La Guayra and escaped, but Monteverde refused to ratify the capitulation.

If Bolívar with his usual activity, had marched on Puerto Cabello, he must have captured it, as the fortifications were dismantled. Instead of this, he vaingloriously marched to receive the ovation which awaited him in Caracas, and gave Monteverde twenty days in which to prepare for defence.

In this campaign, Bolívar showed that though he had had no military education, he possessed the talents of a great revolutionary leader, and the inspiration of genius. At one step he gained a place among the celebrated captains of his time; he drew out his plans quickly and executed them with daring resolution, while he lost no time in securing the fruits of his victories. With 600 men, in ninety days, he had fought six battles, defeated and dispersed 4,500 men, captured fifty guns and three deposits of war material, had re-conquered the whole of western Venezuela from the Cordillera to the sea, and had restored the Republic. Never with such small means was so much accomplished, over so vast an extent of country, in so short a time.

Bolívar entered Caracas in triumph on the 6th August; the bells rang, the cannon roared, and the people shouted in applause of their liberator; his path was strewed with flowers, blessings were showered upon his head. Beautiful girls, belonging to the principal families of the city, dressed in white and wearing the national colours, led his horse by the bridle and crowned him with laurels. The prison doors were opened and the captive Patriots set free, and he did not sully his triumph by one act of vengeance, in spite of his terrible decree of extermination which had been ruthlessly carried out on every field of battle.

Two days later he announced the re-establishment of the Republic, but he did not restore the federal system, to which he was opposed on principle, and which was not consistent with the public safety. He proclaimed himself Dictator with the title of "Liberator," and in this, he showed both foresight and patriotism; the restoration of the old system would have certainly entailed anarchy and defeat.

There were thus two Dictators in Venezuela, Mariño in the East, Bolívar in the West. Mariño sent commissioners to Bolívar to treat concerning the form of government which should be adopted. Bolívar hesitated, he saw the necessity of establishing a firm central authority, and meanwhile Mariño, who had by this time a powerful army, did nothing against the common enemy.

On the 25th August Bolívar laid siege to Puerto Cabello. His Granadian troops stormed the outer defences and drove the garrison into the castle. Then batteries were erected on the coast, which beat off three Spanish brigs of war whose fire had raked the lines of the besiegers. On the night of the 31st an assault was made, but the only result of it was that Zuazola, who commanded an outwork, was made prisoner. Bolívar offered to exchange him for one of his own officers who had been captured. Monteverde refused, whereupon Zuazola was hanged on a gallows in front of the walls.

The Royalists were defeated, but they were not conquered; they soon recovered from their stupor, and reports of reactionary movements came from all sides. Then on the 6th September the Dictator fulminated another decree, his last thunderbolt in this war to the death, which produced one of the most dreadful hecatombs of which history bears record. He declared that all Americans who should even be suspected of being Royalists were traitors to their country. ¡This extreme and ill-advised measure greatly contributed to the defeat of Bolívar in the campaign now commencing. Such is the logic of Destiny!

On the 16th September the frigate *Venganza* arrived at Puerto Cabello from Spain, accompanied by an armed schooner and six transports, with the Granada regiment, 1,200 strong, under command of Colonel Salomón. Bolívar raised the siege and retired to Valencia.

Monteverde, encouraged by the retreat of the Patriots and by the reinforcement he had received, took the field on the 26th September with 1,600 men. But he had no fixed plan and committed the grave mistake of dividing his force. He himself took up a position on the road to Valencia at a place called Las Trincheras, and detached 500 men by another road to the heights of Barbula. Bolívar remained quiet for four days, unable to divine his intentions, and then sent Girardot and D'Eluyar with the Granadian troops against the enemy at Barbula, while a column under Urdaneta went in support. On the 30th September the Royalists were driven from this strong position, but Girardot fell, shot through the head in the moment of victory. His troops, in revenge, asked permission to attack the main body at Las Trincheras by themselves. Bolívar acceded to their request but supported them with 1,000 of his own troops. Monteverde was driven out of the entrenchments he had thrown up, with heavy loss, on the 3rd October. He himself being wounded returned to Puerto Cabello, leaving Salomón in command till he should recover, and the Patriots under D'Eluyar again laid siege to this fortress.

Bolívar, eager for fresh ovations, decreed sumptuous funeral honours to the memory of Girardot, to whose valour both New Granada and Venezuela owed their greatest victories. The citizens wore mourning for a month; his heart was taken out and carried to Caracas to be deposited in the Cathedral, his body was sent to Antioquia, his native province, and his pay was secured to his posterity. Bolívar himself accompanied the funeral procession to Caracas.

On the 14th October, the day of the obsequies, twenty of the civic functionaries of the capital assembled and decreed that Bolívar should be appointed Captain-General of the armies of Venezuela with the title of "Liberator," which he had already bestowed upon himself, and that the inscription "Bolívar, Liberator of Venezuela" should be inscribed over the gateways of all the public offices. Posterity has confirmed this title to him, but its acceptance at that time, when the reaction was gaining ground every day, was a symptom of inordinate personal vanity.

In return for this compliment Bolívar instituted the military order of "The Liberators"; a star with seven rays, symbolical of the seven provinces of the Republic, given as a decoration to those who should merit it by deeds of arms, and which carried with it certain privileges. This order was more democratic than those instituted by O'Higgins and San Martin in Chile and Peru, as it was for lifetime only, and was less aristocratic than the order of Cincinnatus created by Washington.

The time which Bolívar wasted in theatrical displays the Royalists made good use of for their own purposes. Boves was a Spaniard by birth, whose real name was Rodriguez. In his youth he was condemned to eight years penal servitude at Puerto Cabello for piracy, but was released chiefly through the intervention of a man whose name he then adopted in gratitude. He joined the revolution when it first broke out, but being looked upon as disaffected he was thrown into prison at Calabozo till that town was retaken by Antoñanzas, when he joined the Royalists and took part in the butchery at San Juan de los Morros. Morales, his companion and second in command, had served as a volunteer with the Royalists at Barcelona, and was made a sub-lieutenant of artillery by

Monteverde. These two men were both endowed with the warlike instinct, were both distinguished by indefatigable activity and by an iron will; they were just the sort of men to act as leaders of semi-barbarous troops. But Boves, with all his ignorance and brutality, had something of moral elevation about him : he fought for a cause, not for rapine. Morales took an actual pleasure in cruel deeds, and was of insatiable rapacity. These two men were the first to discover the latent strength of the people, which the revolution later on assimilated to itself. Up to this time the revolutionary movement had been confined to the cities and towns; Bolívar with all his perspicacity never suspected that the main strength of the country lay on the plains around them.

When these two men were left on the north bank of the Orinoco by Cajigal they adopted Bolívar's plan of rousing the country by proclamations. They called the Llaneros to arms, offering them bloodshed and booty in the cause of the King, with pain of death to all who disregarded the summons. Each man presented himself on horseback with a lance ; in each district a squadron was formed which took its name. Boves taught them the secret of victory, which was to have no fear of death, to go straight on and never look behind. In a very short time they had 2,500 men embodied, an army of horsemen such as had never yet been seen in America.

Colonel José Yañez, a Canarian, was a man of the same stamp as Boves and Morales, but of greater military skill. After the dispersion of the column by Tiscar, he had retreated to San Fernando on the Apure River, and with some help from Guayana, had there organized an infantry corps of 500 men, which he named the " Numancia" battalion. He also raised two regiments of Llanero cavalry, each 500 strong. With this force he invaded Barinas in September, before the waters had retired from the plains.

Boves opened his campaign by surprising a column of

1,000 men which had been sent against him, near Calabozo, on the 20th September. The cavalry passed over to him, the infantry he routed. He murdered all his prisoners, and then took and sacked the small town of Cura.

Now there appeared upon the scene another singular character, of the iron temperament of Boves, with all his ferocity and courage, who raised a barrier to his impetuous onslaught. Nothing was known of him except that he was a Spaniard who had come to America very young, and had married an American wife. When Bolívar opened his campaign of emancipation, this man had headed the rising at Mérida; then, leaving wife and children, he raised a battalion and devoted himself body and soul to the cause of independence. Throughout the campaign he distinguished himself by his indomitable valour and by his cruelty to prisoners, to whom he gave no quarter. The cause of his hatred to his fellow countrymen is unknown. He was accustomed to say :—

"When the Spaniards are all killed then I will cut my own throat, so that there shall not be one left."

The name of this man was Vicente Campo Elias. At Las Trincheras he was raised to the rank of lieutenant-colonel for conspicuous bravery. This was the man to send against Boves.

He marched from Valencia with 1,000 infantry and 1,500 cavalry. Boves with 2,500 horse, and Morales with 500 infantry, waited for him at a place called Mosquitero, at the entrance to the plains. On the 14th October the armies met. Boves charged the left wing of the Patriots with his usual impetuosity, and carried all before him, but Campo Elias, caring nothing for this, rushed upon the main body of the Royalists, and routed them completely in fifteen minutes. Morales escaped badly wounded, but nearly the whole of his infantry were butchered, and the Llanero horse were cut to pieces. Boves and Morales fled with twenty men beyond the Apure, and the state of the plains rendered pursuit impossible.

Campo Elias contented himself by retaking the town of Calabozo, and killing every man in the place for having given assistance to Boves. Unarmed Venezuelans were butchered by Venezuelan troops at Calabozo in the name of Liberty on the same day on which Bolívar was greeted in Caracas as the Liberator. This cruel deed decided the Llaneros. Seeing that there was no mercy for them, they abandoned their homes and looked to Boves for their revenge. The decree of extermination began to bear fruit.

Ceballos, who commanded at Coro, on hearing that reinforcements had reached Puerto Cabello, drew up a plan for the concerted action of the scattered bands of Royalists. With such men as he could collect, he sallied forth, and after routing two detachments of Patriots took Barquisimeto, where he was attacked by Bolívar and Urdaneta. Bolívar captured the town with a handful of horse, but his main body was totally routed by the Spanish infantry led by Ceballos, who, after his victory, crossed the Cordillera, and at Araure, in the valley of Caracas, effected a junction with the column under Yañez. Salomón, instead of joining him, marched with 1,000 men to the heights of Vigirima, to the west of the city of Caracas, and there entrenched himself.

Bolívar was then at Valencia with the Granadian contingent. He collected what other troops he could; Rivas brought up the garrison of Caracas, with a battalion of 500 students from the University. After two days' fighting, Salomón was on the 25th October driven back to Puerto Cabello with the loss of four guns. Bolívar then turned his attention to Ceballos, and by drawing 1,500 men from the force under Campo Elias, he had by the 1st December collected a force of 3,000 men. Ceballos had 3,500 men and ten guns, posted in a strong position on the slopes of the mountains, at the town of Araure. Here Bolívar attacked him on the 4th December. One Patriot battalion advancing incautiously was cut to pieces, but Bolívar, nothing daunted, brought up the rest of his troops, and ordered a charge with the bayonet, which was his favourite manœuvre. He was no tactician; he hurled his men in masses upon the enemy, and trusted to their valour. Yañez attempted to take the attacking column on the flank with his cavalry, but was himself taken in flank by the Patriot cavalry, and utterly routed. Ceballos, after a stubborn resistance, was completely defeated, losing 500 killed, 400 prisoners, and all his guns. He fled to Guayana, 800 of his infantry escaped in the same direction, and Yañez fled to the Apure with 200 men. This was the first pitched battle won by Bolívar.

After the rout of Barquisimeto, Bolívar had formed the fugitives into a battalion, which, in punishment of their cowardice, he called the "Nameless Battalion," telling them that they should have no flag till they did something to merit one. This corps greatly distinguished itself at the battle of Araure. Bolívar now presented it with the flag of the Numancia battalion, which had been captured in the fight, and renamed it "The Victor of Araure."

Salomón had again taken the field with 1,300 men, but on hearing of the defeat of Araure, he again retired to Coro, harassed on his way by detached parties of the Patriots, and losing two guns and more than half his men.

Bolívar then marched to assist D'Eluyar in the siege of Puerto Cabello. The moment was propitious; the Spanish ships of war had left for the Havana, and Piar, with the flotilla from Cumaná, had established a blockade, cutting off the garrison from all supplies. Monteverde had been dismissed in disgrace from his command; Ceballos, who had been appointed to succeed him, was a fugitive in Guayana, where also was Cajigal, who had been appointed by the Home Government Captain-General of Venezuela, and had as yet done nothing. Still the garrison, which was only 600 strong, held out.

Meantime the dual dictatorship brought forth its natural fruit. The victories of the West were sterile without the concurrence of the army of the East. Mariño refused to combine operations with Bolívar until he was recognised as the supreme ruler of the territory he possessed. The Liberator modestly entreated him to march upon the plains, where Boves and Yañez were recruiting. Far from doing this, though such action was necessary to his own security, he even recalled his flotilla from Puerto Cabello, but Piar listened to the appeals of Bolívar, and continued the blockade. The result was that Bolívar, being unable to attend to the siege of Puerto Cabello and to the war upon the plains at the same time, Boves and Yañez were speedily in a position to assume the offensive. Boves, more especially, with that wonderful energy which hesitated at no means, however terrible they might be, to the end before him, again took the field, two months after his defeat by Campo Elias.

On the 1st November he summoned all able-bodied men to join him, proclaimed war to the knife against the Patriots, decreed that their goods should be distributed among his troops, and, finally, liberated all slaves who would enlist under the banners of the King. The Llaneros, irritated by the massacre of Calabozo, and eager for plunder, flocked in masses to his standard. From Guayana came 100 infantry and one gun. By the middle of December he had 3,000 cavalry, the blades of whose lances were forged from the spikes torn from the railings of windows.

With this horde he descended to the lower plains. On the 14th December he routed a division of 1,000 men at San Marcos, and occupied Calabozo, slaughtering without mercy, and enriching his troops with booty. He then overran the whole plain lying between the windward coast range and the Gulf of Paria. For further operations he needed infantry, and set to work to make some. At the same time Yañez, with some help from Guayana, organized a force of 2,000 men on the Apure, and captured the city of Barinas, while Cajigal and Ceballos raised another army on the leeward coast.

Bolívar was reduced to Caracas and the neighbouring valleys, with a feeble reserve in Valencia, and was constantly harassed by Royalist guerillas. Urdaneta, who had marched on Coro, was forced to return to his assistance.

Mariño, with 3,500 men distributed along the coasts of Barcelona and Cumaná, and in the adjacent valleys, did nothing. All the rest of Venezuela was occupied by Royalists; the country people were everywhere in favour of the reaction, and the Patriots were forced to seek refuge in the cities. The Patriot armies were entirely without guides, no one would give them any information. Despatches to the various commanders could only be forwarded from head-quarters under strong escort. At times only four men out of an escort reached their destination. Public opinion had returned to the state in which it was left by the earthquake of 1812.

Columbian historians attribute this revulsion of feeling to Bolívar's decree of extermination, and to the excesses authorized by him. Bolívar was to fall as Miranda had fallen before him, but from different causes. Ever the logic of Destiny!

CHAPTER XXXIX.

THE SECOND FALL OF VENEZUELA.

1814.

A DICTATORSHIP was a necessity of the time, but the powers of a Dictator to be efficient must be united in one person. Bolívar shared his power with Mariño, the alleged rights of both rested upon force only. To put an end to this anomaly Bolívar determined upon an appeal to public opinion. It was impossible to summon a Congress, he therefore convened an Assembly composed of the civil corporations and of the heads of families of the city of Caracas.

Now was disclosed another phase of his complex character; never in any public man were seen greater contradictions between word and deed. A prey to insatiable ambition he was eager for uncontrolled power, but repudiated it in theory. In South America he was the inventor of the system of resignations, which has had great vogue since his time. He had supreme power in his hands, and resigned it, protesting that he would never again accept it, but took it back on conditions imposed by himself. Throughout his career, he ever invoked the high authority of Congresses as the representatives of public opinion; sometimes he gave way to them, more frequently he imposed his will upon them; but he always sought their sanction for his acts, and so compelled them to share responsibility with him.

To the Assembly he now convened at Caracas, to which by

a convenient fiction he attributed representative authority, he gave an account of his administration, and into its hands he abdicated the power he had bestowed upon himself, only to receive it back again intact. He made three speeches; in the first he abdicated the Dictatorship, and pronounced a warm eulogium upon his own deeds; in the second, he gave a biographical sketch of his own life, and showed from it that it was impossible for him to continue in the exercise of unlimited power; in the third, he again accepted the Dictatorship, which was bestowed upon him without conditions by the acclamations of the Assembly.

His next step was to endeavour to secure the co-operation of Mariño, by recognising his authority in the eastern provinces, and in January, 1814, a treaty was signed between them. But it was too late now, their union merely prolonged the struggle.

Yañez was advancing with 1,000 men by the eastern slopes of the Cordillera. Urdaneta crossed the range, and on the 2nd February met him with 700 men at Ospino. Yañez led a charge of the Llanero horse upon the Patriot infantry, but was killed, and his troops dispersed. His body was cut into fragments, which were sent as trophies to the scenes of his atrocities. Calzada, who took the command, in revenge burned the town of Ospino and then retreated.

Campo Elias was detached with 1,500 men against Boves and his hordes of Llanero horse. He marched to the town of Cura, where it was arranged that he should be joined by Mariño, but Mariño never came. Boves detached Rosete with 1,200 men to Ocumare, a town lying to the west of Caracas, which was feebly defended, and the inhabitants, men, women, and children, were all butchered; even those who had taken refuge in the church found there no safety.

On the 3rd February Campo Elias and Boves met at La Puerta. The Patriots were crushed by overwhelming numbers, and all the infantry perished, but Boves was badly wounded. Campo Elias, with the remains of his force, retreated to the narrow pass of Cabrera in front of Valencia, where he threw up entrenchments.

Morales, who now took command of the Royalists, advanced with 1,000 horse and 300 infantry by the valley of Aragua to Victoria, which city he attacked on the 10th February. Here Rivas was in command of the Patriots, but had hard work to hold the position against the superior numbers of the Royalists, till Campo Elias suddenly appeared at the head of 220 horse, and Morales was beaten off with the loss of all his artillery, and retired to Cura.

Rivas then marched with 800 men upon the town of Charavaye, then occupied by the column under Rosete, and cut the Royalists to pieces, giving no quarter. He then re-took Ocumare, and finding the streets strewn with dead bodies, swore an oath of vengeance, in which oath he was joined by Arismendi, who held the command at Caracas in his absence. This vow was most fearfully fulfilled.

Arismendi finding the prisons of La Guayra full of Spaniards, wrote to Bolívar who was at Valencia, asking instructions, and stating that their presence was a danger to the capital. The answer was an order for the immediate execution of all of them, except such as had taken out letters of naturalization.

"The Secretary of the Liberator is a fool," said Arismendi, "he has put with the *exception* instead of *including.*"

Then with a refinement of cruelty, he set the prisoners to work to erect a great funeral pile on which their bodies should be burned. When the pile was ready the massacre commenced, the prisoners were brought in groups from the dungeons; to the sound of the trumpet the soldiers fell upon them with bayonet, axe, and poniard, and cast their quivering bodies into the flames. Very little powder was burned on the eight days during which the slaughter lasted. Eight hundred and sixty-six victims perished, among them being many who had saved the lives of Patriots at the risk of their own.

These horrible massacres were the natural fruit of Bolívar's decree of extermination. They utterly failed to accomplish their purpose, that of stamping out the spirit of reaction, and only served as a pretext for the perpetration of equally brutal atrocities by the Royalists.

Bolívar, who had only 1,500 infantry and 600 cavalry, could not advance into the open country against Boves, who had at least four times that number of resolute horsemen, but the capital was safe against an assault by such troops. He fortified Valencia and armed a flotilla on the lake, strengthened the pass at Cabrera, occupied Victoria, and threw up field-works at San Mateo, where he established his head-quarters, while he waited for Mariño. The position was well chosen; on the heights which surrounded it stood a country-house which was his own property, to the east of which lay one of the most valuable of his patrimonial estates. But in place of Mariño, Boves, whose wound was by this time healed, appeared in his front on the 25th February, at the head of 2,000 light infantry and 5,000 horse.

Morales was completely routed in an attack on his right flank, and Boves himself was repulsed in an attack on the centre, but captured some outworks on the right. Bolívar sent a reinforcement under Villapol and Campo Elias. Both these leaders were killed, but the son of the former, Captain Villapol, restored the day, drove the Royalists from the positions they had captured, and though badly wounded, held his ground till nightfall. Boves, who was again severely wounded, was carried off the field by his men, and Morales resumed the command.

In this desperate fighting the Royalists had exhausted their ammunition, and were for fifteen days compelled to remain inactive, till on the 11th March Morales again attacked the entrenchments, but was again repulsed. On the 17th Boves again took command, and was on the 20th beaten off in a third attack.

The Patriot magazine was established in the country-house to the rear of the position. On the 25th March

Boves detached a column of infantry to make its way by the heights beyond the Patriot lines, to capture this magazine, while he himself led a general attack in front. The magazine was in charge of a young officer, a native of New Granada, named Ricaurte, who had only fifteen men with him. When this young officer saw the infantry column rushing down upon him from the heights, he knew that it was hopeless to attempt to defend the house. He sent off his men, and remaining alone he waited till the enemy burst in upon him with shouts of triumph, when he fired the magazine, and he himself and the greater part of the Royalist column were blown into the air together.

When Bolívar saw the flight of the small garrison, he thought that all was lost. He dismounted from his horse and ran into the ranks, calling to his soldiers that he would die with them, but the Royalists were so terrified by the sudden destruction of their column of infantry, that they desisted from the attack and withdrew, leaving 800 dead and wounded behind them.

While attacking the lines of San Mateo, Boves had detached a strong column under Rosete to make an attempt upon the capital. Rivas was ill in bed, and 800 of the youth of the city sallied out under Arismendi to meet the enemy on the open plain, but were cut to pieces on the 11th March. Bolívar sent 300 picked troops under Colonel Montilla to the assistance of the garrison. With this reinforcement Rivas managed to organize a column of 900 men, and leading them out in person, lying on a stretcher, he totally defeated Rosete on the 20th March at Ocumare, and the capital was saved.

Cajigal, the new Captain-General, had established his head-quarters at Coro, and had formed a column of 1,000 men from the remnants of various shattered battalions. These troops he placed under command of Ceballos, who drove Urdaneta before him out of Barquisimeto. Urdaneta then endeavoured to hold San Carlos, but was driven thence by Calzada, and took refuge in Valencia, where the war material of the Patriots was stored. Here he received orders from Bolívar to resist to the last extremity, and to send 200 men to aid D'Eluyar in the siege of Puerto Cabello. Urdaneta obeyed orders, but was left with only 280 muskets to make head as he could against the united forces of Ceballos and Calzada, who now attacked Valencia with 3,000 men. The Royalists had no artillery, but by dint of numbers they drove the Patriots from the outworks, and cut off the supply of water from the garrison. Urdaneta called a council of his officers, when it was agreed that if the inner line of defence was forced, the garrison should retire to the artillery barracks and blow the place up. The example of Ricaurte had enflamed their hearts.

Boves for some time made no further attempt on the lines of San Mateo, and the dispirited Llaneros began to desert, but the situation of Bolívar was desperate. His only chance lay in the speedy arrival of Mariño, who was at last advancing by forced marches from the East, and was sweeping the plains in the rear of the Royalists. Then Boves after one more desperate assault upon the lines, which was repulsed, retreated to La Puerta, to stop the advance of Mariño from the plains. But Mariño succeeded in turning this position and established himself at the Boca Chica. Here he was attacked by Boves on the 31st March, but forced him to retreat with a loss of 500 killed, and occupied the city of Victoria.

Ceballos then, fearing an attack on his rear by the united forces of Bolívar and Mariño, raised the siege of Valencia and retired to San Carlos, to await reinforcements which Boves was collecting on the plains. Here he was attacked by Mariño on the 17th April. Mariño was so destitute of military capacity that the troops under his immediate command dispersed at the first volley, but Urdaneta rallied the infantry and retired to Valencia.

Cajigal then brought up a strong reinforcement and took command of the Royalists. Bolívar, after being joined by Rivas with 800 men from Caracas, advanced against him. After some manœuvring the armies met on the plain of Carabobo, and Bolívar won a complete victory. The

Royalists lost 300 killed and all their guns and flags, while the Patriots had only 12 killed and 40 wounded.

Bolívar was victorious over the Spanish generals, but the strength of the people was against him. The indefatigable Boves had received large supplies of arms and ammunition from Guayana, and again rushed upon him from the plains with about 7,000 men, of whom more than 2,000 were infantry. Bolívar, instead of massing his troops to make head against this new danger, detached Mariño against Boves with only 2,300 men, while he sent Urdaneta with 700 men off westward, and another division of 1,100 in pursuit of Cajigal and Ceballos. But this latter corps joined Mariño, who then in complete ignorance of the superior strength of the Royalist leader, determined to wait for Boves at La Puerta, in a most unfavourable position. Bolívar joined him too late to remedy the evil. The Patriots were overwhelmed by a desperate charge of the Llanero horse on the 14th June, and were slaughtered without mercy; at least 1,200 were left dead upon the field; Boves himself reported that 2,800 were killed.

Bolívar fled to Caracas, but instead of making some attempt to reunite his shattered forces, maintained the siege of Puerto Cabello and instructed the garrison of Valencia to hold out to the last extremity. A small detachment of 250 men defending the pass of Cabrera was overwhelmed, every man was killed, and Valencia was forced to capitulate to Boves, who, in spite of his oath to spare the lives of the garrison, butchered them all, and many of the inhabitants of the town also. D'Eluyar being isolated, spiked his guns and embarked his troops on the flotilla. Urdaneta was left alone in the West; Bolívar evacuated Caracas and withdrew to the East, carrying with him all the jewels and specie he could find in the churches, and embarrassed by the multitude of fugitives who fled with him. He reached Aragua with 2,000 men and at once commenced to throw up entrenchments. Mariño sent him 1,000 men under Bermudez from Cumaná, and some supplies of war material.

On the 18th August, the position at Aragua was attacked by Morales with a horde of 8,000 negroes, mulattos, and Indians. The Patriots defended themselves with the resolution of despair, but after two hours fighting, in which entire battalions had perished, Bolívar retreated with a part of his force on Barcelona. Bermudez still held the position for two hours longer, and then fled to Maturin with the remnant of his cavalry. The butchery which followed was frightful, more than 3,000 were killed in cold blood, even the townsfolk who sought refuge in the church had their throats cut in the sacred edifice. The loss of the Royalists was nearly 2,000 in killed and wounded.

Bolívar, Mariño, Rivas, Piar and D'Eluyar met at Cumaná, and resolved to concentrate the resistance at Güiria, a position easily defended, while the flotilla kept open their communications by sea. Bolívar had shipped the treasure brought by him from Caracas on board of these vessels. Bianchi, who was still in command, determined to seize it. Bolívar and Mariño hearing of his intention, embarked with him as he sailed for the island of Margarita. He gave two vessels up to them with all the jewels and two-thirds of the specie, retaining the rest as payment for the prizes he had made, upon which the two Dictators returned to the mainland.

On the 3rd September they landed at Carúpano, where they found that they had been proscribed as traitors who had deserted their comrades, while Rivas and Piar had taken the command. Piar had the intention of treating Bolívar as he had treated Miranda, but Rivas set him at liberty and arrested Mariño. At this juncture Bianchi returned, and by threats saved them both. Bolívar gave up the treasure to Rivas and retired to Curaçoa, leaving behind him an address to the people in which he disdainfully left his justification to the future:—

"I swear to you that this title (Liberator), which your gratitude bestowed upon me when I broke your chains, shall not be in vain. I swear to you that Liberator or dead, I shall ever merit the honour you have done me; no human power can turn me from my course."

When he had gone, Rivas took the supreme command, but the genius of Bolívar was wanting. On the 26th August Cumaná pronounced for the Royalists. Bermudez, entrenched at Maturin, was attacked by Morales with a greatly superior force, but sallying out, utterly routed him, killing 2,000 of his men. He was then joined by Rivas; between them they assembled nearly 5,000 men. Piar, disregarding the orders of Rivas to join him, marched on Cumaná, which he retook and collected 2,000 men, but was then attacked by Boves and totally defeated.

Boves then retook Cumaná, and put every man to death who fell into his hands. It is said that more than a thousand victims perished in this massacre. Cumaná was left a desert. Boves was then joined by Morales, who had reorganized his army, and together they marched on Maturin at the head of 7,000 men. The Patriots sallied out to meet them under the command of Rivas and Bermudez.

With very inferior numbers they met the Royalist army at Urica to the west of Maturin, on the 5th December. Boves drew up his men in two lines and awaited their onslaught. An impetuous charge of the Patriot cavalry broke the right wing of the Royalists, and Boves, ever foremost in a *melée*, was killed by a lance thrust. Morales, with the left and the reserve, restored the combat and gained a complete victory. No quarter was given and the last army of the Republic was destroyed.

Morales was by acclamation named General-in-Chief of the "Windward Army," which was the name which had been given to this Royalist force by its late commander, and lost no time in marching upon Maturin, which city was well fortified and had a good supply of artillery, but the garrison, only 600 in number, was but poorly armed. After an obstinate defence which caused severe losses to the Royalist army, this last bulwark of the Patriots was captured on the 11th December. Bermudez escaped with 200 men, but Rivas flying alone, was overtaken and killed, and his head, covered with the Phrygian cap of Liberty, was exposed in an iron cage on the road from Caracas to La Guayra. According to contemporary writers more than 3,000 victims were slaughtered by Morales after his victory. The peace of the tomb reigned in Venezuela.

Three popular leaders still kept up the flames of insurrection at the head waters of the Orinoco and its tributaries: Zaraza, Monagas, and Cedeño, who afterwards became celebrated as Guerilleros. In the West all was quiet after the rout of La Puerta. The column under Urdaneta, so imprudently detached by Bolívar after Carabobo, was cut off when Boves occupied Valencia. Urdaneta retreated with 1,000 men, and being hotly pressed by Calzada, crossed the frontier into New Granada. He then detached 200 infantry and some cavalry officers to defend the Province of Casanare. This small detachment became the nucleus of the famous Army of the Apure, which changed the destinies of Venezuela, by leading the people to embrace the cause of the revolution. Among these cavalry officers was one named JOSE ANTONIO PAEZ, a man till then unknown, who was soon to become the Achilles of Venezuela, and was to eclipse by his deeds the fabulous prowess of the heroes of Homer.

There now only remained one spot of Venezuelan territory over which still floated the flag of the Republic, the island of Margarita, where Arismendi and Bermudez with some few followers had found asylum.

CHAPTER XL.

THE DISSOLUTION OF NEW GRANADA.

1815—1817.

THE second fall of the Republic of Venezuela was coincident in point of time with the fall of constitutional government in the mother country, and the absolute King of Spain and of the Indies, after subjugating his vassals in the Peninsula, turned his attention to subduing by force of arms his insurgent colonists beyond the seas.

Up to that time, with the exception of New Granada and Venezuela, none of the colonies of Spanish America had declared themselves independent, or had adopted the republican form of government. They made war on those who upheld the Royal standard, but they were governed by rulers of their own choosing in the name of the captive King. Thus, naturally, Venezuela and New Granada were the first of these colonies to receive attention.

In the year 1813 these two colonies had been united by the Spanish authorities under one nominal government, Marshal Montalvo being appointed Viceroy. The Peninsular troops had made but a poor show in the war in Venezuela; the two restorations had been achieved by native troops under the command of Monteverde, Boves, and Morales, who looked with contempt upon the Spanish generals as they condemned their excesses, and who refused all obedience to the colonial authorities. Thus Montalvo looked upon the preponderance of the native element as a source of danger, and as a dishonour to the cause of royalty, and had applied to the Home Government for reinforcements. New Granada was now to be the theatre of war, and thither went Bolívar, either to take part in it or to seek help for another reconquest of Venezuela.

He presented himself to the Congress assembled at Tunja. Camilo Torres, the President, thanked him for his distinguished services, saying that Venezuela was not lost so long as Bolívar lived. He was at once put in command of a corps of 1,800 men, of which Urdaneta's column formed a part, and was sent to reduce Cundinamarca, which still held aloof from the Federal Government. In view of the danger which now threatened the Republic, Congress had appointed a Supreme Junta, whose authority was recognised by all the provinces except Cartagena and Cundinamarca. Santa Fé de Bogotá was the arsenal of the Republic, the subjugation of Cundinamarca was therefore necessary.

Bolívar prosecuted his campaign with his usual activity. At his approach all the towns of Cundinamarca declared in favour of Congress; Bogotá, the capital, where Alvarez, who had been left in command by his nephew, Nariño, when he marched for the South, had entrenched himself, alone offered any resistance. Bolívar laid siege to the city, and by a series of vigorous assaults shut up the garrison in the principal square, and cut off their supply of water. Alvarez was forced to capitulate.

Congress then changed the seat of government to Bogotá; the Republic had at last possession of its own capital, and the Government was greatly strengthened. Bolívar was named Captain-General of the Confederation, his title of Liberator was recognised, and another was bestowed upon him, that of "Illustrious Pacificator." Of course Bolívar made a speech on this occasion, and prophesied that the Army of New Granada would break the chains of all the oppressed peoples of South America.

The new plan of Bolívar was to advance by the coast to Coro. Government gave him three battalions of infantry and a squadron of cavalry, in all 2,000 men, with orders to seek supplies of arms and ammunition at Cartagena. Colonel Castillo, who was Governor of this Province, prompted by his old jealousy of Bolívar, and listening to the counsels of Mariño and Montillo, who had taken refuge at Cartagena, refused these supplies. Bolívar established his head-quarters at the beautiful city of Mompox and remained inactive, passing his time in feasts and parades, and in intrigues against the local government, till his money was spent and he had lost half his troops by sickness and desertion.

Then, with only one gun, he laid siege to Cartagena, the strongest fortress in South America, till a powerful Spanish expedition landed on the coast and brought him to his senses. On the 8th May, 1815, he handed over the relics of his army to Castillo, and took leave of his men in a sentimental address, in which he expressed his sorrow at not being able to share in the triumphs which awaited them. He then withdrew to Jamaica, but ere he went fired a parting shot, declaring :—

"Cartagena prefers her own destruction to the duty of obedience to the Federal Government."

A shot which [recoiled upon himself, for he also had preferred his own destruction to obedience, and had inoculated the Granadian Republic with a new germ of dissolution.

In Jamaica he published a memorial in his own defence, which rather strengthens the case against him. Soon after that, under the signature of "A South American," he published another memorial upon the Revolution in South America, and upon the future organization of the new republics, which is a refutation of the chimerical plan of a Continental monocracy which he attempted to establish later on. In this memorial he advocated the absolute independence of each separate colony, "but New Granada shall unite with Venezuela, and this nation shall be called Columbia." A prophetic vision!

The reinforcements applied for by Montalvo reached

Cumaná early in April. One ship-of-the-line, three frigates, and twenty-one smaller ships of war came in convoy of a fleet of sixty transports, carrying 10,600 men and a siege train. This was the greatest effort which had as yet been made by the mother country to crush the insurrection in South America, and it was the last. The troops were selected from regiments which had fought against the armies of Napoleon, and had been educated in the school of Wellington. They were under the command of Marshal Morillo, the best of all the Spanish generals of that time. Originally a sergeant of marines, he had won his way by distinguished valour to his present high position. He had seen hard service among the Spanish guerillas, and had learned the art of war in the Anglo-Spanish armies. He was no great military genius, but he had respectable talents and was a good fighter. He was popular among the soldiery, but was a strict disciplinarian, and tenacious in his enterprises. He was cruel by system, not from inclination, but was also of a suspicious and passionate temperament. He knew nothing of the country he was sent to pacify, and his instructions gave him no information of any value, being drawn up in complete ignorance of the actual state of South America, and were instinct with contempt for the Creole inhabitants, a contempt in which he also shared.

This expedition was originally intended for the River Plate, but on the fall of Monte Video its destination was changed. At the same time, as Panamá was considered to be the key to the continent, another expedition of 2,500 men was sent, under command of General Miyares, to Vera Cruz for the purpose of securing the Isthmus.

Morillo was instructed to overrun the mainland from Guayana to Darien, first of all reducing the island of Margarita. He was then to take Cartagena, subdue New Granada, and to re-establish order in Venezuela. All this was thought so easy that he was further instructed to send his spare troops to Peru and Mexico. Vast as was this plan, Morillo accomplished it in the time given him for the purpose. In the course of the year 1815 all the insurgent colonies of Spain were reduced to submission, with the exception of the Provinces of the River Plate.

The rest of the instructions were drawn up in terms of benevolence towards the Americans. The atrocities committed under the Royal flag were severely censured, and the troops who had taken part in them were directed to be withdrawn from the theatre of action, but ample power was given to Morillo to deviate from these instructions when he thought it necessary, and he had also permission to suppress the tribunals of justice. Thus everything was left to his discretion.

The first man with whom Morillo spoke in the New World was Morales, who was now master of the east of Venezuela, and had fitted out a flotilla for an attack upon the island of Margarita. Early in April the expedition was sighted from the coast of Cumaná; Morales sailed out to meet it with three brigs, manned by a division of infantry, to place himself at the orders of the general. Camba, the historian, who was present, says that his European soldiers gazed in astonishment upon the decks of these three small vessels as they sailed through the Spanish fleet. They were crowded with dark-skinned men wearing round straw hats, a waistcloth, with a cartridge-box buckled over it, and, in general, no other raiment. If these were the victors what must the vanquished be like! An unfortunate first impression to receive, which gave them a false idea of the work before them. "Venezuela and Caracas were lost after the arrival of first-class troops, who were well commanded."

In accordance with his instructions, Morillo went on to the island of Margarita with all his army, reinforced by three thousand of Morales' troops, shipped on the flotilla. The Patriot cruisers had captured one of the vessels of the convoy, so that the strength of the expedition was known. Bermudez proposed to resist to the last extremity, but finding no support fled to Cartagena. Arismendi gave himself up, and was kindly received by Morillo, who seated him at his own table, apparently forgetting his massacre of eight hundred Spaniards. On the 9th April, 1815, the island was occupied without resistance. Morillo issued a proclamation offering an amnesty to all insurgents who would give themselves up, and kept his word; but fifteen men who gave themselves up to Morales were slaughtered.

The first success and the first disaster of the expedition came together. The ship-of-the-line *San Pedro*, the most powerful vessel of the squadron, caught fire and was a total loss, the military chest and a great quantity of warlike stores being burned with her.

The generous behaviour of Morillo at Margarita procured him a favourable reception at Caracas, where he arrived on the 11th May, but his first act was to levy a forced loan to replace the treasure lost on the *San Pedro*. He then proceeded to confiscate the properties of all who had taken part in the Revolution, and of those who were absent or who were suspected, the amount so taken being estimated at fifteen millions of dollars. General Moxó, a man of cruel and rapacious character, was made Governor of Venezuela; the Audiencia and all the civil tribunals were suppressed, and were replaced by councils of war. A military despotism was established.

Morillo had now 16,000 men under his command, including the native troops. He sent a battalion of light infantry to Puerto Rico, a division of 1,700 men to Peru, 3,000 men were told off as the garrison of Venezuela, and Calzada's division, in Barinas, was reinforced by European troops. Then with 5,000 Europeans and 3,500 native troops under Morales, embarked in fifty-six ships, he sailed on the 12th July for the leeward coast to commence operations against New Granada.

The employment of native troops was in accordance with his instructions, but the measure produced discontent in his ranks. These troops were despised by the Spaniards, and had no wish to leave their native country. More than a thousand of the Llaneros deserted rather than embark. The way in which they were treated aroused in them the native instinct for independence, of which they soon became the most doughty champions.

Morillo landed at Santa Marta, intent upon the capture of Cartagena. The garrison was weak, was short of arms and of provisions, and was cut off from help either by sea or by land, but was nevertheless resolute to resist to the last extremity. The ground was cleared for three leagues round, outlying posts were called in, a flotilla was armed for the defence of the bay, sixty guns were added to the eighty-four already mounted on the batteries, martial law was proclaimed, and all men capable of bearing arms were compelled to serve. The garrison was thus increased to 3,600 men, of whom 1,300 were regular troops. The command was at first given to Castillo, but he was soon after replaced by Bermudez, and Montilla was named Major-General.

Cartagena was then the strongest fortress in America. It was captured by the French in 1697, but when the English, under Admiral Vernon, attacked it in the year 1741 they were beaten off, although they had 9,000 soldiers in addition to a powerful fleet. It was built upon a promontory running into the sea, and is so separated from the mainland by marshes that it may be considered an island—a sort of military Venice. The city proper is situate to the northwest of this promontory, and to the west of it lies a suburb called Getzemani, which communicates with the city by a fortified bridge thrown across a deep canal, and is closed at each end by a stockade. Getzemani is also joined to the mainland by another bridge of similar construction. The fortress, the city, and the suburb, were all enclosed on the land side by high walls and bastions. To the east, beyond the swamps, and about half a mile from the walls, stood a castle on a hill, called San Lázaro, whose fire swept all the city, but was itself under the fire of a fortified hill, called La Popa, which commanded all the approaches. The most accessible part of the city was the bay, which runs from north to south, and is nearly a mile in length. This bay is shut in from the Gulf of Mexico by two islands, which leave only two practicable entrances—the Boca Grande, by which Admiral Vernon penetrated, and which was afterwards closed by orders from Spain, and the Boca Chica, which was defended by two castles on the island and by batteries on the coast. The flotilla consisted of a corvette, seven schooners, and some gunboats, aided in shallow water by a sort of armed rafts called "bongos."

Morillo detached Morales, with his division, across the Magdalena, to blockade the city by land while he blockaded it by sea, his idea being to starve out the garrison.

The heavy rains of the season and frequent tempests made the work of the siege very arduous to the Royalists, filling their hospitals with sick. On the 25th October the city was bombarded, with no other effect than to kill a few women and children. Several assaults were made upon various outworks, which were repulsed, but in November the larger island was captured by Morales. Two batteries were placed upon it and upon the adjacent shore, the fire from which swept the bay and prevented fishing, thus destroying one great resource of the city, where hunger soon proved more formidable than shot and shell. Fevers broke out, rats and hides were eaten by the starving garrison, sentinels were found dead at their posts when parties were sent to relieve them, but no one talked of surrender. At last it was determined to drive from the city two thousand useless mouths, old men, women, and children. It was a procession of spectres; only one-third of them reached the advanced posts of the besiegers, the rest sank down and perished on the way. The survivors were kindly received by the Spaniards, but Morillo wrote to the Patriot leaders that if they did not surrender in three days he would drive the fugitives back into the city. On that day, the 4th December, three hundred persons died of hunger in the streets; it was impossible to hold out longer, but still they would not surrender,

On the night of the 5th the guns on the hill of La Popa, and on the castle of San Lázaro, were spiked. At dawn on the day following, a remnant of two thousand men embarked on the flotilla, crossed the bay under the fire of the Royalist batteries, took on board the garrisons of the batteries at the Boca Chica, and on the 7th put to sea in a storm which dispersed the blockading squadron.

Morillo entered the city on the 6th December, and found it a hospital of dying men, and a cemetery of dead bodies, which lay all about the streets; the very air was poison. The siege had lasted one hundred and eight days. It was calculated that six thousand had died in the city of hunger and disease, besides those who were killed in the various attacks. The loss of the besiegers was nearly three thousand five hundred men.

The victory was stained by an act of barbarism. Morales, who had occupied the batteries at the Boca Chica, on their evacuation by the Patriots, offered an amnesty to all fugitives who would present themselves. Four hundred old men, women, and children, and some fishermen who had hidden in the brushwood covering the island, presented themselves. The throats of every one of them were cut on the seashore by his orders. Morillo was more humane, but Castillo, who had hidden himself, was put to death by his command, and his body was exposed on a gibbet. The same fate was meted out to six of the principal citizens, among them being Garcia Toledo, who had headed the revolution in 1810. At the same time the Inquisition was re-established.

Calzada, advancing from Barinas to aid in the subjugation of New Granada, attempted first to clear the plains of Casanare of the Patriot light horse, but being beaten by them on the 1st October, he crossed the Cordillera with 1,800 infantry and 500 cavalry, routed various detached parties of Patriots who came in his way, and totally defeated their main body at Balaga on the 25th November. He then occupied Pamplona, where he found the streets strewn with the corpses of Spaniards, who had been barbarously murdered by the Patriots when they evacuated that city.

Congress now again made Torres President, with dictatorial powers, and appointed Torices Vice-President, Torres raised an army of 2,500 recruits, with which he forced Calzada, who was advancing on the capital, to retreat to Ocaña. But Calzada, after receiving some reinforcements, turned upon him and completely routed him on the 22nd February. The three Provinces of Pamplona, Socorro, and Antioquia were then occupied by the Royalists, and the capital lay defenceless. Torres resigned, and a physician named Madrid was appointed in his place. He called for volunteers; only six men offered themselves.

Cundinamarca, which had been forced into the Union, had remained disaffected, and now became openly Royalist. The rest of the country was worn out, and was only eager for peace. Congress authorised Madrid to negotiate with Morillo, and dissolved itself. The new President retired to the South with the remnant of the army, and joined the division of Popayán under Mejia, who then marched against a Royalist force under Sámano, which was advancing from Quito, and was totally defeated.

Morillo left a strong garrison at Cartagena and divided the rest of his diminished force into four light columns for the complete subjugation of the country. Bogotá fell without a shot being fired, but while he was at Ocaña with the reserve, news reached him that Venezuela was again in commotion, that a fresh insurrection had broken out in the island of Margarita, and that the emigrants, headed by Bolívar, were preparing an expedition to rekindle the flames of revolution on the mainland. Seriously alarmed, he sent Morales with a division back to Venezuela to secure his base of operations.

Morillo now, for the first time, appreciated the magnitude of the enterprise he had undertaken, and, with rare perspicuity, foresaw its fatal termination. He wrote to the Home Government that, in spite of his success, he could not without reinforcements bring the Llaneros into subjection, and that it was necessary to establish a military government, and so crush rebellion by the use of the same means which had been employed at the time of the conquest. He then published an amnesty to all officers of the revolutionary armies, from captain downwards, who would lay down their arms, but he put to death all superior officers who fell into his hands, quartering their bodies and exposing their heads in cages.

General La Torre, who commanded at Bogotá, published a similar amnesty to civil officials, for which step he was severely censured by Morillo, and in May, 1816, the prisons of the capital were full.

Morillo then went there himself, avoiding a public reception and entering the city by night. La Torre and Calzada were again censured for receiving presents from rebels; the first was, as a punishment, sent off to the plains, and the second to Cúcuta. The amnesty was then annulled, and severe decrees were published against all who should either write or speak on forbidden subjects.

On the 30th May, which was the birthday of the King, the women of the city presented themselves, imploring mercy for their fathers, sons, and husbands. Morillo received them roughly and sent them off with insults. The prisons being insufficient to accommodate the multitude of prisoners, some were confined in the convents. He searched the city archives for pretexts to increase their number, and a military tribunal was established to try them.[*]

Villavicencio, Montufar, Lozano, Camilo Torres, and Torices were executed, being shot in the back as traitors, and their bodies were hung on gibbets. Baraya and Mejia shared the same fate. Caldas, the philosopher, whose scientific labours had won him world-wide fame, was sentenced to death, and when Morillo was entreated to spare the life of so illustrious a man, he answered savagely:—

"Spain has no need of sages."

One hundred and twenty-five victims perished on the scaffold, of whom a fifth part were graduates of the University. The properties of all victims were confiscated; their families were reduced to misery; the entire male population was classified as convicts, and gangs of them were forced to work on the public roads. Truly the system adopted by the Spaniards at the conquest was now reestablished in America in the cause of Spanish absolutism, and for a King who was spoken of by his own mother as "tiger heart and mule head."

Bloodshed and absolute power clouded the mental faculties of Morillo; he dreamed of destroying the Argentine Republic, and of then returning in triumph to Mexico to repeat there the cruelties of Cortes, but the course of events in Venezuela soon opened his eyes. He left a garrison of 3,800 men at Bogotá, Venezuelans and Pastusos, and with 4,000 Spanish troops crossed the Cordillera in November, 1816, taking some prisoners with him to shoot on the frontier line. This march convinced him, for the second time, of his impotence to prosecute his enterprise; by his own confession, he could neither pass the rivers nor procure supplies without the help of the Llaneros who went with him.

General Sámano remained in command at Bogotá. His first act was to erect a gallows in the great square, in front of the windows of his palace, and to set up four execution-posts (banquillos) on the public promenade. One of his first victims was a beautiful young woman, convicted of sending information to the Patriot guerillas on the plains of Casanare. She was shot in the back, with seven men implicated in the same affair. She died encouraging her companions to meet their fate like men, and prophesying that her death would soon be revenged. Under the name of La Pola her memory is still preserved in the songs of her native land.

Morillo, finding Sámano so apt a pupil in his school of terrorism, made him Viceroy in place of Montalvo, whose more humane nature shrank from the perpetration of such cruelties.

CHAPTER XLI.

THE THIRD WAR IN VENEZUELA.

1815—1817.

IN none of the colonies of Spanish America was the struggle for emancipation so stubborn, so heroic, and so tragical, as in Venezuela. In the North of the Continent she was the nucleus of the revolution, gave it both its military power and its political basis, and supplied to it the genius of Bolívar. Twice conquered, she yet arose a third time against her oppressors.

After the rout of Urica, and the catastrophe of Maturin, the remnants of the Republican army of the East were dispersed as guerillas along the banks and about the headwaters of the Orinoco, and on the plains of Barcelona, while the insurrection was still unquelled on the plains of Casanare. A fresh signal for a general revolt was given by the island of Margarita immediately after the departure of Morillo on his expedition against New Granada. The Royalist governor, Colonel Urreistieta, to assert his authority, ordered the arrest of Arismendi. Fifteen hundred of the islanders rose in arms. The governor ordered the troops to give no quarter to the insurgents, gave them permission to pillage as they chose, and burned two towns in accordance with instructions received from General Moxó. The insurgents accepted the challenge of war to the knife. Arismendi put himself at their head, and took possession of the northern half of the island, captured by assault the fort at the Villa del Norte, and put to death the whole of the garrison, who numbered 200 men. Then on the 15th November, 1815, he laid siege to the capital and shut up the governor in the castle of Santa Rosa. His army numbered 4,300 infantry and 200 cavalry, badly armed, but all resolute men.

On the plains of Casanare the scattered groups of guerillas were organized by Paez into an army. José Antonio Paez was a native of Barinas, and was at this time twenty-six years old. He had served bravely throughout the campaign of the reconquest, but had never attracted special notice; now he was to show his great talents as a leader. He was a genuine Creole, of Caucasian race, with some mixture of native blood; a man of herculean strength, a breaker-in of wild horses, and an untiring swimmer. Skilful in the use of lance and sword, in moments of danger he was ever in the front rank, and had great influence over his men, both by his personal and by his moral qualities. They were accustomed to call him "Uncle" when addressing him. If any soldier committed a crime or showed unwillingness to obey orders it was his custom to challenge him to single combat. Whether the challenge were accepted or not he was always the victor, either physically or morally. After the excitement of a battle his nervous system would frequently give way, and he would fall to the ground, apparently lifeless. His plans were always carefully thought out and rapidly executed. He at this time knew neither how to read nor write, and was in no sense a politician, but was of a kindly, generous nature, and of very superior intelligence. In times of peace he was easily led, but in times of danger he led every one. His usual dress was a blouse of blue cloth, with a cloak thrown over his shoulders; a slouched hat, the front rim turned up and decorated with the cockade of Venezuela; and the gaiters of a Llanero. He wore a Toledo sword, and invariably carried a long lance.

Paez was serving as a simple captain with a small corps of Patriots which held the town of Guadalito, when news was brought of the approach of the Spanish governor of Barinas, with 1,100 horse and 300 infantry. The officer in command proposed to retreat. Paez requested permission to remain with one squadron to defend the town. Most of the other officers present approved of the proposition, on which the commander said angrily,

"Then let Paez command you, and those who choose may follow me to Casanare."

Paez, left with 500 men, marched out to meet the enemy, whom he found on the 16th February, 1816, near to the sources of the Apure. Paez, advancing alone to reconnoitre the position, had his horse killed under him by a musket-ball. It was near nightfall; some advised him to wait for daylight.

"It is as dark for them as it is for us," said Paez, and shouted to his men, "Comrades, they have killed my horse. If you will not revenge his death I will revenge him alone, and will die in the enemy's ranks."

The men shouted back that they would go wherever he would lead them. He formed them in two lines and led them on under a heavy fire. Such was the fury of the charge that two-thirds of the Royalist cavalry were driven in confusion from the field. As he led an attack upon their second line his horse was wounded, and burst the girths of the saddle with his plunges. The attack was beaten off. Springing on to the first horse he could catch, Paez rallied his men and again charged at full speed upon the rest of the Royalist cavalry, and bore them down in the rush. While the Patriots pursued the broken cavalry the Spanish infantry retreated through the woods. Four hundred killed and two hundred prisoners were the trophies of the day. Paez treated his prisoners so well that they all voluntarily took service with him.

This brilliant affair attracted the attention of the Llaneros, who were weary of the brutal rule of Boves and Morales, and won them over to the cause of independence.

Paez became at once the first general of cavalry in America. He was the bond of union between the Llaneros and the Patriots. He was proclaimed the chieftain of the plains, and from the recruits who poured in to join his standard he organized the famous Army of the Apure. On taking command he told his men that he would do his best to merit the confidence they had placed in him, but exhorted them above all to put faith in Divine Providence. In September, 1816, he invaded the Province of Barinas.

While the Army of the Apure was thus gathering itself together, the parties of guerillas, scattered along the banks of the Upper Orinoco, and on the eastern plains, also collected, forming divisions of as many as 1,500 men, under Monagas, Saraza and Cedeño. The Governor of Guayana sent a strong column against Cedeño, which was completely routed by him on the 8th March, 1816. A second expedition of 1,500 men, sent in boats up the Orinoco, had no better fortune, and was forced to retire to Angostura, the capital of Guayana.

While Bolívar, in exile at Kingston, Jamaica, was turning over in his mind many plans for renewing the War of Independence, he had a narrow escape from assassination. A slave of his who had followed his fortunes went one night into his room when all was dark, and seeing a man asleep in his hammock, gave him two stabs with a poniard, killing him on the spot. The dead man was found to be a poor emigrant named Amestoy, who, knowing that Bolívar would not sleep at home that night, occupied his room. The slave was caught, and confessed that it was his intention to kill Bolívar, but said not a word about accomplices. He was hung, but it was generally believed that an emissary of General Moxó had paid him to do the deed.

From Jamaica Bolívar crossed to the island of Santo Domingo, hearing on his way of the fall of Cartagena, where, too late, he had been offered the command. The famous mulatto, Alexander Petión, was at that time President of Haiti. He was an ardent partisan of the emancipation of Spanish America, and not only supplied Bolívar with arms for another expedition, but opened a credit for him for the necessary expenses with the house of a wealthy English merchant named Robert Sutherland. Bolívar also met here a Dutch shipbuilder named Luis

Brion, who, becoming deeply interested both in him and in his designs, placed seven armed schooners at his orders, with 3,500 muskets, and offered his life and fortune in the same cause.

Bolívar commenced his preparations early in 1816, at the port of Cayos de San Luis, which has given its name to this famous expedition. There the refugees from Cartagena, and many officers from New Granada and Venezuela had collected. Among them were Piar, Mariño, Bermudez, Montilla, Soublette, the English Colonel MacGregor, who had served with Miranda, Doucoudray-Holstein, and Francisco Zea. There was anarchy among them; many of them refused to recognise the authority of Bolívar. Petión interposed his influence, and Brion declared that he would entrust his ships and armament to no one but to the Liberator. He was at length accepted as leader of the expedition, from which Montilla, who had challenged Bolívar, and Bermudez, who had led the opposition, were excluded.

Brion, with the title of Admiral of Venezuela, took command of the squadron, which sailed from Cayos on the 16th March, 1816. The expedition consisted of 300 men, whom Bolívar afterwards compared to the 300 Spartans of Leonidas, as he compared his reconquest of Venezuela to the redemption of Jerusalem by the Crusaders. They reached the island of Margarita early in May, finding there the Spanish brig *Intrepido* and the schooner *Rita*, which Brion boarded and captured, after a desperate resistance in which three-fourths of their crews were killed. The expedition then disembarked at the port of Juan Griego, the Royalists concentrating their forces at Pampatar and Porlamar.

Bolívar and Arismendi then conjointly convened a meeting of the officers of the Patriot army, and of the principal inhabitants, in the church at La Villa del Norte, in order to name the supreme ruler of the Republic they were about to restore. In accordance with his custom, Bolívar immediately renounced all pretensions to so important a post, which, as he had already arranged the matter with Arismendi, was merely one way of securing his own appointment. On the 7th May he was named "Supreme Chief," with power to do whatever he might find necessary for the salvation of the country. Mariño was named second in command.

On the 8th May Bolívar published a proclamation to the people of Venezuela, announcing that the National Congress would be reinstalled, and authorising the free towns to elect deputies, who should have the same sovereign powers as in the former epoch.

The expedition, reinforced by four ships from the island, then went on to Carupano, on the coast of Paria, capturing two armed vessels of the enemy and the fort, which was abandoned by the garrison. Here Bolívar established his head-quarters on the 1st June.

Rumour had greatly exaggerated the strength of the force he brought with him, but Bolívar made small use of the stupor into which the Royalists were thrown. He detached Piar to Maturin and Mariño to Güiria, but remained himself at Carupano, issuing pompous bulletins, in which he renounced his former system of a war of extermination, as a mistake. Also, in fulfilment of a promise to Petión, he published a decree giving liberty to all slaves, and called the people to arms, but no one joined him. He then convened an assembly of the townsfolk, who at his suggestion decreed the centralization of the powers of government. The federal system was abolished in Venezuela.

But a month of precious time was thus lost. Twenty days after the disembarkation, his advanced posts were driven in, and he was besieged by a division of 1,300 men, while a Spanish squadron threatened his communications by sea. Mariño sent him a strong reinforcement, but Brion refused to risk his ships in an unequal fight with the Spanish squadron. Meantime the guerilla leaders of the East proclaimed him general-in-chief, and desired his presence.

Rejecting the advice of Piar to occupy Guayana as a base of operations, he re-embarked his small force, and again landed on the 5th July at Ocumare, between Caracas and Puerto Cabello. This step can only be explained by his anxiety to rescue his native city from the Royalists, a preoccupation which was to cost him the loss of three campaigns. Again rejecting the advice of his officers, who wished to effect a junction with the guerillas and so form an army, he detached Soublette with the bulk of his men to occupy the pass of Cabrera, and a smaller force along the coast in search of recruits, while he landed a printing press and issued more bulletins, and Brion went off on a cruise leaving him one armed brig and two small schooners.

On the same day on which Bolívar landed at Ocumare, Morales reached Valencia, with the division detached by Morillo after the surrender of Cartagena. In the face of such a superior force, Soublette was compelled to retire to a strong position on the heights of Ocumare. Bolívar went to his assistance with 150 recruits, but the combined force was completely routed by Morales on the 13th July.

MacGregor was then sent off with a detachment southwards to Choroni, while Soublette protected the retreat of Bolívar with the artillery to Ocumare, where he intended to re-embark. While engaged at night in this operation, he received word that the enemy were entering the town. It was a false alarm, Soublette still held his ground, but his men were panic-struck, and Bolívar, without inquiring into the truth of the report, abandoned his sick and wounded, and fled on board the brig where his stores of war material were already in safety. He sailed at once and reached the island of Bonaire on the 16th July. Here he was joined by Brion, and sailed with him for Choroni, where he learned that Soublette and MacGregor had marched inland and had taken refuge in the valleys of Aragua. Returning to Bonaire he there met Bermudez, and with him sailed off to join Mariño at Güiria.

Soublette and MacGregor had joined forces at Choroni,

the latter taking the command. Two days he waited for news of Bolívar and then marched off for the plains with 600 infantry and 30 horse. Dispersing a Royalist detachment which attempted to bar the passage of the hills, he occupied Victoria and routed another detachment under Rosete. On the 1st August he was met by a squadron of Saraza's guerillas, who were in search of him, and on the 2nd August routed another division of 1,200 Royalists at Quebrada-Honda. The next day he was joined by Saraza and Monagas with their divisions of guerillas, and was master of the plains of Barcelona, while Cedeño held his ground on the Upper Orinoco. So was formed the army which was afterwards known as "the Army of the Centre," which, in conjunction with that of the Apure, decided the destinies of Venezuela. Of this army MacGregor was recognised as general-in-chief.

At Güiria Bolívar met with but a sorry reception, the troops of Mariño refused to obey him, and the island of Margarita declined to recognise his authority. Bermudez charged him with cowardice for deserting his soldiers when in danger. Amid threats and jeers he was forced to re-embark and returned to Haití, where he was coldly received by Petión. The people were incensed against him and had lost all faith in him. Nevertheless, Bolívar was the man not only for the revolution in Columbia, but for the emancipation of South America. None so well as he could rise superior to adverse fortune, none had such power as he over the petty chieftains, none but he could organize the discordant elements of the revolution into the strength of a warlike nation. Spite of his ignorance of military tactics and of his puerile vanity, he was the genius of the revolution in the North of the Continent. The sacred fire of liberty and of patriotism burned within him and inspired him. As he himself said, he would yet merit the title of Liberator. History owes to him this justice as she turns this disgraceful page.

After the departure of Bolívar, Mariño was named general of the army at Güiria, with Bermudez as his second in command, but his authority did not extend beyond the peninsula of Paria.

After occupying the plains of Barcelona, MacGregor marched upon the city. A Royalist force, which, under the command of Colonel Lopez, occupied the town of Aragua, sallied out to meet him. The action was hotly contested, but was decided by desperate charges of the Llanero horse led by Saraza and Monagas, and by a bayonet charge led by MacGregor in person. The Royalists lost 500 killed, 300 prisoners, and one gun.

Barcelona was evacuated by the Royalists on the 12th September, after they had murdered many of the townsfolk and plundered many of the houses, but MacGregor was now threatened by Morales, who had advanced to Aragua with 3,000 men. He sent to Arismendi, Mariño, and Piar for assistance. Piar, who was then besieging Cumaná, came at once with all his troops and took the command. On the 27th September the two armies met at the Playon del Juncal, near to Barcelona. MacGregor, supported by the fire of Piar's artillery, led a bayonet charge which decided the day. The Royalists were totally routed, with a loss of 300 killed and 400 prisoners. After this victory MacGregor, worn out with fatigue and unwilling to brook the domineering ways of Piar, withdrew to Margarita.

Paez, by skilful manœuvres, forced his old opponent, Colonel Lopez, to retreat to the line of the Apure in October. The town of San Fernando on this river was the key of the plains; he resolved to seize it, but had no boats in which to cross the river. The Royalists had a flotilla of four "flecheras"* and seven long-boats, manned by 400 men. An officer named Peña had committed some fault. Paez ordered him as a punishment to get himself killed by the enemy. He crossed the river in a canoe with eight men, at midday, and threw the Royalist camp into

* A "flechera" is a flat-bottomed boat, capable of carrying one or two guns, and is very swift. Managed by Venezuelan boatmen, they rendered great service in this war.

confusion. In the skirmishes which followed, Colonel Lopez was killed and the Patriots seized seven boats. Paez then crossed the river, and in December laid siege to San Fernando. There he received news that La Torre and Morillo were on the march from New Granada to the plains watered by the Arauca and Apure.

Mariño and Bermudez were engaged in the siege of Cumaná, aided by the flotilla from Margarita. The Spanish garrison was about to evacuate the city, when the Royalist force on the island abandoned it and came to their assistance. The Patriots were forced to raise the siege.

At the close of the year 1816 the Patriot armies had gained many advantages, but they felt the need of a head to give cohesion to their efforts. With the army of the centre were many of the partisans of Bolívar. Backed by Arismendi they induced the army to demand his recall. Assisted by Petión and by Brion he organized another expedition, sailed from Haití on the 21st December, and reached Barcelona at the same time as Arismendi, who brought a strong reinforcement from the island of Margarita.

But the Army of the Centre was no longer there. Piar had seen from the beginning that descents on the coasts and incursions on to the plains would lead to no satisfactory result, that the Orinoco was the true line of action, and that Guayana was the true base of operations. Bolívar, without any plan, had hovered round Caracas like a moth round a candle, and had burned his wings. Even Cedeño, the rude guerilla, had seen more clearly, as was shown by his success on the Upper Orinoco. Morillo himself had seen the same thing, and ere leaving New Granada had written to the Home Government, impressing upon them the importance of preserving the line of the Orinoco. Piar, after the victory of Juncal, found himself in command of an army, and at once proceeded to carry out his idea, thus saving the Patriot cause by forcing Bolívar to give up his pursuit of a phantom at Caracas. He left a small garrison at Barcelona, left the guerillas to defend the plains, and marched for Guayana.

The Royalists had a powerful flotilla on the Orinoco, and had fortified Angostura, which was the capital of Guayana. Piar cut down trees in the woods and made small boats, captured two boats from the enemy, and forced the passage of the Cauca in front of the Royalist camp. The guerillas, under Cedeño, swam the river on horseback, fighting with the crews of the Royalist gun-boats as they passed, and on reaching the opposite shore charged upon the encampment, driving out the enemy before them.

Piar then marched upon Angostura, but was repulsed in every attempt to take the city by assault. Desisting for a time, he passed behind the city to the mission station at Coroní, where supplies were plentiful. One of his officers cut the throats of twenty-two friars who were given into his custody, and received no reprimand for his barbarity. In fact this cruel deed greatly increased the popularity of the Patriots in the country round about, as these friars were hated by their Indian neophytes.

At Coroní Piar established a regular administration, which was of great service to the Patriot cause, as the armies were by it afterwards regularly supplied with cattle and corn. By these successes Piar acquired great fame, which for a time eclipsed even that of Bolívar himself.

All the Patriot leaders had now done something except Bolívar, but when he assumed the command for the second time he was another man: more grave and more thoughtful than he had been. But he was not yet a true soldier; he still took audacity for inspiration, and launched forth on enterprises without first of all adapting the means to the end desired. Immediately on landing at Barcelona he issued a proclamation that he was about to liberate the Province of Caracas, and in twenty hours set forth on his expedition with a force of 600 men. A Royalist detachment lay in his way in an entrenched position on the river Unare. Without any reconnaissance Bolívar rushed at it.

Forty horse fell upon his rear, threw his attacking column into confusion and totally destroyed it.

The Liberator was lost again. He was now in a worse plight than when he fled from Carúpano. He wrote to Piar and Cedeño to abandon their attempt on Guayana, and to Paez, Monagas, and Saraza that they should come to the protection of Barcelona. All this was utter folly, for Morillo, with 4,000 men, already covered the approach to Caracas, and La Torre, with Calzada, occupied the higher plains. Meantime he fortified himself in Barcelona, and mustered 600 more recruits. He turned the Franciscan convent into a regular citadel and sent for Mariño. Mariño, forgetting his jealousy, marched from Cumaná and joined him with 1,200 men. Bolívar then left 700 men in Barcelona, and naming Aragua as the point of concentration for the scattered forces of the Patriots, he went off to Guayana to persuade Piar to join him in an invasion of Caracas.

On the 7th April, 1817, Barcelona was attacked and taken by the Royalists, who cut the throats of the whole of the garrison, and in addition killed 300 old men, women, and sick. Mariño retreated to the peninsula of Paria and again declared himself independent, while Bermudez and other leaders got together 500 men and awaited orders from Bolívar on the plains.

The Liberator, attended by fifteen officers, met Piar near Angostura and found that he was already in possession of all the open country. The behaviour of the negro general was noble and patriotic. He showed no jealousy of his superior, who had come to seize the laurels which he had won in spite of him, and set to work to show him that Guayana must be the base of a successful campaign. The veil fell from the eyes of Bolívar; for the first time he saw before him the true theatre of the war. Leaving Monagas to hold the plains of Barcelona with his guerillas, he summoned Bermudez, Arismendi, and Saraza to join him, and the revolution was saved, thanks to Piar.

The Royalists held the coastline from Coro to Cumaná with the army of Caracas, 5,000 strong. The divisions of

La Torre and Calzada, 4,000 picked troops, with 1,500 Llanero horse, had concentrated at Guadalito on the Apure, and in January had forced Paez to raise the siege of San Fernando. Paez sent a small force against them to draw them on. La Torre, who had no idea of his force, fell into the trap, and advanced with all his army on to a wide plain covered with dry reeds. Here the fugitives were joined by the main body, and facing about, charged furiously upon the Royalist cavalry, dispersed them completely, and then by repeated charges forced the infantry to form square. Then Paez, with fifty men whom he had detailed for the purpose, set fire to the reeds all round them. Fortunately for them they found a marsh, into which they plunged, with the mud up to their waists, until the fire burned itself out, when they hurriedly retreated, leaving Paez in possession of the whole country round.

This famous deed of arms confirmed the authority of Paez over the Llaneros, and put him into a position to overrun the Province of Barinas. He concluded his glorious campaign by placing himself voluntarily at the orders of Bolívar, on condition that he might still protect the province he had conquered. Morillo, who was well aware of the importance of the Province of Guayana, detached La Torre with a strong force to drive out the Patriots, while he marched with 3,000 men to reduce the island of Margarita.

La Torre embarked his force at San Fernando and descended the Apure and the Orinoco to Angostura, without meeting any resistance, and manœuvred to draw Piar from the Missions of Coroní, hoping then to capture them by crossing the river at Angostura. But Piar divined his intentions, and leaving a reserve of horses on the right bank, he marched by the left bank to the vicinity of Angostura, then, after nightfall, leaving his camp-fires burning, he rapidly countermarched to his former position.

La Torre crossed the river as he had proposed, but was met by Piar at San Felix on the 11th April, 1817. The Spanish infantry, advancing in three columns with cavalry on the flanks, were received by volleys of musketry and showers of arrows. The Patriots, among whom were 1,200 Indians from the Missions, armed with bows and pikes, then charged, and a furious hand to hand fight ensued, in which the Spaniards were totally routed. La Torre escaped with seventeen men, but all the rest of his Spanish troops were killed. Piar spared the lives of all the Creoles among the Royalists who would join his ranks.

Bolívar, on his return from an expedition to the plains, where he had a narrow escape from falling in with Morillo, then on the march for Margarita, found himself at the head of a respectable army. All the Patriot leaders now recognised his authority except Mariño, who summoned a Congress at Cariaco, of which Zea and Admiral Brion were members. This Congress appointed an executive Junta, of which Bolívar was named one, and gave Mariño the title of general-in-chief.

Morillo soon put an end to this farce; he overran the peninsula of Paria, sank the Patriot flotilla, and dispersed Mariño's army, shooting all prisoners taken. Those who escaped, headed by Urdaneta and Colonel SUCRE, a name soon to become famous, went to join Bolívar in Guayana, while Mariño, with a few followers, fled to Maturin.

Until the Patriots had the dominion of the Orinoco their tenure of Guayana was insecure. Bolívar armed and organized a flotilla of flecheras, but what was more to the purpose, Brion again came to assist him with five brigs, some schooners and more flecheras from Margarita. These vessels were commanded by a mulatto named Diaz.

One part of the Royalist flotilla was engaged in the defence of Angostura and Guayana Vieja, which still held out; the other guarded the mouth of the Orinoco under the protection of the forts. Diaz being sent by Brion to explore the position of this latter detachment, was attacked by sixteen Royalist flecheras, and lost two of his boats. With three flecheras which remained to him, he then attacked the Royalists, recovered his two boats, captured two of theirs, sank five, and compelled the rest to retreat in confusion. Brion then entered the river under full sail.

At the approach of Brion, La Torre evacuated Angostura and was soon afterwards obliged by hunger to abandon Guayana Vieja, the last position held by the Royalists in Guayana. The remnant of his army, which now numbered only 600 men, he embarked on 32 vessels and gained the open sea in safety.

Piar, though he had recognized the authority of Bolívar, was in his heart disaffected and entered into a conspiracy with Mariño to restrict his authority by the appointment of a Junta of War; he also gained over Arismendi to his views. Bolívar prudently quelled this attempt at sedition by counsels and threats conveyed privately to the conspirators. Piar, in alarm, asked leave to withdraw from the army on pretext of illness, and retired to Upata, where he continued his intrigues till Bolívar wrote a friendly letter to him asking him to desist. He then fled to Maturin and concerted with Mariño a plan of independent action.

The position of Bolívar was now one of great danger; the troops of the army of Guayana were for the most part men of colour, Piar was very popular with them, and was accused of an intention to produce among them a mutiny of race. Bolívar gave orders to Cedeño to arrest Piar. The negro chieftain made no resistance, and was brought to Angostura for trial by a court-martial, under the presidency of Brion. He was sentenced to death for disobedience, sedition, and desertion.

Bolívar confirmed the sentence and he was shot in the great square of Angostura on the 16th October, 1817, dying as bravely as he had lived. If not an act of justice, this execution was warranted by necessity. It was the only means of preventing a civil war, which would have ended in the destruction of the army.

Mariño was still in arms at Cumaná with 400 men. Bolívar sent Bermudez with his corps to arrest him. Bermudez being an old friend of Mariño's, procured his banishment. Bolívar was now rid of opposition, but still his power was far from being well consolidated.

CHAPTER XLII.

THE REORGANIZATION OF VENEZUELA.

1817—1819.

THE Home Government, on hearing of the third insurrection on the island of Margarita, sent a reinforcement of 2,800 men under the command of General Canterac. Morillo on his way to that island with his 3,000 men met Canterac at Barcelona, and, embarking his troops in twenty vessels, sailed with him for Margarita.

Brion had left the island with his flotilla for the Orinoco. Arismendi was also absent, and General Gomez, who had been left in command, had but 1,100 infantry badly equipped, 200 cavalry, and some few artillerymen.

On the 15th July the troops effected a landing under the protection of the guns of the squadron. Canterac had thought that the mere sight of his fresh troops would suffice to disperse the insurgents, but his division suffered a heavy loss ere they could make good their footing on the island.

Morillo's first step was to publish a proclamation, in which he offered pardon to all insurgents who would lay down their arms, but threatened all who should resist with extermination. Gomez rejected the offer of pardon and made every preparation for a stubborn resistance, strengthening the fortified positions, and piling up heaps of stones on the heights for want of better ammunition.

The castles of Porlamar and Pampatar were evacuated by the Patriots after a slight resistance, but they spiked the guns and concentrated their forces in the city of Asuncion. Morillo marched inland to cut them off from the north of the island, and was met on the 31st July by a body of 500 Patriots who had entrenched themselves on very broken ground, covered with brushwood, at a place called Matasiete. It took Morillo eight hours of hard fighting to drive them from this position, but his losses were so heavy that he was forced to return the next day to Pampatar. He then occupied the town of San Juan, which is situate in a break in the range of hills which divides the island, and so cut off the communications of the main body of the Patriots with the port of Juan Griego, where their flotilla was stationed. On the 8th August the fort which protected the town was taken by assault after a desperate resistance. The garrison of this fort only consisted originally of 200 men, the survivors of whom fled to a lake near by, and refusing to surrender were massacred, Morillo killing eighteen of them with his own hand. The scene of this butchery is known to this day as "The Lake of the Martyrs."

Had Morillo persevered there is no doubt that he would have conquered the whole island, but adverse intelligence recalled him to the mainland. After losing 1,000 men he re-embarked the rest, and on the 20th August, 1817, established his head-quarters at Caracas.

Morillo now adopted a more humane policy. He published a general amnesty, abolished the military tribunals, and re-established the Audiencia and the Civil Courts. The aspect of the war had changed greatly in his absence. Paez had invaded Barinas, taken the capital of that province, and had routed a strong Royalist division at San Carlos, sacking the town and shooting all his European prisoners. But the plains were now covered with water, so nothing could be done against him. Bolívar had possession of the line of the Orinoco. Saraza's guerillas, strengthened by an infantry corps, protected the right flank of Paez. Monagas occupied the plains of Barcelona, and the Province of Cumaná was held by Bermudez.

Canterac was sent off to Peru with his sorely diminished division. The garrison of Caracas and the division of La Torre held the line of the coast. Aldama, with another division, covered the line of the Lower Apure and protected San Fernando, and Calzada, with a light cavalry division, disputed with Paez the possession of the Province of Barinas. The peninsula of Paria, and the cities of Cumaná and Barcelona were held by 800 men, and the rest of the Royalist forces were distributed in various forts along the coast. Neither party had any plan of operations, both were waiting to see what the other would do.

Bolívar was at this time the one conspicuous figure in America. He received a despatch from the Director of the United Provinces of La Plata congratulating him upon his success, and prophesying the speedy union of their arms in the same cause. Bolívar replied by an address to the Argentine people:—

"The Republic of Venezuela, though plunged in mourning, offers you brotherhood. When, covered with laurels, she has crushed the tyrants who profane her soil, then she will invite your concurrence, that our emblem be the UNION of South America."

As steps towards constitutional government by the installation of a Congress Bolívar established a High Court of Justice, and on the 30th October presided at the opening of a Council of State to which he entrusted the management of civil affairs in his absence, hoping to strengthen his authority by "the first of all forces, public opinion."

Bolívar then ascended the Orinoco with 1,500 well equipped troops, and crossed to the left bank, at about a hundred miles from Angostura. His intention was to join Saraza, who had 2,500 men, and with his aid to crush Morillo and retake Caracas. At the same time he wrote to Paez to co-operate in the scheme by advancing from Barinas. But on the 2nd December Saraza allowed himself to be surprised and completely routed by La Torre at Hogaza. The Patriots suffered a loss of 1,200 killed with three guns and all their flags, while the Royalists had only

200 killed and wounded, among the latter being La Torre himself.

Bolívar was forced to recross the Orinoco and return to Angostura. Then with some reinforcements he again ascended the river to join Paez, who, on the advance of Morillo and La Torre had prudently retired to Calabozo. The two commanders having united their forces marched with 2,000 infantry and 2,000 cavalry on San Fernando.

On reaching the river Apure, Bolívar looked in vain for the boats which Paez had promised to provide, while on the opposite side were a number of canoes under guard of a Royalist gunboat and three armed flecheras. Bolívar was dressed in a green spencer with red facings and three rows of buttons; on his head was a dragoon's helmet, which had been sent him as a sample; he wore Llanero gaiters, and carried in his hand a short lance with a black pennon adorned with a skull and cross bones, under which might be read the inscription " Liberty or Death."

" Where are your boats ? " asked Bolívar of Paez.

" There they are," said Paez, pointing to the enemy's boats.

" How shall we take them ? "

" With cavalry," answered Paez.

" And where are these horse marines ? " asked Bolívar.

Paez turned to his guard of honour, and picking out fifty men under Colonel Aramendi, he put himself at their head, shouting :—

"Into the water, boys! Follow your Uncle!"

Then putting spurs to his horse he plunged into the river, followed by his men lance in hand, and yelling to frighten off the alligators which swarmed around them.

The armed boats opened fire upon them, but without effect; the terrified crews jumped overboard, and fourteen boats were captured.

" If I had not seen it, I never would have believed it possible! " said Bolívar.

Bolívar simply established a blockade of San Fernando, and marched without loss of time against Morillo, who had assembled 1,600 infantry and 300 horsemen near to Calabozo. His movements were so rapid that Morillo was taken by surprise on the morning of the 10th February, 1818, and was himself involved in the rout of his cavalry, and borne from the field by the fugitives. One company of light infantry covered the retreat, and perished to the last man. Morillo shut himself up in Calabozo, which was defended by four redoubts, while Bolívar withdrew to rest his men.

Morillo, without cavalry and without supplies, saw that resistance was hopeless; he buried his guns, and on the night of the 14th February marched off towards Sombrero on the river Guarico, taking his sick and wounded with him. At midday, on the 15th, he was overtaken by Bolívar with his cavalry. The horsemen could make no impression on the solid columns of the Spanish infantry, but they delayed their march and so gave time for the Patriot infantry to come up. During the night which followed Morillo continued his retreat, and the next day reached the wooded country about Sombrero. Here he took up a strong position on the river Guarico, where he repulsed several attacks of the Patriot infantry, and after nightfall, by a forced march, reached the valleys of Aragua.

Bolívar, still with Caracas on the brain, retired to Calabozo, where he had a stormy conference with Paez. The Llanero chieftain insisted that to attempt an offensive campaign while the fortress of San Fernando was still held by the Royalists was to lose the command of the plains. Bolívar let Paez depart with his division, but marched himself with 1,000 raw infantry and 1,200 horse for the valleys of Aragua, where he greatly increased his force by recruits. At Victoria he established a reserve under Urdaneta, and detached his cavalry and 200 infantry to occupy the pass at Cabrera. Morillo, who had concentrated his forces at Valencia, surprised Saraza at Cabrera, routed Monagas at Maracay on the road to Caracas, and advanced upon Victoria. Bolívar was compelled to make a hasty retreat.

He halted at La Puerta, for him a most ominous position, and was there attacked on the morning of the 16th March by the Royalist vanguard under Morales. He succeeded in repulsing this attack, but Morillo, in person, led up the main body, and though himself wounded, very quickly drove the Patriots from the field, with the loss of 400 killed and 600 wounded.

Bolívar lost in this battle even his private papers, and seemed to have lost his head also. He exposed himself in the most reckless manner wherever the fight was hottest, seeming to court death as some expiation of the errors he had committed. Fortunately for him, on the 6th March Paez had captured San Fernando, with twenty guns, eighteen armed vessels, and seventy-three flecheras, and now came to his assistance; as did also Cedeño with his guerillas.

La Torre, who had taken command of the Royalists, found another army in front of him when he advanced to Calabozo. He retreated to the heights of Ortiz on the river Poga, which command the entrance to the valleys. Here he was attacked by Bolívar and Paez with 800 infantry and 2,000 horse. The strength of his position enabled him to repulse several assaults, after which he prudently retreated to Cura, and later on to San Carlos.

Bolívar then detached Paez against San Carlos, and marched with the bulk of his force further to the West, always aiming at Caracas. Paez was met at Cojedes by La Torre with a very superior force. Carried away by his impetuosity, he charged at the head of one squadron, and bore down all before him, but found on his return to the field that his army had disappeared. Overwhelmed by numbers the infantry had been cut to pieces, the cavalry had fled. Paez returned to San Fernando with less than half the force with which he had commenced the campaign.

Still worse fortune befell Bolívar. He abandoned the plains and advanced into a country swarming with detached parties of Royalists. He, with his staff, were attacked at night as they slept in hammocks in a wood. He threw off his green spencer and brass helmet and

C C

escaped on foot, but wandered about all alone till next day, when he fell in with his dispersed troops, flying from their encampment where they had been surprised, and ultimately rejoined Paez at San Fernando.

Bolívar, downcast and sick but not disheartened, immediately set to work to raise fresh troops, and sent Cedeño with 1,300 men to re-occupy the plains of Calabozo. Cedeño was cut to pieces by Morales, who then advanced towards the Apure, but was there totally routed by Paez on the 28th May, 1818. Then came on the rainy season, and both parties were forced to remain in quarters. The Patriot army no longer existed, all the infantry had disappeared, the arms were ruined and the ammunition was exhausted. The Liberator had lost both his credit as a general and his civil authority. All threw upon him the blame for the ill-success of the Patriot arms, and time, which has enhanced his glory, confirms in this instance the judgment of his contemporaries. But there was yet the nucleus of an army on the Apure, and Guayana was still secure.

The position of the Royalists was not much better. Morillo had 12,000 men scattered about in detachments, but he had neither money, arms, nor supplies. As he himself reported to the Viceroy of Peru:—

"Twelve pitched battles, in which the best officers and troops of the enemy have fallèn, have not lowered their pride or lessened the vigour of their attacks upon us."

The Spanish squadron lay idle at Puerto Cabello, while Argentine and Venezuelan privateers scoured the Carribean Sea with the ports of Margarita as their head-quarters.

In the East the Patriot arms had been equally unfortunate. Mariño, recalled by his partisans and supported by Gomez, Governor of Margarita, had again established himself at Cumaná and openly renounced all allegiance to the Liberator. Bermudez, who remained faithful, was routed and driven across the Orinoco with the loss of his artillery. Monagas was isolated on the plains of Barcelona.

Bolívar returned to Angostura, leaving Paez in command of the Army of the Apure, and with indomitable energy set to work to create a new army. He raised recruits in the Missions of Coroni, re-organized the divisions of Saraza and Monagas, while Bermudez recruited his forces in Guayana. Brion brought him 5,000 muskets and a large supply of military stores from the West India Islands. He also effected a reconciliation with Mariño and made him general of the Army of Cumaná. The Army of the Apure, at the instigation of Colonel Wilson, an Englishman who had joined it with a contingent of volunteers, proclaimed Paez general-in-chief. This appointment was confirmed by the Llaneros, who adored him, but Paez, taking no notice of this, assisted the Liberator in every way he could.

Bolívar then sent General Santander, with 1,200 muskets and a group of officers, to raise a new army in the Province of Casanare, from the parties of Patriots scattered on the plains, with orders to threaten the frontier of New Granada, which step had very important results.

Santander was a native of New Granada, he had served through all the campaigns of the revolution, and was a well-educated man of great intelligence.

Bolívar also issued a prophetic proclamation to the people of New Granada :—

"The day of America has come. No human power can stay the course of Nature guided by Providence. Before the sun has again run his annual course altars to Liberty will arise throughout your land."

Bolívar's next step was to re-ascend the Orinoco with twenty vessels and some infantry to reinforce the Army of the Apure. He had a friendly interview with Paez, and leaving him in command, returned to Angostura to attend to the claims of civil government.

The country was not satisfied with the arbitrary government of one man, and demanded some sort of popular representation. Bolívar calmly reviewed the situation and acquiesced. He re-organized the Council of State, which

had fallen to pieces in his absence, and charged it with the convention of a Constituent Congress. An electoral scheme was drawn up on the basis of joining Venezuela and New Granada in one Republic, and on the 22nd October, 1818, Bolívar published this plan in a proclamation, in which as usual he renounced all claim to the supreme power, but contradicted himself by saying:—
"The first day of peace will be the last of my authority."

The world was beginning now to turn its eyes to the great movement in Spanish America. The figure of Bolívar stood forth prominently. San Martin had fought and won the Battle of Maipó, and was preparing for the conquest of Peru. O'Higgins wrote from Chile to Bolívar, recognising him as a champion in the cause of America:—

"The cause which Chile defends is the same in which Buenos Ayres, New Granada, Mexico, and Venezuela are engaged; it is that of the whole Continent of America."

Spain solicited the intervention of the European Powers to bring about a reconciliation. Bolívar replied by a solemn declaration:—

"That the Republic of Venezuela, by right Divine and human, is emancipated from the Spanish nation; that she neither had solicited nor would admit, the mediation of the Great Powers; that she would only treat with Spain as with an equal; and that the people of Venezuela, in defence of their sovereign rights, were resolved to bury themselves under its ruins, if Spain, Europe, and all the world were to unite to keep them under Spanish domination."

On the 15th February, 1819, the second Congress of Venezuela was solemnly installed at Angostura. Into its hands the Dictator resigned his absolute power, and in a speech disclosed for the first time his plan of constitutional organization, the union of Venezuela and New Granada in one nation. He spoke in favour of democratic government, and against the system of federation, as organically weak. At the same time he showed that no Democracy had ever had the stability of Monarchies and Aristocracies, and held up the constitution of England as a model, at once Republican and Conservative. He proposed an hereditary Senate as the base of the constitutional edifice. In regard to the executive, the idea of a life President, which he had learned from his master, Simon Rodriguez, was in his head, but he dared not as yet propose it, it would not have met with any support:—

"The executive power in a Republic must be strong, for all conspire against it. In a Monarchy the power should rest in the legislature, for all conspire in favour of the monarch."

On the 10th February, 1819, Congress unanimously elected him President, and from that day he always respected the liberty and opinions of that body; although he still remained *de facto* Dictator, he appealed to them in every emergency. When he abandoned Congress he fell.

Congress established a life Senate in place of the hereditary Senate proposed by Bolívar, and adopted a centralized form of government; fixed the presidential term at four years, the President being eligible for re-election once but not oftener; and arranged the other public offices on the republican system. This constitution had yet to be submitted to the vote of the people; this was at present impossible, and it never was actually adopted, the framework alone being established.

By decree, unlimited powers were granted to the President in all provinces which were the theatre of war, and it was also decreed that the Vice-President should have no authority over the armies. This was in fact the creation of a military dictatorship.

Bolívar delegated his power to Don Francisco Antonio Zea, with the title of Vice-President. Zea being a native of New Granada, this appointment formed a link between the sister colonies. Bolívar then took the field, followed by a battalion of 500 English, under command of Colonel Elsom, which had been raised in England in the preceding year.

Often have we made mention of European officers and men in the Patriot armies, more especially of Englishmen. Venezuela, spite of the virile strength of her men, and of their heroic efforts during eight years of struggle against the disciplined armies of Spain, was the only Republic of South America to seek the help of foreign volunteers, and which had in her pay entire corps of foreign soldiers commanded by their own officers. Bolívar was something of a cosmopolitan, and had none of the prejudices of his fellow-countrymen against foreigners. More a soldier by instinct than by education, he knew that results are only to be obtained by method and discipline. He saw how San Martin, with an army well organized and well led, had triumphed over the best of the Spanish troops, and understood that he himself needed a more solid nucleus for his armies than the light horsemen of the plains, and a better disciplined infantry, to ensure success. Taught by his late disasters, which were the result both of his own imprudence and of the lack of cohesion in his troops, he was convinced that without a properly disciplined army any advantage he might gain would be ephemeral, and that if he did eventually triumph, he would stand as a conqueror over ruins. Learning these lessons, he grew from a mere warrior to be a great captain; without the science and mathematical precision of San Martin, but with greater boldness and with a heavier crop of laurels.

In 1815 endeavours had been made to raise an auxiliary corps of Irish, but it was only in 1817 that a system of enlisting volunteers was instituted in England, through the agency of Don Luis Lopez Mendez, who was at that time the representative of Venezuela in London. Without this assistance and efficient co-operation, Bolívar averred that he would have accomplished nothing in the famous campaign of 1819, for which he was now preparing.

The soldiers received a bounty of $80 on enlisting, were paid two shillings a day and rations, and were to receive at the conclusion of the war $500 and an allotment of land.

In the year 1817, various English and German officers made contracts with Mendez to take to Venezuela organized corps of artillery, lancers, hussars, and rifles. The first expedition to leave England consisted of 120 hussars and lancers, under Colonel Hippisley. Their brilliant uniforms gave them more the appearance of a theatrical troupe than a body of soldiers going on active service; nevertheless they became the basis of a corps of regular cavalry.

Colonel Wilson and Colonel Skeenen organized another corps of cavalry, but Skeenen with 300 men suffered shipwreck on the coast of France. Campbell took out the nucleus of a battalion of riflemen, which afterwards did good service in Columbia; and a subaltern named Gilmour, with the title of Colonel, and with 90 men, formed the basis of a brigade of artillery.

Such enlistments were contrary to law in England, but in 1818 and in 1819 the number of volunteers increased considerably. General English, who had gone through the Peninsular War with Wellington, contracted for a division of 1,200 English, which about this time reached the Island of Margarita, and subsequently became the celebrated Carabobo battalion. The 500 men under Colonel Elsom, who accompanied Bolívar to the Apure, were at first called the "British Legion," but were afterwards named the "Albion" battalion. Colonel Elsom had also brought out 300 Germans under Colonel Uzlar, who had been enlisted at Brussels, which corps was landed at Margarita.

General MacGregor, of whom we already know something, brought a foreign legion of 800 men. Besides smaller contingents, General Devereux, who had initiated the idea, brought an Irish legion, in which a son of the great Irish Tribune, O'Connell, was an officer.

On hearing of the arrival of General English and others at Margarita, Bolívar sent Urdaneta there to organize them. Urdaneta found 1,200 English and 300 Germans. These troops were destined for operations on the coast of

Cumaná and Caracas, but were at this time almost in open mutiny against their officers. They were brought to order by the exertions of Colonel Montilla, who had become reconciled to Bolívar. He was the last of Bolívar's enemies to become reconciled, and from this time to the end stood faithfully by him. Montilla had served in Spain, and had travelled much in Europe; he spoke the languages of these foreigners and understood their customs. He was also energetic and was possessed of some military skill. These acquirements gave him considerable influence over the auxiliaries, which he turned to good account.

On the 30th January, 1819, Morillo paraded 6,500 men, in seven battalions and sixteen squadrons, all perfectly equipped, and opened the campaign by advancing on San Fernando. Paez burned that city on his approach, and retired south of the Arauca with 4,000 men, among whom was a squadron of English dragoons. The Royalists dragged canoes with them across the plains, and on the 4th February forced the passage of the river.

Paez then changed his tactics: he sent his infantry to the rear, and remained himself facing the enemy, with 1,500 men well mounted. Morillo saw small parties of the enemy, who hovered on his flanks and rear, but who fled from him over the vast plain whenever they were attacked. He detached Morales with 3,000 men to reconnoitre and to drive in cattle. On the 14th February one of his squadrons was so occupied when Paez suddenly rushed upon it with 1,200 men, chased the fugitives to the encampment, charged the reserve, and then retired at full speed. After nightfall he again appeared in the rear. Morillo wearied out his troops in ineffectual pursuit, till after nine days of marchings to and fro upon the immense plain, he retreated to the Apure. He then threw up fresh entrenchments at San Fernando, and making that place his head-quarters, detached divisions to occupy Barinas, Calabozo, and Sombrero. At this juncture Bolívar arrived, and at once assumed the offensive, but had the worst of it in two small affairs, and prudently withdrew beyond the Arauco.

Again Morillo advanced. On the 3rd April Paez, with 150 picked horsemen, swam the river and galloped towards the camp. Eight hundred of the Royalist cavalry, with two small guns, sallied out to meet him. He slowly retreated, drawing them on to a place called "Las Queseras del Medio," where a battalion of infantry lay in ambush by the river. Then splitting his men into groups of twenty, he charged the enemy on all sides, forcing them under the fire of the infantry, and recrossed the river with two killed and a few wounded, leaving the plain strewn with the dead of the enemy.* Morillo again retreated, and the rains put an end to further operations.

Bolívar, ever impatient of inactivity, heard at this time that Santander had raised 1,200 infantry and 600 horse in Casanare, and had driven back a Royalist army of 2,300 men under Colonel Barreiro, who had marched against him from New Granada. This gave him an idea; he resolved to cross the Cordillera and save Venezuela by reconquering New Granada. He summoned a council of war, and the idea was received with enthusiasm by his officers. It was decided that Paez, with a part of the army, should attract the attention of Morillo and of the Army of New Granada upon the plains of Barinas; that Urdaneta and Montilla should embark the auxiliaries on the vessels of Brion's squadron, and should make a descent on the coasts of Caracas, menacing the rear of the Royalist army; while he with the rest of the Army of the Apure, and with the forces of Santander, should cross the Cordillera, and capture the capital of New Granada.

This was the greatest stroke of strategy that had emanated from the fertile genius of Bolívar. It changed the whole aspect of affairs, and had a similar effect to the passage of the Andes by San Martin.

* See Appendix VI.

CHAPTER XLIII.

BOYACA—COLUMBIA—CARABOBO.

1819-1822.

IN order to join Santander in Casanare Bolívar had to cross an immense plain, covered at this season with water, and had to swim seven deep rivers, taking his war material with him. Then lay before him the most difficult part of his enterprise, the passage of the snow-covered Cordillera in the depth of winter. All this he accomplished.

He joined Santander at the foot of the Andes, at the sources of the river Casanare, on the 11th June, 1819. His army now comprised four battalions of infantry, one of which, the "Albion," was composed entirely of English, two squadrons of lancers, and one of carabineers, with a regiment called the "Guides of Apure," part of which was English also. Two thousand five hundred men, well armed, but nearly naked.

Santander led the van with the Casanare division, and entered the mountain defiles by a road which leads to the centre of the Province of Tunja. This point was held by Colonel Barreiro with 2,000 infantry and 400 horse, with advanced posts on the Cordillera. A reserve of 1,000 men was stationed at Bogotá; at Cartagena, and in the valley of Cauca were other detachments, and there was still another Royalist army at Quito. Bolívar, who had fewer men, trusted much to the effect of surprise, and counted upon the support of the inhabitants.

As the invading army left the plains for the mountains

the scene changed. The snowy peaks of the eastern range of the Cordillera appeared in the distance, while instead of the peaceful lake through which they had waded they were met by great masses of water tumbling from the heights. The roads ran along the edges of precipices, and were bordered by gigantic trees, upon whose tops rested the clouds, which dissolved themselves in incessant rain. After four days' march the horses were foundered; an entire squadron of Llaneros deserted on finding themselves on foot. The torrents were crossed on narrow trembling bridges, formed of trunks of trees, or by means of the aerial "taravitas." Where they were fordable the current was so strong that the infantry had to pass two by two, with their arms thrown round each others shoulders, and woe to him who lost his footing, he lost his life too. Bolívar frequently passed and repassed these torrents on horseback, carrying behind him the sick and weakly, or the women who accompanied his men.

The temperature was moist and warm; life was supportable by the aid of a little firewood; but as they ascended the mountain the scene changed again. Immense rocks piled one upon another, and hills of snow, bounded the view on every side; below lay the clouds, veiling the depths of the abyss; an ice-cold wind cut through the stoutest clothing. At these heights no other noise is heard than that of the roaring torrents left behind, and the scream of the condor circling round the snowy peaks above. Vegetation disappears, only lichens are to be seen clinging to the rocks, and a tall plant bearing plumes instead of leaves, and crowned with yellow flowers, like to a funeral torch. To make the scene more dreary yet, the path was marked out by crosses erected in memory of travellers who had perished by the way.

On entering this glacial region the provisions gave out, the cattle they had brought with them as their chief resource could go no further. They reached the summit by the Paya pass, where a battalion could hold an entire army in check. It was held by an outpost of 300 men, who were dislodged by the vanguard under Santander without much difficulty.

Now the men began to murmur, and Bolívar called a council of war, to which he showed that still greater difficulties yet lay before them, and asked if they would persevere or not. All were of opinion that they should go on, a decision which infused fresh spirit into the weary troops.

In this passage more than a hundred men died of cold, fifty of whom were English; no horse had survived. It was necessary to leave the spare arms, and even some of those that were carried by the soldiers. It was a mere skeleton of an army which reached the beautiful valley of Sagamoso, in the heart of the Province of Tunja, on the 6th July, 1819. From this point Bolívar sent back assistance to the stragglers left behind, collected horses, detached parties to scour the country around, and communicated with some few guerillas who still roamed about. The enemy, knowing nothing of his numbers, took up strong positions, and remained on the defensive.

But Bolívar could not remain long inactive. Barreiro occupied a position which commanded the main road to Bogotá; it was necessary to attack him before he could receive reinforcements from that city or from Morillo. No sooner had he his army once more in hand than by a skilful flank movement Bolívar established himself on Barreiro's rear, in a country abounding in resources. The Royalists were forced to evacuate their entrenchments, and a hard fought but indecisive action took place in the swamps of Vargas on the 25th July, after which Bolívar recrossed the Sagamoso river, and forced Barreiro to again change his position. Then, deceiving him by a retreat in the daytime, he rapidly countermarched by night, and on the 5th August captured the city of Tunja, where he found good store of arms and war material, and placed himself between Barreiro's force and the army of Bogotá.

Barreiro, finding his communications cut, marched resolutely on the capital; but it was too late. Bolívar had command of all the roads, and seeing that the Royalists were advancing by the shortest route, which crosses the small river Boyacá by a bridge, he posted his army on the right bank and waited for them.

The battle of the 7th August commenced upon the bridge itself, where the Spanish skirmishers were driven back. Barreiro then formed his infantry in columns, with cavalry on the flanks, throwing out a battalion of light infantry on the right, whose fire might enfilade the attacking column of the Patriots. The Patriot centre and right wing drove in an advanced party of Royalist infantry, and crossing a shallow stream threw themselves upon the left flank of the Royalist army, while the left wing and the cavalry attacked in front. The Royalist cavalry fled, the infantry retreated to a fresh position, but on a second attack threw down their arms. The vanguard, under Santander, accounted for all who were not with the main body.

The victory was complete. Anzuátegui, who led the infantry of the right and centre, and Rondon, who led the final charge of the Llanero horse, were the heroes of the day. The English auxiliaries were seen for the first time under fire, and showed that British solidity for which they were always famous. The trophies of the victory were 1,600 prisoners, including Barreiro himself, and 37 officers, 100 killed, and all the artillery and small arms.

Boyacá is, after Maipó, the great battle of South America. It gave the preponderance to the Patriot arms in the North of the Continent, as Maipó had done in the South. It gave New Granada to the Patriots, and isolated Morillo in Venezuela.

Bogotá was panic-stricken. Sámano fled with 200 men to Cartagena, abandoning the archives and nearly a million dollars in the treasury. The rest of the garrison retreated under Colonel Calzada to the North. Bolívar, with a small escort, entered the capital in triumph on the 10th August, amid the shouts and blessings of the populace. This victory was not stained with blood. Bolívar was no longer the man of 1813 and 1814. He shot one only of the prisoners he took, the man who had headed the mutiny at Puerto Cabello in 1812. By incessant activity, he soon became master of the whole country, which responded with enthusiasm to his call. He raised new battalions and organized a fresh army to make head against Morillo.

Where Bolívar triumphed there could be no lack of honours. Washington and San Martin avoided ostentatious demonstrations of gratitude, but Bolívar delighted in them. The municipality of Bogotá gave him a cross of honour, a triumphal entry, and a crown of laurel. A picture of Liberty supported by Bolívar was set up in the council chamber, and it was decreed that the anniversary of the great battle should be celebrated for ever. The crown of laurel sat well upon his head, upon that of Washington it would have been a caricature.

But, great as was Bolívar's vanity, there was room also in his head for great ideas. Making use of the ample powers conferred upon him by the Congress of Venezuela he founded the Republic of Columbia, which was the dream of his life, and named Santander Vice-President of New Granada.

During a temporary absence of Bolívar, Santander shot the thirty-eight Royalist officers who were taken prisoners at Boyacá, with Barreiro at their head, and finished off the hecatomb with a countryman who had protested against it on seeing the blood-stained benches. Santander justified his cruelty by saying that it was done in retaliation of similar barbarities committed by Barreiro; but some said it was done in revenge for the death of his mother, occasioned by the privations she had suffered while hiding herself from the persecutions of Sámano.

Bolívar returned to Angostura on the 11th December, and found that affairs had greatly changed there during his absence. Zea had been deposed by a revolution, and Arismendi was now Vice-President. Mariño was General-in-Chief, and he himself was branded as a deserter for having undertaken the reconquest of New Granada without authority from Congress. The news of Boyacá had fallen as a thunderbolt among the disaffected, and his return quelled them utterly. He acted with great magnanimity, pardoned everything, resumed his authority, and announced to Congress the union of Venezuela and New Granada, calling upon it to give legal consistency to an accomplished fact.

Congress, enlarged by the addition of five New Granadian deputies from the Province of Casanare, decreed the establishment of the REPUBLIC OF COLUMBIA, in three great departments: Venezuela, Quito, and Cundinamarca, each ruled by a Vice-President. A new city, which should be called Bolívar, was to be the capital. The tri-coloured flag raised by Miranda in 1806 was to be the flag of the new nation. A Constituent Congress was convened, to assemble at Cúcuta on the frontier of Venezuela. Bolívar was named provisional President of Columbia, Santander Vice-President of Cundinamarca, and Roscio Vice-President of Venezuela. The day of the installation of the Republic was fixed for the 25th December.

This great political business being settled, war again called for the attention of the Liberator. The Spanish armies in the north and west of Venezuela, and in Quito and Cartagena, amounted altogether to nearly 20,000 men, and reinforcements were expected from Spain. The new Republic was still beset by dangers, while the strength of the country was well-nigh exhausted.

Urdaneta and Montilla had been unfortunate in their expedition. Urdaneta captured Barcelona on the 17th July, but being there attacked by very superior forces was compelled to re-embark his men and retire to Paria, where with some reinforcements he made an attack on Cumaná on the 5th August, but was beaten off and withdrew to Maturín, with a greatly diminished force. MacGregor took Portobello on the 10th April, but was soon after driven out again with heavy loss. On the 5th October he took Rio Hacha, but the conduct of his troops was so bad that the citizens rose in arms against them, and forced him to re-embark. Happily at this time the first division of the Irish Legion, 1,200 strong, reached the island of Margarita. Bolívar placed them under the command of Montilla, with orders to threaten Cartagena and co-operate with the Army of New Granada on the Lower Magdalena, while the Army of the Apure advanced from the plains of Caracas upon the capital.

Paez had invaded Barinas with cavalry, but was soon forced to retire, after which Diaz captured ten armed flecheras on the Apure river, and on the 30th September the Patriots retook San Fernando, which gave them complete command of the Orinoco.

Morillo, thunderstruck by the invasion of New Granada, remained inactive at Calabozo, and simply detached La Torre with 1,000 men to the valley of Cúcuta, whence he was driven back by the division under Soublette, which crossed the hills against him from Pamplona.

Soublette then joined Paez on the plains in his advance upon Caracas. Bolívar reinforced them with two battalions of infantry, one of which was English, and sent a strong column of Venezuelan troops, under Colonel Valdez, to the south of New Granada, in order to act against Quito. Morillo, uncertain what to do, confined his attention to securing his base of operations in the western provinces of Venezuela.

Happily for America, and for Spain also, the reinforcements expected from Europe never arrived. They could but have prolonged the struggle. The revolution of 1820 prevented them from leaving the mother country. The new policy of Spain was felt as much in the north as in the south of the Continent. At the same time that San Martin broke up the armistice of Miraflores, Bolívar signed one with Morillo at Trujillo. When negotiations for peace recommenced as Punchauca, hostilities were renewed in Venezuela.

The armistice signed by Bolívar and Morillo on the 25th November, 1820, was of great service to the Patriots, giving them much-needed breathing time, in which the country recovered somewhat from the exhaustion produced by the long continuance of the struggle, and the institutions of the new Republic became to some degree consolidated. Now that the establishment of constitutional government in Spain gave hopes of a possible reconciliation, commissioners were sent to the mother country to treat for peace, and Morillo, despairing of ultimate success, resigned his command and returned to Europe, leaving La Torre as General-in-Chief of the Royalist armies.

The armistice was badly observed by both parties, more especially so by the Patriots. While it was still in force, and while the commissioners from Columbia were at Madrid, on the 28th January, 1821, the Province of Maracaibo declared itself independent, and made overtures for a union with the Republic of Columbia. La Torre declared that he should look upon the occupation of this province by the Patriots as an act of hostility. Bolívar acknowledged that such would be the case, but stated that the Revolution itself was an accomplished fact, and as such he had a right to support it. The armistice was accordingly declared to be at an end on the 28th April, 1821.

During this interval of repose the Patriot armies had been considerably strengthened. While the armistice still lasted Montilla had taken Rio Hacha and Santa Marta, and was now besieging Cartagena with 3,000 men. Bolívar had 5,000 men at Barinas, and Paez was in his rear with 4,000 more. Bermudez with 2,000 men threatened Caracas from the East; the army of New Granada held the valley of the Magdalena. La Torre had 9,000 men besides the garrisons of the towns on the coast, but his communications were interrupted by the revolution in Maracaibo.

Bermudez after retaking Caracas and meeting with varied fortune in desultory skirmishes, was compelled to retire, but his operations were of great effect in occupying the attention of a considerable portion of the Royalist army. Bolívar established his head-quarters at San Carlos, where he was joined by Urdaneta's division and part of the cavalry of the Army of the Apure, and then marched with 6,000 men in search of the enemy. La Torre had 5,000 men under his immediate orders, including a strong body of cavalry commanded by Morales, but, uncertain of Bolívar's intentions, he detached two battalions of infantry and one squadron of cavalry to reinforce a Royalist division which was stationed at Barquisimeto, thus materially weakening his force on the eve of a decisive action. The rest of his army he drew up on the wide plain of Carabobo, at the foot of the passes leading through the Cordillera.

Bolívar, after surprising the principal pass, on the 23rd June, occupied the heights looking down upon the plain. He could only descend at the risk of having his troops cut up in detail before they could deploy on open ground. As Bolívar hesitated, a guide told him of another road which would lead him to the flank of the enemy. The next morning he detached Paez, with 1,500 horse, the Apure battalion, and the British legion, to attack the right flank of the Royalists, while he with the bulk of the army remained on the heights ready to descend by the main pass when the coast was clear.

The exit from the smaller pass was through a belt of woods and across a stream, commanded by a hillock which was occupied by a detachment of Royalists. The Apure battalion was in front, led by Paez in person. La Torre, with three battalions and under cover of a heavy fire of artillery, attacked this battalion as it left the pass, and threw it into disorder, but the British legion, led by Colonel Ferrier, came quickly to its assistance, deployed in line, and with the front rank kneeling poured in so heavy a fire that the advance of the Royalists was checked. The Apure rallied, and the cavalry charged on the right flank. Ferrier, having burned all his cartridges, led on his men with the bayonet and drove the enemy before him, while the Llanero horse rode them down, and their ranks were disordered by the flight of their own cavalry. One battalion stubbornly kept its formation, and repulsed every charge made upon it during a retreat of twenty miles until it rejoined the rest of the routed army, which took refuge in Puerto Cabello.*

This battle, the complement of that of Boyacá, which has been called the Columbian Waterloo, secured for ever the independence of Venezuela and New Granada, as Maipó and the expedition to Peru had secured that of the South; the three battles combining to prepare the definitive triumph of the emancipation of South America.

Bolívar entered Caracas for the second time in triumph; no one could now deny him the glory of being the Liberator of his country. His retention of the supreme power, both civil and military, was more than ever a necessity. This was exactly the moment he chose for another resignation; but there was a reason for it.

The Constituent Congress was convened at Cúcuta on the 6th May. It was composed entirely of civilians, of whom the greater number were lawyers, and was radically republican, opposed both to the abuses of military rule and to the anti-democratic theories of the Liberator. His resignation was thus at once a protest against accusations made against him, and an indirect way of influencing public opinion.

Congress took no notice of his resignation, but quietly debated and enacted the Constitution of Columbia. It decided that the President should hold office for four years and should not be eligible for re-election; that the General-in-Chief of the army should, while on active service, have no political power, which was equivalent to the abolition of the military dictatorship; and that the Constitution should not be reformed for ten years. It only adopted the ideas of Bolívar in one respect, which was in the establishment of a centralized system of government. His plans of a life presidency and of an hereditary Senate, as also the life Senate decreed by the Congress of Angostura, were rejected. Bogotá was declared the capital of the Republic; Bolívar, "as he feared," was named President, and Santander Vice-President.

* See Appendix VII.

Bolívar repeated his resignation, but added that he would yield if Congress persisted. Congress did persist, upon which he made an eloquent speech, in which he said :—

"A man, such as I am, is a dangerous citizen under a popular government. I wish to be a simple citizen in order to be free, and that all may be so likewise."

The Dictator of Columbia, reduced in theory to the position of a Constitutional President, showed on this occasion, as on all others, that though ambitious he was not a despot, and had no wish to be. He swore the Constitution and proclaimed it, and devoting himself to his military duties left the administration in the hands of the Vice-President, but on the 9th October, 1821, he procured the passage of a law by Congress which gave him absolute power over the army, and empowered him to organize, as he pleased, the Provinces he might liberate until he saw fit to place them under the Constitution of the Republic.

On the 1st October, 1821, Cartagena capitulated to Montilla after a siege of fourteen months. The Provinces of Panama and Veraguas, situate on the Isthmus, immediately declared themselves independent, and announced their intention of joining the Republic of Columbia. On the 28th November the fortresses of Chagres and Portobello fell into the hands of the Patriots. In Venezuela the Spaniards, with 5,000 men, now held only Cumaná and Puerto Cabello on the Windward Coast. In order to round off the territory of Columbia it was now only necessary to subjugate Quito. Thither converged the victorious armies of Bolívar from the North, and those of San Martin from the South. San Martin was already in possession of one half of Peru, and had one foot on Guayaquil.

On the 1st August, 1822, Bolívar left Cúcuta for the South. Before going he divided Venezuela into three military departments under Mariño, Paez, and Bermudez, placing them under the superior orders of Soublette. On the 16th October Cumaná surrendered to Bermudez. Puerto Cabello was still held by a Royalist garrison of

4,000 men under Morales, who, at this time, succeeded La Torre in command. Morales displayed such activity and energy as for a time changed the aspect of the war. With 1,200 men he went by sea to Maracaibo, took that city on the 7th September, and on the 12th November routed a division of 1,000 men under Montilla. Then he overran the Province of Santa Marta, and on the 3rd December occupied the Province of Coro. But in January, 1823, Santa Marta was retaken by Montilla, and Coro by Soublette. Colonel Padilla with a Patriot flotilla, which had greatly aided in the capture of Cartagena, entered Lake Maracaibo under the fire of the forts, and on the 24th July totally defeated the Spanish squadron which was there stationed. On the 3rd August Morales capitulated.

Puerto Cabello was taken by assault by Paez on the 7th and 8th November, 1823, and the war in this part of the Continent was at an end.

CHAPTER XLIV.

THE WAR IN QUITO.

1821—1822.

AFTER the battle of Boyacá, the defeated Royalists had retreated to the Highland Provinces of Pasto and Patia, in the south of Columbia, and were there strongly reinforced by Aymerich, Captain-General of Quito. General Valdez was sent against them, with three battalions of infantry, one of which was the Albion. On the 6th June, 1820, Valdez was attacked by 1,100 infantry under Calzada at the town of Pitayo to the north-west of Popayán. His vanguard was driven in, but the Albion re-established the fight, and decided the day by an impetuous charge with the bayonet; the Royalists retreated to Patia.

Valdez being reinforced, then occupied the city of Popayán with an army of 2,300 men, which was soon reduced to 1,000 by sickness and desertion. Then in January, 1821, in obedience to positive orders from Bolívar, he marched into the Province of Pasto. The Patianos, as was their custom, gave him free passage, but closed in upon his rear, cutting his communications with Popayán. He marched upon the city of Pasto, surrounded by enemies. Colonel Garcia who had succeeded Calzada in command, waited for him with 850 men in the pass of Jenay, and on the 2nd February, completely defeated him. The Albion battalion suffered very heavily in this action, and it was only the armistice of Trujillo which saved Valdez from total destruction.

On the resumption of hostilities, General Torres, who

had succeeded Valdez in command, was forced by Garcia to shut himself up in Popayán. He afterwards marched with 1,800 men upon Pasto, but suffered such heavy losses by sickness and desertion, that he was compelled to retreat, and in August he abandoned Popayán.

The Royalists of Patia and Pasto, aided from Quito, might have prolonged the war indefinitely but that the operations of San Martin and Cochrane threw their base open to attack, and the revolution of Guayaquil cut off all communication between Quito and the Pacific. Bolívar saw this, and as Quito was not included in the armistice of Trujillo, determined to attack from the South as well as from the North, and at the same time open for himself a road to the Pacific. Looking about for an officer to whom he could entrust the undertaking, he chose General Sucre, who was at that time Minister of War of the Republic of Columbia.

Sucre was a native of Cumaná, had received a scientific education, and had served from his early youth in all the campaigns of the revolution of Venezuela, under Miranda, Piar, and Bolívar. Bolívar said of him:—

"Sucre has the best organized head in all Columbia."

San Martin, who never met him, wrote of him in after years, that he was one of the most noteworthy men produced by the Republic of Columbia, and of greater military skill than even Bolívar himself.

The mission confided to Sucre was both political and military. He was to aid the new State of Guayaquil against the Royalists, and was to induce her to join the Republic of Columbia. At Popayán he collected a thousand of the dispersed troops, and reached Guayaquil by sea in May, 1821. He found that the majority of the people were in favour of union with Peru, and that they had already suffered defeat in their first brush with the Royalists.

At this juncture the flotilla and a battalion of native troops revolted in the name of the King. Sucre put down the movement, and thus became master of the situation, and commander-in-chief of all the forces.

At the head of a combined army, Sucre then marched against the Royalists, who under Aymerich were descending the mountain slopes from Quito, in two separate columns. One of these columns he totally defeated at Yahuachí on the 19th August, and compelled the other, which was led by Aymerich himself, to return to Quito with heavy loss. He then ascended the slopes of Chimborazo and occupied the plateau of Ambato, but was here attacked by Colonel Gonzalez with very superior forces, and was completely defeated, with a loss of 300 killed and 640 prisoners. He himself was wounded, and returned to his former position with a remnant of his force. Here he was fortunately reinforced by a battalion of 500 Columbian infantry, and as Aymerich did not follow up the victory, held his ground, till on the 20th November he arranged an armistice of ninety days.

At this time the Royalists, whose total force of regular troops amounted to 3,000 men, in the Provinces of Cuenca, Quito, and Pasto, received a reinforcement of 800 men, under General Murgeón, who had been appointed Viceroy of New Granada on the death of Sámano. Murgeón had arrived from Europe at Puerto Cabello with a smaller force, which being increased by La Torre, he led across the Isthmus to Panamá, whence he went by sea to Atacames, and from there marched for sixty miles through a dense forest and then over the Cordillera to Quito, where he arrived on the 24th December, 1821, and took the command.

When New Granada was secure, Bolívar wrote to O'Higgins that :—"The Army of Columbia was about to march on Quito with orders to co-operate with the Argentine-Chileno Army in their operations against Lima," but after that, affairs in the North distracted his attention. After the fall of Cartagena, he wrote to San Martin, proposing to take 4,000 men across the isthmus, and by sea to Peru, to aid him in crushing the Royalists in the centre of their power, leaving them in their positions on the equatorial Andes till afterwards. But the defeat suffered by Sucre, and the arrival of Murgeón, determined him first of all to prosecute the war in the south of Columbia.

Under the name of the "Columbian Guard," Bolívar had organized an army, with which he incorporated at Popayán the remnants of the division of General Torres, raising his total force to about 3,000 men. During his march through a hostile country, he was compelled to leave 1,000 sick in the hospitals, and with the rest reached the frontiers of Quito on the 24th March, 1822. Avoiding a conflict with the Pastusos, which had so often proved fatal to the Patriot arms, he turned to the right and tried to find a pass over the River Guáitara, a mountain torrent whose course lies at the bottom of an almost impassable abyss. Finding one suspension bridge cut, he marched to the left in search of another, and on the 7th April came upon the Royalist army under Garcia, strongly posted between the river and the volcano of Pasto. It was already past noon, but Bolívar seeing that to retreat was impossible, attacked the enemy at once. He drew up his army on the plain of Bomboná, and sent a column against the left wing of the enemy, where the ground presented fewer difficulties than on their right and centre. This column being repulsed, then attacked the centre of the position and was almost annihilated in the attempt to force its way through an abatis which covered this part of the Royalist line. Meantime another column, directed against the right wing of the Royalists, had detached a battalion of light infantry, which climbed the face of the mountain and secured a commanding position on the flank of the enemy, on which Bolívar made another attack upon the centre with a battalion drawn from the reserve. This attack was also repulsed, but when night came on the Royalists hurriedly retreated, abandoning their artillery. The Patriots were left masters of the field, but it was a Phyrric victory, they had lost 600 men in killed and wounded, while the loss of the Royalists was not over 250.

Bolívar remained for eight days encamped on the plateau of Bomboná, and then retreated, leaving 300 sick and wounded behind him. During the retreat his losses were very heavy, but at Patia he received reinforcements from Popayán. The climate and the people were both against him ; two months he remained inactive, uncertain what to do, when news reached him that Sucre, aided by a contingent of Argentine-Peruvian troops, sent to his assistance by San Martin, had taken Quito. The moment had arrived in which the two revolutions of the North and of the South of the Continent joined hands on the Equator, in accordance with the plan of San Martin.

On the eve of setting out on his first expedition against Quito, Sucre had written to San Martin asking for his cooperation. After his defeat at Ambato, he wrote again, this time to the Peruvian Minister of War, showing the danger which threatened Guayaquil. From Columbia he received a reinforcement of 500 men, but this was quite insufficient to enable him to take the field. Again he wrote to the Protector of Peru, and San Martin now resolved to give him efficient help.

General Arenales, who was president of the department of Trujillo, had a division stationed on the Peruvian frontier of Quito. San Martin sent him orders to march with it to the assistance of Sucre. Arenales was ill, and declined the command, which was then bestowed upon Colonel Santa Cruz, and by a convention the Republic of Columbia undertook to pay the troops, and to supply the places of all who might fall in war. The auxiliary division consisted of about 1,200 men, among them being one squadron of the mounted grenadiers, under command of Lieutenant-Colonel Juan Lavalle.

Sucre left Guayaquil with such troops as he had, and joined the auxiliaries in the Province of Cuenca in February, 1822, forming an army of 2,000 men, and in March went in search of the enemy. While on the march Colonel Santa Cruz received a despatch from the Government of Peru directing him to withdraw from the army at once with his contingent, which strange order arose from the misunderstanding concerning Guayaquil. Santa Cruz showed the despatch to Sucre, who forbade him to act upon it, telling him that he was no longer under the orders of the Protector. Fortunately the officers of the contingent upheld the authority of Sucre, whose firmness on this occasion prevented a great disaster, and a few days later a despatch was received from San Martin himself cancelling the order.

The situation of the Royalists was now very difficult. The Army of Quito, though numbering 2,000 good soldiers, was isolated, and might defend the mountain passes, but was powerless to take the offensive. The affair at Bomboná had greatly depressed the spirits of the Pastusos. Murgeón had died of despair on seeing the untoward course of events, and Aymerich was again in command.

Aymerich detached Colonel Lopez with 1,500 men to protect the western passes. Lopez stationed himself at Rio Bamba, but was out-manœuvred by Sucre, who entered the valley at the foot of Chimborazo. In accordance with his instructions, Lopez avoided an action, and slowly retreated from one impregnable position to another, till on the 21st April, 1822, Sucre managed to gain his rear by an undefended pass. The Royalists retreated to another position behind the town of Rio Bamba. As they were marching, Lavalle took advantage of a faulty manœuvre, and with ninety-six grenadiers charged the whole of their cavalry, 420 in number, and drove them in confusion upon the positions held by their infantry. Then retreating at full trot, he was joined by thirty Columbian dragoons. The Royalist horse having rallied, came down upon him at full gallop, upon which he wheeled round, charged them again, and completely routed them, with a loss of 52 killed and 40 wounded. One Argentine and one Columbian were killed and twenty were wounded, and the Royalist horse were of no further use in that campaign.

The infantry continued their retreat to the inaccessible position of Jalupano. Then Sucre, by a flank march of four days over the snow-covered heights of Cotopaxi, gained the valley of Chilló, 14 miles from Quito, but found the enemy again in an inaccessible position between him and the city. On the night of the 23rd May, during heavy rain, the Patriot army defiled by a narrow road, covered with loose stones, over the slopes of the volcano of Pichincha, and at eight o'clock the next morning reached the heights overlooking the city of Quito, where the steep mountain side below them was covered by a forest of trees and brushwood.

Before the whole army had reached this position the Royalists had ascended the mountain side, and rushed out of the forest upon the 2nd battalion of Peru, which led the van. Colonel Olazabal, who was in command, stubbornly held his ground till his ammunition was exhausted. The position was held by one battalion after another, as it came up, so long as any cartridges were left, but the reserve ammunition was far in the rear, and the Royalists gained ground. A Columbian regiment charged with the bayonet and recovered the position. Then the Royalists advancing under shelter of the trees, endeavoured to turn the left flank of the Patriots, but were in their turn taken in flank by three companies of the Albion battalion and driven back in confusion. Colonel Cordova then brought up his regiment of Columbian infantry, and, with the aid of the Albion, drove the Royalists down the steep mountain side in utter rout. On such ground the cavalry on neither side could come into action, but the Royalist horse, drawn up as a reserve in the suburbs of the city, was attacked later on by the Patriot cavalry and dispersed.

Sucre then summoned the city to surrender. Next day, the 25th May, 1822, Aymerich capitulated. The Royalists lost 160 officers and 1,100 men taken prisoners, 400 killed and 190 wounded, 14 guns, and all their flags. The Patriots had 200 killed, of whom half belonged to the auxiliaries from Peru, and 140 wounded.

The victory of Pichincha was the seal of the continental alliance, and concluded the war in the North. Garcia, with his isolated force, capitulated to Bolívar, but the indomitable Pastusos refused to lay down their arms till

Garcia appealed to Padilla, Bishop of Popayán, who had hitherto, both by his preaching and by his example, encouraged them in their fanatic loyalty to the King of Spain. Thanks to Bishop Padilla, a capitulation was agreed upon, by which these brave mountaineers were secured in possession of all their local laws and customs.

The Liberator entered Pasto in triumph, and thence, on the 8th June, addressed a bulletin to the Columbian people:—

"From the banks of the Orinoco to the Andes of Peru the liberating army, marching from one triumph to another, has covered with its protecting arms the whole of Columbia. Share with me the ocean of joy which bathes my heart, and raise in your own hearts altars to this army which has conquered for you glory, peace, and liberty."

The deification of the armies of Columbia inaugurated prætorianism' in South America, which was soon to press heavily upon the independent States, and was to bring the career of Bolívar to an end. The soldiery began to look upon the people they had freed as upon men whom they had conquered. The victors of Pichincha declared that Quito was annexed to Columbia. The municipality protested, and were banished from the city. Nevertheless, Bolívar on his arrival was received with enthusiasm. On the 16th June he made a triumphal entry, and was presented with a laurel wreath of gold, the third he had received in commemoration of his victories.

The two Liberators of the North and of the South were now about to meet on the dividing line' of their several campaigns. Their triumphant armies converged upon Peru. History presents no other example of so vast a military combination, carried out with steady perseverance for twelve long years, ending in the concentration of the forces of an entire continent upon one strategical point, which concentration gave the final victory.

CHAPTER XLV.

GUAYAQUIL.

1822.

UP to this time the struggle for emancipation, both in the South and in the North of the Continent had been the result of the instinctive desire for independence which was common to all the people of Spanish America, but towards the conclusion of this struggle, the peculiar idiosyncracy of each separate people began to show itself in action, and the ideas and personal interests of different leaders came into collision. Nevertheless the fundamental principles of the Revolution remained unchanged. The movement was essentially Republican, based on local autonomy. The monarchical ideas of San Martin, and the dreams of Bolívar of a continental union, left not a trace behind. The popular movements of the North and of the South of the Continent, joined hands at Quito; the diverse principles of the two great leaders came into conflict at Guayaquil.

When the Province of Guayaquil declared herself independent, she placed herself under the protection of the troops of San Martin and Bolívar, and became an apple of discord between the two leaders. Both accepted the Protectorate, San Martin with the idea of annexing the Province to Peru, Bolívar with the intention of annexing it to Columbia. In November, 1820, San Martin sent Guido and Luzuriaga to negotiate a treaty of alliance, which should place the province under his control; when they arrived the situation had changed. Guayaquil had sent 1,500 men against Quito, under the command of Luis Urdaneta, an officer from Venezuela. Urdaneta easily overran the Province of Cuenca, but on advancing towards the capital was met on the plateau of Ambato by Colonel Gonzalez, with 600 regular troops, and was completely defeated, on the 20th November. An Argentine officer named Garcia rallied the dispersed troops and led them back against the enemy, but was also routed on the 3rd January, 1821. Garcia was taken prisoner, and being put to death, his head was exposed in an iron cage at one of the entrances of the capital.

The city of Guayaquil was thrown into consternation at this disaster, but the commissioners were well received, and Luzuriaga being placed in command of the remaining troops, checked the advance of the enemy, until the rainy season covered the low grounds with water and put an end to military operations; after which the commissioners returned to Peru, without having made any definite arrangement.

The division of Sucre, sent by Bolívar, arrived in May, 1821, and for a time the influence of Columbia prevailed, but the defeat of Sucre and the retreat of Bolívar from Pasto, turned the eyes of the people again to San Martin, who had by this time taken the city of Lima. It was then that San Martin decided to take a part in the war in Quito, and sent the contingent which did such good service at Pichincha.

On the 16th December, 1821, the district of Puerto Viejo declared itself a part of Columbia, and was supported by the Columbian officers. The Junta of Guayaquil pronounced this an act of rebellion, and resolved on measures of repression. Civil war appeared imminent, when Sucre interposed, and by calming the zeal of his subordinates, restored tranquillity.

On the 30th November, 1821, Salazar had arrived as Peruvian Minister, with instructions from the Protector to adopt a waiting policy, which, in the face of a resolute opposition, was to ensure defeat. The Junta, which, as also the majority of the people, was in favour of annexation to Peru, complained to Salazar of the overbearing conduct of the Columbian troops, on which La Mar was sent from Peru to take command of the provincial forces.

Bolívar, who was resolved to include in the new Republic of Columbia the whole of the late Viceroyalty of New Granada, now sent Don Joaquin Mosquera to Peru as Minister of Columbia, to arrange the question of limits, and on the eve of marching against Quito, sent a note to the Junta, saying that "the Government of Guayaquil knows that it cannot remain an independent State; that Columbia cannot give up any of her legitimate rights; and that there was no human power which could deprive her of a hand's breadth of her territory."

The Province of Guayaquil had been at various times a dependency of the Viceroyalty of Peru, but on the formation of the Viceroyalty of New Granada it became definitely an integral part of Quito, which was a dependency of the new Viceroyalty. During the disturbances of 1809 and 1810, Abascal, Viceroy of Peru, had for military purposes taken charge of the province, as he had done of the outlying districts of Upper Peru, which belonged to the Viceroyalty of the River Plate. But this arrangement came to an end in 1819, by a decree from the Court of Madrid. Without Guayaquil Quito was cut off from all communication with the Pacific.

The Junta of Guayaquil appealed to San Martin, who replied that if they boldly declared Guayaquil an independent State he would assist them by force if necessary, but that he would make no complaint if they chose to join the Republic of Columbia. At the same time he wrote to Bolívar, asking him to let the people decide for themselves.

The attitude adopted by Bolívar was one of defiance; that adopted by San Martin, if more correct, was not baséd either on good policy or on good military tactics. Bolívar could not recede without consenting to the mutilation of Columbia, a republic of his own creation. The direct intervention of San Martin endangered an open rupture between them, which would upset the plans of both.

Under these sinister auspices took place the interview previously arranged between San Martin and Bolívar, at Guayaquil, which had been postponed in consequence of the exigencies of the war.

CHAPTER XLVI.

THE INTERVIEW AT GUAYAQUIL.

1822.

ONCE only do astronomers record the meeting of two comets at the point of intersection of their eccentric orbits. Almost as rare in the records of mankind is the meeting of two men who have made the history there recorded.

After Washington, San Martin and Bolívar are the only two men of the New World whose names figure in the catalogue of the heroes of humanity at large. They were greater as liberators than as men of thought, but the influence of the deeds accomplished by them yet lives and works in their posterity.

Events are the logical sequence of causes which have preceded them, nevertheless they are moulded by the influence of individuals. If Columbus had never lived, America would at some later date have been discovered by some one else. If Cromwell had never lived the Revolution would have occurred in England all the same, but without him it would not have triumphed. The emancipation of the British colonies of North America must in any case have produced a great Republic, but it was Washington who impressed upon the democracy the seal of his moral greatness. The French Revolution was the natural outcome of what had preceded it, but had it been directed by others than those who did direct it the result might have been better. The insurrection in South America was a spontaneous movement, resulting from historical antecedents and from the circumstances of the time, but the triumph would have been delayed, and the losses in the struggle would have been greater, but for the genius of San Martin and Bolívar, who directed the discordant elements to one definite end.

San Martin acted more from calculation than from inspiration, Bolívar more from instinct than from method, yet both were necessary, each in his own place. While they went with the current they were mere agents, but they laid hold of the forces that were in action, condensed them, and impelled them to act on one general plan by them devised, which was unseen by the masses. And they worked in concert, the idea of San Martin being carried to a successful ending by Bolívar. Neither could alone have achieved the emancipation of the Continent.

Now these two men were to meet for the first time, under the fiery arch of the Equator, with the ocean on one hand, on the other the giant range of the Andes. The world listens intently and hears nothing of what they say. One quietly disappears, saying words which have no meaning in them; the other as quietly takes his place. For twenty years all is mystery; then the veil is partially drawn aside, and it is seen that there is no mystery, that nothing had happened save what everyone knew was certain to befall. Only now that the masks have fallen we can read in the character of each one of them the motives which made the one relentless in his purpose and forced abdication on the other.

San Martin sent an auxiliary force to aid in the war in Quito without making conditions of any kind, and expected to receive help in Peru on the same terms, but after Pichincha, Bolívar was master of the situation, and could dictate his own terms. San Martin indulged the illusion that he was still one of the arbiters of South America, that Bolívar would share with him his political and his military power, and that in conference they would arrange together the destinies of the nations by them emancipated. Without other plan, he sought that interview with the Liberator which was to decide his own destiny and was to paralyze his career.

Guayaquil was the only province of the late Viceroyalty of New Granada which was not yet absorbed in the new Republic of Columbia. With this acquisition her territory would stretch from the Atlantic to the Pacific, and Bolívar would lay his powerful hand upon Peru, "the last battle-field of America" as San Martin expressed it. Bolívar was now arbiter of the destinies of South America, and could not tolerate opposition from San Martin. His policy, a union of personal ambition with grand designs of emancipation, now began to show itself.

At Quito he saw for the first time the troops of San Martin, and could compare them with his own. He marked their soldierly bearing and strict discipline, more especially he noted the Argentine mounted grenadiers, and saw that, compared with them, his own Llaneros, brave as had been their deeds, were but an undisciplined mob of horsemen. From that time there arose in his heart that jealousy of Argentine influence which was presently to mould his policy.

At a banquet given in his honour at Quito he exclaimed in his enthusiasm :—

"The day is not far distant when I will carry the flag of Columbia triumphant to Argentina."

Five Argentine officers were present, and Juan Lavalle, rising to his feet, proposed a toast :—

"To the independence of America, and of the Argentine Republic."

There were no more toasts.

On the 11th July Bolívar entered Guayaquil, under triumphal arches inscribed with his name. The gunboats on the river hauled down the white and blue flag of Guayaquil and hoisted the tri-colour of Columbia.

"What, so soon!" he exclaimed, thinking this was a signal for the incorporation of the Province. But when the boats had fired a salute up again went the white and blue flag, and was hailed by a unanimous shout of, " Viva Guayquil independiente ! "

He replaced his cocked hat, which he had till then carried in his hand, and the procession went on, but the incident excited much comment in the city, and especially in the Peruvian legation.

The intentions of Bolívar were no secret ; he had brought 1,500 men with him, who occupied the city. Within twenty-four hours of his triumphal entry a deputation of his partisans waited upon the municipality and asked them to proclaim the Province a part of the Republic of Columbia. They refused, alleging that the decision of the question lay with the representatives of the people, who were then in Assembly. The application was repeated, and was again refused.

On the 13th July an appeal was made to Bolívar himself. Bolívar sent his secretary to the Junta and an aide-de-camp to the Assembly, to announce to them that in consequence of the anarchy which prevailed he had assumed the supreme power, and had annexed the Province to Columbia. The Junta resigned and fled on board the Peruvian squadron, then lying at anchor in the harbour. San Martin had sent this squadron in support of his own partisans, thinking that Bolívar was yet in Quito, but the Liberator had been too quick for him.

On the 25th July San Martin himself arrived in the schooner *Macedonia*. Bolívar sent off two of his aides-de-camp to salute him, and to offer him hospitality "on Columbian soil." The next day he disembarked amid files of silent soldiery and crowds of enthusiastic people. Bolívar, dressed in full uniform and surrounded by his staff, awaited him at a house which had been prepared for him. The two heroes met, and embraced for the first and last time, at the foot of the staircase, and turning, entered the house arm-in-arm. In the salon the Liberator presented his generals; then the authorities of the city came to bid him welcome. A deputation of ladies presented an address to him; then a beautiful girl of eighteen years of age placed a laurel wreath of gold upon his head. San Martin, little accustomed to such theatrical ceremonies, flushed and took the crown from his head, but said that he would keep it for the sake of the patriotic sentiment that inspired the gift, and for the sake of those who bestowed it, in memory of these happy days.

The two representatives of the Revolution being left alone, walked up and down the salon together, but what they said to each other could not be heard by those in the ante-room. Bolívar appeared to be agitated, San Martin was calm and self-possessed. They shut the door and talked together for more than an hour and a half. Bolívar then retired, impenetrable, and grave as a sphinx. San Martin accompanied him to the foot of the staircase, and they took a friendly leave of each other. Later on the Protector paid a visit to the Liberator, one of mere ceremony, which lasted only half an hour.

The next day, the 27th, San Martin sent his baggage on board the schooner, saying that he should sail after attending the great ball given in his honour, and at one P.M. went again to call on the Liberator, remaining closeted with him for four hours.

At five P.M. they sat down together to a splendid banquet. When the time for toasts arrived, Bolivar stood up and proposed one:—

"To the two greatest men of South America—General San Martin and myself."

San Martin then proposed another:—

"To the speedy conclusion of the war; *to the organization of the different Republics of the Continent;* and to the health of the Liberator of Columbia;" words that indicated the thoughts which occupied his mind.

They then passed to the ball-room, where Bolívar gave himself up with juvenile ardour to the delights of the waltz, of which he was passionately fond. The rude behaviour of the Columbian officers, who were roughly reproved by Bolívar, gave a grotesque aspect to the scene.

DEPARTURE OF SAN MARTIN.

San Martin looked coldly on, evidently pre-occupied with thoughts of a much more serious nature. At one A.M. he called his aide-de-camp, Guido, to him, and said :—
"Let us go ; I cannot stand this riot."

Bolívar had already taken leave of him ; a chamberlain showed them out by a private door, and accompanied them to the landing place. An hour afterwards the *Macedonia* was under way.

The next day San Martin rose early and was silent and pre-occupied. After breakfast, as he was walking the deck, he exclaimed :—

"The Liberator has been too quick for us."

On reaching Callao he commissioned General Cruz to write to O'Higgins :—

"The Liberator is not the man we took him to be ; " words which are a compendium of the results of the interview. Of what passed between them no account was published, but at that time there were only two questions which could be discussed between them : the conclusion of the war, and the political organization of the new States.

What occurred at the famous conference at Tilsit is as well known as though all the world had been there to listen ; the interview at Guayaquil is still more easy to reproduce, illuminated as the subject is by later disclosures from the pen of San Martin himself.

The unsteady glance and ill-concealed vanity of Bolívar produced repulsion in San Martin, who read his character at once, but Bolívar, full of himself, failed to penetrate the calm exterior of San Martin ; he learned nothing of his ideas, and looked upon him as one who owed his victories to fortune more than to genius.

Bolívar had in his head a confused plan for the consolidation of America, in which everything was to hinge upon his own personality. San Martin, who had no personal ambition, said of him :—

"His feats of arms entitle him to be considered the most extraordinary character that South America has produced ; of a constancy to which difficulties only add strength."

But he had none of the frankness of a soldier, and disclosed nothing of these plans to San Martin; there was, therefore, nothing to discuss between them—on that point they could treat only of facts already accomplished.

San Martin expatiated upon the importance of bringing the war to an end. Three or four thousand Columbian troops, placed at his orders, would enable him to finish it in three months. Bolívar offered him only three battalions, and the war lasted for yet another three years. San Martin then offered to serve under him, if he would only take a sufficient force with him. Bolívar declined the offer, alleging that he could not leave Columbian territory without special authority from Congress. San Martin then saw that the Liberator would not make common cause with him, that one or the other must give way, and it is probable that he then formed the resolution of retiring from the scene.

The organization of the new States was the only other subject on which they could exchange opinions. Doubtless San Martin set forth his reasons for believing that in the establishment of independent monarchies lay the solution of the question, the people not being yet so educated in the principles of self-government as to be capable of sustaining the common responsibility of democratic rule, and Bolívar would scout the idea, showing that monarchy was a European, not an American institution; his own power, as the head of a republic, was greater than that of any constitutional king. Deep in his mind lay the teachings of his old master, Simon Rodriguez, who had taught him that the bestowal of all offices for life was the means whereby stability could be given to democracy. The result of this talk was seen in the toast which San Martin proposed at the subsequent banquet:—

"To the REPUBLICS of South America."

Was there more than this? Likely enough. The reserve which both maintained on the subject for so many years is an indication that such was the case. San Martin foresaw the failure of his scheme, and silence became a patriotic duty, lest he should place arms in the hands of the enemy. Bolívar, recognising the moral superiority of his rival, felt abashed in the presence of such abnegation, and cared not to speak of that which could only throw a slur upon his own fame.

On the return of San Martin to Peru, he announced publicly his satisfaction with the result of the interview, the conclusion of a South American alliance, and the speedy arrival of a reinforcement of three battalions of Columbian troops. But immediately afterwards he wrote to Bolívar, setting forth the great numerical superiority of the Royalist forces, and showing that much more efficient help was needed to put an end to the war. He concluded with these remarkable words :—

"My decision is irrevocable. I have convened the first Congress of Peru; the day after its installation I shall leave for Chile, convinced that my presence is the only obstacle which keeps you from coming to Peru with your army.

"For me it would have been the height of happiness to have concluded the War of Independence under the orders of a General to whom America owes her liberty. Destiny has decreed otherwise, and I must resign myself to it."

This letter explains one of the principal causes of his retirement from public life, and may be considered as his political testament. He yields his self-imposed task into the hands of a more fortunate rival, congratulating him upon the glory of finishing the great work.

By the bearer of this letter he also sent Bolívar a fowling-piece, a brace of pistols, and a war-horse to carry him on his next campaign, with this special note ;—

"Receive, General, this remembrance from the first of your admirers, with the expression of my sincere desire that you may have the glory of finishing the war for the independence of South America."

History records not in her pages an act of self-abnegation executed with more conscientiousness and with greater modesty.

CHAPTER XLVII.

THE ABDICATION OF SAN MARTIN.

1822.

DURING the absence of San Martin at Guayaquil an event had occurred at Lima which must have confirmed him in his intention of retiring from public life. The people had risen against the Government, and though the movement was not directed against him, it showed him the instability of his power. Before his departure the Council of State had consulted him as to what they should do in case of the death or incapacity of his delegate, Torre-Tagle. San Martin left with them a sealed paper, in which he appointed General Alvarado to that post in case it became vacant.

On the 25th July fifty citizens of Lima, at the instigation of Riva-Agüero, presented a petition to Torre-Tagle, asking him to dismiss his minister Monteagudo, whose tyrannical procedures and private immoralities had disgusted everyone. At the same time they addressed a note to the municipality, asking them for support in delivering the city and the country at large from "the oppression and despotism under which they suffered"; and one of their number was sent to notify the Government that in case this petition was not complied with they would convene an open Cabildo.

Riva-Agüero, who was president of the municipality, acceded to their request, and demanded the immediate imprisonment of the obnoxious minister. Government replied that they would take the matter into consideration next day.

At half past ten at night the people assembled in crowds at the gates of the municipal building and round the government house, calling loudly for the deposition of the minister. Monteagudo resigned. The municipality demanded his imprisonment, which was decreed, and Monteagudo remained under arrest in his own house.

Meantime the army remained quietly in barracks, Alvarado not choosing to interfere, although he wrote to the municipality that if the disorders continued he might be compelled to take steps to restore tranquillity. But the popular excitement day by day increased. As one of their own leaders said, "The peace-loving Peruvians appeared to have changed into raging lions." National sentiment was aroused against the foreigners who ruled them, republican sentiment against the monarchical proposals of the Government. Fly-sheets of the most seditious tendency circulated from hand to hand.

On the 29th the municipality again met and demanded the banishment of Monteagudo. He was banished.

On the 20th August San Martin returned, and was received with enthusiasm by the people. Riva-Agüero and the principal leaders presented themselves and assured him of their adhesion, but he was not deceived. He saw that they were tired of his rule, that the army was no longer devoted to him, that he had erred in the choice of his deputy, and of his ministers, and that he himself was no longer necessary, and might even become an obstacle to the complete independence of the country. He could only re-establish his authority by means of repression, which were repugnant to him; he preferred to leave the Peruvians to work out their destiny for themselves. Then it was that he wrote the memorable letter to Bolívar, of which mention was made in the last chapter.

Also he wrote to O'Higgins, alleging bad health as the cause of his retirement:—

" I am tired of hearing them call me tyrant, that I wish

to make myself King, Emperor, the Devil. On the other hand, my health is broken, this climate is killing me. My youth was sacrificed to the service of Spain, my manhood to my own country. I think I have now the right to dispose of my old age."

Twenty-five years later the publication of his letter to Bolívar disclosed the true motive of his retirement. He sacrificed himself from duty, and from necessity, and kept silence.

But he did not purpose to leave Peru defenceless. He set to work with the greatest activity to place the army on the best possible footing. At the end of August he had more than 11,000 men under arms, and expected 1,000 men from Chile to join in an expedition against the intermediate ports, and drew up a plan for the next campaign, which would probably have been decisive if he had led the troops himself.

On the 20th September, 1822, the first Constituent Congress of Peru was installed with great pomp. San Martin, in its presence, took off the bi-coloured sash he wore as the emblem of his authority, made a short speech, laid six folded sheets of paper upon the table, and retired amid the plaudits of the Assembly. The first sheet being opened was found to be a renunciation of all future command.

Congress passed a vote of thanks "to the first soldier of Liberty," and named him generalissimo of the land and naval forces of the Republic, with a pension of 12,000 dollars a-year.

San Martin accepted the title and the pension, but refused to serve, giving good reasons therefor:—

"My presence in Peru after the powers I have wielded would be inconsistent with the dignity of Congress, and with my own. I have kept the promise I made to Peru, but if some day her liberty be in danger I shall glory in joining as a citizen in her defence."

Congress then voted him the title of " Founder of the Liberty of Peru," with the right to wear the sash he had laid down, and with the rank of Captain-General; decreed to him the same pension as Washington had enjoyed; that a statue should be erected to him with inscriptions commemorative of his services; that a bust of him should be placed in the National Library he had established; and that he should receive all the honours due to one of the actual executive.

Up to this time San Martin had said no word to anyone of his intention to leave the country, but that same evening at his country-house he told Guido, who had gone there with him. Guido expostulated with him, and tried all means to dissuade him from his intention, till at last he told him in confidence his real reasons for going :—

" There is not room in Peru for both Bolívar and myself. He will shrink from nothing to come to Peru; it may not be in my power to avoid a conflict if I am here. Let him come, so that America may triumph. It shall not be San Martin who will give a day of delight to the enemy."

It was ten o'clock; his orderly announced that all was ready; the General embraced his faithful friend, mounted on horseback, and rode away through the darkness. Next morning Guido found a letter of farewell from him lying at the head of his bed, and Alvarado received another, but San Martin had embarked that same night on the brig *Belgrano*, and had left Peru for ever.

All that he took with him were 120 doubloons, the standard of Pizarro, and the golden bell of the Inquisition of Lima. In Chile he had the farm which had been given him, and a small sum of money left with a friend, most of which was lost. The Government of Peru, hearing of his poverty, sent him 2,000 dollars, with which, after an illness of two months in Chile, he crossed to Mendoza early in 1823, and while living there as a farmer, heard of the banishment of O'Higgins, and of the death of his own wife.

The reasons for his sudden departure were for long a mystery to all, except to Bolívar and to Guido. Some looked upon it as an act of self-abnegation, some as one of desertion. Time has solved the problem. The step was taken after mature reflection, and was the result of deep insight into his own character, into those of the men about him, and into surrounding circumstances. Bolívar was master of the situation, he recognised this fact, and left the field open for him to put the seal to their joint labours in his own way.

On the night of his departure he issued a farewell address to the Peruvian people, in which no mention was made of these facts. He gave no sufficient reason for so leaving them, and this caused much obloquy to be thrown upon his name. But he did so wittingly, for the disclosure of the true character of Bolívar would have predisposed the Peruvians against him, and his aid was necessary to their complete deliverance.

The public life of San Martin ends here, but the remains of the army which he had organized for the liberation of Chile, continued its glorious career in Peru until the emancipation of South America was accomplished.

CHAPTER XLVIII.

THE FIRST NATIONAL GOVERNMENT OF PERU.

1822—1823.

ONE of the heaviest charges brought by his contemporaries against San Martin, and which history has repeated, is the precipitate manner of his retirement from Peru. He left his army under the command of a General without prestige; he left the country in the hands of a Government which had no authority; and he made no provision for an efficient Government. If he had delayed his departure until he had arranged all this it is probable that he would never have gone at all. The fact is that he left everything in a state of complete disorganization. It was more than an abdication, he abandoned the country.

Congress instead of appointing at once an efficient executive appointed a governing Junta of three of its own members, two of whom were foreigners. General La Mar, a native of Quito, was President; his colleagues were Don Felipe Alvarado, a brother of the Argentine General, and Don Manuel Salazar y Baquijano, Count of Vista Florida, a citizen of Lima, and a leader of society. The selection pleased nobody. The popular party, headed by Riva-Agüero, commenced to conspire. The new Government had no support, save in Congress itself. Abandoned by the Protector, the only hope of Peru was now in the Liberator.

Bolívar no sooner saw the coast clear than he wrote to the new Government offering them a reinforcement of 4,000

men, and promising, if these were not sufficient, six or
eight thousand more. Bolívar had not seen that San
Martin was eager to open the way for him; San Martin
had failed to see that by rousing the national spirit of the
Peruvians he had shut them off from help. Government
suspected the intentions of Bolívar, and coldly declined his
proffered assistance. The answer was long in coming, and
Bolívar in alarm wrote to General Castillo, the commander
of the Columbian contingent, not to incur any risk of defeat,
but rather to retire on Columbia, and afterwards notified
these instructions to the Government of Peru.

Jealousy of foreign influence then induced Congress to
decree that all vacancies in the civil, military, and naval
services should be filled by Peruvians alone, and then set
to work to debate what constitution they should give to
the country.

The nation was named "The Peruvian Republic;" the
constitution was drawn up on the basis of popular
sovereignty, and a special clause was inserted providing that
executive offices should be neither for life nor hereditary,
which was directed against Bolívar.

The plan drawn up by San Martin for the ensuing campaign depended upon the efficient co-operation of two
armies; one acting in the South under Alvarado, the other
in the Centre under Arenales.

The whole line of the main Cordillera was held by the
Royalists, but the Patriots commanding the sea had the
choice of the point of attack. The bulk of the Royalists,
under Canterac, occupied the Centre of their line from
Jauja to Huancayo. Arequipa was weakly garrisoned.
La Serna had his head-quarters at Cuzco with a reserve at
Puno. Olañeto was at Potosí, and Valdés was fully
occupied in Upper Peru by Lanza the guerilla chieftain.
Consequently, a simultaneous attack from the South and
Centre would place the main army between two fires.
This plan was adopted by Government.

The Army of the South, consisting of 1,700 Argentines,
1,200 Chilians, and about 1,600 Peruvians, with ten light

field pieces, embarked on transports at Callao in September. Alvarado wished to take the Columbian contingent also, but Castillo refused to go. The expedition did not sail till October, and was fifty-seven days on the voyage; a most unfavourable commencement which presaged a catastrophe.

On the 3rd December the convoy reached Arica, but Alvarado sent one battalion to Iquiqui, which landed there on the 7th. Miller, with a very small force, had performed wonders in the previous campaign in this district, but Alvarado remained three weeks at Arica without doing anything. He consulted Miller, who told him anything was right if it was only done quickly. He then detached Miller with 120 men further north to make a diversion, and occupied Tacna with a strong vanguard under General Martinez. These long delays had given the Royalists time to concentrate their forces, and the indefatigable Valdés, with a flying column of 800 men, descended the hills, crossed the sandy plain, and on the 1st January, 1823, encamped in a fertile valley about twelve miles from the city. The Patriots were so superior in number that his position was one of great peril; nevertheless he put on a bold front, and while Martinez was wasting time in an attempt to surround him, he succeeded in effecting his retreat during the night and the following day to the foot of the hills at Moquegua.

On the 13th January Alvarado occupied the valley of Locumba, but again by dilatory movements lost his chance of overwhelming a small force of Royalists which had been detached by Valdés to watch him. Valdés, who was expecting Canterac with a strong force, allowed Alvarado to occupy the city of Moquegua on the 18th without resistance, but then prepared to dispute his further progress.

Beyond Moquegua the ground rises in abrupt steps which give great facilities for defence. The Royalist skirmishers covered the heights, and detached parties lay in ambush in the hollows. One by one they were driven from these positions, but at Torata Valdés drew up his force in line of battle. On the afternoon of the 19th the two armies faced each other, and the Patriots advanced to the attack. A Spanish battalion in skirmishing order covered the centre, and at the same moment the heights beyond were occupied by an advanced party of Canterac's division, whose shouts of "Viva el Rey!" re-echoed from the mountain sides. Canterac strengthened his right flank and beat back a vigorous attack of the left wing of the Patriots, upon which the whole Royalist line advanced and drove the Patriot infantry, who had exhausted their ammunition, before them in utter rout with great slaughter. The Patriots lost about 500 men killed and wounded, the Royalists about half that number. The Peruvian legion, which was now for the first time under fire, distinguished itself by its steady behaviour.

The routed battalions rallied under the fire of their artillery, but during the following night the whole army retreated, and encamped next day at Moquegua, seventeen miles from the field of battle. The ammunition was nearly exhausted. Alvarado summoned a council of war, but the advice of his officers was so discordant, that before he had formed any resolution the enemy was again in his front on the 21st.

Alvarado then took up a strong position, with his left resting upon the suburbs of the city, and his line extending along the ridge of a steep declivity, broken in the centre by a road which was swept by the fire of his artillery. His right rested upon a bare hill. Valdés, with two battalions and two squadrons of horse, seized this hill and turned the right flank of the Patriots, while the rest of the Royalist cavalry menaced the left, and Canterac led the main body against the ridge. Alvarado wheeled back his right wing, and for a short time the Patriots held their ground with great determination, but were at length driven from the position and totally routed with a loss of 700 in killed and wounded, and 1,000 prisoners. The mounted grenadiers, led by Lavalle, made two desperate charges to cover the retreat, but were in their turn overwhelmed by the Royalist horse.

About 1,000 men reached Ilo with General Martinez, and embarking there, returned to Lima. Alvarado went to Iquiqui in search of the detachment he had left there, and on the 14th February landed a small party on shore, which was all either captured or destroyed by Olañeta, who had occupied the city. Alvarado then invited Olañeta to a conference concerning the prisoners, and found this general to be so disaffected to the Viceroy and his adherents, whom he styled "traitorous Liberals," that he declared his intention of separating from them and confining himself to the defence of Upper Peru for the King.

Miller, with his 120 men, accomplished more than all the rest of the army; he alarmed all the South, and kept the whole reserve under Caratala in check.

Meantime Arenales lost much time in endeavouring to persuade General Castillo to incorporate his auxiliaries with the army he was organizing for the attack on the centre of the Royalists. Castillo refused to join at first, on the plea that success was doubtful, and then demanded that a Peruvian should be appointed to command the allied army. His demand being refused, he then asked permission to retire altogether from the country. Government, anxious to free itself from so arrogant an ally, furnished transports, and the Columbian contingent left Peru for Guayaquil, taking with it the Numancia battalion, 600 strong, which Bolívar had claimed, as being a Columbian corps. This Columbian contingent had cost Peru 190,000 dollars and had been of no service whatever.

Nevertheless Arenales, who hoped to make up by speed for paucity of numbers, had organized a column of 2,000 men, when Martinez arrived with a remnant of the Army of the South. The news brought by him produced great irritation, but by no means disheartened the people, who were confident of ultimate success. Their anger was turned against Government; the army encamped at Miraflores was almost in open revolt. Arenales was asked to put himself at the head of the movement, but this stout soldier would have none of it, and giving up the command to Santa Cruz left Peru for ever.

The leaders of the army headed by General Martinez, on the 26th February, 1823, presented an address to Congress, asking that Riva-Agüero might be placed at the head of the Executive. The city militia supported them. Congress yielded, and on the 27th Riva-Agüero was named President of the Republic, and afterwards Grand Marshal of the armies, although he was simply a colonel of militia and had never been under fire.

Riva-Agüero was a true representative of the people, and his popularity was enhanced by his activity and by the skill shown in the first measures he adopted. He reorganized the army, making Santa Cruz general-in-chief, and Martinez general of the division of the Andes and Chile. He reopened relations with Chile, and wrote to Bolívar accepting the help which Congress had refused. Bolívar made a treaty with him, in which he promised 6,000 men, who were to be equipped and paid by Peru. Chile promised a further contingent of from 2,000 to 2,500 men, and 1,500 muskets in addition. San Martin in Mendoza pushed on the organization of an Argentine division, which was to operate on the frontiers of Salta, under the orders of Urdininea. At the same time news was received that the Peruvian commissioners, in London, had abandoned their monarchical schemes, and had effected a loan of *one million two hundred thousand pounds sterling*, which was ratified by Congress.

Before two months had passed Peru had an army of 5,000 men ready for the field, in addition to the Argentine and Chilian auxiliaries, who were 2,500 more. Riva-Agüero determined upon another expedition to the intermediate ports, directed against Arequipa and Puno, while another army, composed of troops of the four Allied Nations, should advance by Jauja upon the centre, a repetition of the previous plan. Bolívar approved of the plan when his opinion was asked, and promised his 6,000 men. Chile again promised a fresh contingent, which should be sent to the south of Peru, and offered to supply horses for the expedition. The Royalists, ignorant of these preparations, made ready on their part for an attack upon Lima.

Five thousand Peruvian troops left Callao in May for the South under General Santa Cruz, with Colonel Gamarra as chief of the staff. For the first time Peru had an army of her own, commanded by Peruvian generals. Before leaving, Santa Cruz presented himself to Congress and swore to return triumphant or to die. He did neither the one thing nor the other.

Santa Cruz showed more activity than Alvarado had done. On the 17th June the convoy reached Arica. On that same day Canterac, with an army of 9,000 men, rushed down from the Highlands and captured Lima. The expedition was thus isolated, but the move was a false one on the part of the Royalists.

Bolívar did not share in the general confidence, he was more clear sighted than most others, as is seen in a notable letter which he wrote at this time to General Sucre. He had concentrated his forces at Guayaquil, and on hearing of the disasters of Torata and Moquegua, before signing the treaty of which we have already made mention, he at once sent off an expedition of 3,000 men under Sucre, with instructions to gain possession of the fortresses of Callao at any cost. Sucre, whom he called "his right arm," was also named minister plenipotentiary to Peru, and was sent to prepare the way for the accomplishment of the secret designs of the Liberator, who saw that Peru would soon be in a condition to welcome him as her saviour.

The occupation of Lima by the Royalists was a mistake, it gave them no military advantage while Callao and the ocean were held by the Patriots. The Government fled to Callao, and the army collected under shelter of the guns of that fortress. Sucre was made general-in-chief. Congress dispersed; some of the members went over to the enemy; but a minority, who were hostile to Riva-Agüero, kept together, and sent for Bolívar on the 19th Juue, 1823, giving him the title of Generalissimo and ample powers for the salvation of the country. Riva-Agüero retained the title of President, but was sent out of the way to Trujillo.

Bolívar accepted the invitation, saying that "for a long time his heart had yearned towards Peru." Pending his arrival Sucre exercised his powers as his representative; the secret wish of Bolívar was accomplished, he was master of Peru.

The Viceroy soon perceived the mistake he had made, and recalled his army from Lima. On the 16th July Canterac evacuated the city, and returned to the Highlands unmolested. On the 20th Sucre sailed southwards with 3,000 Columbians and Chilians and a squadron of Peruvian cavalry, leaving an army of Peruvians, Argentines, and Columbians at Lima with orders to occupy Jauja and secure the line of the Apurimac. His intention was to combine the movements of the three armies, with Arequipa as the base of his operations, and to advance on Cuzco with 8,000 or 12,000 men, but when he reached the south coast Santa Cruz was already far inland. He then landed at Quilca and marched on Arequipa; but the same day Santa Cruz had fought a battle of doubtful result on the borders of Lake Titicaca.

Santa Cruz had changed the plan. Instead of keeping his army together he had divided it into two columns, directed against Upper Peru. With the first he landed near Ilo, and advanced to Moquegua, while the second, under command of Gamarra, landed at Arica, and occupied Tacna. Here he remained till the middle of July, awaiting the Chilian contingent; but as it did not come he, on the 13th July, ascended the Cordillera, crossed the Desaguadero by the bridge of the Inca without opposition, and on the 8th August occupied the city of La Paz. Gamarra at the same time marched by the Tacora road, crossed the Desaguadero lower down, and occupied the city of Oruro, which is about 170 miles from La Paz.

Olañeta, who was retreating towards Potosí with 1,500

men, was almost surprised by Gamarra, of whose movements he knew nothing, and withdrew to the South. Gamarra was then joined by Lanza, the Guerilla chieftain, with 600 men, and learned that Urdininea, with the Argentine division, was advancing from Salta; but he lost the opportunity of destroying Olañeta, which was part of the plan of Santa Cruz, by remaining inactive at Oruro.

Santa Cruz, hearing that La Serna was concentrating his scattered divisions at Puno, then turned back to cover the line of the Desaguadero, and stationed himself on the left bank at the bridge of the Inca. Valdés advanced against him with 2,000 men, but finding the bridge was defended by artillery, he withdrew to the town of Zepita. Santa Cruz crossed the bridge and went after him, and overtook him in a strong position between the mountains and the lake of Titicaca. By a feigned retreat he drew Valdés into the plain, where two Peruvian squadrons cut the Royalist horse to pieces, but the attack upon the infantry was less successful, and night put a stop to the action. Both sides claimed the victory, but Valdés retreated, and soon after Santa Cruz returned to his position on the Desaguadero. This was the first and last battle of the expedition.

La Serna joined Valdés at Zepita, and crossed the Desaguadero with 4,500 men. Santa Cruz retreated before him, and on the 8th September joined Gamarra to the south of Oruro. He then manœuvred to prevent a junction between La Serna and Olañeta, who was returning from Potosí with 2,500 men, but La Serna by a flank march over the heights succeeded in effecting the junction on the 14th September. Santa Cruz thought himself lost, and without attempting to bring on an action in which the chances would have been in his favour, retreated precipitately. The retreat soon became a flight, arms and baggage were thrown away, and he recrossed the Desaguadero utterly routed, without fighting and without even seeing an enemy. He left a company of infantry with two guns to defend the bridge, who capitulated to the Royalist vanguard at the first summons. Barely 1,000 men reached the coast, and the Chilian contingent, which just then arrived, returned at once to their own country.

Sucre, seeking to affect a junction with Santa Cruz, had shown in the prosecution of his arduous task both the prudence and the ability of a master in the art of war. At Arequipa he heard of the fight at Zepita, and marched on Puno supposing that Santa Cruz was still holding his ground at the bridge of the Inca, but was met by the intelligence of the total dispersion of the Patriot army, and of the concentration of the Royalists. Placing himself so as to cover the flight of the fugitives, he steadily retreated and re-embarked at Quilca.

Before the result of the first expedition to the intermediate ports was known, two of the admirers of San Martin had written to him in his retirement at Mendoza, telling him that "the hand of San Martin alone can crown his work and give liberty to Peru." Even Riva-Agüero wrote to him, beseeching him to return to public life. After the disasters of Torata and Moquegua, the eyes of all Peruvians were turned to their late Protector, and a multitude of letters to the same effect reached him in his solitude. The new Government of Chile wrote to him that posterity would forget his immense services unless he completed his work. After the failure of the second expedition a council of Peruvian officers, headed by General Porto Carrero and Admiral Guise, with the authorization of Riva-Agüero, passed a resolution that all Peruvians of every class called upon their Protector to fly to their assistance, now that their country was in danger. Guido wrote to him that all Patriots looked to him for help. Riva-Agüero, who had quarrelled with Congress, and was opposed to the alliance with Columbia, offered him the supreme power, by a special messenger. But San Martin had no faith in Riva-Agüero, and wrote to him to re-establish the authority of Congress, and on his refusal, rejected his offers with disdain.

Riva-Agüero, in his semi-exile at Trujillo, had dissolved

Congress, and on the 19th July had convened a Senate of his own selection, but he had no support in public opinion. On the 6th July thirteen members of the late Congress met at Lima, called up some substitutes, formed themselves into a sovereign Congress, appointed Torre-Tagle chief of the Executive, and on the 8th August declared Riva-Agüero an outlaw. He replied by declaring them traitors and their decrees null and void. He then collected an army of some sort, proposed an armistice to the Spaniards and offered to dismiss the auxiliaries. But the auxiliaries refused to recognise his authority, and the Columbian troops called upon him to lay down the command.

Then came Bolívar. The castles of Callao thundered him a welcome; Lima decked herself in flags in his honour. He landed in Peru on the 1st September; no American ever received so enthusiastic a reception. Congress made an appearance of consulting him, but in reality only awaited his orders. As at Caracas, at Angostura, in New Granada, and at Cúcuta, he renounced all claim to civil power, placing only his sword at their disposal. Congress paid no attention to these empty phrases, invested him as Liberator with supreme authority, both military and civil, and voted him an annual salary of 50,000 dollars, which, with his usual disinterestedness, he declined to touch.

At a banquet which followed, the name of San Martin was not mentioned among the many toasts proposed. Whereupon Bolívar rising to his feet proposed one himself:—

"To the good genius of America, which brought General San Martin with his liberating army from the banks of La Plata to the shores of Peru; and to General O'Higgins who had sent him on from Chile."

Then as the banquet drew to an end, he proposed another :—

"That the peoples of America may never raise a throne upon their soil."

At night as he entered the theatre, the whole audience rose to their feet. He occupied the official box with the

President, under a drapery of the festooned flags of Peru and Columbia.

Procter, an English traveller who was present on this occasion, thus describes him:—

"He is very thin, but his whole person shows great activity. His features are well formed, but are worn by fatigue and anxiety. The fire of his black eyes draws attention at once. Never did the exterior give a more exact idea of the man himself. Egoism, determination, activity, intrigue, and a persevering spirit, are clearly expressed in his bearing, and in each movement of his body."

Bolívar's first care was to put an end to the dispute with Riva-Agüero, but finding all friendly overtures unsuccessful, he resolved upon using force. The country seemed on the verge of a civil war, when his own troops mutinied against the ex-President. He disappeared from public life, and the danger was averted.

Bolívar remained absolute master of Peru. He thought that all America was now his.

CHAPTER XLIX.

JUNIN—AYACUCHO.

1823—1824.

THE day-dreams of men often mould the course of their lives. The day-dream of Bolívar was the unification of South America. It was in pursuance of this dream that he created a great military power, and carried his arms in triumph over half the Continent. His first step was the creation of Columbia. Then he dreamed of a South American Confederation, ruled by an international assembly, after the manner of the Achaian League of ancient Greece; and, at last, of a monocracy under the protection of Columbian bayonets. Then the dream became delirium.

In the treaties with Chile and Peru, forming an alliance offensive and defensive, it was stipulated by Bolívar:—

"That an Assembly should be convened of the American States, composed of plenipotentiaries, with the object of establishing on a solid basis intimate relations between each and all of them, which may serve as a council when great questions arise, as a point of contact in common danger, as an interpreter of treaties in case of a misunderstanding, and as an arbitrator and conciliator in disputes and difficulties."

On the field of diplomacy the Liberator of Columbia came for the first time in contact with Don Bernardino Rivadavia, the highest personification of the Liberalism of South America. One was at the head of four great States, the other was the constitutional minister of a province.

Bolívar aspired to the laurel crown of an American Cæsar, Rivadavia to that of a pacific liberator.

Rivadavia was at this time the soul of the Provinces of La Plata, which were separated by political shipwreck. The Argentine Republic, exhausted by her great struggle for the independence of America, and prostrated by civil conflict, took no more part in the continental war, but her soldiers still fought for her in far-off lands; her integral parts, in spite of separation, had still cohesion and sought reunion. A centre of attraction was wanting to this constellation of fourteen wandering stars—Buenos Ayres provided that centre. Rivadavia welded this province into a State, which became the organic cell of national life. On the small theatre of a province, the representative system of a republic was seen for the first time at work in South America. These institutions, which were then a novelty in the world, except in the United States and partially in England, showed to the peoples of South America what the republican system was; from Buenos Ayres they spread over the entire Continent.

The Argentine Republic was then threatened with the war which broke out two years later. The new Empire of Brazil had occupied by force the Banda Oriental, which was one of the United Provinces; the Government of Buenos Ayres, inspired by Rivadavia, faced the question with all its consequences. In these circumstances, in January, 1823, Don Joaquin Mosquera arrived in Buenos Ayres as minister plenipotentiary of Columbia. Rivadavia was provisionally in charge of the Government. He rejected at once the idea of a Congress with power to decide international disputes. The treaty was reduced to a defensive alliance, in support of their independence from Spanish or from any other foreign domination. As Rivadavia explained to the Legislature:—

"The treaty proposed by Columbia did not fulfil the requisite conditions, since it only recognised the existence of governments and not their legitimacy."

The idea of Rivadavia was to complete the triumph of

the revolution by a peaceful understanding with the mother country, in which all the late colonies should unite.

When King Ferdinand, in 1820, sent a royal commission to the River Plate with the object of "putting an end to differences existing between members of the same family," the Government of Buenos Ayres replied that it could listen to no proposition which was not based upon the recognition of independence, which declaration served as a precedent.

The treaty with Columbia was signed on the 8th March, 1823, was ratified by the Government of Columbia on the 10th June, 1824, and by the Argentine Congress on the 7th June, 1825.

Almost simultaneously with Mosquera, there arrived in Buenos Ayres two new commissioners from the King of Spain. The Spanish Cortes, re-installed at Cadiz in 1820, was composed of Liberals, who saw that these ancient colonies could not be subjected by force, and attempted to settle the question by negotiation. These commissioners brought no proper credentials, but were simply appointed by the King, under Liberal pressure, to listen to proposals, and to arrange provisional treaties of commerce. Their real object was to divide the different republics which were at war with Spain. Buenos Ayres was looked upon as the centre of the revolutionary spirit; the commissioners were instructed to recognise the independence of the United Provinces, and so to separate them from Peru and Columbia.

Rivadavia drew up a resolution which was sanctioned at once by the Legislature:—

"Government shall negotiate no treaties of neutrality, of peace, nor of commerce with Spain, until after the cessation of war in all the new States of the American Continent, and not until after the recognition of their independence."

On this basis an arrangement was drawn up, in which a suspension of hostilities for eighteen months was stipulated, during which time the Province of Buenos Ayres should negotiate the acquiescence of the other American governments.

Meantime commercial relations were re-established with Spain, contraband of war being excepted. But it was an illusion on the part of Rivadavia to hope that the question with Spain could be settled by any other mode than by arms.

There was yet a further stipulation. As France had voted 20 millions of dollars in aid of the restoration of absolutism in Spain, in agreement with the Holy Alliance, from which England was already separated, the Government of Buenos Ayres was authorized to negotiate for an equal sum among the States of America " to uphold the representative system in Spain." Don Felix Alzaga was, with this object, appointed plenipotentiary to the Governments of Chile, Peru, and Columbia. At the same time General Las Heras was sent as a commissioner to the Royalist authorities in Peru, to arrange an armistice with them, in conjunction with General Arenales, who was at that time in command on the northern frontier.

Buenos Ayres, in spite of the dangers which surrounded her, thus performed her duty to her sister States, boldly confronting the alliance of the absolute kings, and thereby gained the goodwill of England; but the convention was rejected in Chile through the intervention of the Columbian minister. Alzaga then went on to Peru and presented it to both Presidents, to Torre-Tagle and to Riva-Agüero. The first made use of it to open a traitorous correspondence with the Royalists, the other used it as a plea for arranging an armistice of his own, and for sending back the Columbian auxiliaries; but, strange to say, it was accepted by Bolívar as a way out of his difficulties, he merely stipulating that it should, first of all, be ratified by the Spaniards. His object was to gain time for the arrival of reinforcements from Columbia.

At the beginning of 1824 the situation of the Patriots in Peru was very precarious. The Royalists had 18,000 men, flushed with recent victories; the Patriots had only half that number. At this juncture an event happened which had for a time most disastrous effects upon the fortunes of Peru. Just as the Spaniards were making a last effort to regain the dominion of the Pacific the Patriots lost the fortress of Callao, while, almost simultaneously, President Torre-Tagle passed over to the Royalists, taking with him a part of the national forces, and the Spaniards re-occupied Lima.

The Argentine contingent was very discontented; the Peruvians were jealous of them and treated them as foreigners, tolerated only on account of their services. They were badly clothed and fed, their pay was both irregular and insufficient; the Government by whose authority they had become an army no longer existed; the general to whom they owed their existence had deserted them. In March, 1823, they had applied for protection to the Government of Buenos Ayres, and had been adopted by the Province, then the only representative of the nation.

Bolívar commenced to prepare for offensive operations by concentrating his forces at Pativilca, about 140 miles to the north of Lima, and withdrawing most of the Columbian garrison from Callao, supplied their place with the Rio de la Plata regiment and the 11th battalion of the Andes, putting the whole garrison under command of General Alvarado.

On the night of the 4th February, 1824, the rank and file of the garrison mutinied under two Argentine sergeants, named Moyano and Oliva, and imprisoned their officers. Their first demands were for 100,000 dollars as arrears of pay, and that they should be sent back to their own country. While Government hesitated to accede to these terms the spirit of insubordination gained strength among the soldiery, their own leaders could not prevent excesses. Among other Spanish prisoners in the dungeons, was a Colonel Casariego, whom Oliva had known in Chile; the two sergeants took counsel with him, and by his advice released the Spanish prisoners and put their own officers in the dungeons. He then persuaded them that their situation was desperate, and that their only chance of safety lay in embracing the Royalist cause and hoisting the Spanish flag. The troops were reorganized and placed under Spanish officers. Moyano was made a colonel and Oliva a lieutenant-colonel, all sergeants and corporals were promoted, and a messenger was sent to Canterac placing the fortress at his disposal.

On the 7th February the flag of Spain was raised on one of the towers. A negro soldier of the Rio de la Plata regiment, a native of Buenos Ayres, known by the nickname of "Falucho," refused to mount guard over the flag against which he had so often fought. He broke his musket against the flag-staff, and was shot, shouting—"Viva Buenos Ayres!"

The mounted grenadiers who were encamped in the valley of Cañete, mutinied also, and marched to join their comrades at Callao on the 14th February, but when they saw the Spanish flag flying over the walls they released their officers. One hundred and twenty of them returned to their allegiance, and represented their country in the liberating armies to the end of the war. Thus by mutiny and by treachery was dissolved the celebrated Army of the Andes.

As soon as Canterac heard of the mutiny at Callao, he sent a strong division under Monet from the Highlands, which joined the division of Rodil in the valley of Ica and marched on Lima. Torre-Tagle, who with his Minister of War, was in secret correspondence with the Royalists, joined them with some Peruvian troops, and issued a proclamation against Bolívar.

The Royalists were now masters of the Highlands, and of all the centre and south of Peru, and aimed at the dominion of the sea as well. A part of the Peruvian squadron was stationed at Callao. Admiral Guise with the *Protector* frigate and four armed boats, entered the port under the fire of the forts, boarded the frigate *Guayas*, formerly *Venganza*, and burned her, as also the *Santa Rosa*, and some merchant vessels, on the 25th February. The brig of war *Balcarce* was the only vessel saved, but the Royalists were expecting two Spanish frigates.

Bolívar issued terrible decrees for the evacuation of Lima, which were not obeyed, but on the 10th February Congress appointed him Dictator.

Monet occupied Lima without resistance, but did not remain there. He left Rodil in command at Callao, and returned to the Highlands, taking the officers of the former garrison with him as prisoners.

These officers, 160 in number, were forced to march on foot up the mountain passes to Jauja. On the third night, as they were passing through a narrow defile, two of them, by preconcerted arrangement, slipped into a ditch where they could not be seen, the two who were next them concealing their retreat so that the evasion was not discovered till they reached the next halt. Monet ordered two of the prisoners to be shot in place of those who had escaped. They were all drawn up in line by General Camba, and told to draw lots, which were presented to them in a helmet. Several lots had been drawn blank, when two officers stepped forward saying that they were the men who had concealed the escape of the fugitives. With one exception all the other officers called for the drawing to go on, but Camba decided that these two should pay the forfeit of their lives, and they were shot.

One of them, Domingo Millan, was a native of Tucuman, and of middle age. He drew out from the lining of his uniform coat the medals of Tucuman and Salta, pinned them on his breast, and died shouting, "Viva la Patria!" The other, Manuel Prudon, was a native of Buenos Ayres, and only twenty-four years of age. He died with the calmness of a martyr, shouting, "Viva Buenos Ayres!"

Bolívar had fallen dangerously ill at his head-quarters at Pativilca; for six days he lay unconscious. When he was yet in the first stage of convalescence, news reached him of the mutiny of Callao, and of the treason of Torre-Tagle. Mosquera went to visit him, and found him seated in a rocking-chair in the orchard, his head tied up in a white handkerchief. He was deadly pale, and his voice was hollow with weakness.

" What do you think of doing now ? " asked Mosquera.

" Of triumphing," replied he, undauntedly. Misfortune only seemed to strengthen his spirit.

He retreated with 7,000 men to Trujillo, made the Southern Provinces of Columbia his base of operations, and wrote to Vice-President Santander asking for reinforcements:

"The interests of all America are at stake; nothing must be trusted to probabilities, still less to chance or fortune."

On the 11th May, 1824, Congress authorised a levy of 50,000 men, and 3,000 men were sent to join him at once. Before the enemy suspected that he was about to move, he had concentrated his army at the foot of the northern Cordillera, in three divisions of infantry, under Cordoba, Lara, and La Mar, and one of cavalry, under Necochea. Sucre was chief of the staff.

At this time Olañeta, who was in Upper Peru with 4,000 men, refused any longer to obey the orders of the Viceroy. He had heard from Buenos Ayres that, by the help of France, Ferdinand had abolished the Constitution of 1820, and was once more an absolute king. La Serna sent Valdés against him, and some severe fighting took place between them, in which Valdés had the advantage, when he was recalled by the Viceroy.

Bolívar took advantage of the absence of Valdés to commence operations, and marched on Jauja by the road which had twice led Arenales to victory, covering his advance by a cloud of Peruvian guerillas, under whose protection Sucre marked out the daily route of the army, and provided supplies. Bolívar ascended the range at its highest point in the direction of Pasco, hoping to surprise the enemy, and on the 2nd August passed 9,000 men in review about twenty-five miles from that city, on which occasion he was accompanied by O'Higgins and by Monteagudo, who had returned from exile. On the 4th Miller, who had been detached with a party of cavalry, brought word that Canterac was advancing from Jauja with all his army.

To the south of Pasco, at the head-waters of the Rio Grande, commences the great lake of Reyes, which lies between the two ranges of the Cordillera, and occupies all the low ground as far as the entrance of the valley of Jauja. On its eastern bank there runs a level road, on the western bank is another which leads to Junin, and is much rougher. At the southern extremity of the lake lies the plain of Junin, broken by numerous hillocks, and cut up by streams and marshes filled by the overflow from the lake.

On the 1st August Canterac had advanced with his cavalry along the eastern road to reconnoitre, and learned to his surprise that Bolívar was already on the other side the lake. He retreated rapidly, and rejoined his infantry on the 5th August. On the 6th, at two o'clock in the afternoon, he found himself face to face with the Patriot army on the plain of Junin. Their infantry held the heights beyond, while their cavalry appeared about to charge him. Bolívar had marched along the eastern slopes of the western range, halting only in strong positions, showing a cautiousness which was not usual with him. On seeing the Royalist army, he sent Necochea in front with 900 horse. The ground was so contracted by a hill on one side and by a marsh on the other, that at five o'clock Necochea had only two squadrons of Columbian horse on the plain, when he was attacked by the whole of the Royalist cavalry, 1,300 strong, led by Canterac in person.

The Columbian lancers received the charge with great steadiness, but were driven back upon their supports, who were still entangled in the defile. The Royalist horse, greatly disordered by their rapid advance, entered the defile with the fugitives. Necochea, pierced by seven lance wounds, was trampled under foot and made prisoner. Colonel Suarez, with the first squadron of Peruvian hussars, had drawn his men into an angle of the marsh, and, letting the rout pass by, charged the pursuers in the rear. The fugitives were rallied by Miller, who led them again to the charge, and drove the Royalists from the field. In forty-five minutes the whole affair was over, and not a shot was fired. The Royalists lost 250 killed by lance and sabre; the Patriots lost 150 between killed and wounded, and rescued Necochea. The fugitives took shelter under the fire of their infantry, which at once retreated.

Such was the celebrated action of Junin, which broke the prestige of the Royalist army, and prepared the way for the final triumph. Bolívar, who had seen the rout of the first squadrons, thought he had lost his cavalry, and returned to the infantry, who were a league behind. He only learned the defeat of the enemy from a pencil note sent him by Miller after sundown. The hussars who did such good service were afterwards styled the Hussars of Junin, in reward for their gallant behaviour.

Canterac, who was greatly disheartened by this disaster, which was chiefly the result of his own precipitate conduct in charging without a reserve over ground of which he knew nothing, evacuated the valley of Jauja, and retreated so rapidly that in two days he was more than a hundred miles from the scene of the action, and his infantry was quite worn out; but he did not stop until he had crossed the Apurimac, more than five hundred miles from Junin, and lost between 2,000 and 3,000 men by desertion on the way. La Serna sent him a reinforcement of 1,500 men, and recalled Valdés to Cuzco. Canterac had fled from his own shadow, for he was not pursued.

Bolívar rested for three days on the field of battle, took ten days to occupy the valley of Jauja, and remained nearly a month at Huamanga. In September he crossed the river Pampas, an affluent of the Apurimac, and threatened Cuzco from the sources of that river, his right flank being covered by a spur from the Cordillera, but did not consider himself strong enough to attempt anything more now that the rainy season was at hand. He also learned that a loan, projected by San Martin, had been successfully launched in London, and that a million dollars were expected immediately. Leaving Sucre in command, he returned to Lima in October.

Before leaving he received notice that on the 28th July the Congress of Columbia had abrogated the law conferring extraordinary powers upon him, which he might no longer exercise now that he was in a foreign country. This was the first sign of Parliamentary resistance to his autocratic tendencies. The Liberals now formed a powerful party in Congress under the leadership of Vice-President Santander, who thought more of the interests of New Granada than of those of the Republic at large.

Bolívar received the blow with dignity, comprehending that he had brought it upon himself by taking charge of the government of a foreign state, and notified Sucre that he would only interfere in military operations as President of Peru. Sucre, who was not ambitious, and was devoted to Bolívar, advised him to pay no attention to the new law, and declared that he himself would have no direct communication with the Government of Columbia, looking to Bolívar alone for orders. Both kept their promises, Bolívar leaving complete liberty of action to Sucre, who followed his instructions except in the conduct of military operations, in which he knew that his talents were superior to those of the Liberator.

Bolívar again established his head-quarters at Pativilca, but found matters much changed for the worse. The arrival of the Spanish ship-of-the-line *Asia* and of the 20-gun brig *Aquiles* had given the naval preponderance to the Royalists. These ships were joined by a corvette and a brig from Chiloe, and there was one brig already at Callao, which Guise had failed to capture. After an exchange of shots with the Spaniards, Guise, with the Peruvian squadron, was forced to seek shelter at Guayaquil.

A detachment of the Patriot army had been defeated

near Lima; Chile remained inactive; but Bolívar, still undaunted, collected such forces as he could assemble at Pativilca, and urgently requested a further reinforcement of 6,000 men from Columbia in aid of Sucre, whose position was very precarious.

Bolívar also returned to his old project of an American Congress, summoning it to meet on the 7th December at Panama, as the most central point for all the world, and addressed circulars to that effect to the Governments of Mexico, Columbia, Guatemala, Buenos Ayres, Chile, Brazil, and later on to the United States.

While occupied in these dreams, he heard that the Royalists had advanced from Cuzco, manœuvring to cut off the retreat of Sucre; then there was silence. Eight days afterwards the fate of America was decided at Ayacucho.

Upon one point only Bolívar and Sucre were not agreed. Bolívar had left instructions with Sucre to keep his army together at all risks; but he, thinking his position a dangerous one, spread his troops over the whole district, and advanced himself, with a light division, as far as Mamará on the road to Cuzco, and from there sent Miller on with the grenadiers to reconnoitre. When Bolívar heard of these manœuvres he wrote to Sucre impressing upon him his maxim that—

"Union is strength. You expose yourself to the loss of a battle for the sake of occupying some more leagues of territory. The liberty of Peru will not be won by occupying land, but by a victory upon it."

Sucre replied, saying that he would obey orders; but had only just sent off the letter when he received advice from Miller that the enemy was advancing in mass, and only twenty-five miles distant. His army was spread over an extent of ninety miles; before he could concentrate the Royalists were in his rear. As he retreated he received a further despatch from Bolívar authorising him to fight if he thought it necessary.

Sucre had under-estimated the strength of the Royalists.

By calling in the outlying divisions La Serna had, on the 24th October, assembled 10,000 men, in three divisions of infantry under Canterac, Valdés, and Monet, and one of cavalry, which he commanded himself, with ten guns. Sucre had only 7,000 men and two guns.

La Serna manœuvred to cut off Sucre from his base, moving in a semicircle of which the Patriots held the centre. Sucre was thus enabled to concentrate his forces, and choose for himself the field of battle. He retreated on Huamanga, but on the 24th November, at the river Pampas, he found that the enemy by forced marches was there before him. The river lay between them. Three days were spent in manœuvres, after which Sucre crossed the river, but on the 2nd December found the heights of Matará in his front already occupied by the Royalists. Wheeling rapidly to his right, he passed by a gorge towards the valley of Acrocos, but his rearguard under Lara was overtaken in the pass by Valdés. One Columbian battalion was cut to pieces, and two more were dispersed with the loss of a gun on the 3rd December; but the further advance of the Royalists was checked by the main body stationed on the heights beyond. The two armies encamped for the night with the gorge between them.

The next day Sucre gained the valley of Acrocos and offered battle. But La Serna, anxious to cut him off from Jauja, marched round the left flank of the Patriots and again gained their rear, cutting all the bridges and closing the defiles to prevent their retreat. The people of the valleys rose in favour of the Royalists. A Patriot column, advancing from Jauja to join Sucre, was driven back; his sick were killed in the hospitals; and he had lost 600 men in the retreat. For him it was now victory or death.

He drew up his army in the valley of Ayacucho, his flanks resting on the mountain ranges to the east and to the west, while the Royalists occupied the heights in front. Cordoba commanded on the right, Miller in the centre, and La Mar on the left, and a reserve of three battalions was commanded by Lara.

On the morning of Thursday, the 9th December, 1824, the sun rose gloriously over the peaks of the eastern Cordillera. Sucre galloped from end to end of his line, telling his men that on their valour that day hung the destinies of South America. At nine in the morning the Royalists descended from the heights to the attack. At ten o'clock they debouched upon the plain, and the left and centre advanced in mass, led by the Viceroy himself. The Royalist right, under Valdés, was the first to engage, and drove in the Patriot skirmishers; but the Peruvian infantry stood firm, and a battalion of Columbians was sent to aid them.

Sucre then ordered Cordoba to charge with the right wing, supported by Miller's cavalry. The young general, who was only twenty-five years of age, advanced rapidly in two parallel columns, and threw himself with great impetuosity upon the Royalist centre. Eight squadrons of Royalist cavalry who charged him were driven back by the Columbian horse under Silva. Monet, whose division had not yet been engaged, came to the assistance of the left centre, but was attacked by the reserve under Lara, and driven back in confusion. Three more squadrons were then thrown forward, and were exterminated by the Columbian lancers. La Serna strove in vain to rally his disordered soldiery; he was borne from his horse with six wounds, and made prisoner, with more than 1,000 of his men.

Meantime Valdés had turned the left flank of the Patriots, and the Peruvian division, under La Mar, began to give way, when the Columbian battalion came to their assistance, followed by the Peruvian hussars and the Argentine grenadiers, led by Miller, who charged with such fury that the Royalist infantry were thrown into confusion, and all the guns were captured.

It was one o'clock, Valdés in despair, sat down on a rock, waiting for death; but his officers forced him away, back to the heights, where many of the Royalist generals were already assembled, with such troops as they could collect. Canterac took the command, and capitulated with Sucre. The war of independence was at an end, emancipation was secured. In the words of a poet:

> "We passed one thousand years
> In one hour at Ayacucho."

Ayacucho is known in America as the Battle of the Generals. Fourteen Spanish generals, with all their subordinate officers, gave up their swords this day. The Royalists lost 1,400 killed and 700 wounded; the Patriots 300 killed and 600 wounded. One-fourth of all who entered into action were placed *hors-de-combat*.

Ayacucho crowned the joint work of San Martin and Bolívar. The victories of Chacabuco and Maipó were united to those of Boyacá and Carabobo, with the golden link forged at Ayacucho by the genius of Sucre.

CHAPTER L.

APOGEE, DECLINE, AND FALL OF BOLIVAR.

1824—1830.

The victory of Ayacucho put an end to the War of Independence in South America. All the Royalist forces in Lower Peru capitulated, with the exception of those under command of Rodil, who with a garrison of 2,200 men, held Callao for a year longer. Besieged by land and blockaded by sea, he surrendered in January, 1826, "after the garrison had eaten all the horses, cats, and dogs in the place."*

In Upper Peru the cities of Cuzco, Arequipa, and Puno opened their gates to the victor, who crossed the Desaguadero, and was received in triumph at La Paz, Oruro, Potosí, and Chuquisaca. The Royalist army under Olañeta was dissolved by a mutiny, in which that General was killed, and Sucre, after overrunning the country, convened an Assembly to decide upon its future policy.

The Spanish squadron abandoned the coasts of Peru and dispersed in the Pacific. The island of Chiloe was the last position held by the Spaniards, but soon shared the fate of Callao. The poet of the century, perched in imagination on the summit of Chimborazo, cast his eyes over the New World and saw not one enslaved people.

Bolívar was now at the apogee of his glorious career, his name was famous throughout the world, South America acclaimed him as her Liberator. The exaggerated honours which were paid to him were but clouds of impure incense

* "The English in South America." By M. G. Mulhall.

which could not obscure his real heroism, and which a breath of common sense would have dispersed. He had the power to solve the political problem in a manner which would have made him the equal of Washington, but it was not in his nature so to do. He lacked the moral strength to keep a cool head at the height to which he had attained. As was the case with San Martin, the apogee of his career marked the commencement of his decline.

One of the most noteworthy phenomena of the revolution in South America is the contrast between the qualities of the leaders and the instincts of the masses of the people. Emancipation came in the process of natural evolution, organized and directed by popular leaders, who had only one principle in common with those they led, the instinct of independence. They devoted their attention to mechanical facts, and for the most part knew nothing of the hidden forces of the movement they professed to guide.

The revolution in South America was twofold in its action, internal and external. One force was directed against the common enemy, the other against the elementary organism of the peoples themselves. The spirit of South America was genuinely democratic, so could not be other than republican. The first development was into anarchy, from which was to arise a new national life. To check this anarchy monarchical projects were hatched in the United Provinces, which resulted in their dissolution. The idea of establishing a monarchy in Peru destroyed the moral power of San Martin. The empire of Mexico furnished proof enough of the error of this plan. The prolonged dictatorship of O'Higgins in Chile brought him to the ground. The oligarchical theories of Bolívar, which tended to monocracy, were rejected by Congresses of Republicans, and brought about his fall. The Liberators, with all their power and all their glory, could not turn the revolution from its natural sphere of action; the day they ceased to go with it they were cast aside as obstacles to the march of progress.

When the independence of America was secured at

Ayacucho, the mission of Bolívar as a Liberator came to an end. His duty, his honour, and even his interest, called upon him to retire from Peru, leaving the redeemed peoples to work out their own destinies. Monteagudo was the only one to give him such advice. On the night of the 28th January, 1825, Monteagudo was assassinated in a lonely street in Lima. His death is a mystery; by some it is attributed to political enmity, by some to private revenge. Bolívar in person conducted the enquiry into the matter, and kept the secret to himself.

Among the papers left by Monteagudo was found an essay upon the necessity of a general federation of the Spanish-speaking peoples of South America, based upon the plan of the Congress of Panama. An alliance of the republics of the New World was proposed, as a counterpoise to the Holy Alliance of the sovereigns of Europe. Suspicion was thrown upon the designs of the new empire of Brazil; Chile and the Argentine Republic were accused of lukewarmness in the common cause; and it was suggested that an appeal for help should be addressed to Great Britain and to the United States.

Bolívar adopted the idea as a development of his own plan, and again summoned a Congress at Panama, in the hope of organizing it himself. The United States accepted the invitation to send representatives, on condition of being permitted to remain neutral; England also, but only in order to have witnesses of her own to what went on; Brazil as a mere form; and the Argentine Republic and Chile, with reservations. Deputies from Peru, Mexico, Columbia, and Guatemala were the only ones who attended the Congress. When this shadowy Congress escaped from his influence Bolívar compared it to "that fool of a Greek, who, standing on a rock, pretended to guide the ships sailing round him."

His next step was, for the fourth time, to send in his resignation as President of Columbia. Congress declined to receive it with unanimity, but in silence. At the same time he sent two commissioners to Vice-President Santander to announce his intention of "proceeding to Argentine territory to establish the independence of South America by assisting the Patriots." Santander replied by reminding him that Congress had only authorised him to carry on war outside the territory of Columbia "for the security of the Republic of Peru."

His third theatrical step was to resign the dictatorship of Peru, and to accept it again for reasons directly contrary to those on which he had based his resignation, and with the farcical condition that "the odious word dictatorship" should be no longer used. Congress also voted him a million of dollars as a reward for his services, which he refused for himself, but accepted in the name of various charities, to which they were never applied.* The servility of the Congress of Peru was repugnant even to Bolívar, and was censured by his Columbian partisans.

The general Assembly of the Provinces of Upper Peru, convened by Sucre, went even further than Congress had done. They declared Bolívar to be "the first-born son of the New World, the saviour of the people," and on the 19th July, 1825, placed themselves under the protection of his sword and of his wisdom. They declared themselves independent of Lower Peru, called their country the "Republic of Bolívar," and placed the supreme executive power in his hands so long as he should reside among them, Sucre acting as his delegate in his absence. This Assembly then dissolved, and on the 6th October a Constituent Assembly was convened, which applied to Bolívar for a Constitution, and for a garrison of 2,000 Columbian troops.

In July Bolívar offered to help the Chilians to drive the Spaniards from the island of Chiloe. They declined other help than a subsidy, which did not meet his views, as his design was to bring them under his sway by the help of Columbian troops. From the Congress of Columbia he had procured authority to take the Peruvian fleet and army

* The amount thus voted was, after his death, paid to the heirs of Bolívar.

to Columbia, under pretext of defending it from a French invasion, and so brought upon himself an accusation that he wished to oppress her with foreign bayonets. His policy tended to the establishment of a Prætorian Empire, an uncrowned monarchy supported by a standing army.

Leaving Lower Peru under the rule of a Council he then went to Upper Peru. His journey from Lima to Potosí was one triumphal march. The cities presented him with golden keys, and with war-horses equipped with golden harness. At Arequipa General Alvarado gave a rural banquet in his honour, at which the Argentine "Asado" was the principal dish. There was abundance of claret to wash down the roast beef, but he asked for champagne, in which he indulged to an extent not usual with him. A toast was given to the unification of South America, on which he remarked that he would soon tread Argentine soil. Colonel Dehesa, also excited by wine, told him :—

"My countrymen do not welcome Dictators to their territory."

Bolívar sprang upon the table in a fury, and crushing glasses and plates under the heels of his boots, shouted—

"Thus will I trample upon the Argentine Republic."

An ebullition of temper roused by the opposition of the press of Buenos Ayres to his anti-democratic plans.

At Potosí he was met by General Alvear and Dr. Diaz Velez, envoys sent by the Argentine Government to congratulate him on his successes. He thanked them but refused to treat further with them, alleging as an excuse the absence of his Minister of Foreign Affairs. Afterwards, on learning that the Brazilians had occupied two provinces of Upper Peru, he managed to dispense with the aid of this official.

When at Arequipa, he had offered General Alvarado to send 6,000 men to aid the Argentines in the war with which they were threatened by Brazil. Alvarado had declined the offer. This incident now gave a plausible pretext for his interference in the question. On the 18th and 19th October he held private conferences with the

Argentine envoys, which greatly enlightened them as to his extravagant ideas. Among other proposals he asked permission to cross Argentine territory with a Columbian army to overturn the despotism of Dr. Francia in Paraguay, which could not be granted, as all Argentine governments had steadily followed a policy of non-intervention in the internal affairs of other nations.

He met them again at Chuquisaca, but the interview had no definite result, and the occupation of the Province of Tarija, which was formerly one of the United Provinces, by Columbian troops, nearly produced an open rupture.

Rivadavia, who was about that time elected President of the United Provinces, looked upon Bolívar and his army as a danger, but the idea of his armed intervention in Argentine affairs was welcomed by the Opposition press of Buenos Ayres. They echoed his words that:—

"The Argentine Republic could not triumph alone over the Emperor of Brazil, and could not even organize itself without the help of the genius of America."

But the Liberal press commenced to analyze the tendencies of the proposed Monocracy, and their words found echo in the public opinion of Bolivia, Peru, and Columbia. Chile was the first state to join the United Provinces in open opposition to his views.

Bolívar then returned to Lima, and on the 25th May, 1826, sent to Upper Peru a draft of a constitution for the REPUBLIC OF BOLIVIA.

All the works of Bolívar, both political and military, are so impressed with his own character that it has been necessary to invent special words to express them. His system of warfare was a *mélange* of the warlike propensities of the indigenous races with European discipline. With little knowledge of tactics, and with less strategy, he gained his victories by audacity, by impetuosity in attack, and by unfailing constancy in defeat, somewhat after the style of Charles XII. His power was symbolized by a new title, involving a permanent Dictatorship; he called himself the LIBERATOR. His policy was neither democratic, nor aristocratic, nor autocratic; the historian has had to invent a word to describe it, MONOCRATIC. For the new Republic formed in Upper Peru he invented a new name, derived from his own, BOLIVIA.

The constitution drawn up by him for the new State is an amalgam of ancient traditions with modern practice. It has something of the Greek Republic, something of Roman Cæsarism, something of the English Monarchy, something of the consular constitution of Napoleon. The base of the system is a President, nominated for life, with power to name his successor, and elected by a representative assembly, appointed by an electoral body. The legislative power was shared by three chambers, one of which exercised a species of censorship over the other two, like to that of the Council of the Areopagos of Athens.

With some slight modifications, this constitution was adopted by the Constituent Assembly, and Sucre was elected President, but with power subordinate to that of the Liberator when he was there.

But Bolivia was too small a sphere of action for Bolívar. For the realisation of his plan it was now necessary to impose the same constitution upon Peru and Columbia, binding the three States together by one supreme authority, vested in his own person as the Liberator.

When the Congress of Peru re-assembled there appeared in it a new national party, opposed to the Dictatorship and to the continued presence of Columbian troops. Government then found that the elections were irregular, and fifty-two of the deputies asked for their own dissolution. At the same time the discovery of a conspiracy against the Dictator sent some victims into banishment, and brought others to the scaffold.

While preparations were being made for a new election, Bolívar threatened to leave Peru to its fate. With the most abject servility all classes besought him not to desert them; one high dignitary actually asked him to set his foot on his neck that he might have the honour of bearing the weight of the greatest man of the age. Still he remained obdurate, until a deputation of ladies waited upon him, to whom he gracefully yielded, and so brought the farce to an end.

The Electoral College of Lima met on the 6th August, and within a hedge of Columbian bayonets voted with unanimity the abrogation of the Constitution of 1823, and the adoption of the Bolivian Constitution. The example was followed by the Provincial Colleges, the new Constitution became law, and Bolívar was acclaimed perpetual President. Of course he declined the honour, but accepted it as soon as it was offered to him a second time.

Now for Columbia. But meantime his idea had achieved a further development, "The Grand Confederation of the Andes." Bolivia was to remain as one unit, Peru was to be divided into two, and Columbia into four States, each one with a President for life, satellites to the central power of the Liberator. Sucre pronounced in favour of the new plan, Santander accepted it, and the Columbian leaders offered it the support of their swords. On this basis a treaty was signed between Bolivia and Peru, giving the two nations one Federal Congress, to which each should send nine deputies; but a special clause was added, that at the death of the Liberator each Republic should be at liberty to withdraw from the union.

"My funeral will then be as sanguinary as that of Alexander," said Bolívar.

Much must be forgiven to Bolívar for the good by him accomplished. He did not wish to be a tyrant, but he did not understand that a people cannot be at once half free and half enslaved. His plan of a Monocracy was a reaction against the Revolution and against the independence of the new Republics; it was a return to another colonial system, even worse than the one which had been destroyed. The paternal government of a distant and hereditary monarch was a less evil than would be a government dependent upon the life of one man. A crown had been offered to Bolívar, he had rejected the idea with scorn, but he now demanded a power greater than that of any king.

H H

Engaged in these dreams Bolívar had led for two years in Lima the voluptuous life of an Eastern prince, when evil news reached him from his native country, which he had apparently quite forgotten. The Venezuelans, with Paez at their head, had risen against the general Government, and had demanded federal autonomy. In New Granada the Liberal press vigorously attacked the principle of Monocracy. In September, 1826, he went to Guayaquil and resumed his absolute powers as President of the Republic of Columbia. From there he went on to Bogotá, and was met by a deputation of the people and of the authorities, who assured him "that he could count upon their obedience under the Constitution and under the laws which he had sworn to respect and uphold." He answered angrily that he expected a welcome and not advice.

After that he went on to Venezuela, where he made terms with Paez, and agreed to a reform of the Constitution of Cúcuta, which in 1821 he had sworn should remain unchanged for ten years. But public opinion no longer supported him; the Liberal press of Bogotá, under the influence of Santander, fiercely attacked his policy.

On the 6th February, 1827, he again sent in his resignation. His example was followed by Santander. Congress declined to accept either resignation, but Bolívar's was declined by 56 votes against 24, while Santander's was declined by 70 against 4. Both retained their offices, but from this time he and Santander became the heads of two antagonistic parties.

While affairs were in this state in Columbia, the people of Peru and Bolivia, aided by the garrisons of Columbian troops, deposed their life Presidents. Sucre made some attempt to re-establish his power, but being attacked by a Peruvian army under Gamarra, he withdrew from Bolivia in October, 1827, taking the Columbian troops with him. The news of these events was received with rejoicing at Bogotá; Santander pronounced his approval of the con duct of the troops. All were tired of Bolívar.

Columbia had been an efficient war machine in the hands of Bolívar by which the independence of South America was secured, but was an anachronism as a nation. The interests of the different sections were antagonistic, and the military organization given to the country only strengthened the germs of disorder. Venezuela and New Granada were geographically marked out as independent nations. Quito from historical antecedents aspired to autonomy. Had Bolívar abstained from his dreams of conquest, and devoted his energies to the consolidation of his own country, he might perhaps have organized it into one nation under a federal form of government, but that was not a task suited to his genius. When his own bayonets turned against him he went so far as to despair of the Republican system altogether, and sought the protection of a foreign King for the last fragment of his shattered Monocracy.

On the 9th April, 1828, he assembled a Convention at Ocaña for the reform of the Constitution of 1821. The partisans of Santander were in a majority, and the Convention was dissolved on the 10th June by the desertion of the partisans of Bolívar.

On the 13th June a popular Junta assembled at Bogotá, at which General Cordoba proposed the re-establishment of the Dictatorship in the person of Bolívar. Bolívar accepted the office, and suppressed that of Vice-President. Military rule became dominant, those who opposed the measure were banished as disturbers of public order, the study of political economy was prohibited in the Universities, and liberty of the press was suspended, but Bolívar promised to convene another Constituent Congress a year from that time. According to Gervinus, the Liberator now tore off the mask and showed the vulgar ambition which lay beneath, yet he was not a tyrant, he was simply a despot driving he knew not whither.

The young men talked of the dagger of Brutus, but an attempt to assassinate him failed, and the principal conspirators died on the gibbet. Santander, who had joined the conspiracy but had opposed the assassination, was sent into exile.

The Columbian troops which had mutinied in Peru brought civil war to Guayaquil. Rebellion broke out in the Province of Pasto. Bolívar declared war against Peru. Peru sent a fleet and an army and captured Guayaquil.* Their army was defeated by Sucre, but Bolívar, after losing 3,000 men in the marshes in an attempt to retake the city, made peace.

Bolívar had appealed in vain to the Ministers of the United States and of Great Britain to interfere for the prevention of anarchy. He now proposed to Colonel Campbell, the British chargé d'affaires, to appoint a Prince of some one of the reigning families of Europe King of Columbia. Many of the chief dignitaries of Bogotá accepted this idea, and came to an understanding on the point with Messrs Campbell and Bresson, the diplomatic agents of Great Britain and France, but Bolívar, three months after he knew of this, suddenly told them in September, 1829, that the idea could not be carried out, and that it was necessary to separate Venezuela from Columbia.

The idea of a monarchy found no acceptance with the people. On the 14th September a rebellion, headed by General Cordoba, broke out at Antioquia, but was crushed, and Cordoba was brutally murdered. At the end of this year, Venezuela declared herself an independent Republic, under the Presidency of General Paez, and pronounced sentence of perpetual exile against Bolívar.

On the 30th January, 1830, Bolívar convened at Bogotá the Constituent Congress he had promised, and concluded his message :—

"I blush to say that independence is the only good thing we have gained by the sacrifice of all else."

He then retired to his country-house at Fucha; never-

* Admiral Guise, who commanded the Peruvian fleet, was killed in the attack.—TR.

theless a party, strong both in Congress and among the people, desired his re-election, and he for some time expected it, but seeing that the bulk even of his old friends opposed it, he on the 27th April sent in a formal resignation, couched in very simple terms, which was accepted.

Don Joaquin Mosquera, leader of the Liberal party, was elected President, but Congress decreed that Bolívar "was the first and best citizen of Columbia," and assigned him a pension of 30,000 dollars a year, for his great wealth had all disappeared.

EPILOGUE.

POSTERITY has pronounced judgment upon the two liberators of South America, upon SAN MARTIN and upon BOLIVAR.

They were both great men, the greatest after Washington that America has produced. Both fulfilled their mission. The one gave the first signal for a continental war, the other carried it to a glorious termination. Without San Martin at the South and Bolívar at the North it is impossible to conceive how the forces of the revolution could have worked together towards one end; neither is it possible to conceive how one could have completed his task without the other. Nevertheless, as politicians both went astray; neither reached the level of the public opinion of their day, and both failed to comprehend the instincts of the masses they led. They were military leaders only, and knew not how to direct the organic evolution of the peoples.

Time, which dissipates false and enhances true glory, has thrown much light upon matters which during their lifetime seemed obscure. Their outlines are now seen clearly against the horizon of history; they stand forth as symbols of the epoch which gave birth to a new republican world, the greatest political phenomenon of the nineteenth century.

The Argentine Republic and Chile, led by San Martin, were victorious in the South, and carried their arms from sea to sea, and from the temperate zone to the equator.

There the entire forces of the revolution of South America joined hands; there the two liberators embraced, and separated for ever.

Columbia, led by Bolívar, gave victory to the revolution in the North; secured the independence of Peru and Bolivia, and guaranteed that of the other Republics of the Southern Continent. San Martin yielded the completion of the task to Bolívar, and by his abdication gave a high example of civic virtue. Bolívar crowned the work; the triumph belongs to both. Their fate was equal, both died in exile.

The fate of the emancipators of South America is tragical. The first revolutionists of La Paz and of Quito died on the scaffold. Miranda, the apostle of liberty, betrayed by his own people to his enemies, died alone and naked in a dungeon. Moreno, the priest of the Argentine revolution, and the teacher of the democratic idea, died at sea and found a grave in the ocean. Hidalgo, the first popular leader of Mexico, was executed as a criminal. Belgrano, the first champion of Argentine independence, who saved the revolution at Tucuman and Salta, died obscurely, while civil war raged round him. O'Higgins, the hero of Chile, died in exile, as Carrera his rival had done before him. Iturbide, the real liberator of Mexico, fell a victim to his own ambition. Montufar, the leader of the revolution in Quito, and his comrade Villavicencio, promoter of that of Cartagena, were strangled. The first Presidents of New Granada, Lozano and Torres, fell sacrifices to the restoration of colonial terrorism. Piar, who found the true base for the insurrection in Columbia, was shot by Bolívar, to whom he had shown the way to victory. Rivadavia, the civil genius of South America, who gave form to her representative institutions, died in exile. Sucre, the conqueror of Ayacucho, was murdered by his own men on a lonely road. Bolívar and San Martin died in banishment.

San Martin when he saw that his life's work was accomplished, left Mendoza for Buenos Ayres, where he was received with indifference and contempt. Neither country wife, nor home, was left to him, there was not even a place in the Argentine Army for the man who had led the armies of three Republics to victory. At the close of the year 1823 he took his orphan daughter in his arms and retired into exile. In Europe he found himself penniless. Five years later he returned to Buenos Ayres, seeking to end his days in his native country; the war with Brazil had just concluded.

On the 12th February, 1829, the anniversary of his triumphs at San Lorenzo and at Chacabuco, the ship which carried him anchored in the roadstead, and he was greeted with this contemptuous denunciation in the city press:—

"General San Martin has returned to his native country after five years' absence, but after knowing that peace was concluded with the Emperor of Brazil."

His answer had been given two thousand years before, by the mouth of Scipio, when he was insulted by his fellow countrymen on the anniversary of one of his great battles:—

"On such a day as this I saved Rome."

San Martin did not repeat this answer, he returned in silence into exile. His reply was given from the tomb many years later:—

"I desire that my heart may rest in Buenos Ayres."

Bolívar, after his last resignation was accepted, retired to the neighbourhood of Cartagena, and there heard of the death of Sucre, who had written to him two years previously, that unless they withdrew in time they would lose their heads. He was dying, but still indulged ambitious designs. He had prophesied anarchy and it came. He looked on complacently, and even encouraged it, but was greatly mortified by a notification from his friend Mosquera, that Venezuela demanded his banishment as a condition of peace.

"No, no, I will not go dishonoured," he exclaimed.

His partisans said that he alone could restore quietude, and they seemed right. Part of Venezuela and New Granada rose in arms to demand the re-establishment of his dictatorship. Quito and Guayaquil separated from

Columbia, and in May, 1830, formed themselves into an independent State, under the name of THE REPUBLIC OF ECUADOR.

At Bogotá the Government of Mosquera was upset, and civil war broke out. The friends of Bolívar, triumphant in the capital under Urdaneta, called upon him to put himself at their head, and to re-establish the Union of Columbia. He was weak enough to accept the invitation. Death saved him from the disgrace of becoming a leader in an internecine war between States to which he had given independence.

His sickness increasing, he retired to Santa Marta to breathe the fresh sea air. At the Quinta of San Pedro, seven miles from that city, he breathed his last. Seated in an arm-chair to receive extreme unction, his last words addressed to the Columbian people, which had been written down to his dictation, were read over to him :—

"My wishes are for the happiness of my country. If my death weaken the divisions, and help to consolidate union, I shall go to the tomb content."

He added in a hoarse voice :—

"Yes, to the tomb, to which I am sent by my fellow-citizens, but I forgive them. Oh! that I could take with me the consolation of knowing that they will keep united."

These were the last sensible words that he was heard to speak. Delirium supervened, and he died on the 17th December, 1831, at the age of forty-seven years four months and twenty-three days.

In October, 1832, San Martin, then resident in France, was attacked by cholera. He was living in great poverty on the proceeds of the sale of the house given him by the Argentine Congress after the victory of Maipó. He thought he was to die in a hospital. The Spanish banker Aguada, who had been a comrade of his in the Peninsular War, came to his assistance, saved his life, and relieved his distress. He gave him the small country-house of Grand Bourg, on the banks of the Seine, close to that old elm which, according to tradition, was planted by the soldiers

of Henry IV., when besieging Paris. There, surrounded
by trees and flowers which he tended himself, he passed
many quiet years, complaining sometimes of the ingratitude
of men, deploring the sad state of the peoples for whom he
had done so much, but never despairing of their destiny.
Once only did his old enthusiasm blaze out. He thought
the independence and honour of his country were threatened by France and England in the questions of 1845—1849, and came from his seclusion to show that America
could not be conquered by Europe. Subsequently, in his
will, he left his sword to the Argentine Dictator:—

"As a proof of the satisfaction with which I, as an
Argentine, have seen the firmness of General Rozas in
defending the honour of the Republic against the unjust
pretensions of the foreigners who sought her humiliation."

As the end approached, his eyes were obscured by
cataract. Reading, which was with him a passion, was
forbidden him. He went to Boulogne to breathe the sea
air, as Bolívar had done. On the 13th August, 1850, as
he was standing on the beach, gazing with dim eyes over
the Channel, he felt the first mortal symptom. He pressed
his hand to his heart, and with a feeble smile said to his
faithful daughter:—" C'est l'orage qui mene au port." On
the 17th of the same month he died in her arms, at the age
of seventy-two years and six months.

Chile and the Argentine Republic have raised statues to
him. Peru owes him one, which she has decreed. The
Argentine people, now united and consolidated as he
desired, brought back his mortal remains to his own
country, and in May, 1880, laid them to rest in the Cathedral
of Buenos Ayres, as those of the greatest man among them.

In San Martin and Bolívar were combined, in unequal
proportions, the two elements which make history: the
active element which produces immediate effect in deeds,
and the passive element from which springs the future. The
effect of their combination marks the present and influences
posterity. The political work of Bolívar died with him;
that of San Martin lives after him; South America has

organized itself as foreshadowed by his genius, within the geographical lines he drew out with his sword.

The Argentine Republic instructed her General:—

"That no idea of oppression or conquest carried her arms beyond her territory; that the independence of the United Provinces was the purpose of the campaign."

Thus, when Chile was free, alliance was made with her on the basis of their mutual independence. Nations were emancipated and left to work out their destinies themselves. This was the work of San Martin as a liberator, and has produced an international equilibrium in South America, to which Europe has not yet attained,

A very different plan was followed by Bolívar. Under his leadership frontiers disappeared; Venezuela, New Granada, and Quito, became one giant nation, powerful for war, but intrinsically weak from lack of geographical and social cohesion. Bolívar freed Peru from Spain, only to make her a parasite of Columbia, and of Upper Peru he made a feudal territory dependent upon himself. He tried to establish a monocratic empire in opposition to natural laws and to the tendencies of the Revolution; to bring back the colonial system in defiance of the democratic instincts of the people.

In Bolivia the two systems met face to face. The Argentine Republic, true to her principles, yielded her historic rights over that territory and recognised the independence of Upper Peru, but she barred the further progress of Bolívar, who sought to impose his own system on Paraguay. The ephemeral structure of the monocracy fell to pieces by its own weight, and the whole of the Continent became definitely organized on the geographical system represented by San Martin.

The glory of Bolívar is imperishable, and his action as a liberator was more decisive in his day, but none of his designs or of his ideals survived him. The work of San Martin remains an enduring monument to his memory.

The chief characteristic of San Martin was his disinterestedness. He struggles, destroys, and rebuilds as he can; he commands, obeys, abdicates, and condemns himself to eternal silence and eternal exile. Seldom has the influence of one man had more decisive effect on the destinies of a people. The greatness of those who attain to immortality is not measured by their talents, but by the effect exercised by their memory upon the conscience of humanity, making it vibrate from generation to generation with a passion or with an idea. Of such was San Martin, whose influence still lives, not by reason of any genius he possessed, but by reason of his character.

San Martin conceived great plans, political and military, which appeared at first to be folly, but when believed in became facts. He organized disciplined armies, and infused into them his own spirit. He founded republics, not for his own aggrandisement, but that men might live in freedom. He made himself powerful, only that by this power he might accomplish his destined task; he abdicated and went into exile, not from egoism or from cowardice, but in homage to his own principles and for the sake of his cause. He is the first captain in the New World, the only one who has given lessons in modern strategy on a new theatre of war. With all his intellectual deficiencies and his political errors the Revolution of South America has produced no other who was his equal.

Faithful to the maxims of his life, HE WAS THAT WHICH HE OUGHT TO BE, and rather than be that which he ought not to be he preferred TO BE NOTHING. For this his name shall be immortal.

TRANSLATOR'S APPENDIX.

I.

"THE sole purpose for which the Americans existed was held to be that of collecting together the precious metals for the Spaniards; and if the wild horses and cattle which overrun the country could have been trained to perform this office the inhabitants might have been altogether dispensed with, and the colonial system would then have been perfect. Unfortunately, however, for that system, the South Americans . . . finding that the Spaniards neither could nor would furnish them with an adequate supply of European products, invited the assistance of other nations. To this call the other nations were not slow to listen, and in process of time there was established one of the most extraordinary systems of organized smuggling which the world ever saw. This was known under the name of the contraband or forced trade, and was carried on in armed vessels, well manned, and prepared to fight their way to the coast, and to resist the coast blockades of Spain. This singular system of warlike commerce was conducted by the Dutch, Portuguese, French, English, and latterly by the North Americans. In this way goods to an immense value were distributed over South America, and . . . along with the goods no small portion of knowledge found entrance, in spite of the increased exertions of the Inquisition. . . . Many foreigners, too, by means of bribes and other arts, succeeded in getting into the country, so that the progress of intelligence was encouraged, to the utter despair of the Spaniards, who knew no other method of governing the colonies but that of brute force."—From the *Journal of Captain Basil Hall, R.N., F.R.S., on the Coasts of Chile, Peru, and Mexico, in the years 1820, 1821, 1822.*

II.

Captain Basil Hall, who paid a visit to San Martin, in the month of June, 1821, on board the schooner *Montezuma*, then at anchor in the Callao Roads, thus describes his personal appearance:—

"General San Martin is a tall, erect, well-proportioned, handsome man, with a large aquiline nose, thick black hair and immense bushy whiskers, extending from ear to ear under the chin; his complexion is deep olive, and his eye, which is large, prominent, and piercing, jet black; his whole appearance being highly military. He is thoroughly well bred, and unaffectedly simple in his manners; exceedingly cordial and engaging, and possessed evidently of great kindliness of disposition; in short, I have never seen any person the enchantment of whose address was more irresistible."

III.

"It has been stated that the filling of the tubes was, from motives of parsimony, entrusted to Spanish prisoners, who, as was found on examination, had embraced every opportunity of inserting handfuls of sand, sawdust, and even manure at intervals in the tubes, thus impeding the progress of combustion; whilst in the majority of instances they had so thoroughly mixed the neutralizing matter with the ingredients supplied, that the charge would not ignite at all, the result being complete failure in the object of the expedition."—*Autobiography of a Seaman*, by Lord Dundonald.

IV.

" . . . This bridge is curious from its simplicity, and from the close resemblance it bears to the iron bridges of suspension recently introduced into England, to which, in principle, it is precisely similar. It consists of a narrow roadway of planks, laid crosswise, with their ends resting on straight ropes, suspended by means of short lines to a set of thicker ropes drawn across the stream from bank to bank.

These strong sustaining cords are six in number, three at each side of the bridge, and hang in flat curves, one above another, the short vertical lines supporting the roadway being so disposed as to distribute the weight equally. The main or suspending ropes are firmly secured to the angles of the rock on one side at the height of thirty feet from the stream; but the opposite bank being low, it has been found necessary to correct the consequent inclination in some degree, by carrying the ropes over a high wooden framework, and attaching them afterwards to trees and to posts driven into the bank. The clear span from the frame or pier on one side to the face of the rock on the other is one hundred and twenty-three feet. The materials being very elastic the bridge waved up and down with our weight, and vibrated from side to side in so alarming a manner that, at the recommendation of the guide, we dismounted and drove our horses, one by one, before us; but it must be owned, neither man nor horse appeared much at ease during the passage."—*Journal of Captain Basil Hall.*

V.

" . . . How far his professions were sincere, or, if sincere, his plans were wise, it is now very difficult to say. They certainly appeared to many people very judicious at the time, and they were uniformly followed by the success which he anticipated.

" . . . On the 25th June I had an interview with General San Martin, on board a little schooner anchored in Callao Roads. . . . There was little at first sight in his appearance to engage attention; but when he rose up and began to speak, his great superiority over every other person I had seen in South America was sufficiently apparent. He received us in a very homely style, on the deck of his vessel, dressed in a surtout coat and a large fur cap, seated at a table made of a few loose planks laid along the top of two empty casks.

" . . . Several persons came on board privately from Lima, to discuss the state of affairs, upon which occasion his views and feelings were distinctly stated: and I saw nothing in his conduct afterwards to cast a doubt upon the sincerity with which he then spoke. The contest in Peru, he said, was not of an ordinary description; not a war of conquest and glory, but entirely of opinion; it was a war of new and liberal principles against prejudice, bigotry, and tyranny. People ask why I don't march to Lima at once; so I might, and instantly would, were it suitable to my views, which it is not. I do not want military renown; I have no ambition to be the conqueror of Peru; I want solely to liberate the country from oppression. Of what use would Lima be to me, if the inhabitants were hostile in political sentiment? How could the cause of independence be advanced by my holding Lima, or even the whole country, in military possession? Far different are my views. I wish to have all men thinking with me, and do not choose to advance a step beyond the march of public opinion.

" . . . I have been gaining, day by day, fresh allies in the hearts of the people, the only certain allies in such a war.

" . . . Public opinion is an engine newly introduced into this country; the Spaniards, who are utterly incapable of directing it, have prohibited its use; but they shall now experience its strength and importance.

" . . . When all was quiet in the capital I went to Callao, and hearing that San Martin was in the Roads, waited on him on board his yacht. I found him possessed of correct information as to all that was passing; but he seemed in no hurry to enter the city, and appeared, above all things, anxious to avoid any appearance of acting the part of a conqueror. 'For the last ten years,' said he, 'I have been unremittingly employed against the Spaniards, or rather, in favour of this country, for I am not against any one who is not hostile to the cause of independence. All I wish is that this country should be managed by itself, and by itself alone. As to the manner in which it is to be governed that belongs not at all to me. I propose simply to give the people the means of declaring themselves independent, and of establishing a suitable form of government; after which I shall consider I have done enough, and leave them.' "—*Journal of Captain Basil Hall.*

VI.

In January, 1891, a number of Venezuelans presented the city of New York with a painting commemorative of this deed of arms, in token of their gratitude for honours paid to the memory of their hero, who died an exile in that city.

This painting is thus described in the *Tribune* :—

"The canvas is 9½ by 15½ feet in size, and was brought to this country mounted and handsomely framed. It represents the famous cavalry manœuvre of General Paez at the battle of Queseras del Medio. In this battle General Paez took 119 men, about half his force, and started to meet the Spanish cavalry. As the latter advanced Paez turned his men in full retreat toward a thicket where he had concealed the rest of his force. At the ambuscade Paez suddenly turned and charged the Spaniards, who fled in terror. The artist has pictured the scene at this moment. The general is mounted on a superb horse, which he has pulled sharply back on its haunches as he gives the order, 'Vuelvan cara!' (face about), On one side are his troopers, rough-looking fellows, carrying long-handled spears; their clothing, saddles, trappings, and equipments are all characteristic of their country. In the distance the Spanish cavalry are seen charging, in ignorance of the trap into which they are about to fall. The Venezuelan artist, Michelena, who received his education in Paris, has found abundant room for vivid colouring in the tropical landscape and sky, and the gaudy garments of his figures."

VII.

The following account of the battle of Carabobo was written by an officer of the British legion, and was published in *All the Year Round*.

"We halted at dusk on the 23rd at the foot of the ridge. The rain fell in torrents all night, and reminded us of the night before Waterloo. Next morning the sky was cloudless when we stood to arms, and presently Bolívar sent us the order to advance. We were moving to get round the enemy's right flank, where his guns and infantry were partly hidden by trees and broken ground. Bolívar, after reconnoitring, ordered us to attack by a deep ravine between the Spanish infantry and artillery. The enemy's guns opened fire and our men began to fall. Meantime the Bravos de Apure had advanced within pistol-shot of the Spaniards, and received such a murderous volley from 3,000 muskets that they broke and fled back in disorder upon us.

"It was a critical moment, but we managed to keep our ground till the fugitives had got through our ranks back into the ravine, and then our grenadier company, gallantly led by Captain Minchin, formed up and poured in their fire upon the Spaniards, who were only a few paces from them. Checked by this volley, the enemy fell back a little, while our men, pressing eagerly on, formed and delivered their fire, company after company.

"Receding before our fire and the long line of British bayonets, the Spaniards fell back to the position from which they had rushed in pursuit of the Apure Bravos. But from thence they kept up a tremendous fire upon us, which we returned as rapidly as we could. As they outnumbered us in the ratio of four to one, and were strongly posted and supported by guns, we waited for reinforcements before storming their position. Not a man, however, came to help us, and after an hour passed in this manner our ammunition failed. It then really seemed to be all over with us. We tried as best we could to make signals of our distress; the men kept springing their ramrods, and Colonel Thomas Ferrier, our commanding officer, apprized General Paez of our situation, and called on him to get up a supply of cartridges. It came at last, but by this many of our officers and men had fallen, and among them Colonel Ferrier. You may imagine we were not long in breaking open the ammunition boxes; the men numbered off anew, and after delivering a couple of volleys we prepared to charge. At this moment our cavalry, passing as before by our right flank, charged, with General Paez at their head. They went on very gallantly, but soon came galloping back, and passed again to our rear, without having done any execution on the enemy, while they had themselves suffered considerably.

"Why Bolívar at this time, and indeed during the period since our first advance, sent us no support I have never been able to guess. Whatever the motive, it is certain that the second and third divisions of the army quietly looked on while we were being slaughtered, and made no attempt to help us. The curses of our men were loud and deep, but seeing that they must not expect any help they made up their minds to carry the enemy's position or perish. Out of nine hundred men we had not above six hundred left. Captain Scott, who succeeded Colonel Ferrier, had fallen, and had bequeathed the command to Captain Minchin; and the colours of the regiment had seven times changed hands, and had been literally cut to ribands, and dyed with the blood of the gallant fellows who carried them. But, in spite of all this, the word was passed to charge with the bayonet, and on we went, keeping our line as steadily as on a parade day, and with a loud "hurrah" we were upon them. I must do the Spaniards the justice to say that they met us gallantly, and the struggle was for a brief time fierce, and the event doubtful. But the bayonet in the hands of British soldiers, more especially such a forlorn hope as we were, is irresistible. The Spaniards, five to one as they were, began to give ground, and at last broke and fled.

"Then it was, and not till then, that two companies of the Tiradores came up to our help, and our cavalry, hitherto of little use, fiercely pursued the retreating enemy.

*   *   *   *   *   *

"The remains of the corps passed before the Liberator with trailed arms at double quick, and received with a cheer, but without halting, his words, 'Salvadores de mi Patria!'"

BIOGRAPHICAL NOTES.

ALVARADO was in the year 1827 banished from Peru in consequence of the jealousy of the Peruvians of their Argentine allies. In 1829 he was for a month Governor of Mendoza, but was driven out by Aldao. In 1831 he was for a short time Governor of Salta, and again in 1855. He died in that city in the year 1872.

ARENALES.—This stout old soldier was from 1824 to 1827 Governor of Salta, where the remnants of the Royalist army of Olañeta surrendered to him in 1825. He died in Bolivia in the year 1831.

BROWN.—William Brown was born at Foxford, Co. Mayo, Ireland, in the year 1777, and made his first appearance in the River Plate as master of a trading brig which was wrecked at Ensenada. He afterwards established the first regular sailing packet between Buenos Ayres and Monte Video, but two years later adopted a career more in accordance with his daring genius. In 1814 he took command of the first naval squadron fitted out by the Government of Buenos Ayres. His first exploit was the capture of the island of Martin Garcia, after which he attacked and defeated the Spanish fleet stationed at Monte Video; and his subsequent blockade of that port compelled the garrison to surrender to General Alvear, who was then besieging the city. After his cruise in the Pacific, recounted in Chapter X., he went to the West Indies, where his ship was seized and confiscated by the British naval authorities, on the plea that he was a pirate. After a vain attempt to procure redress in England he returned to Buenos Ayres, where he lived quietly, till in January, 1826, he again took command of the Argentine squadron, and drove off the Brazilian fleet, which was blockading Buenos Ayres. During this and the following year he fought several desperate actions against greatly superior forces, and invariably came off with honour. In 1842 he was in command of the Argentine squadron, which totally destroyed the Uruguayan flotilla at Costa Brava, which was led by Garibaldi, and afterwards blockaded the port of Monte Video, till in August, 1845, his ships were confiscated by the British and French naval squadrons, without any declaration of war.

After that he lived in retirement at his country-house in the suburbs of the city of Buenos Ayres, till the 3rd May, 1857, when he died, surrounded by his family, and was buried at the cemetery of the Recoleta, where a fine monument to his memory was afterwards erected by his widow.

COCHRANE, the eldest son of the ninth Earl of Dundonald, was born at Annesfield, Lanarkshire, on the 14th December, 1775. After leaving Chile he entered the service of Brazil, and again distinguished himself by deeds of daring, which were as ill-requited as were his exploits on the Pacific. In 1825 he returned to England, where he found his popularity had grown during his absence, but soon after joined in the struggle for the independence of Greece, when for the first time in his career he found no opportunity of distinguishing himself.

At the accession of William IV., he received tardy and imperfect reparation for the injustice from which he had suffered. His rank in the British Navy was restored to him, and in 1831 he succeeded his father in the Earldom of Dundonald. In 1841 he became Vice-Admiral of the Blue. During the Crimean War he presented to Government a plan for the total destruction of the Russian fleet, which was not accepted. He died at Kensington on the 30th October, 1860, and was buried in Westminster Abbey.

GÜEMES was Governor of Salta from May, 1815, to May, 1820. In the former year he made himself master of the city and Province of Jujui also, and refused to recognise the authority of the National Government, and even went so far as to harass the march of the Army of the North, which was then retreating from Upper Peru, under command of General Rondeau. But the citizens of Jujui refused to obey him, and he was outlawed by Rondeau, who seized the city of Salta, but came to a peaceable understanding with him in the following year.

In 1821 he led an expedition from Salta against Tucuman, in conjunction with another expedition from Jujui, but was defeated. On his return he found the citizens of Salta in insurrection against him, but their army passed over to him, and he easily re-established his authority. In June of that year the city of Salta was captured by a party of Royalists under Valdés. After nightfall he rode with a small escort into the principal square, not knowing what had occurred, and was received by a volley. He was severely wounded, but kept his seat in the saddle, and returned to his encampment, where he died ten days afterwards.

LAS HERAS was in April, 1824, elected Governor of the Province of Buenos Ayres, in succession to Don Martin Rodriguez, under whose beneficent rule the country had made great progress. Las Heras followed in the steps of his predecessor, but was in March, 1826, deposed by the National Constituent Congress, which assumed the powers of a sovereign congress, and decreed the federalization of the province. Las Heras refused to listen to those of his friends who wished him to resist this unconstitutional proceeding, and retired into private life. He died in Chile in the year 1866, in the eighty-sixth year of his age.

LAVALLE, after the conclusion of the War of Independence, returned to Buenos Ayres, and commanded a division in the Argentine army, which was sent against Brazil in the year 1826. At Ituzaingo he again displayed the same reckless daring for which he was distinguished in Chile and in Peru. In November, 1828, he returned to Buenos Ayres, after the conclusion of the war, in command of the first division of the army, and encamped to the north of the city. On the 1st December he headed a revolt by which Don Manuel Dorrego, who was then Governor, was deposed, and was named Provisional Governor in his stead. On the 9th of the same month he completely defeated the Government forces at Navarro, and on the 13th ordered the summary execution of Dorrego, who had been taken prisoner the day previous. On the 26th April in the following year he was attacked at the Puente Marquez by greatly superior forces under Rozas and Lopez, but maintained the unequal fight till sundown. He eventually came to terms with Rozas, and retired to Monte Video. Some years afterwards he joined the Argentine refugees in that city in a conspiracy against the Dictatorship of Rozas, and in 1840 headed an expedition into Argentine territory, where, after several defeats, he was on the 9th October, 1841, killed by a scouting party of Government troops near to the Bolivian frontier.

MILLER was born at Wingham, Kent, in the year 1796. For four years he served in the Royal Artillery, under Wellington, in Spain. In the year 1817 he went out to Buenos Ayres with the intention of engaging in commercial pursuits, but was diverted from that intention by an English lady then resident in that city, who said to him, "Were I a young man I would never abandon the profession of arms for one of mere money-making." He was presented to Don Juan Martin Pueyrredon, who gave him a letter of introduction to General San Martin, who gave him a commission in the artillery under Colonel Plaza, with whom he was present at the disaster of Cancha-Rayada.

In 1826 Miller returned to England, and met with a very flattering reception. In 1844, and again in 1851, he represented the British Government in the Sandwich Islands. In the latter year he returned to Peru, where he enjoyed the title of Grand Marshal of Ayacucho, and died on board H.M.S. *Naiad* at Callao on the 31st October, 1861, and was buried in the English cemetery. Before his burial two bullets were extracted from his body, which showed the marks of twenty-two wounds.

NECOCHEA was banished from Peru in 1826, at the same time as Alvarado and other Argentine officers, but afterwards returned to Lima, and died at Miraflores near to that city in the year 1849. He also was a Marshal in the Peruvian army.

O'HIGGINS never returned to Chile after his banishment, and died at Lima on the 24th October, 1842, in the seventy-third year of his age. In the year 1869 his remains were taken back to his native country, and in 1872 an equestrian statue of him was erected in the great square of Santiago.

PAEZ.—In the year 1831 Paez was elected first Constitutional President of the Independent Republic of Venezuela, and remained in office for four years. In 1838 he was again elected President, and was presented by Congress with a sword of honour. He also in the same year received another sword of honour from William IV., King of Great Britain and Ireland. In 1842 he brought back the remains of Bolívar from New Granada, and buried them with great pomp at Caracas, the natal city of the Liberator. In 1843 he again retired into private life, but in 1850 took part in a revolutionary movement, brought on by the mal-administration of President Monagas, in consequence of which he was banished from the country, and retired to the city of New York, where he died in the year 1874. His remains were some years afterwards taken back to his native country, and re-interred with the honours due to his illustrious services.

INDEX.

Abascal, 96, 117, 118, 166, 225, 226, 416
Action of America upon Europe, 25
────── the Revolution, 459
Affiliation of the Revolution of South America, 13
Aldao, 125, 247, 248, 261, 262
Alvarez Jonte, 86, 192, 228
Alvear, 34, 36, 44, 47, 50, 61, 62, 78, 79, 110, 462
Alvarado, 127, 137, 147, 170, 176, 178, 183, 195, 215, 217, 218, 241, 242, 250, 251, 285, 426, 427, 429, 432, 433, 434, 435, 437, 447, 462
Arenales, 67, 69, 234, 241, 243, 246, 247, 248, 251, 261, 262, 263, 276, 410, 432, 435, 446, 485
Arismendi, 327, 345, 352, 357, 365, 369, 373, 374, 376, 380, 398
Armistice of Punchauca, 256
────── Trujillo, 400
Army of the Andes, 125, 136, 448
────── Apure, 368, 400
────── Centre, 372, 374
Arrival of Morillo's Expedition at Cumaná, 356
Assassination of Rodriguez, 183
────── Monteagudo, 460
Atero, 140, 141
Aymerich, 237, 320, 406, 408, 411, 412

Balcarce, A. G., 61, 125, 164
────── Marcos, 61, 102, 169, 177, 194
Barañao, 103, 148

Baraya, 317, 319, 363
Barreiro, 393, 394, 396, 397, 398
Battle of Ambato, 408, 415
────── Aragua, 373
────── Araure, 340
────── Ayacucho, 456
────── Ayohuma, 61
────── Balaga, 361
────── Barbula, 335
────── Boca-Chica, 348
────── Bomboná, 409
────── Boyacà, 397
────── Calabozo, 384
────── Carabobo, 348, 402
────── Cepeda, 218
────── Chacabuco, 147
────── Cojedes, 385
────── El Cerrito, 53
────── El Gavilán, 153
────── El Roble, 101
────── Guadalito, 367, 377
────── Hogaza, 382
────── Huamanga, 248
────── Jenay, 406
────── Junin, 451
────── La Florida, 70
────── La Puerta, 344, 349, 385
────── Las Trincheras, 335
────── Las Queseras del Medio, 393
────── Maipó, 106, 177, 178, 179
────── Matasiete, 381
────── Mocha, 319
────── Moquegua, 434
────── Mosquitero, 338
────── Ocumare, 347, 371
────── Ospino, 344

K K

490 INDEX.

Battle of Pasco, 247
——— Quebrada-Honda, 372
——— Pichincha, 412
——— Pitayo, 406
——— Playon del Juncal, 373
——— Salta, 60
——— San Carlos, 98
——— San Felix, 377
——— San Lorenzo, 58
——— San Marcos, 341
——— Suipacha, 37
——— Torata, 434
——— Tucuman, 50
——— Unare, 375
——— Urica, 351
——— Vargas, 396
——— Vilcapugio, 61
——— Yahuachí, 408
——— Zepita, 439
Beauchef, 156, 207, 208
Belgrano, 49, 52, 60, 61, 62, 73, 129, 163, 214, 471
Beltrán, 127, 140, 142
Bermudez, José F., 325, 328, 349, 350, 351, 352, 357, 359, 369, 372, 374, 376, 379, 381, 386, 387, 401, 404
——— Bernardo, 325, 328
Blanco-Encalada, 104, 178, 188, 190, 191, 193, 200, 202, 203, 291
Bogado, 59
Bolívar, 118, 143, 164, 180, 185, 196, 231, 233, 236, 252, 270, 282, 285, 293, 294, 295
——— His person, parentage, and education, 301; his marriage, return, and second trip to Europe, 301; his mission to London, 302; his character, 303; meets Miranda, 303; returns with him to Caracas, 304; is present at the capture of Valencia, 306; is placed in command at Puerto-Cabello, 309; is deserted by his troops and flies, 309; at La Guayra he with others imprisons Miranda, 311; he is allowed to leave the country, 311; retires to Curaçoa, 321, is appointed to a command by Cartagena, 321; commences to show his genius, 321; conceives the idea of reconquering Venezuela, 322; crosses the mountains and wins his first victory, 322; publishes a memorial, 322; Government accepts his idea, 329; makes him a brigadier-general, 330; he publishes a decree of extermination against Spaniards, 330; and defeats the Royalists in several engagements, 332; synopsis of his campaign, 333; he enters Caracas in triumph, 333; and gives himself the title of "Liberator," 334; he lays siege to Puerto-Cabello, 334; fulminates another decree against American Royalists, 334; defeats the Royalists at Las Trincheras, 335; institutes the military order of "The Liberators," 336; is defeated at Barquisimeto, 339; concentrates his troops and defeats Ceballos at Araure, 340; he marches to Puerto-Cabello, 340; is compelled to retire on Valencia, 342; he convenes an Assembly at Caracas, 343; resigns his Dictatorship but is reappointed, 344; makes a treaty with Mariño, 344; entrenches himself at San Mateo, 346; and repulses several attacks, 346; defeats Cajigal at Carabobo, 348; but is himself defeated by Boves at La Puerta, 349; and retreats to Aragua, 349; but is driven out by Morales and retires on Barcelona, 350; embarks at Güiria to protect treasure, and returns to find himself proscribed as a traitor, on which he gives up the treasure and retires to Curaçoa, 350; he returns to New Granada, 354; is put in command of a force sent against Cundinamarca, takes Bogotá, and is named Captain-General, 354; lays siege to Cartagena, 355; he retires to Jamaica, 355;

INDEX. 491

Bolívar—*continued*.
publishes a memorial, 355; narrowly escapes assassination, 368; goes to Santo Domingo, 368; organizes an expedition at Cayos de San Luis and sails for the mainland, 369; is named "Supreme Chief" at Margarita, 370; addresses a proclamation to the people of Venezuela, 370; decrees liberty to slaves, 370; from Carúpano sails to Ocumare, 371; is defeated by Morales and flies to Bonaire, 371; and from Güiria returns to Haiti, 372; is recalled to Barcelona, 374; is defeated at Unare, 375; goes to Guayana, 376; is appointed to a Junta, 378; he organises a flotilla, 378; discovers a conspiracy against him and shoots Piar, 379; sends an address to the Argentine people, 382; goes up the Orinoco, 382; drives Morillo before him from Calabozo, 384; and marches to Aragua, 384; is defeated by Morillo at La Puerta, 385; receives reinforcements and drives La Torre to San Carlos, 385; his men are dispersed in a night attack, 385; returns to Angostura, 387; sends Santander to occupy Casanare, 387; prepares for the convention of a Congress, 388; and declines the intervention of the Great Powers, 388; is elected President of Venezuela, 389; he recruits auxiliary troops in Europe, 390; and resolves to reconquer New Granada, 393; he joins Santander in Casanare, 394; and crosses the Andes, 395; encamps at Sagamoso, 396; fights an indecisive action at Vargas, 396; and wins a complete victory at Boyacá, 397; he enters Bogotá in triumph, 397; and returns to Angostura, 398; Congress decrees the establishment of the Republic of Columbia, 399; Bolívar is named provisional President, 399; he arranges an armistice with Morillo, 400; reopens the campaign and wins a decisive victory at Carabobo, 402; he enters Caracas in triumph, 403; and is named President of Columbia, 403; he sends Sucre to Guayaquil, 407; proposes to aid San Martin, 408; Marches on Quito, 409; wins the battle of Bombona, 409; and retreats to Patia, 409; enters Quito in triumph, 413; and goes on to Guayaquil, 420; annexes that province to Columbia, 421; he receives San Martin as an honoured guest, 421; his conference with San Martin, 422; he offers to assist Peru, 431, 436; sends Sucre to Peru with 3,000 men, 437; enters Lima in triumph, 441; Proctor's description of him, 442; his projects, 443; concentrates his forces at Pativilca, 447; is appointed Dictator, 449; he retreats to Trujillo, 450; marches on Jauja, 450; his cavalry routs the Royalist horse at Junin, 451; he returns to Lima and the Congress of Columbia abrogates his extraordinary powers, 453; he again collects troops at Pativilca, 454; summons an American Congress, 454, 460; his resignation is declined, 461; tendency of his policy, 462; his triumphal march to Potosí, 462; he confers with Argentine envoys, 463; founds the Republic of Bolivia, 463; character of his work, 463; Conspiracy against him at Lima, 464; is appointed perpetual President, 465; draws up a plan for a "Grand confederation of the Andes," 465; he returns to Bogotá, 466; summons a Convention at Ocaña, 467; becomes a military Dictator and narrowly escapes assassination, 467; declares war against Peru, 468; he resigns office, 469; his life in

INDEX.

Bolívar—*continued*.
retirement, 472; his death, 473;
his remains are brought back to
Caracas and buried there with
great pomp by Paez in 1842, 488
Borgoño, 178, 199
Boves, 308, 328, 336, 337, 338, 341,
344, 346, 347, 348, 349, 351, 353
Bowles, Captain, 164, 166
Brandzen, 235
Brayer, 155, 168, 172. 176
Brown, 78, 120, 121, 122, 484
Brion, 369, 370, 372, 374, 378, 380,
387, 393
Buchardo, 121, 122

Cabot, 137, 139
Cajigal, 306, 326, 328, 331, 337,
340, 341, 347, 348, 349
Callao, description of, 201
———— first attack on, 201
———— second attack on, 204
Caldas the philosopher, 363
Calzada, 344, 347, 348, 352, 358,
361, 362, 363, 376, 377, 382, 397,
406
Camba, 229, 233, 234, 258, 266
Campbell, 391
Campo-Elias, 338, 344, 345, 346
Cancha-rayada, 104, 170
Cangallo burned, 248, 293
Canning, 6
Canterac, 243, 250, 258, 260, 263,
264, 278, 279, 280, 281, 282, 289,
292, 294, 380, 382, 432, 433, 434,
437, 448, 451, 452, 455, 457
Capture of the *Esmeralda*, 237
——————— *Intrepido* and *Rita*,
369
——————— *Maria Isabel*, 191
——————— *Resolucion*, 273
——————— Barcelona, 376, 399
——————— Barinas, 332, 341, 381
——————— Bogotá, 354
——————— Calabozo, 339, 341
——————— Caracas, 333, 401
——————— Chagres and Portobelo,
404
——————— Chiloe, 458
——————— Coro, 405
——————— Cumaná, 328, 351, 404
——————— Guayaquil, 468

Capture of Lima, 437
———————— Maracaibo, 405
———————— Maturin, 325, 352
———————— Mérida, 330
———————— Pamplona, 361
———————— Popayán, 406
———————— Puerto-Cabello, 405
———————— San Carlos, 347
———————— San Fernando, 385, 400
———————— Santa Marta, 405
———————— Trujillo, 330
———————— Valdivia, 208
———————— Valencia, 306, 308, 332,
349
———————— Victoria, 372
Carrera, José Miguel, 34, 61, 91, 92,
93, 97, 98, 99, 100, 101,
102, 103, 106, 107, 109,
110, 124, 158, 195, 276
———— Juan, José, 91, 92, 93,
99, 100, 101, 102, 162,
181
———— Luis, 91, 92, 93, 98, 100,
103, 106, 162, 181
———— Doña Javiera, 91, 162, 195
———— Ignacio, 96
Castillo-Rada, 322, 329, 355, 359,
361
Ceballos, 331, 339, 340, 341, 347,
348, 349
Cedeño, 352, 368, 374, 375, 376,
379, 385, 386
Chacabuco, description of Plain of,
144, 145
Character of Arenales, 263
——————— Paez, 366
——————— Sucre, 407
Charles, Colonel, killed at Pisco,
205
Chillán, 97, 99, 101, 103
Chiloe, 97, 98, 101, 151, 209, 458
Chincha, fever at, 266
Civil war in Chile, 106
———————— New Granada, 320, 355
Cochrane, 192, 193, 200, 201, 202,
203, 204, 206, 207, 208,
209, 212, 219, 231, 232,
234, 236, 237, 238, 239,
240, 251, 265, 266, 267,
269, 270, 272, 273, 277,
280, 287, 288, 289, 290,
291, 485

INDEX. 493

Cochrane attempts a private treaty with La Mar, 273
Colonial Policy, 10
Colonisation of Spanish America, 7
——————— North America, 9
——————— Chile, 80
Concepçion, 97, 100, 101, 104, 194
Condarco, 128, 129, 130, 159, 188, 192
Conde, 126, 137, 156
Confiscations of Spanish property, 266, 267, 276, 295
Conference at Chuquisaca, 463
——————— Guayaquil, 422, 424
——————— Miraflores, 233, 258
——————— Potosí, 462
——————— Punchauca, 255, 256, 257
——————— Retes, 250, 251
Congress at Angostura, 388
——————— Bogotá, 315, 468
——————— Caracas, 305
——————— Cariaco, 378
——————— Cúcuta, 403
——————— Ibague, 316
——————— Lima, 428, 441
——————— Santiago, 88
——————— Tucuman, 128
Congreve rockets made in Valparaiso, 203, 478
Conspiracy of the Carreras, 159, 162
——————— to betray Callao, 265
Constitution of 1812, 25
Convention of Rancagua, 218
Cordillera of the Andes, 132
Córdoba, 412, 450, 455, 456, 467, 468
Cost of the war to Spain, 185
Cramer, 126, 137
Creole, the, of South America, 21
Cruelties of the Royalists, 324, 325, 338, 344, 349, 350, 351, 352, 361, 363, 376, 381
——————— the Patriots, 327, 328, 330, 339, 345, 361, 375, 381, 398

D'Albe, 155, 176, 240
Declaration of Independence at Bogotá, 316

Declaration of Independence at Caracas, 305
——————— Cartagena, 316
——————— Guayaquil, 237
——————— Lima, 272
——————— Maracaibo, 401
——————— Panama, 404
——————— Santiago, 168
——————— Tucuman, 129
——————— Veraguas, 404
——————— by Ecuador, 473
——————— Venezuela, 468
D'Eluyar, 330, 335, 340, 349, 350
Description of Callao, 201
——————— Cartagena, 359
——————— Chacabuco, 144, 145
——————— "Flecheras," 373
——————— Island of Margarita, 326
——————— Peru, 223, 245
——————— Royalist levies by Camba, 357
——————— "Taravitas," 321
——————— the Northern Zone, 296, 299
——————— the Plain of Maipó, 175
——————— Upper Peru, 65
——————— Valdivia, 206
Dehesa, 170, 246, 247, 462
Devereux, 391
Disaster at Ica, 294
Dispersion of Cancha-rayada, 170
——————— El Desaguadero, 439
Dorrego, 73, 88

Earthquake, the great, of 1812, 37, 307
Effect of the Revolution, 28
Elections, first in Perú, 227
Emancipation of North America, 11
English, 391
Escalada, 137, 147, 177, 195
Europe, state of, in fifteenth century, 6
Evacuation of Margarita, 374
——————— Talcahuano, 180
Execution of Carrera, Juan José, 181
——————— Luis 181

Execution of Carrera, José Miguel, 276
———— Patriot prisoners, 449
———— Royalist prisoners, 398
———— La Pola, 364
———— Piar, 397
———— San Bruno, 149
———— Torres, &c., 363
———— Two conspirators in Buenos Ayres, 195
Expedition from Cayos, 369
———————— Haiti, 374
———————— Triste, 325
———————— of Canterac, 380
———————— Morillo, 356
Exploits of the Chilian Squadron, 188, 190, 192

Falucho, death of, 448
Fate of the Emancipators of South America, 471
Ferrier, 402
Flag of Army of the Andes, 130
——— Chile, 95
——— Columbia, 399
——— Mexico, 254
——— Peru, 234
——— Venezuela, 305
Flecheras, Description of, 373
Flotilla, Patriot, destroyed at Lorondo, 307
Foreign Auxiliaries in Venezuela, 390, 391
Formation of the Chilian Navy, 186, 187
Freyre, Ramon, 121, 122, 137, 140, 152, 153, 154, 168, 178, 180, 194, 207, 219

Gainza, 103, 104, 105
Gamarra, 229, 261, 262, 294, 437, 438, 439, 466
Garcia del Rio, 255, 274, 286, 288
Gauchos, the, of Salta, 75
Gilmour, 391
Girardot, 330, 332, 335
Godoy Cruz, 138, 163, 218
Guayaquil, 236, 294, 317, 318, 404, 407, 410, 414, 416
Güemes, Martin, 74, 76, 166, 229, 485

Guido, 125, 161, 172, 199, 250, 255, 414, 429
Guise, 191, 205, 219, 238, 239, 288, 291, 440, 448, 453, 468

Hall, Captain Basil, 258
Heroism of Ricaurte, 347
Hillyar, 105
Hippesley, 391
Horse Marines, 383

Institution of "The Legion of Merit," by O'Higgins, 161
Institution of "The Order of the Sun," by San Martin, 283
Institution of "The Order of the Liberators," by Bolívar, 336
Instructions given to Morillo, 356
International Law, A New, 2
Interview between San Martin and La Serna, 257
Interview between San Martin and Bolívar, 422
Invasion of Spain by Napoleon, 23
Irizarri, 103, 161, 196
Iturbide, 253, 254, 255

Jujui, 75

Lautaro Lodge, see "Sociedad."
La Aurora de Chile, newspaper, 95
Lafayette, 6
La Mar, 273, 280, 282, 416, 431, 450, 455, 456
Lanza, 267, 292, 432, 439
La Pola, death of, 364
Las Heras, 102, 103, 106, 107, 110, 124, 137, 140, 141, 142, 152, 153, 155, 156, 171, 173, 174, 176, 177, 179, 218, 219, 232, 273, 274, 281, 285, 446, 486
La Serna, 166, 226, 229, 242, 243, 250, 251, 255, 257, 258, 259, 261, 263, 274, 278, 292, 293, 295, 432, 439, 450, 452, 455
La Torre, 363, 374, 376, 377, 378, 379, 382, 383, 385, 400, 401, 402, 405, 408
Lavalle, Juan, 141, 246, 247, 410, 411, 420, 434, 486

INDEX.

Liberal ideas, effect of, on the Royalist armies, 229, 249
Liberating army of Peru, 230
Lima, the Capua of the liberating army, 277
Lircay, treaty of, 105
Llaneros, the, 299, 337, 339, 341, 348, 358, 362, 364, 367, 373, 377, 387
Loriga, 250, 251, 278, 292
Loss of the *Intrepido*, 208
―――― *San Martin*, 269
―――― *San Pedro*, 358
Lozano, 316, 363, 471
Luzuriaga, 163, 414, 415

Macaulay, 318
Macduff, Lord, 36
MacGregor, 369, 372, 373, 391, 399
Mackenna, 97, 99, 100, 103, 104, 105
Manning, 156
March of Canterac across a desert, 278
Marcó del Pont, 119, 130, 134, 135, 140, 145, 148, 149, 198
Mariño, 325, 327, 331, 334, 341, 342, 343, 344, 346, 348, 349, 350, 351, 355, 369, 370, 372, 373, 374, 376, 378, 379, 386, 398, 404
Maroto, 145, 146, 149, 292
Martinez, Enrique, 141, 218, 433, 435, 436
Massacre of a boat's crew, 240
―――― at Calabozo, 308, 339
―――――― Juan Griego, 381
―――――― La Guayra, 345
―――――― Ocumare, 344
―――――― Pasto, 319
―――――― Quito, 313
―――――― San José, 308
―――――― San Juan de los Morros, 308
Medina, 153, 177
Melian, 137, 142
Mendoza, 109
Mendez, Luis, 301, 390, 391
Mercurio Peruano, newspaper, 224
Mexico, 21, 105, 252, 253, 254, 300
Miller, 187, 190, 203, 204, 205, 206, 208, 209, 251, 262, 265, 266, 267, 268, 269, 281, 431, 435, 450, 452, 454, 455, 456, 487
Miranda, early life of, 16; he establishes a secret society in London, 17; his first attempt at revolution, 18; he meets Bolívar in London, 303; and returns with him to Caracas, 304; his cordial reception, 304; is appointed to draw up a constitution, 304; he organises a political club, 305; he is sent against Valencia, 305; which he captures, 306; he is named Dictator, 308; he marches on Valencia and entrenches himself, 308; he retreats to Victoria, 309; repels several attacks on his position, 309; the slaves rise against the Patriots, 309; the Patriots lose faith in him, 310; he capitulates and withdraws to La Guayra, 310; he is made prisoner by his officers, 311; and is sent to Spain, where he dies in a dungeon, 311, 471
Mission of Alzaga from Buenos Ayres, 446
Monagas, 352, 368, 372, 373, 375, 381, 384, 386, 387
Monarchy, attempts at, in South America, 26, 185, 213, 234, 257, 286, 468
Montalvo, 320, 353, 355, 364
Monteagudo, 48, 50, 181, 183, 198, 272, 274, 275, 283, 286, 288, 295, 426, 427, 450, 460
Monteverde, 306, 307, 308, 309, 310, 311, 325, 326, 332, 334, 335, 337, 353
Monte Video, 52, 54, 60, 78, 86
Montilla, 347, 355, 359, 369, 392, 393, 399, 400, 401, 405
Montufar, 315, 317, 318, 363, 471
Morales, 328, 336, 337, 338, 345, 346, 350, 351, 352, 353, 357, 358, 360, 361, 362, 372, 373, 386, 392, 402, 405
Moral Revolution of South America, 15
Morgado, 153, 177, 198
Morillo, 112, 116, 180, 233, 252, 356, 357, 358, 359, 360, 361, 362,

363, 364, 365, 374, 376, 377, 378, 380, 381, 382, 383, 384, 392, 393, 396, 397, 400
Morla, 177, 197, 198
Mosquera, 416, 444, 445, 469, 472, 473
Mounted Grenadiers, the, 44, 54, 124, 420, 448
Murdering Expedition of Briceño, 329
Murder of Castillo de Ruiz, 319
———— General Solano, 33
———————————— Córdoba, 468
Murgeón, 408, 409, 411
Mutiny at Callao, 447
———— San Juan, 217

Nariño, 15, 316, 319, 320, 321
Naval capacities of Chile, 186
Necochea, 127, 137, 141, 147, 148, 450, 451, 487
New Granada, characteristics of, 313

O'Brien, 158, 176, 179, 183
———— Captain, 187
Occupation of Lima, 259
O'Connell, 391
O'Donohu, 255
O'Higgins, 83, 89, 93, 97, 99, 100, 101, 102, 103, 104, 105, 106, 107, 109, 110, 127, 137, 140, 145, 146, 147, 148, 152, 153, 154, 155, 159, 161, 162, 167, 168, 169, 170, 171, 172, 173, 176, 178, 181, 190, 195, 196, 199, 218, 289, 290, 295, 388, 429, 450, 471, 487
Olañeta, 229, 432, 435, 439, 450, 458
Ordoñez, 148, 151, 152, 153, 154, 155, 167, 169, 170, 175, 177, 178, 179, 197, 198
O'Reilly, 247
Osorio, 106, 117, 118, 167, 168, 169, 174, 175, 176, 178, 179, 180, 183

Paez, 352, 366, 367, 373, 374, 376, 377, 381, 382, 383, 384, 385, 387, 392, 393, 400, 401, 402, 404, 405, 466, 468, 487
Pareja, 96, 98

Parliamentary system established in Chile, 88
Parroissien, 128, 286
Passage of the Andes by San Martin, 140, 141
———————————— Bolívar, 395, 396
Peru, description of, 223, 224, 225, 245
Peruvian Infantry, the, 66
Petión, 368, 369, 370, 372
Pezuela, 69, 73, 75, 77, 116, 118, 166, 180, 201, 226, 229, 233, 234, 241, 249, 250
Piar, 325, 326, 328, 329, 350, 351, 369, 370, 371, 373, 374, 375, 376, 377, 378, 379, 471
Pitt, his sympathy with America, 17
Plan of Iguala, the, 254, 255
Plan, the, of Emancipation, 2
Poinsett, 95, 97
Posadas, 62
Prætorianism, advent of, 413
Preparations in Spain for a last expedition, 211
Primo de Rivera, 168, 169, 170, 175, 177, 197, 198
Pringles, 198, 241, 242
Proclamations, 230, 231, 232, 234, 260, 330, 370, 380, 387, 388, 413
Proctor's description of Bolívar, 442
Pueyrredón, 129, 137, 158, 159, 161, 163, 185, 199
Pumacahua, 227, 228
Public Library endowed by San Martin at Santiago, 150

Quimper, 232, 233, 246
Quintana, 160, 161, 163, 171, 178
Quiroga, 198
Quito, 22, 233, 236, 270, 293, 300, 312, 313, 317, 318, 319, 400, 404, 407, 408, 410, 411, 412, 413, 467

Races, the, of South America, 19
Rancagua, 106, 218
Reaction at Bogotá, 362
———— Coro and Maracaibo, 300, 304, 306
———— Guayana, 307
Recognition of new Republics by United States, 5

INDEX. 497

Representative system, the first, established in South America at Buenos Ayres, 444
Repulse at Angostura, 375
—————— Chiloe, 209
—————— Coro, 304
—————— Guarico, 384
—————— Ortiz, 385
—————— San Carlos, 348
—————— San Mateo, 347
—————— Valencia, 306
—————— Victoria, 308
Revolt of the Canarians at Caracas, 305
Revolt at Valencia, 305
Revolt on Island of Margarita, 327, 365
Revolution, first throes of, in South America, 21
—————— of 1812, Buenos Ayres, 51
—————— of 1820, in Spain, 216
—————— at Bogotá, 314
—————— Caracas, 300
—————— Cartagena, 313
—————— Casanare, 313
—————— Guayaquil, 236
—————— Maracaibo, 401
—————— Pamplona, 314
—————— Santiago, 83
—————— Socorro, 314
—————— Trujillo, 243
Ricafort, 248, 261, 262, 273
Riva-Aguero, 274, 426, 427, 431, 436, 437, 440, 441, 442, 446
Rivadavia, 161, 443, 444, 445, 446, 463, 471
Rivas, 332, 339, 345, 347, 348, 350, 351, 352
Robertson, William Parish, 56
Rodil, 174, 179, 448, 449, 458
Rodriguez, Manuel, 120, 135, 152, 163, 172, 182, 183
—————— Simon, tutor of Bolívar, 301, 302, 424
Rondeau, 53, 61, 110, 116, 211, 212, 213, 214, 217
Royalist Armies, strength of, 229
Royal Commission from Spain, 445
Rozas, Juan Martinez de, 82, 86, 87, 90, 93, 95
Ruiz de Castillo, 300, 313, 318, 319

Salta, Province of, 75
Sámano, 180, 319, 320, 364, 397, 398, 408
Sanchez, 98, 99, 100, 101, 103, 148, 152, 180, 191, 194, 282
San Juan, 109
San Luis, 109
San Martin, his birth and parentage, 31; he joins the Spanish army, 32; his campaigns against the French, 35; he returns to Buenos Ayres, 36; his personal appearance, 39; he organizes the mounted grenadiers, 44; he founds the Lautaro Lodge, 47; he joins in the revolution of 1812, 51; he fights the action of San Lorenzo, 58; and takes command of the Army of the North, 62; he entrenches a camp at Tucuman, 73; he draws up a secret plan of campaign, 79; he is appointed Governor of Cuyo, 79; reaches Mendoza, 109; is elected Governor by the Cabildos, 111; he establishes spies in Chile, 119; and organises the Army of the Andes, 125; he treats with the Indians, 134; the equipment of the army, 136; he marches from Mendoza, 139; encamps in the valley of Putaendo, 142; wins the battle of Chacabuco, 147; and occupies Santiago, 148; he endows a public library and returns to Buenos Ayres, 150; arranges for a fleet on the Pacific and for an alliance with Chile, 158; he marches against Osorio, 168; his army is dispersed at Cancha-rayada, 170; he reorganizes the army at Maipó, 173; and wins a complete victory, 177, 178, 179; he again visits Buenos Ayres, 184; he plans an expedition to Periu, 196; and withdraws a part of his army from Chile, 196; disregards the orders of Government, 214, 215; and returns to Chile, 216; he convenes a meeting of officers at

San Martin—*continued*.
Rancagua, 218 ; is appointed generalissimo of the united army, 219 ; on the eve of sailing he issues a proclamation to his fellow-countrymen, 230 ; the instructions given him by the Chilian Government, 231 ; his plan of campaign, 231 ; he lands at Pisco, 232 ; treats with the Viceroy, 233 ; he establishes by decree the flag and escutcheon of the Republic of Peru, 234 ; re-embarks, leaving Arenales behind him, 234 ; his plans, political and military, 234 ; he sails past Callao, 235 ; lands a detachment at Ancon, 235 ; and sails for Huacho, 240 ; lands and encamps in the valley of Huara, 240 ; the "Numancia" battalion deserts to him, 242 ; he is joined by the northern provinces, 243 ; he advances to Retes, 243 ; is joined by Arenales, and retires, 244 ; he publishes a "Provisional Regulation," 244 ; is invited to a conference by La Serna, 250 ; he arranges an armistice, 257 ; and meets the Viceroy, 257 ; he enters Lima, 259 ; recalls Arenales from the Highlands, 264 ; he sends Cochrane and Miller to the south, 266 ; his position, 271 ; he convenes a meeting of citizens, 272 ; and adopts the title "Protector of Peru," 274 ; he issues rigorous decrees against the Spaniards, 275 ; the Royalists attempt to relieve Callao, 278 ; he sees Cochrane for the last time, 280 ; he declines to attack Canterac, 280 ; he organises a Peruvian army, 283 ; institutes the "Order of the Sun," 283 ; the municipality of Lima gives a subsidy to the officers of the army, 284 ; he discovers a conspiracy against him, 284 ; his ideas of legislation, 285 ; his dispute with Cochrane, 287 ; he summons a Congress, 293 ; sends another expedition to Ica, 293 ; attempts to treat with the Viceroy, 295 ; he sends a contingent to assist Sucre, 410 ; sails to Guayaquil, 421 ; he meets Bolívar, 421 ; his conference with him, 422 ; he returns to Peru, 423 ; his opinion of Bolívar, 423 ; his letter to Bolívar, 425 ; his letter to O'Higgins, 427 ; he draws up a plan for a new campaign, and opens the first Congress of Peru, 428 ; his abdication, 428 ; leaves Peru for ever, 429 ; and retires to Mendoza, 429 ; he organizes an auxiliary force, 436 ; he is besought to return to Peru, 440 ; returns to Buenos Ayres, 471 ; goes to Europe, 472 ; returns to be insulted, and goes back, 472 ; is assisted by Aguada, 473 ; he bequeaths his sword to Rozas, 474 ; his death, 474 ; his remains are brought back to Buenos Ayres, 474
San Martin, Maria Mercedes de, 149, 199, 472, 474
Santa Cruz, 410, 436, 437, 438, 439, 440
Santa Cruz de la Sierra, 65
Santander, 387, 393, 394, 398, 450, 453, 461, 466, 468
Saraza, 352, 368, 372, 373, 376, 381, 382, 384, 387
Sequence of causes, the, 418
Ships burned at Callao by Guise, 448
Siege of Callao, 272, 273, 280, 282, 458
————— Cartagena, 360, 361, 401, 404
————— Chillán, 100
————— Cumaná, 374
————— Puerto-Cabello, 334, 335, 340, 348, 349
————— Rancagua, 107
————— San Fernando, 374, 377
————— Talcahuano, 155, 156
————— Valencia, 348
Skeenen, 391

INDEX.

Skirmish at Achupallas, 141
———— Carora, 306
———— Chancay, 236, 241
———— Guachipas, 76
———— Guardia-Vieja, 141
———— Mirave, 268
———— Rio Bamba, 411
———— San Fernando, 374
———— San José, 308
———— Wasca, 246
Sociedad de Lautaro, 33, 47, 50, 60, 125, 149, 160, 163, 184, 199, 211
Soler, 124, 137, 140, 141, 145, 146, 147
Soublette, 369, 372, 400
Spano, Colonel, death of, 103
Spry, 191, 219, 288
Successes of Nariño, 320
Sucre, 378, 407, 408, 410, 411, 415, 437, 438, 440, 450, 453, 454, 455, 456, 457, 458, 461, 464, 465, 466, 468, 471, 472
Surrender of the *Prueba* and *Venganza*, 290
———— Valencia, 305
Sutherland, Robert, 368

Talca, 97, 103, 104, 152, 167, 168, 169
Talcahuano, 97, 104, 106, 152, 154, 155, 167, 179, 194
"Taravitas," 321
Thompson, 178

Torices, 317, 321, 322, 362, 363
Torres, Camilo, 314, 320, 322, 323, 330, 354, 361, 363, 471
Torre-Tagle, 243, 293, 294, 295, 426, 441, 446, 447, 448
Tragedy of San Luis, 197, 198
Treaty between Columbia and the Argentine Congress, 445
Tristan, 293, 294

University of Lima, 225
Upper Peru, 22, 61, 62, 65, 227, 300
Urdaneta, 332, 335, 342, 344, 347, 348, 349, 352, 354, 378, 391, 393, 399, 401, 473
Uzlar, 391

Valdés, 229, 235, 241, 250, 258, 261, 262, 278, 279, 294, 432, 433, 434, 439, 450, 452, 455, 456
Valdivia, 97, 98, 101, 151, 195, 206, 207, 208
Venezuela, 24, 299

Warnes, 67, 69
Wellesley, Marquis of, 302
Wilson, 387, 391

Yañez, 337, 339, 340, 341, 344

Zapiola, 34, 36, 44, 127, 137, 146, 147, 177, 180, 194
Zea, 369, 378, 389, 398
Zuazola, 325, 334

THE END.

PRINTED BY J. S. VIRTUE AND CO., LIMITED, CITY ROAD, LONDON.

www.ingramcontent.com/pod-product-compliance
Lightning Source LLC
Chambersburg PA
CBHW020857020526
44116CB00029B/333